CROP CIRCLES
REVEALED
LANGUAGE OF THE LIGHT SYMBOLS

JUDITH MOORE
& BARBARA LAMB

A 1993 crop circle: swirled center with standing stalks.

CROP CIRCLES

REVEALED

LANGUAGE OF THE LIGHT SYMBOLS

3 LIGHT
Technology
PUBLISHING

edited by Ashley E. Costanzo
Ann Cowles
Laura Monroe
designed by Michael Russell
cover illustration by Doug Taylor
computer enhancement of starglyphs
by Philip Senart

ISBN 1-891824-32-5

Published by

 **Light Technology**
Publishing
P.O. Box 3540
Flagstaff, AZ 86003
1-800-450-0985
e-mail: publishing@lighttechnology.net
www.lighttechnology.com

DEDICATION

*This book is dedicated to the unseen creators of genuine crop
circles, with gratitude for their messages of hope and inspiration.*

—BARBARA LAMB

*I wish to lovingly dedicate this book to a prophetic woman:
my dear mother and my best friend, Irene Allander.
Her motto was, "Because I have known the torment
of thirst, I dig a spring that others may drink."
This book is also dedicated to Ola, a spiritual elder,
a Cherokee grandmother.*

—JUDITH MOORE

Barbara Lamb and Judy Moore in the *Celtic Cross* crop circle at Milton Hill Farm, Milton Laibourne, near Pewsey, Wiltshire County, July 2000.

TABLE OF CONTENTS

ACKNOWLEDGMENTS

Barbara Lamb

I would like to express my great appreciation and thanks to all the crop circle researchers and writers who have contributed to this synthesis of information about the crop circle phenomenon, and to all those people whose ideas have enriched me yet which I have not directly incorporated into this writing. Some of those whom I have not cited are Francine Blake, Jazz Rasool and Barbara Hand Clow.

I thank the genuine crop circle creative intelligence for going to the effort again and again to give us these patterns in our crop fields, which inspire us with their beauty, arouse our curiosity and wake us up to new information and perspectives. I apologize to the true circlemakers for not including in this writing *all* of their fine creations because of limitations of space.

I thank all of the photographers who made the many expensive flights to provide beautiful photographs of crop circles, which preserve the archives of this precious phenomenon. I acknowledge Steve Alexander, Lucy Pringle, Colin Andrews, Busty Taylor, Steve Patterson, Ron Russell, Michael Glickman and Patricia Murray, Karen Cushing, Andrew King, Peter Sorensen, N. Hillier, Ulrich Kox and Petr Novak. I especially thank Lucy Pringle, Karen Cushing and Andrew King, who generously donated their photographs to this book.

My appreciation goes to the people who provided drawings of the crop circles, many of which I have included to illustrate various points, especially Peter Sorensen, Colin Andrews and Pat Palgrave-Moore. Additional thanks go to Richard Andrews, R, Armstrong, Beth Davis, Isabelle Kingston, Lucy Pringle, Leonie Starr, Busty Taylor and George Wingfield. I acknowledge them also for their continuing research in and over the fields of England during the several crop-growing months each year.

I offer a special acknowledgment to everyone who has enriched crop circle theories and interpretations by offering us insights about the solid geometry, geometric theorems and sacred geometry exhibited in the crop circle formations. The list includes Gerald S. Hawkins, John Martineau, Michael Glickman, Freddy Silva, Rod Bearcloud Berry, Peter Sorensen, Brian Grist, Bert Janssen and John Michell. My apologies to anyone else contributing to this aspect of the work whom I have failed to mention.

I give enthusiastic kudos to Mark J. Fussell and Stuart Dike of the Crop Circle Connector Internet Web site for including and updating pictures and information about each crop circle about which they have been informed. They donate great amounts of time, effort and personal expense to visit as many crop circles as they can, taking their effective "pole shot" photographs and writing field reports. They include this information about crop circles in England and in other countries on their Web site, and it is shared with crop circle enthusiasts worldwide. This is a much welcomed and appreciated service.

I especially commend the fine people who have organized the crop circle conferences in England that I have attended so enthusiastically: Francine Blake, Roland and Clare Pargeter, and currently Andy Thomas, Karen Douglas and Sheila Martin. Their hard work and initiative provide an inestimable enrichment for me and for the crop circle community.

My personal appreciation extends to friends who have accompanied me on many adventures in the giant treasure hunt of finding and experiencing crop circles firsthand: Shawn Randall, Cariel Quinly, Denni Clarke, Patricia Hill, Karen Cushing, ilyes, Peter Sorensen, Valja Roseman, Wendy Allen, Margaret Moore, Chet and Kallista Snow, Jean Booth, Andrea Corsick, Gil Holt and Nonie Michelli. I am grateful for the loving support and encouragement of my dear husband, Warren Lamb, my son, Chris Peterson, and my daughters, Jennifer Catozzi and Erica Dornan.

I deeply appreciate the channeling of transmissions by Judy Moore, which bring significant insights and messages about the crop circles from high spiritual sources. This information helps us to understand at deep levels the large movements going on today and into the future, involving humanity, the Earth and the cosmos. I thank Judy for all she has introduced to me in the spiritual realm and for bringing my awareness more than ever before to the specialness and sacredness of the Wiltshire landscape. I honor her lightheartedness, her humor and her very generous nature, and I thank her for carrying my heavy backpack into all the crop circles we explored together! In my opinion, the transmissions she relays to us are at the heart of the matter.

Judith Moore

There are so many I would like to thank. First and foremost, I wish to thank Creator God, J.C., the I Am That I Am, with my entire mind, body, spirit and soul. I am but a salt shaker, a tool—hopefully, a good one; of my own self, I am nothing. Blessed be the Tunkashilas [Native American word for spirit beings], angels and archangels, and spirit and animal guides and teachers, with special honor paid to my spiritual guides: Laiolin, the Great Cobra and Quonob, the spirit of Bald Mountain. Thank you, Quonob, for my soul connection to Charm Springs and for protecting me throughout my life. And a special thank you to the circlemakers, the tools of this mystery who have worked to bring this gift to the world.

I wish to thank my children for having patience with me. I want to thank my grandchildren for the love they give me. Thank you, Randy Hansen, for your loving support as my companion. I could not have completed this work without your help. I want to acknowledge my granddaughter Ann, a lightworker and a wonderful twelve year old. I wish to acknowledge my former husband of twenty-eight years, Dr. J. Michael Moore, D.O. Thank you to my loving parents, Paul and Irene Allander, who taught me to love and honor the Earth Mother and to never turn my back on my fellow man.

Barbara Lamb, thank you for your vision. I want to acknowledge your fine work as a bridge of understanding and trust for all of us star beings. Thank you, Phillip Senart, for your hard work on the graphic design and refinement of the star glyphs. Thank you for giving freely of your time and services to make this project possible.

My many and enduring thanks go to Peter Paget for his editorial work from the viewpoint of an ET researcher. Your work to create a glossary of scientific terms was invaluable. Thank you, Pat Reitemeier, for your mentorship and editing skills; you encouraged me from the start.

I want to thank my dear sister-friend, Tika, who spent many hours editing, cooking my meals and helping the family when I couldn't. She is a willing tool of Creator God and wonderful lightworker. Rand, thank you for being my teacher and helping me prepare for this important mission. Thank you, Grandmother Star. You are my cosmic mentor and have supported me in vital ways. Special thanks goes to Taskara of the Mayan Center in Los Angeles. He worked with me in many capacities and was the initiator of this book. Taskara, wherever you are, my prayers are with you.

A special acknowledgment to my Brother Standing Elk and the Star Nation. I can't say anything good enough about him, so I won't try.

I stand to honor our elders named and unnamed: Ollie Napesnie, Grandma Bertha Grove, Allegra Ahlquist, Shirley Tassencourt, Star Flaniken, Barrie Ryan, Nana Gaia, Marion, Shirley Khabbaz, Mary Diamond, Pauline Mitchelle and the dear Grandmothers' Council. A special thanks to Kit Wilson; she taught me more than she will ever know.

With deepest respect, I wish to thank my Uncle Tony Shearer, the "man for all seasons." To him I dedicate the song, "To Reach the Unreachable Star," from the play, *Don Quixote, Man of La Mancha*. He has given his life in service to Mother Earth and the mending of the Sacred Hoop. He is a teacher, flute player, poet, prophet and the bringer of the dawn. Thank you, my dear sweet one, for being my friend and for guiding my journey these past years. Mitakyue Oyasin [Native American phrase meaning "all my relations"].

LIST OF PLATES

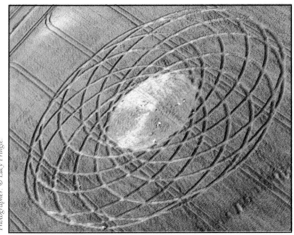

Photographer: © Lucy Pringle.

PLATE 1. July 11, 1997, Woodborough Hill, Alton Priors, Wiltshire County, wheat crop, 300-350 feet in diameter.

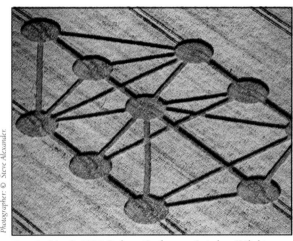

Photographer: © Steve Alexander.

PLATE 2. May 3, 1997, Barbury Castle, near Swindon, Wiltshire County, "The Key to the Kabbalah," oilseed canola crop.

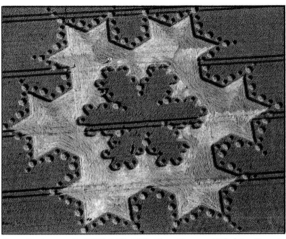

Photographer: © Steve Alexander.

PLATE 3. August 8, 1997, Milk Hill, Alton Barnes, Wiltshire County, wheat crop.

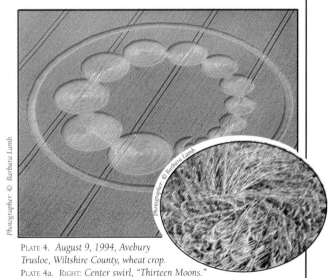

Photographer: © Barbara Lamb.

Photographer: © Barbara Lamb.

PLATE 4. *August 9, 1994, Avebury Trusloe, Wiltshire County, wheat crop.*
PLATE 4a. RIGHT: *Center swirl, "Thirteen Moons."*

Photographer: © Steve Alexander.

Photographer: © Barbara Lamb.

PLATE 5. August 10 and 11, 1994, Avebury, Wiltshire County, wheat crop.
PLATE 5a. RIGHT: Aerial view.

Photographer: © Barbara Lamb.

PLATE 6. July 17, 1991, Barbury Castle, near Swindon, Wiltshire County, wheat crop.

Photographer: © Karen Cushing.

Photographer: © Barbara Lamb.

PLATE 7. July 21, 1998, Beckhampton, Wiltshire County, wheat crop, 300' x 450'.
PLATE 7a. RIGHT: Standing tufts in "Stingray."

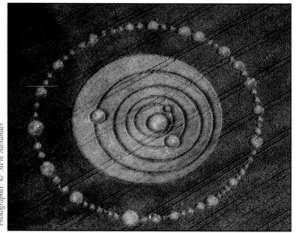

Photographer: © Steve Alexander.

PLATE 8. June 26, 1995, Longwood Warren, near Winchester, Hampshire County, wheat crop.

Photographer: © Steve Alexander.

PLATE 9. May 31, 1999, "Menorah," below Barbury Castle, near Swindon, Wiltshire County, barley crop.

Photographer: © Steve Alexander.

PLATE 10. June 19, 1999, next to Silbury Hill, Wiltshire County, wheat crop.

Photographer: © Steve Alexander.

PLATE 11. June 20, 1999, Avebury Trusloe, Wiltshire County, wheat crop.

Photographer: © Karen Cushing.

PLATE 12. June 23, 1999, West Overton, Wiltshire County, wheat crop.

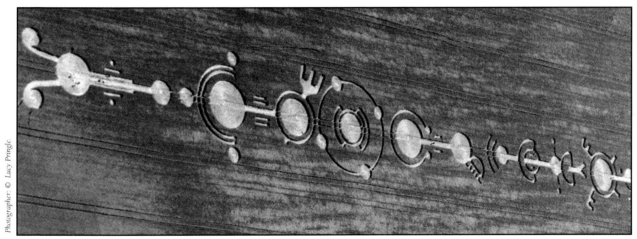

PLATE 13. June 12, 1999, East Field, Alton Barnes, Wiltshire County, barley crop.

PLATE 14. June 12, 1999, East Field, Alton Barnes, Wiltshire County, barley crop.

PLATE 15. June 23, 1999, "The Cube" at Allington Down, Wiltshire County, wheat crop.

PLATE 16. July 15, 1999, Honey Street, Alton Barnes, Wiltshire County, wheat crop.

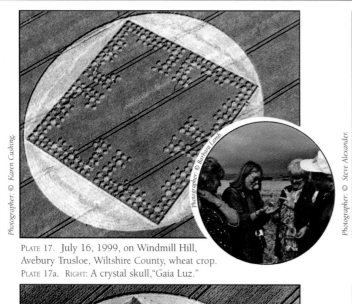

Photographer: © Karen Cushing.

Photographer: © Barbara Lamb.

PLATE 17. July 16, 1999, on Windmill Hill, Avebury Trusloe, Wiltshire County, wheat crop.
PLATE 17a. RIGHT: A crystal skull, "Gaia Luz."

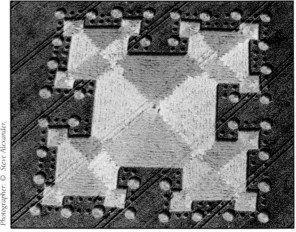

Photographer: © Steve Alexander.

PLATE 18. August 4, 1999, West Kennett Longbarrow, Wiltshire County, wheat crop.

Photographer: © Karen Cushing.

Photographer: © Barbara Lamb.

PLATE 19. July 18, 1999, Cherhill Down, Wiltshire County, wheat crop.
PLATE 19A. RIGHT: Anomalous light in Cherhill formation.

Photographer: © Karen Cushing.

PLATE 20. July 21, 1999, Liddington Castle, east of Chiseldon, Wiltshire County, wheat crop.

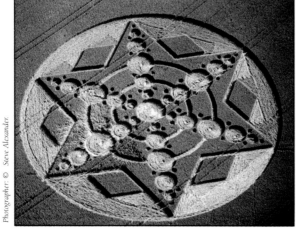

Photographer: © Steve Alexander.

PLATE 21. July 19, 1999, Devil's Den, near Fyfield, Manton and Marlborough, Wiltshire County, wheat crop, 250 feet in diameter.

Photographer: © Barbara Lamb.

Photographer: © Barbara Lamb.

PLATE 21a. Devil's Den crop circle, near Fyfield, Wiltshire.
PLATE 21b. RIGHT: Swirl, Devil's Den.

PLATE 22. July 24, 1999, across the A4 road from Silbury Hill, Wiltshire County, wheat crop.

PLATE 25. July 31, 1999, at Roundway, Devizes, Wiltshire County, wheat crop.

PLATE 23. July 28, 1999, at Beckhampton, Wiltshire County, wheat crop.
PLATE 23a. RIGHT: Overlapping flows of wheat.

PLATE 24. July 23, 1999, Barbury Castle, near Swindon, Wiltshire County, wheat crop.
PLATE 24a. RIGHT: Valja Roseman at Barbury Castle crop circle.

PLATE 24b. Rippled lay of wheat, Barbury Castle crop circle.

Photographer: © Karen Cushing.

Photographer: © Lucy Pringle.

PLATE 26. July 4, 1999, below Hackpen Hill, near Broad Hinton, Wiltshire County.
PLATE 26a. RIGHT: Overlooking crop circle.

Photographer: © Lucy Pringle.

PLATE 27. July 11, 1999, Rockley Down, Wiltshire County, wheat crop.

Photographer: © Steve Alexander.

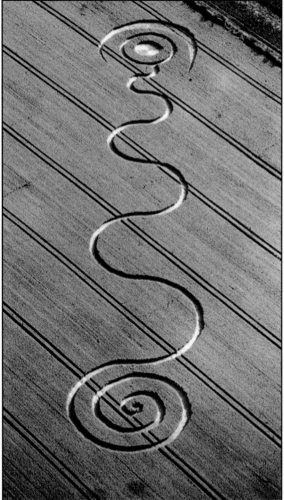

PLATE 29. August 5, 1999, Barbury Castle, near Swindon, Wiltshire County, wheat crop.

Photographer: © Karen Cushing.

PLATE 28. July 20, 1999, Allington Down, Wiltshire County, wheat crop.

Photographer: © Karen Cushing.

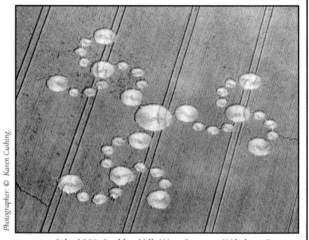

PLATE 30. July 1999, Lurkley Hill, West Overton, Wiltshire County, wheat crop.

PLATE 31. August 6, 1999, Bishops Cannings, Wiltshire County, wheat crop.

PLATE 33. July 22, 1999, Meon Woke, Hampshire County, wheat crop.

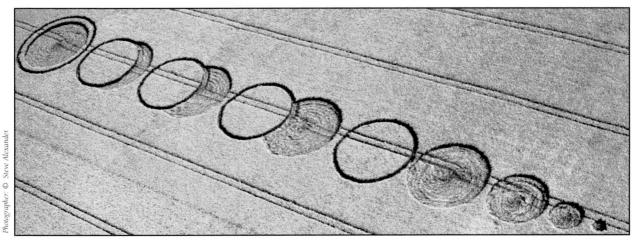

PLATE 32. May 2, 1999, Middle Wallop, Hampshire County, oilseed canola (rapeseed) crop.

PLATE 34. July 12, 1999, Wanford, Hampshire County, wheat crop.

PLATE 35. June 21, 1999, East End, near West Meon, Hampshire County, barley crop.

PLATE 36. May 30, 1999, Penton Grafton, Hampshire County, barley crop.

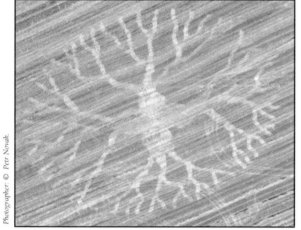

PLATE 38. July 21, 1999, Novy Jicin, North Moravia, Czech Republic, wheat crop.

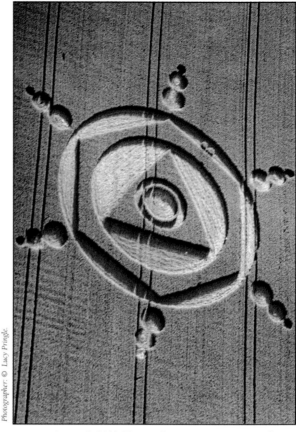

PLATE 37. August 3, 1999, Henwood, near East Meon, Hampshire County, wheat crop.

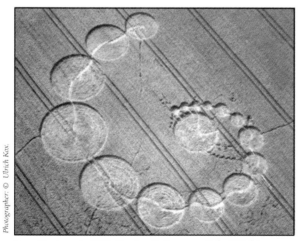

PLATE 39. August 1999, Newton St. Loe, near Bath, Wiltshire County, wheat crop.

PLATE 40. June 20, 1999, Trottiscliffe, near Maidstone, Kent, wheat crop.

Photographer: © Lucy Pringle.

Photographer: © Kate Dash.

PLATE 41. July 14, 2000, West Stowell, Wiltshire County, wheat crop.
PLATE 41a. RIGHT: Light sphere approaching Golden Ball Hill.

Photographer: © Lucy Pringle.

PLATE 42. June 19, 2000, South Field, Alton Priors, Wiltshire County, barley crop.

Photographer: © Lucy Pringle.

Photographer: © Judy Moore.

PLATE 43. July 16, 2000, Avebury Down, Wiltshire County, wheat crop.
PLATE 43a. RIGHT: Boy sleeping at the center of Avebury Down circle.

Photographer: © Karen Cushing.

PLATE 44. July 16, 2000, Picked Hill, near Wilcot, Wiltshire County, wheat crop.

Photographer: © Lucy Pringle.

Photographer: © Barbara Lamb.

PLATE 45. July 19, 2000, Milton Lilbourne, Wiltshire County, wheat crop.
PLATE 45a. RIGHT: Ground level of "Celtic Cross."

Photographer: © Barbara Lamb.

Photographer: © Barbara Lamb.

PLATE 45b. Barbara Lamb and Judy Moore in the "Celtic Cross" crop circle at Milton Hill Farm, Milton Lilbourne, near Pewsey, Wiltshire.
PLATE 45c. RIGHT: "Celtic Cross" crop circle, Milton Hill Farm.

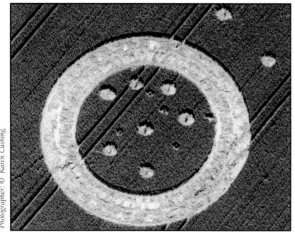

Photographer: © Karen Cushing.

PLATE 46. July 16, 2000, Old Shaw Village, near Lockeridge, Wiltshire County, wheat crop.

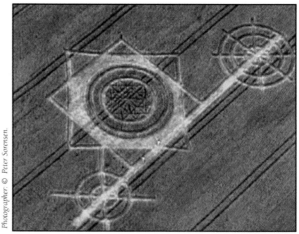

Photographer: © Peter Sorensen.

PLATE 47. July 30, 2000, Blackland, near Calne, Wiltshire County, wheat crop.

Photographer: © Lucy Pringle.

PLATE 48. June 18, 2000, Windmill Hill, Avebury Trusloe, Wiltshire County, barley crop.

Photographer: © Karen Cushing.
Photographer: © Lucy Pringle.

PLATE 49. July 1, 2000, Milk Hill, Alton Barnes, Wiltshire County, wheat crop.
PLATE 49a. RIGHT: Farmer Hues, owner of the "Rose Window" field.

Photographer: © Lucy Pringle.
Photographer: © Barbara Lamb.

PLATE 50. July 22, 2000, Avebury Trusloe, Wiltshire County, wheat crop.
PLATE 50a. RIGHT: Cross section.

Photographer: © Barbara Lamb.
Photographer: © Barbara Lamb.

PLATE 50b. John Clements doing hands-on healing.
PLATE 50c. Boy in diamond shaped cross section.

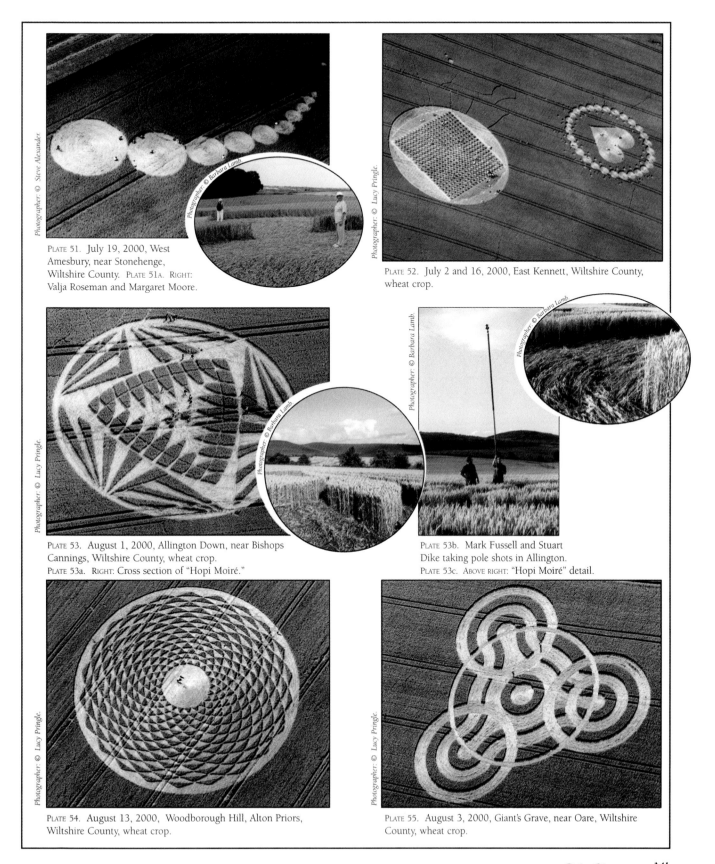

Photographer: © Steve Alexander

Photographer: © Barbara Lamb.

PLATE 51. July 19, 2000, West Amesbury, near Stonehenge, Wiltshire County. PLATE 51A. RIGHT: Valja Roseman and Margaret Moore.

Photographer: © Lucy Pringle.

PLATE 52. July 2 and 16, 2000, East Kennett, Wiltshire County, wheat crop.

Photographer: © Lucy Pringle.

Photographer: © Barbara Lamb.

Photographer: © Barbara Lamb.

PLATE 53. August 1, 2000, Allington Down, near Bishops Cannings, Wiltshire County, wheat crop.
PLATE 53a. RIGHT: Cross section of "Hopi Moiré."

PLATE 53b. Mark Fussell and Stuart Dike taking pole shots in Allington.
PLATE 53c. ABOVE RIGHT: "Hopi Moiré" detail.

Photographer: © Lucy Pringle.

PLATE 54. August 13, 2000, Woodborough Hill, Alton Priors, Wiltshire County, wheat crop.

Photographer: © Lucy Pringle.

PLATE 55. August 3, 2000, Giant's Grave, near Oare, Wiltshire County, wheat crop.

Photographer: © Lucy Pringle.

PLATE 56. August 11, 2000, Clench, Wiltshire County, wheat crop.

Photographer: © Lucy Pringle.

PLATE 57. August 5 and 13, 2000, Broadbury Banks, near Wilsford, Wiltshire County, wheat crop.

Photographer: © Lucy Pringle.

Photographer: © Barbara Lamb.

PLATE 58. June 26, 2000, Bishops Cannings, Wiltshire County, wheat crop.
PLATE 58a. RIGHT: Standing tuft in "Bells and Stars" crop circle.

Photographer: © Steve Alexander.

PLATE 59. June 18, 2000, Bishops Cannings Down, near Beckhampton, Wiltshire County, wheat crop.

Photographer: © Lucy Pringle.

PLATE 60. July 26, 2000, North Down, near Beckhampton, Wiltshire County, wheat crop.

Photographer: © Lucy Pringle.

PLATE 61. August 25, 2000, West Overton Hill, Wiltshire County, wheat crop.

Photographer: © Lucy Pringle.

Photographer: © Barbara Lamb.

Photographer: © Barbara Lamb.

PLATE 62. July 26, 2000, near Bishops Cannings, on A361, Wiltshire County, wheat crop.
PLATE 62a. RIGHT: A standing pyramid center.

PLATE 62b. "Pattern of Curves" crop circle.

Photographer: © Lucy Pringle.

PLATE 63. July 14 and 30, 2000, Bishops Sutton, Hampshire County, wheat crop.

Photographer: © Lucy Pringle.

PLATE 64. July 1, 2000, Stephen Castle Down, Upham, Hampshire County, oat crop.

Photographer: © Lucy Pringle.

PLATE 65. August 13, 2000, Chilbolton, near Andover, Hampshire County, wheat crop.

Photographer: © Andrew King.

PLATE 66. July 28, 2000, Telegraph Hill, near Pegsdon, Icknield Way, Bedfordshire, wheat crop.

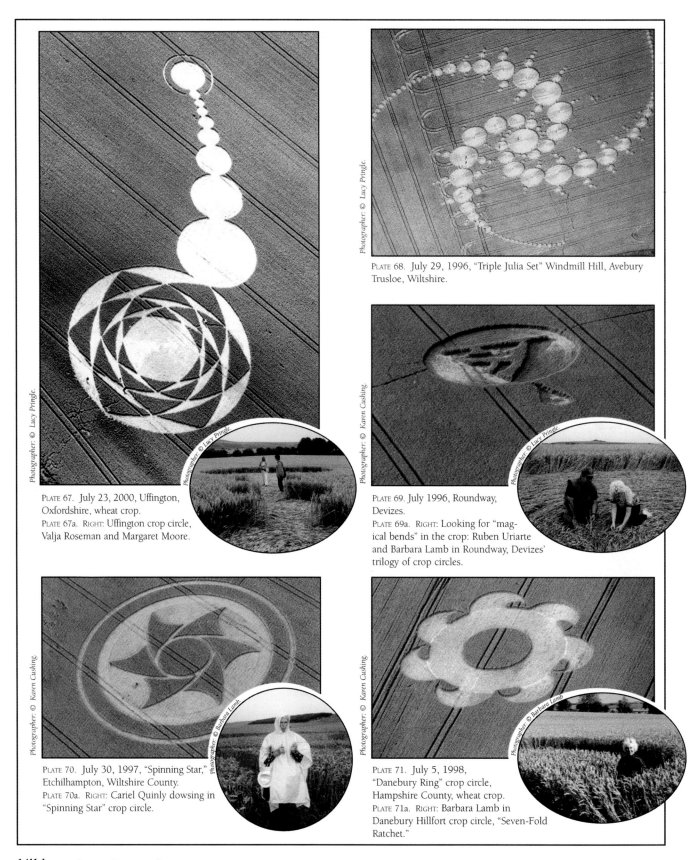

PLATE 68. July 29, 1996, "Triple Julia Set" Windmill Hill, Avebury Trusloe, Wiltshire.

PLATE 67. July 23, 2000, Uffington, Oxfordshire, wheat crop.
PLATE 67a. RIGHT: Uffington crop circle, Valja Roseman and Margaret Moore.

PLATE 69. July 1996, Roundway, Devizes.
PLATE 69a. RIGHT: Looking for "magical bends" in the crop: Ruben Uriarte and Barbara Lamb in Roundway, Devizes' trilogy of crop circles.

PLATE 70. July 30, 1997, "Spinning Star," Etchilhampton, Wiltshire County.
PLATE 70a. RIGHT: Cariel Quinly dowsing in "Spinning Star" crop circle.

PLATE 71. July 5, 1998, "Danebury Ring" crop circle, Hampshire County, wheat crop.
PLATE 71a. RIGHT: Barbara Lamb in Danebury Hillfort crop circle, "Seven-Fold Ratchet."

Photographer: © Albert Ridgley.

PLATE 72. Heart of crop circle territory: the White Horse on Milk Hill, Alton Barnes, Wiltshire County.

Photographer: © Barbara Lamb.

PLATE 73. July 1998, "The Green Man" and the crop circles on the ceiling of the crop circle room at the Barge Inn.

PLATE 73a. RIGHT: Germans studying the crop circle bulletin board at the Barge Inn.

Photographer: © Barbara Lamb.

PLATE 74. July 2000, Silbury Hill, from West Kennett Longbarrow looking over a harvested field.

Photographer: © Karen Cushing.

Photographer: © Barbara Lamb.

Photographer: © Barbara Lamb.

PLATE 75. July 23, 1998, "Silbury Hill II," Wiltshire County.

PLATE 75a. RIGHT: Hunting for "magical bends" in stalks.

PLATE 75b. LOWER RIGHT: Small circle center in crop circle next to Silbury Hill.

Photographer: © Barbara Lamb.

Photographer: © Barbara Lamb.

PLATE 76. August 1994, cutting through "Galaxy" circle, West Stowell, Wiltshire County.
PLATE 76A. RIGHT: Shawn Randall, Alton Priors, Wiltshire.

Photographer: © Barbara Lamb.

PLATE 77. July 1999, Francine Blake and Rod Bearcloud Berry climbing barbed-wire fence to get to a crop circle.

Photographer: © Karen Cushing.

PLATE 78. July 10, 1998, Lockeridge "Dragon," Wiltshire County, wheat crop.

Photographer: © Karen Cushing.

PLATE 79. August 6, 1998, Lockeridge, West Stowell, Wiltshire County, wheat crop.

Photographer: © Karen Cushing.

PLATE 80. July 4, 1998, Dadford, near Silverstone, Buckinghamshire, wheat crop.

Photographer: © Sharyl Noday.

PLATE 81. A 1993 crop circle: swirled center with standing stalks.

INTRODUCTION

Imagine you are driving up to the entrance of the Barge Inn on a balmy July evening in rural southern England. It's still twilight, and the stars are just appearing. You are about to enter another world.

The Barge Inn, an unprepossessing little pub at the end of a dead-end road in Honey Street, next to Alton Barnes, Wiltshire County, is the gathering place for crop circle enthusiasts, or *croppies*, from all over the world. This is a central information source for news about the spotting of new crop circles as well as a haven for the irresistible urge to share—and to mirror—the experiences of physically entering the formations.

If you enter the backroom, immediately your eye is caught by a map of southern England pinned on the wall and covered with colored stickers showing the locations of the season's crop circles. As reports of the new crop circles are tracked, veterans remember the crop circles made in the same or nearby fields in past years, and plans are made for visiting them, meditating in them and recording them to scale with drawings, surveys and computer graphics.

As the conversations ebb and flow nearby, you hear tantalizing fragments about intuitions received during meditations, the effects of the energies on dowsing rods and batteries, and what it feels like to stand in a new crop circle and know at the core of your being that no human could have created such miraculous constructions. Unfamiliar—or possibly familiar—terms strike your ears, such as Fibonacci spirals, fractals, Mandelbrots, the Golden Mean, vortices, synchronicities and other terms of mythology and sacred geometry. And over and under and through all the words spoken in several accents and languages, you can pick up the feelings of excitement, awe and curiosity about the crop circles and their makers, whether the speakers are on their first or twentieth visit.

Welcome to the world of crop circles, one of the most tantalizing phenomena in our world today. It is difficult not to be captivated by their beauty and complexity and by the questions and issues they provoke, including the query that becomes more pressing every day: What other intelligent life forms are out there trying to communicate with us? What are their intentions? What is the communication system between them, the Earth and humanity? Consider this: Groups of croppies have meditated together on visual patterns and projected the intention that crop circles would be made of those images. And that has happened. What do events like that do to our world-view? Send to our view of the cosmos?

We, Barbara Lamb and Judy Moore, felt impelled to gather together information available on crop circles, especially those in southern England that Barbara has been visiting for ten years and that captivated Judy before her visit in the summer of 1999. It is impossible to ignore the synchronicity of the proliferation of crop circles near Stonehenge, Silbury Hill and other ancient sacred sites. We wanted to share with you the awe, the anticipation, the passion, the reverence, the beauty, the questions, the theories, the comraderie of the croppies, the pictures. Judy has channeled general information about the crop circle phenomenon as well as specifics about a number of crop formations that her source, Laiolin, selected. Laiolin is a thirteen-dimensional being of great wisdom and awareness with whom Judy is merged.

The information in this book has come from many sources, human and otherwise. Unfortunately, we have lost track of some of the sources of our information over the years. We would hear a theory about a crop circle and it felt right intuitively, so we incorporated it. Several years and many crop circles later we might have forgotten who first stated that point of view, at what convention or on what evening sitting in the Barge Inn or in a crop circle after a meditation. Many ideas grew synergistically from what we would consider group consciousness, and often it has been difficult to give credit to any one individual. We apologize to anyone who recognizes that he or she is the original source of a fact or idea and we did not provide accurate acknowledgment. Please contact us so we can provide more accurate information in later editions of this book.

Humanity is changing. Our perspectives are broadening rapidly in this age of Internet communication, satellite TV and videotapes. We believe that the crop circles—and the reactions they have generated—have much to add to humanity's growth spurt in consciousness. We are pleased to contribute to the growth spurt with this book on crop circles. We thank the many beings, terrestrial and extraterrestrial, who have enriched our understanding of the crop circles and, at the same time, our understanding of what it means to be human on planet Earth at this time when we believe it is becoming impossible to deny or ignore that *we are not alone.*

Barbara Lamb

In tracing the roots of how I became involved in writing this book, I recognize that I have had a lifelong curiosity about what is behind all that we see and know in our physical lives, and what is real. I always have had a strong sense that this physical world is not all there is and that there must be much more to reality than what we ordinarily know. This led me to the study of philosophy at Mount Holyoke College in Massachusetts. Years later, I became a licensed psychotherapist and movement therapist, dedicated to bringing people whatever is behind the scenes, causing people's symptoms and difficulties.

My five years of professional training as a regression therapist through the Association for Past Life Research and Therapies opened me up to the multidimensional aspects of our beingness. In regression work, my clients revisited previous lifetimes and in many cases relived experiences they had had with extraterrestrial beings (ETs) during this and previous lives. Sometimes they regressed to actually being a member of these other species themselves. A few of them channeled extraterrestrials or multidimensional beings in my office. Thus my perspective of reality and of the cosmos—full of other beings—expanded.

My own personal experiences corroborated my awareness of beings on many levels of existence. In 1968, I had an unexpected spirit visitation by my deceased favorite aunt, which led me to know that beings existing in other levels or dimensions of reality can visit us and communicate with us. This enlightening experience was repeated years later with my deceased father, mother and brother.

When I saw my first tiny picture of a crop circle in the program guide of the 1990 Whole Life Expo in Los Angeles and read the title of the lecture, "Crop Circles in England," I flashed on the notion of ET beings coming to Earth and giving physical evidence of their existence. I was thrilled. That lecture, given by Erik Beckjord, inspired me to commit to going to England the following summer to see these amazing crop formations for myself. Since then, I have driven around southwest England every summer, exploring as many crop circles as possible. I began exploring with my English husband, Warren, and next with my son, Chris. Later, I continued exploring as a speaker with Power Places Tours and with my friend Shawn Randall, and finally for a few years on my own and with various friends. I intend to continue these explorations as long as the phenomenon continues and my body allows.

After my first crop circle visits in 1991, I began to speak to groups of people about the amazing phenomenon of crop circles. The enthusiastic responses to these lectures encouraged me to continue researching and sharing this information. Over the past ten years, I have spoken at hundreds of groups and conferences in the United States and England and have been on numerous television and radio shows and Internet broadcasts. Many people have asked when I was going to write a book about crop circles, but I considered myself too busy to commit the time to do it.

In October 1999, I serendipitously met Judy Moore at a Star Knowledge Conference where I was lecturing about crop circles. She had previously known nothing about the circles but was fascinated with my color photographs. She began channeling wonderful information about a few of these patterns, receiving information from the thirteenth-dimensional source with whom she had merged (Laiolin). Then and there we decided to collaborate in writing a book about crop formations—she with the channeled transmissions and I with the history and information on crop circles from the "Earth" point of view.

I have provided the written research: information from my years of experience within the crop circles and at crop circle conferences, the photographs and the black-and-white figure drawings of crop circles that illustrate my text. Judy has provided the extraordinary transmissions of information for sixty-seven crop formations and the accompanying channeled star glyph drawings. Precious perspectives about the huge forces at work are offered by highly conscious beings who are working to help us save humanity and the Earth and to help us evolve in consciousness and spirituality.

When Judy and I came together in October 1999, our mission was to share with as many people as possible our information about the amazing crop circle phenomenon. We responded intuitively to the significance of these lovely symbols that appear in crop fields worldwide. We each have the conviction that these symbols have profound meaning and that the intelligence behind them is trying to tell us something important for the betterment of humanity. We elected to focus primarily on crop circles in England, which hosts a numerous and complex array of formations each year.

We like the balance we each provide in this sharing—I, with my ten years of personal crop circle research in England and years of reading and study of the phenomenon, and Judy's high-level, insightful transmissions of information about the crop circles from a higher-dimensional source. Judy also contributes a sensitive awareness of the sacred monuments and natural features that magnetize crop circles to them. She wrote most of the material about the historical and mythological significance of the sacred sites. Our trip to crop circle territory in England in the summer of 2000 expanded my appreciation for the relationship between crop circles and those special areas, and deepened her understanding of the connection of Earth energies with spiritual energies and consciousness. We believe that together we offer an important balance of perspective on the crop circle phenomenon.

We both have a painful awareness of the challenging situations and dynamics that humanity and the Earth itself are going through. We know that humans could either grievously impair or destroy life on this planet or help it evolve into a higher consciousness, a greater refinement of vibrations and a more decent, loving, enlightened way of living amongst ourselves and with our cosmic siblings and neighbors. Through our individual experiences, we are convinced that there are evolved, enlightened beings out there in the cosmos and in higher dimensions, aware of us mortals in crisis on Earth and trying to help us advance and become participating, contributing members of the multidimensional cosmic community.

Judith Moore

The mysterious phenomenon of the crop circles has entered the very core of my being. For a time, I, like many other people, did not particularly pay attention to the circles. I knew they were special and beautiful, but I hadn't read a book or attended a lecture on the subject until I met Barbara Lamb.

Barbara was lecturing on the crop circles at a Star Knowledge Conference in Pomona, California, in November 1999. I had been doing altered-state work, activating energies at sacred sites with Taskara, a man who runs a Mayan Center in Los Angeles. An arrangement was made for me to do a reading for Barbara Lamb while I was viewing crop circle pictures with her. As I channeled Laiolin, I held Taskara's Mayan fetish that he calls Tolktan [see Appendix B, "Tolktan Speaks"].

We were all amazed as, with each picture shown, the star beings gave an interpretive transmission. At the same time, I drew the image of the star glyphs on paper. We were told in the channeled session that the star glyphs are from the archives of the Great Central Sun, or the Records of Ra. They are the language of creation, a hieroglyphic cosmic language of light.

In that reading, we realized that we were being given an important gift by the star beings; we had a lot of work to do. The star beings who chose me to be the messenger of this information also insisted that I did not read Barbara's section of the book until I had finished all of the transmissions in my section.

The process of bringing in the channeled transmissions was very intense. Since I have channeled Laiolin since 1992, I am accustomed to the energies of being in an altered state. However, the work I had to do to bring in the crop circle transmissions affected me physically in a profound way, often requiring the ingestion of minerals and rest after each transmission. The star beings have explained that the transmissions enter the right hemisphere of my brain as light frequencies, encoded within the images of the glyph. These are first translated into images my brain can recognize, then into English by the left hemisphere of my brain. This is why I get so tired when I am doing the work, even though I am being funded with extra energy to support me.

Initially, I recorded the transmissions on a tape recorder and then transcribed them, which is a lot of work. After the first nineteen glyphs were complete, Laiolin told me that I was to learn to type in a trance, which would facilitate the process. This requires the simultaneous use of the left and right hemispheres of the brain; it took practice and a lot of spell-checking. After a while, I discovered that it was quite easy as my skills of using the right and left hemispheres improved to a state of ease.

My ascension process has also quickened over this year. I have observed a deep state of emotional and spiritual peace. My intuitive skills have improved, I am more grounded when doing altered state work than I have ever been, and my health has markedly improved. Overall, I can honestly say that this project has been incredibly beneficial to me. All of the transmissions of the crop circles for 1999 were done in my home in New Mexico. I was told by the star beings that the first thirty-five transmissions had to be completed between the solar eclipse and the lunar eclipse in January 2000.

The content of the transmissions astounded us. Barbara has a great deal of experience in this field and has told me that to her knowledge the capacity of the work is entirely unique. We soon realized that the information had to be published. At that time, I had never visited the crop circles in Great Britain.

▶ *July 19, 2000, Judy in "Heart Circle" crop circle.*

▼ *Star glyph dowsed by Margaret.*

The more I worked, the more intrigued I became. As summer approached, I decided to join Barbara Lamb on her annual trip to do research in Great Britain. We had submitted the manuscript to a publisher and were going to do a second book about the summer 2000 experiences. We later decided to incorporate the summer 2000 crop circles in the original book as well as the incredible crop circles that appeared after I left.

During this journey, the work took on new dimensions. Though I received amazing validation of my transmissions from the lectures at the two crop circle symposiums I attended, it astounded me how much more material was covered in my transmissions. The star beings have chosen me as a messenger, and for this I am truly grateful. I had no idea that there were theories about the very subject matter contained in these transmissions. Yet the transmissions go far deeper than anything I have read or studied since beginning the channeling. I haven't ever taken a course in physics, advanced geometry or quantum physics.

The weeks in Great Britain were filled with wonderful crop circle experiences; I am truly a "croppie," now. I participated in many wonderful prayers and ceremonies for world peace and visited ancient sacred sites and sacred churches. I even got married in a crop circle. I became an active part of the phenomenon.

Literally, everyone you meet has the same question: "Do you think it is man-made?" I do not care who made them. In my opinion, it is an ET-assisted phenomenon of the collective consciousness. The truth is, no one knows for sure if star beings didn't telepathically guide the "man-made" ones, and no one can figure it out. It is a mystery.

After visiting crop circle country, I definitely understand why so many crop circles are appearing in Wiltshire County. It feels like heaven on Earth. As I close my eyes, I see the lovely countryside, sacred sites, sacred springs, ancient holy churches, beautiful gardens and green fields—canvases ripe for creation. And then there's the Barge Inn, the meeting place for all the incredibly interesting people who come from great distances to explore the crop circles. We stayed at Well Cottage in Alton Barnes, a little piece of heaven. Just for the record, the Brits are great cooks. I'll take pub food any day over a chain restaurant in the United States.

It is amazing to me that I did not know the mythological history of Silbury Hill when I did transmission twenty-two. Once you read the transmissions, you will see that the theme of the birthing of Gaia (Mother Earth) is a crucial part of the entire manuscript. In the U.K., I met J. D. Wakefield, the author of *Legendary Landscapes*. I eagerly read this important book and realized the link between the mythology of the birthing goddess and the channeled material in my manuscript. I believe there is a deep link between the mythological history of this area and the apparition of the crop circles.

Crop circle country is filled with intrigue and mystery. The experience of sitting in a crop circle and creating a star glyph on site was very powerful. The star glyphs for crop circles forty-one through fifty-two, fifty-eight, fifty-nine, sixty-three and sixty-four were completed on site. On July 19, we entered a crop circle in West Lavington and I created a star glyph that appeared with remarkable likeness on July 26, 2000. The day the crop circle appeared, I was on my way to St. Michael's Mount.

Another intriguing experience involves dowsing. When we entered a circle, Barbara and our companions would dowse the energies while I did the star glyph. Just for fun, I asked Margaret, a lady from South Africa, to dowse one of my star glyphs. She got distinctive dowsing results, showing that part of the glyph dowsed with male energy and part with female energy. At breakfast the next morning at Well Cottage, I met a lady from the British Society of Dowsers. Just for fun, I asked her to dowse the images, without mentioning our previous findings. Her dowsing was exactly like Margaret's. The conclusion was that the star glyphs emanate a consistent energy field that can be detected with dowsing.

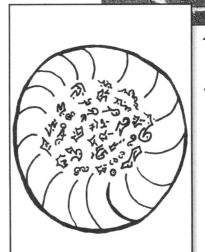

Photographer: © Lucy Pringle.

▲ *July 26, 2000, North Down, near Beckhampton*

◀ *Star glyph dowsed by Margaret.*

Appendixes A, B and C contain a variety of important information that might not appear to be directly related to the crop circles. The star beings have instructed me to include these teachings for the reader who wishes to delve deeper into the cosmic principles related to the phenomenon.

One last note concerning the use of the word "evolution" in the text: Please do not associate this word with Darwin's theory of evolution. This word is used merely to convey the concept of a process related to the evolvement of humanity over the ages. Clarification is likewise needed for the use of the word "mutation." It is defined as the evolution of the perfect blueprint of the Eden principle. *The Keys of Enoch* refers to this as the Adamic man, or the blueprint of what God intended man to be.

BECOMING A CHANNEL

The channeled transmissions are telepathically received from the star beings via Laiolin, a cosmic being of light. She is extraterrestrial and multidimensional. Throughout the years, she has referred to communications with the mothership. She is a member of the Galactic Federation and the Council of Abborah.

I also have a mystical connection to the Great Cobra, a high-level being of great benevolence who has appeared in history linked with such spiritual beings as Quetzalcóatl and Buddha. During a trance journey in 1995, she came as my teacher. The first place I ever saw the star glyphs was in the antechamber of her cave during a trance journey over three years ago. When I am doing the transmissions of the star glyphs, I meditate and go to the Cave of the Great Cobra's antechamber, where I receive the images of the star glyphs. It is not surprising to me that the mythology of the area is intensely connected to serpentine energy.

I am a spiritual interpreter, or a sensitive, and a conscious-merge channel for Laiolin. (The term "spiritual interpreter" refers to the fact that my work is broader than just channeling. I receive visions, telepathic transmissions from sacred entities, remote view and much more.) I am the oracle; Laiolin is the starbeing who brings the transmissions through me. She is a keeper of the Records of Ra, the cosmic records of creation of the Great Central Sun, which include Mother Earth. Laiolin has explained to me that she is a thirteenth-dimensional ambassador of the Central Sun and a member of the Council of Abborah and the Galactic Federation. She taught me that there are twelve solar temples around the Central Sun and that the thirteenth is within the Central Sun. Laiolin has taught me about the mystical history of the House of David, or the cosmic Christ consciousness. Her mission is to awaken the House of David in the third dimension. The channeled history of the House of David is presented in Appendix B. It is not directly related to the crop circles, but it is pertinent to understanding the messages of the circlemakers.

I became coexistent with Laiolin in March of 1992. I don't channel and leave my body; I visually experience the information and am co-conscious while I am in trance. The day I merged with Laiolin was a beautiful spring day. I was receiving Hakomi therapy. I was in a deep meditation when she appeared to me as a cosmic being of light, or an angel. She told me that in her dimension she is pure light. She came in the angelic form to assist me in relating to my experience. In her essence, she is neither male nor female; her gender was chosen to facilitate the process of communication. Laiolin is a higher-dimensional aspect of myself.

She asked me if I wanted to help heal the planet. As a child, I had made a vow to be of service to my people. It was an easy choice to make, and I agreed to work with her. She activated my heart chakra, and I had a very intense light experience. She gave me three gifts: strength without power, protection without defense and battle without war.

At that point of my life, I was engaged in an intense journey for inner healing—what is referred to as dancing with your shadow. I call it my journey from fear to freedom. During this time, Laiolin facilitated my healing journey. I have even been up on starships for healing experiences.

For the next two years, she introduced me to the skills of being a conscious-merge channel. It was a pretty big shock because I really had not read about or been very interested in channels or channeling. I began to receive high-level transmissions that were validated by independent sources afterward. About a year later, Barbara Marciniak, a channel and the author of *Bringers of the Dawn*, came to Santa Fe for a conference. While listening to her, I realized that the channeled information was not new to me. It was information that Laiolin had taught me. Other sources of verification came from reading books including *The Celestine Prophecy, Awakening to Zero Point* and *The Pleiadian Agenda*. I realized that I was receiving important information and decided to pursue the journey. It is important to mention that in all things I am protected by the heart of Christ Jesus.

After these two years, Laiolin told me that I would have a year to sample the work by doing channelings for family and friends. At the end of this year, Laiolin ask me if I wanted to continue the training process. I agreed to continue. She told me that I would have a year of initiations and preparation for my vows to serve in this capacity. I was told that I must take a vow not to drink alcohol or use recreational drugs, not to lie, not to steal, not to participate in violence for entertainment and not to participate in the abuse of sexual energy. Later, I learned that these are similar to the five precepts of Buddhism.

I then entered a four-year period of intense experiential learning and initiation. During this time, I had experiences where I believe I was taken on ships. Once I was told telepathically that on the ship, my brain's neurosynapses were expanded and I was prepared to receive large amounts of electromagnetic frequencies. My health has improved, and I have attained a deep feeling of inner peace. This training/initiation process spanned eight years, a period that I believe prepared me to be the cosmic messenger for these transmissions.

I am deeply humbled by the opportunity to serve in such a powerful way. My prayer is that you the reader will benefit from this information, for each of us is an important part of the creation of the new world of peace and the emergence of heaven on Earth.

A COMPREHENSIVE LOOK AT THE CROP CIRCLE PHENOMENON

BARBARA LAMB

WHERE CROP CIRCLES ARE FOUND

A crop circle is a design or pattern laid gently down in a growing crop, leaving the surrounding crop, the *standing crop*, growing normally. Each stalk of the crop in a crop formation is gently bent over near ground level. There is no crushing, squashing, bruising, cutting, breaking, burning or damaging of the crops in any way. In fact, the plants remain in perfect condition, and they continue to grow parallel to the ground, coming to full maturity and ripening. The contrast between the laid-down stalks against the surrounding standing stalks is what makes the crop circle noticeable, drawing the attention of people passing by or flying overhead. These patterns occur most frequently in cultivated crops such as wheat, oilseed canola (rapeseed), barley, oats, hay, corn, rye, potato, spinach and rice, and in leguminous plants including soy. They appear in grassy fields, heather, fields of wildflowers and beds of reeds. They also occur in winter crops such as beets and kale. In Mexico, they appear in sugar cane. In China and Japan, crop circles are found in rice paddies, a circle of swirled plants with the water drained out.

AUGUST 1994, BARBARA LAMB IN THE "GALAXY" CROP CIRCLE, WEST STOWELL, WILTSHIRE COUNTY.

1999, MARLBOROUGH, WILTSHIRE COUNTY.

This phenomenon is full of surprises. No one knows in which country or field a crop circle will next appear, what the design will be, how beautifully and perfectly the stalks will be laid down, what the energies will be, how many crop circles will appear that year or when the season of crop circles will begin and end. No one knows at the beginning of the season, each spring, if crop circles will appear at all. This phenomenon is a gift we should not take for granted.

No one knows in advance what the theme of the designs will be, or whether or not they will trigger recognition in the eye of the beholder and evoke a sense of meaning and significance. No one knows how much energy people will feel in the crop circles or what kinds of anomalies will occur in or near them before, during or after their appearance. Enthusiasts who are artists, or who are artistically inclined, eagerly await the new designs, hoping for new and beautiful motifs to emerge. Geometricians guess at the next intricate or meaningful formulas that will dazzle their minds. Scientists await the next clues that might help them unravel the mystery of the circles. Metaphysically and spiritually inclined seekers anticipate what kinds of inspiring symbols might appear to raise their consciousness. These surprises and mysteries continue to stimulate crop circle enthusiasts and encourage them to remain faithfully involved in the subject.

In this book, I focus primarily on crop formations in southern England, as this is the region in which the overwhelming majority of crop circles appear each year. Not only are crop circles more numerous in England, but in many people's opinion, they are the most beautiful and complex in design, the most recognizable in symbolic meaning and the most meticulous and accomplished in execution. However, crop circles occur wherever there are fields of crops, especially cereal (grain) crops. An estimated thirty-five to forty-five countries have been receiving these unusual formations, notably the United States, Canada, Mexico, countries in South America, Australia, New Zealand, Ireland, Holland, Austria, Germany, Italy, Spain, Israel, the Czech Republic, Scandinavia, Russia, China, Japan and parts of Africa..

Unfortunately, no widely identified database or reporting center is known to people worldwide, especially in rural areas. Due to the incomplete reporting of crop circles worldwide, and even in England, it is difficult to assess how many crop circles have appeared over the years. It generally is estimated by researchers that between the early 1980s through the year 2000, nearly nine thousand crop circles or more complex formations have appeared worldwide. The numbers of crop circles occurring in England have increased through the 1980s and 1990s. In 1999, a record-breaking three hundred crop formations were discovered, which some people felt was an honoring farewell to the twentieth century and a magnificent welcoming to the new millennium.

THE SPECIAL WILTSHIRE COUNTY AREA

Many people wonder why England, specifically, is the site for ninety to ninety-five percent of the crop circles that we know about in the world, and why the formations occur mostly in the "Wessex Triangle," the area of southern England between Winchester, Warminster and Wantage, including Wiltshire, Hampshire and Sussex Counties. A few crop circles each year are scattered around Kent County, Staffordshire, Oxfordshire and other agricultural areas of England. Occasionally, a crop circle appears right next to a major motorway in plain sight of motorists speeding by, as if the creators deliberately wanted their artwork to be seen by many people.

Many researchers have noted that crop circles often appear near ancient sacred sites and megalithic stones that were located on active ley lines and vortices of Earth energy. These were believed to be powerful, magical locations on which the ancient people grounded and projected energies by building large stone monuments. These energy points appear to attract the making of crop circles. It is hypothesized that the circlemakers need the ley lines and energy vortices to make their formations, or they are trying to infuse or activate latent energy in the Earth by adding crop formations there.

VALE OF PEWSEY HILLS, THE SERPENTINE/GODDESS HILLS IN CROP CIRCLE TERRITORY, ALTON BARNES, WILTSHIRE COUNTY.

The ancient sites in Wiltshire County that frequently attract crop circles are Stonehenge, the Avebury complex, Silbury Hill, the Sanctuary of ancient wooden posts, the Avenue of Stones leading from Avebury toward Silbury Hill, West Kennett Longbarrow, Adam's Grave, the Oliver's Castle hillfort, the ancient ring at Alton Priors, Danebury Ring (an ancient hillfort), tumulus mounds, sacred springs, mystical churches and large white chalk horses carved into steep hillsides. There are nine chalk horses in Wiltshire County, carved during various centuries beginning in prehistoric times in chalk laid down in the Upper Cretaceous geological period. The ancient peoples in this area believed horses were spirits of the solar cycle and carried the souls of the dead to the underworld. In the following discussion, several excellent books were used as references about the Wiltshire area sacred sites and the ley line energies present there: *Mysterious Britain* (Janet and Colin Bord), *The Silbury Treasure* (Michael Dames), *The Sun and the Serpent* (Hamish Miller and Paul Broadhurst) and *Legendary Landscapes: Secrets of Ancient Wiltshire Revealed* (John and Julie Wakefield). Readers interested in more in-depth information are referred to these texts. The common mythological themes of these sacred sites are concentrated on the Goddess, the Maiden, the Hag, the Pregnant Goddess and the Serpent.

JULY 1998, BARBARA LAMB IN CHERHILL "WHITE HORSE" CROP CIRCLE.

Silbury Hill is considered by many people to be the heart of crop circle territory. Since the 1970s, it has consistently attracted crop formations in nearby fields. A noticeable feature for miles around, Silbury Hill is 130 feet high from the base. In the winter months it is surrounded by a ring of water, which gives it a mystical look. This ring is a carefully constructed moat that creates an outline of a reclining woman. Although Silbury Hill has a round shape on the outside and is covered with soil and grass, the underlying structure of the hill actually is a *ziggurat*, or step pyramid with six steps, similar to South America's pyramids. It was the largest man-made earthwork in Neolithic Europe and is one of two conical pyramids in England, estimated to be comparable in volume to the second pyramid at Giza. Silbury Hill was built approximately five thousand years ago, about the same time as the placing of the enormous megalithic stones at Avebury. It was constructed of alternate layers of limestone and soil (organic and inorganic materials), like Wilhelm Reich's orgone accumulator chambers. Never used as a tomb, it seems to be some sort of battery storage cell, which attracts anomalous spheres and shafts of light, UFOs and even beings of light. It is thought to be an attractor and transducer of energy.

Silbury Hill was a major site for fertility rituals and for worshipping the goddess of harvest. For centuries it was known as the Hill of Mars. In their book, *The Sun and the Serpent*, Hamish Miller and Paul Broadhurst write about the mystical area around Silbury Hill, with its sacred springs and its energy lines running through the Earth—lines called serpent lines or ley lines. Ancient people performed Beltane rituals here. "The whole crux of the Beltane ritual was to do with timing and we had often wondered how great numbers of people, assembled for the Mayday rite, could be co-ordinated in the dark to arrive at the Henge at the correct time. Silbury was the answer. It was the communications centre. From its flattened summit, both ends of the Serpent Temple were intervisible. It was a stage where the symbolic rites were performed, watched by all those who participated in a ritual spread over an entire sacred landscape. At the appropriate moment, signals could be given to the two extremities of the serpent's body, triggering a process that would fuse the energies from its tail to other, country-wide currents that linked sacred sites up and down the land. At a time determined by the cycles of the heavens, the energies of the Sun would stream down an alignment of shrines, positioned according to their function, to create an orgasmic coupling of male and female energies throughout the land" (Miller and Broadhurst 1998, 203).

It is noteworthy that in 1988, a large grouping of fifty-eight crop circles, forming quincunx or quadruplet designs, appeared over a period of weeks in the field across from Silbury Hill. They were placed on the female energy line called the Mary Line, which runs between Silbury Hill and nearby sacred Swallowhead Spring. On May 4, 1998, a crop circle 222 feet in diameter called the "Beltane Ring" appeared at that same location, seeming to honor the ancient rituals performed in that area during prehistoric times.

In *The Silbury Treasure*, Michael Dames states, "Silbury is the Great Goddess, pregnant. . . . The Hill or womb is (naturally) composed of material derived almost entirely from the mother's body, i.e. the quarry. Mother Earth gave rise to Silbury Hill, and in the process revealed her whole body. . . . What is more, she appears squatting in the Neolithic birth

SWALLOWHEAD SPRING, A SACRED SPRING NEAR SILBURY HILL.

position, ready to give birth to the unborn child within Silbury Hill, the child of a million forms and names . . ." (Dames 1976, 54-55). In these modern times, the crop formations with their individual sacred geometric identities are her children.

Isabelle Kingston, a well-respected English psychic and trance channel, has channeled that spiritual power from other dimensions is drawn down into Silbury Hill, which is the hill of the shining beings, or the Watchers, who came to ancient wise people. They began helpful work on Earth and directed the building of Silbury Hill. In fact, the word "Sil" comes from the word meaning shining being. The foundations of the ancient structures were laid to help humanity at a later, cataclysmic time—which probably is now (Kingston 1991, 150).

Another kind of crop circle site is a mound surrounded by a moat. Silbury Hill and Old Sarum (near Salisbury and Stonehenge) both feature steep man-made hills with flat tops, surrounded by water-filled ditches. It is believed that these locations are an important part of the ley line system. The ring of water draws attention to convergences of ley lines (power points) by reflecting in the water light from the sky and perhaps reflecting the light of beacons from the top of the mound when seen at a distance from higher ground.

Using deer antlers for tools, ancient people deliberately remolded the countryside as an integral part of their way of life. "By sculpturing the forms of the hills and downs they could enhance and magnify those currents of natural energies that flowed, and still do flow, through the body of the earth, and by the use of sound, movement, and above all thought, in the form of solemn and joyful ceremonies they could manipulate the vibrations in order to bring the bountiful and vital life force flowing through the land and the people" (Bord and Bord 1984, 204).

Across the road from Silbury Hill is West Kennett Longbarrow, the largest stone mound and chamber in England, where pre-Celtic peoples buried their dead. This was the site of elaborate rituals concerning death and rebirth and provided a symbolic womb from which the dead ancestors could be reborn. In prehistoric mythology, the Mother goddess who gave birth to all life became the Hag goddess who presided over the dead (Wakefield and Wakefield 1999, 79).

This and other longbarrows always seem to have attracted animals and people. Created in ways similar to Wilhelm Reich's orgone chambers or boxes, the longbarrows had a positive effect upon life forms with their accumulation of strong energies. Longbarrows were cairns for early people who entered into the darkness to communicate with ancestors and the spirit of the place. They would ask questions and create new happenings with thought in these enclosed, womblike stone structures, which were often built over underground water sites and energy lines. Thus would their thoughts be consolidated and transmitted.

West Kennett Longbarrow has attracted many crop circles since the 1980s, as well as many anomalous glowing lights. It is widely believed that

JULY 1999, ISABELLE KINGSTON.

BARBARA LAMB PLACING PRAYER ON SACRED TREE BY WEST KENNETT LONGBARROW BURIAL MOUNDS. THIS IS A TRADITIONAL WAY TO HONOR THE ANCESTORS OF THESE SACRED SITES.

all ancient megalithic sites serve as beacons and attractors of energy and of both physical and nonphysical visitors from space. The whole Wessex area has been imbued with a sense of mystery for many centuries. King Arthur is said to have spent time here, and mysterious large black cats, dogs, ghosts and witches have been seen here.

In the heart of the Wiltshire crop circle territory is the tiny village of Alton Barnes, located near Silbury Hill, West Kennett Longbarrow, Swallowhead Spring and the Avebury complex. The fields around Alton Barnes have birthed many crop circles over the years. Here, as in Avebury, there is a recurrent theme of the Goddess in local mythology. The hills just north of Alton Barnes are undulating and serpentine for several miles running east and west. They look like a huge woman or goddess lying in repose, with certain features of this lovely landscape forming the appearance of her breast (Adam's Grave), pregnant stomach (Knap Hill) and vulva (a small alcove just to the east of Knap Hill). This alcove is in a confluence of underground waters and has two thick copses of trees. It has

Photographer: © Judith K. Moore.

THIS LOVELY OLD SAXON CHURCH IS LOCATED NEAR THE AVEBURY STONE CIRCLE, IN THE VILLAGE OF AVEBURY.

been and still is used for sacred Celtic ceremonies and ritual practices, celebrating fertility, the harvest and the Goddess. This "Alton Goddess" stretched across the area landscape even has a carved pathway or trench that looks like a serpentine umbilical cord running down the hillside and into the well-known East Field, where many of the major crop circles have appeared over the years. Again, this landscape suggests that the Goddess is giving birth to the crop circles as her children.

A small longbarrow on top of one of these hills is called Adam's Grave, which is next to the Milk Hill barrow. It is said that if anyone circles around Adam's Grave on foot seven or nine times, he will awaken the giant. Is this a myth, or is there an ancient force within these sacred formations that is waiting to awaken?

The view from the top of Knap Hill is wonderful. One can see the lay of the lush, gentle landscape for miles. A lovely little Saxon church can be seen in the village of Alton Priors. Here on a bronze plaque behind the altar is a depiction of a man, presumably a lord, resurrecting from a tomb. Is this a Christian way of representing the legend of the giant rising from nearby Adam's Grave? This could be a link to Adam and Eve and the return to Eden, or the emergence of heaven on Earth.

Beneath a trap door in the floor of this little church is a holed Sarcen stone. In Wiltshire, the old name for Sarcen stones is *bridestones*. What are the mystical powers of ancient stones like this one that merit a church being built over them and a trap door being installed to permit access? Here, as in other places in the world, the church was built over an ancient holy site. Perhaps the true mystical nature of the site has been

Photographer: © Judith K. Moore.

BAPTISMAL ALTAR COVER IN SAXON CHURCH, AVEBURY.

lost or destroyed in an effort on the part of the church leaders to suppress the natural Earth religions and their pagan wisdom. This church was built near a holy spring where people still go to make offerings. The water is alleged to have curative powers. This underground water is part of the moisture that is drawn from the Earth for the formation of local crop circles.

The view from nearby pyramid-shaped Picked Hill is splendid. From the top, one can see the entire sacred landscape in a 360-degree circle. The valley is surrounded by undulating hills, like Knap Hill, and forms a circle that opens to the south. This geography gives the appearance of a womb with the cervix opening to the south. Within this womb are countless sacred sites, churches, springs—and crop circles.

Dowsers and sensitive individuals repeatedly detect that crop circles are placed over ley lines, which are active lines of energy that run along the Earth near the surface of the ground. They are similar in function, it is thought, to the acupuncture meridians running in lines through the human body. Just as the acupuncture points in the body are known to be locations where the energy flows can be regulated and reversed and the body treated for cures, the points where ley lines cross—which contain temples, churches and sacred places—attract rituals and ceremonies that help regulate and heal the energy flows in the Earth.

These invisible lines, which are detected by dowsing, pendulums, the hands of psychically sensitive people and by various other kinds of equipment, have been known and revered by people since ancient times. The ancient people lived right on the ground and used to walk long distances on these lines to find their way from one location to another. It is believed that their awareness of these lines activated the energies along them. They marked the points where energy lines crossed each other or converged by erecting huge megalithic stones. The stones reminded people where the ley line energies were the strongest. Probably these stones increased the energies at these points as well.

The modern founder of the ley line theory was Alfred Watkins, inventor and natural scientist, who in 1925 discovered "old straight tracks" through the English landscape that connected natural features such as small ponds, springs, underground streams and rivers, islands in lakes, notches in hillsides and prehistoric man-made features such as mounds, tumuli (small round hills containing large standing stones), moats and hand-carved hillforts, ditches, dikes, rings of land and rings of stones, longbarrows, mizmazes, beacons marked by large stones, giant earthworks called castles or camps, holy wells, crossroads with place names given to them and ancient wayside crosses. Three to four thousand years later, sacred structures were built on many of these sites: churches, hermitages, chapels, cathedrals, abbeys, circles of standing stones, large stones with holes in them and deliberately planted copses of trees. All of these features are noted on contemporary ordinance survey maps. Wherever stretches of ancient roads follow the same line between some of these features, those tracks most likely follow a ley line (Devereux and Thomson 1979).

In *The Sun and the Serpent*, Miller and Broadhurst write: "All the great

JULY 1998, ANCIENT STONE DOLMEN AT DEVIL'S DEN CROP CIRCLE AT MANTON, NEAR MARLBOROUGH, WILTSHIRE COUNTY.

monuments we had come across had been erected according to clearly defined principles, each place with its precise function. The crossing points of the male and female energies of the Earth were the sense organs of the land, receiving impulses of energy that were harmonized by the Earth itself. The special nature of these places, which often strike people as having a powerfully magical atmosphere, is also indicated by the energy field that is dowseable where the currents anchor themselves deep into the surface of the planet. . . . Stone circles, many of which had once possessed avenues leading to them, marked particularly important places where the influence of the Earth Spirit could be concentrated or channeled out into the surrounding countryside through its hidden network of veins and arteries" (Miller and Broadhurst 1998, 204).

The powerful Michael and Mary grid lines of energy run from the southwestern tip of England to the northeastern coast, undulating and crossing each other in the Wessex Triangle region, their paths marked with stone circles, mumps, tors and St. Michael churches. The powerful Mary Line intersects Silbury Hill and nearby Swallowhead Spring, connecting these two powerful sites with the entire energetic system of the Michael and Mary Lines. Many of the crop circles are placed along these lines (Carr-Smith 1999, 24:8). Perhaps the Michael and Mary Lines serve as a generator to pull in the energies used for the sacred activities in this area (Holden and Scott 1991, 92).

Swallowhead Spring, near Silbury Hill and West Kennett Longbarrow, echoes the theme of death and rebirth by the surging of waters from deep within the Earth just prior to the coming of spring. This ancient spring has been the site of sacred rites for thousands of years. Another possible indicator or symbol that the Silbury Hill area is the energetic center for England comes from the fact that the Downs surrounding Avebury is the location of the confluence of the three main watersheds in England (Wakefield and Wakefield 1999, 82).

The Avenue of Stones, leading out in two directions from the Avebury stone circles and giant Avebury Henge, is serpentine in shape, like cosmic snakes. The symbol of the snake is linked to fertility and power, generally masculine in nature, but also to the concept of transformation. In many indigenous cultures and Asian mythologies, the snake transmutes poison; therefore the shamans with their snake medicine have incredible healing powers over the spiritual poisons of the dark forces. One well-known example is Quetzalcóatl, the winged serpent god of Mexico, who promised to return to abolish human sacrifice.

Derek Carvell discovered during his research in Northumberland, England, near the Scottish border, that all the crop circles that have appeared in that area point to where ancient standing stones used to be. He learned this by studying the ordinance survey maps of the area from the 1800s. Unfortunately, these standing stones have been removed over the centuries for constructing stone buildings. He thinks that the circlemakers are trying to draw our attention to the importance of these ancient stones and perhaps to the Earth energies they marked. These stone monuments had all been placed in a straight line, as were all the crop circles in that area (Carvell 2000).

Most crop circles seem to be placed intentionally where they can be seen easily by people: on the sides of hills where they can be seen from a road below or above or from across a valley, or on flat ground where they can be seen from higher on a hillside. Once in a while, a crop circle is placed in a more remote location accessible only by hiking. However, these often are locations that people visit anyway for other purposes, such as ancient hillforts, rings or castles. Each crop circle is open for anyone to enter, unless the farmer who owns the land prohibits people from trespassing on his property. Many people experience the crop circle itself as welcoming, almost as if inviting and drawing visitors to come inside its special energy field.

THE INFLUENCE OF WATER AND WEATHER ON CROP CIRCLES

Some scientists and geologists have determined that under many crop circles are geological aquifers composed of very porous limestone, sandstone and chalk. This substratum absorbs water from the abundant English rain and easily yields water. They also notice that many crop circles are placed over underground streams and other water sources, or where the water table is high. Jenny Clark, a member of the British Society of Dowsers (the Earth Energies Group), told me that their dowsing always shows that crop circles are placed over underground water. Colin Andrews and Freddy Silva, two long-standing crop circle researchers, also have found a relationship between formations and underground watersheds through analyzing infrared photographs (Andrews 1995/96, 4:14). Jim Lyons reported at the 1996 Glastonbury Symposium that researchers Steven Page and Glenn Broughton have found that the chalk and greensand under many crop circles hold water.

This underground water is necessary for the steam effect that seems to be involved in the making of crop circles. Some crop circle scientists theorize that when heat of 500 degrees Fahrenheit or higher is applied to the plants as abundant moisture is being drawn up from under the soil, the plants become pliable enough to be gently bent over at ground level without any cracking, breaking or killing, and then to be swirled or shaped to form a variety of patterns. As an indication that this water element could be very important to the making of crop circles, when a pronounced drought in Wiltshire County in 1995 lowered the water table, fewer formations appeared in that region that year. More crop circles occurred in neighboring Hampshire County, where conditions were somewhat more humid.

Crop circles appear during the season when the crop has reached a height of at least a foot from the ground. Otherwise, the pattern would not form much of a contrast with the standing crop and would be difficult to see. In southern England, crop circles usually begin to appear in the young green crops in May, although in 1999, they began at the earliest date so far, April 3. New crop formations continue to appear as long as there are growing crops that have not been harvested. Harvesting usually is completed by the end of August or early September, depending on the weather. When the weather is dry for a period of time, the crop ripens, dries and needs to be harvested sooner. The crop will not be harvested if it is wet. In some summers, such as 1995, the drought caused the early harvesting of many crop circles, and researchers who arrived during late July were disappointed to find many of the formations already gone. Usually, new crop circles appear through the middle of August, but visitors need to take the weather into account when planning visits to the crop circle area.

JULY 1999, CHERHILL CROP CIRCLE, WILTSHIRE COUNTY.

Crop circles have been formed in many different kinds of weather: in calm conditions on clear sunny days as well as in wind, rain, fog and storms. They can appear during the daytime, although most of the crop circles are formed during the night in the relatively short period of complete darkness between 11:00 P.M. and 3:30 A.M. Crop circles made during heavy rainstorms are just as beautiful as ones made during dry weather and show no signs of mud or damage. However, once someone walks into an existing crop circle, dents in the crop are formed by every footstep, tiny blossoms of the crop are crushed and the stems of the plants are broken where they are bent over near the ground. Such damage is looked for when assessing whether a crop formation has been *hoaxed*, the term in general use for formations made by humans.

THE REACTIONS OF FARMERS

Farmers react in various ways to the appearance of a crop circle in the agricultural crops that provide their income. Some feel especially honored, even blessed, by a crop circle's appearance on their land and welcome interested visitors as long as they do not leave litter or damage the crop. Some believe the formations were created by some mysterious higher force, and they want to learn more about this mysterious intelligence. Others feel baffled by this phenomenon. They try to ignore a crop circle in their fields and hope that not too many visitors will come around.

Some farmers see a crop circle as an opportunity to collect some money from visitors to make up for the loss of their crop—the laid down crop is difficult or even impossible to harvest and represents a loss of important income—and charge an entrance fee of one to three British pounds (equivalent roughly to $1.55–$5.70 U.S. dollars). Sometimes this money is collected at the entrance to the field by family members or friends, or by the posting of a "charity box" with a courteous note asking for donations. In 1999, the very agreeable farmer of the Hackpen Hill formation, James Hussy, built a little wooden bridge over the ditch at the side of the road to facilitate visitors entering his field, erected a charity box and posted information about the crop circle therein. He even offered directions for which tramway line (tractor track) to use to easily find the crop formation. He was open to learning as much as he could from visitors who were informed about this phenomenon.

Other farmers feel very hostile about having a crop circle in their fields and assume it was covertly placed there as a negative prank by bums or cocky young rebels from a pub. A few farmers have considered the crop circle on their land to be "the work of the devil" and mowed it down as soon as possible. In fact, some crop formations have been photographed only once or just a few times before they were mowed down. Considerate crop circle researchers go out of their way to locate the farmer in whose field a crop circle resides to obtain permission to enter his land. If denied permission, they do not press the issue. One farmer in the mid-1990s became a believer when from his kitchen window at midday he witnessed a large swirl of greenish/blackish light vigorously spiral up from the crop circle and suddenly disappear.

THE ATTRACTION OF THE CROP CIRCLES

Every summer, a variety of people interested in crop circles gather from all over the world in the Wiltshire area of England. They have been described as "a tribe returning," and many report experiencing a special bonding with each other. Most are drawn by the mystery and scope of this phenomenon—the curiosity, the jolting absurdity of these lovely designs of such magnitude suddenly appearing overnight in farmers' crop fields. A single circle can measure from twenty inches to a few hundred feet in diameter. Long pictograms composed of circles, rings, keys and other design elements have stretched over fields for distances up to eight-tenths of a mile. Occasionally, formations cross roads and continue in other fields, although they incorporate the road in the design rather than sprawl haphazardly from one field to another. Crop circles are mind-boggling to many people, especially since these designs are beautifully wrought, contain varying kinds of energies and provide a variety of effects on people, animals and equipment.

JULY 1999, ANDREW WHEDER, DENNI CLARKE AND DOE KELLY AT THE GLASTONBURY SYMPOSIUM.

Photographer: © Barbara Lamb.

Their mystique tantalizes many people. Mystery has a way of sparking people's interest and even devotion. Mystique has been used by shamans throughout history to draw people in and to bring them to greater realizations. People wonder why these crop circles are occurring, by whom and how they are made, and why they are appearing now and in such numbers. They wonder why they show up in some fields, geographic areas and countries, and not others.

Most people who are drawn to crop circles respond to the beauty and symmetry of the designs and to the exactness and perfection with which each stalk is laid down and swirled or shaped. Some are attracted to the

Photographer: © Barbara Lamb.

NORTH AVEBURY DOWN CROP CIRCLE: WENDY ALLEN WATCHING JUDY MOORE CHANNEL THE STAR GLYPH FOR THIS CROP CIRCLE AND BARBARA LAMB BASKING IN THE GOOD ENERGY.

symbols that are evident in these patterns and enjoy pondering their meaning and significance. Some sense messages that seem to be intended for them personally. Crop circles seem to stimulate and awaken many people to a higher consciousness, a different sense of reality and a greater focus on spirituality. To some, crop circles seem to provide tangible evidence of supernatural intelligence and presence, enabling them to enter a sacred space and experience it to their heart's content. People appreciate that crop circles are not fleeting, transient or ephemeral as some anomalous or spiritual experiences are, such as visions, spirit visitations and appearances of angels and/or extraterrestrial (ET) beings.

Many people drawn to UFO phenomena are drawn to crop circles, seeking evidence of ET involvement and hoping for ET contact. Some have been rewarded by seeing what look like spaceships, humanoid ETs, spirit beings, strange lights and other inexplicable phenomena.

Crop circles seem to invite, welcome and allow each visitor to have his or her own unique experience over a period of time. Experiences in crop circles, no doubt, happen on various levels, some of which people are consciously aware and some of which they are not. From the rational and scientific interest to the intuitive, feeling experience, each visitor creates a memory. Some people are satisfied with visiting only one or two crop circles. However, an amazing number of visitors want to experience more, as I did, and attempt to return every summer. Those who cannot return in person are eager to see photos, videos and television shows, to attend lectures and to read articles and news from the Internet. Active communication networks via e-mail and e-mail lists disseminate current information and opinions.

Many people have an immediate strong reaction when they see their first crop circle in a field or when they see their first photo or drawing of a crop circle. The attraction feels irresistible, and they want to know more about the phenomenon. I was one of those people. In 1990, I saw my first small photo of a crop circle in the printed program of the Whole Life Expo in Los Angeles, California. I had a very strong reaction and immediately committed myself to attending the lecture on crop circles in England. I felt tingles and a surge of light within myself, accompanied by feelings of amazement, wonder, curiosity and awe. I instantly wondered if someone out of our usual understanding of reality was trying to get our attention, to communicate something of importance through the strange designs in the fields. After only a few minutes of hearing the lecture and seeing video footage of amazing long formations of strange yet lovely designs, I made my decision to visit crop circles in England that forthcoming summer of 1991. I knew I had passed the point of no return, and I felt compelled to check it out for myself. I have been visiting crop circles in England each summer since then, and I feel as dedicated now to exploring the phenomenon as when I began.

Crop circle glyphs seem hauntingly familiar to many people, yet they cannot always put their finger on what the symbols remind them of. The symbols appear to be part of the collective consciousness of humanity, which we tap into frequently but often without recognizing the source of our awareness. Mick Hardy writes, "There are many rock carvings all over the world that contain many characteristics contained in the Crop Glyphs. These are known as endotic images and they are a product of the human brain when it's in a hypnogogic state. They can also appear in one's consciousness shortly after one has ingested LSD or something similar. This is related to one's consciousness, which is ultimately what the Crop Formations are all about" (Hardy 1999, 24:7).

PORTRAYING AND STUDYING THE CROP CIRCLE DESIGNS

Scientifically inclined individuals can be attracted to crop circles by the challenge of doing focused scientific research according to their own discipline—perhaps attempting to figure out how the formations are created or what the energy configurations and effects are. They rigorously use various kinds of scientific instruments, record their data diligently and draw conclusions from their backgrounds in mechanics, mechanical or electrical engineering, physics, mathematics, geometry, architecture, geology, archaeology, dowsing and other disciplines. For example, David Tilt and Richard Andrews have added to our knowledge of crop circles by drawing the energy lines going through and radiating from the centers of certain formations.

Researchers have chosen several methods to accurately represent the crop formations, including meticulous surveys on the ground, hand drawings, aerial photographs and computer graphics. Since crop formations are large and complex and the configurations have mathematical and geometrical significance, accuracy in the proportions is essential but difficult to achieve from the ground. Photographs taken from small airplanes, helicopters, open microlite craft and occasionally hot air balloons have been very important in conveying the scope, complexity and beauty of the formations. Andreas Müller and J. F. Langrish have surveyed and drawn crop formation designs. These drawings are matched up with photographs of the same crop circles taken from the air. Other people have spent untold hours carefully drawing to scale the crop circle designs with computer graphics programs. Individuals who have contributed visual representations of the crop formations include Peter Sorensen, Wolfgang Schindler, Bert Janssen, John Martineau, Michael Glickman, Richard Adams, Cariel Quinly, Lucy Pringle, Peter Baillie, Terence Meaden, Colin Andrews, Nigel Tomsett, Debbie Pardoe, Stuart Dike, Jens Rowold, Rodney Ashby, Kris Weber Sherwood, Graham Tucker, David Godwin and John Sayer. The dissemination of these beautiful images has contributed significantly to the worldwide burgeoning awareness of the crop circle phenomenon.

JULY 14, 2000, STUART DIKE AND MIKE FUSSELL WITH THEIR PHOTOGRAPHY EQUIPMENT.

Photographer: © Barbara Lamb.

Accurate images have facilitated geometrical analyses of the designs. Numerous individuals have contributed to the appreciation of the crop circle phenomenon by their analyses of the underlying geometrical significance of the patterns. Notable contributors are Gerald Hawkins, Michael Glickman, John Martineau, Wolfgang Schindler, Bert Janssen, Rod Bearcloud Berry, Martin Noakes, Robert Seaman and Dana Thibault.

PILGRIMAGE TO CROP CIRCLE COUNTRY

The experience of finding crop circles is an adventure in itself, often full of synchronicities. Off and on there are telephone hot-line numbers peo-

Photographer: © Barbara Lamb.

1999, THE BARGE INN.

ple can call for information on where crop circles have been appearing. People who visit crop circle territory with a guided group rely on the leader to collect the information and obtain permission from the farmers to enter their land. Individuals and pairs on their own most often visit the Barge Inn, a pub in the tiny town of Honey Street, next to the town of Alton Barnes in Wiltshire County. A room at the Barge is devoted to the posting of information about the crop circles already found during that season, with aerial photographs, drawings and commentaries. A large map is posted on the wall—much like a map in a war room during active military campaigns—on which the locations of the crop circles are marked with small stickers. The *croppies* (crop circle researchers and enthusiasts) congregate there, exchange information about the latest finds and speculate about the meaning of each pattern and of the phenomenon overall. Sometimes video footage of the newest crop circles is shown, especially by Peter Sorensen. Other times sketches, black and white computer renditions of crop circle designs, photos and photo albums are shown to anyone sitting nearby. Stories circulate about sightings of anomalous phenomena witnessed over the crop fields, and directions to crop circle locations are shared and traded. The large campground in back of the Barge also is a fertile ground for sharing information, enthusiasms and speculation. Andreas Müller and Frank Laumen usually drive around the Wiltshire crop circle territory early each morning, searching for new formations made during the night, and then report their findings to anyone waiting at the Barge Inn.

From there, searching for crop circles is like a giant treasure hunt ranging over the large landscape. Small country roads confuse one's sense of direction. There are no signs obligingly pointing the way to the nearest crop formation, which adds to the sense of adventure. Once within a crop circle, people often meet up with other enthusiasts, and they share news of the formations they have already visited and how to find them. It seems as if one formation leads to another and another. Often when I want to run into a certain person or to learn information about a particular subject, that person will show up within a few minutes or will be in the next crop circle visited or in the next eating venue. Thoughts seem to travel telepathi-

Photographer: © Barbara Lamb.

JULY 1999, WENDY ALLEN AND VALJA ROSEMAN CLIMBING OVER BARBED WIRE TO GET TO A CROP CIRCLE.

cally from one formation to another, and people seem to flow into the same time and place miraculously. It happens again and again. The whole process is a flow of synchronicities. Things seem to work out precisely as they should in a very freeform mode of operation.

CHARACTERISTICS OF THE LAY OF THE CROP

Once inside a crop circle, there are wonders to behold in the laid-down crop itself. The *floor pattern*, or the way the crop is laid down and shaped into patterns, is a very important part of the mystery and marvel. Some researchers believe the details of the construction are even more wondrous than the overall shape or symbolism in the pattern.

Most often, the plants within a circle are swirled in clockwise or counterclockwise directions, but sometimes they are moved into *S*-shaped patterns or splayed out radially from the center. Other times, they are swirled in one direction from the center, but near the edge of the circle they reverse direction and run back in the other direction. In some formations, they form arcs and curves that create intricate patterns within the complex shape of the crop circle itself. Sometimes the stalks bend at exacting angles to form straight lines and corners in the pattern. In some crop circles, a pathway of laid crop is bent to form a right-angle turn into a perpendicular pathway. Often the crop that was laid down in a straight pathway flows over the crop that already had been laid down in a direction perpendicular to that pathway. Sometimes, two pathways merge together from different directions. At these junctions, my dowsing rods consistently indicate amplified energy.

The variations of the lay of the crop are as numerous as the variations of crop circle designs themselves. In some formations *whorls* are present; that is, strands of the laid-down crop are twisted together like loose rope and follow in the direction of the swirl. In some large areas of laid-down crop, the stalks look like lovely long, flowing ripples, much like sand on the bottom of streams of running water. One would think water had flowed around the standing shapes of the crop, leaving eddies, contraflows and little ripples. In many crop circles, the stalks give a clear indication of how and where the energy flowed in making the pattern. Stalks in genuine formations usually are laid down gracefully and evenly. Some floor patterns show how various layers of the crop have been laid down one on top of the other, often heading in different directions and creating a basket-weave effect. Some layers of crop appear to be intertwined, almost braided. Occasionally, a narrow pathway of stalks is detected under the main lay of the crop that might be swirled in a number of ways, as if the circlemakers first drew guidelines for the ensuing circle. Crop circles

JULY 1998, CENTER SWIRL OF EAST FIELD "SEVENFOLD KOCH SNOWFLAKE" CROP CIRCLE, ALTON BARNES, WILTSHIRE COUNTY.

JULY 2000, UNUSUAL STANDING CENTER IN PICKED HILL CROP CIRCLE, WILTSHIRE COUNTY.

2000 "PATTERN OF CURVES" CROP CIRCLE NEAR BISHOPS CANNINGS, WILTSHIRE COUNTY. SHAWN RANDALL INSPECTING A PYRAMID-SHAPED CENTER.

made from 1976 through 1993 were made with the technique of laying the crop down to make the design, leaving the surrounding standing crop as the border or contrast. Beginning in 1994, an additional technique was introduced: laying down the crop around standing shapes that formed the main aspects of the design. Both of these techniques continue to be used to date.

The centers of circles and large formations show great variety as well. We have seen fans, twisted ropes of standing crop, knots, nests, standing tufts of varying thickness, pyramids, teepees, simple swirls, radial swirls and S swirls. Some centers are flat to the ground, laid down smoothly and tightly swirled; others are swirled with a looser, more relaxed look. Other centers are more three-dimensional, slightly twisted and raised a few inches from the ground like bird nests. Some centers are flat at the starting point, surrounded by a raised ring of stalks, as if the center is being protected or emphasized. Many circles have standing tufts of stalks, ranging from only two or three strands slightly swirled together upright to columns of stalks of varying thickness. Some of these tufts stand straight upward like columns, and some splay out at varying angles. When one sees the intricacy of some of the centers, it seems quite obvious that there is no way that circle could have been man-made.

In one very large crop formation, the Beckhampton "Manta Ray" of July 1998, each of the fifty-four small circles trailing off from the main part of the large design had its own unique kind of center [figure 1] [plate 7]. A 1999 trapezoidal-shaped crop circle across from Silbury Hill had four nested centers in the single formation [plate 22]. Also in 1999, the West Kennett Longbarrow crop circle had a center that stood up like a prominent nipple [plate 18]. In 2000, a raised beehive-shaped center was created in the Picked Hill formation [plate 44], and a pyramid-shaped grouping of wheat stood up from the middle of a semicircular swirl in the Bishops Cannings crop circle [plate 62]. Two nestlike centers stood in the middle of the Woodborough Hill "Moiré" design [plate 54], known as the "Sunflower" or "Crown Chakra."

In some formations that are not circular in shape, the lay of the crop is executed masterfully, radiating out from a flatly swirled center and ingeniously bent to form straight and triangular shapes at the outside edges, as in the Silbury Hill "Koch Snowflake" or "Star of David" formation of July 1998 [figure 2] and in the "Inside-Out Koch Snowflake" pattern of August 17, 1998, below Hackpen Hill, north of Avebury [figure 3]. In the 2000 crop formation at East Kennett, instead of a center swirl, the whole pattern was formed by wheat laid down in straight lines but in alternate directions, leaving a pattern of standing square shapes [plate 52]. In the 2000 "Celtic Cross" crop circle at Milton Lilbourne [plate 45], the crop was laid in four different directions in each of the four circles, around a swirled center. Also, in the ring that encircled the pattern, wheat ran in one direction right next to wheat running in the opposite direction. In the

JULY 17, 2000, NORTH AVEBURY DOWN CROP CIRCLE. INTERESTING LAY IN ONE OF THE THREE LARGE "PETAL" SHAPES.

2000 "Moiré Magnetics," or "Magnetic Field," pattern at Avebury Trusloe, the center of the design was standing crop and there were two additional centers closer to the edge of the design [plate 50]. With each year, new variations of centers and intricate lays of the crop continue to appear and dazzle the mind.

Some crop formations contain no actual circles at all, some contain one or a few circles and some formations contain many circles. Fine examples of the latter are the 1999 Devil's Den formation near Marlborough, Wiltshire [plate 21], which contained at least ninety-six circles; the 1995 "Solar System" formation near Arlesford in Hampshire [plate 8], which contained sixty-eight circles; and the 1999 formation at Windmill Hill, which contained 288 circles [plate 17]. In these formations, each circle was swirled and centered in a different way. It appears as if each circle was designed and laid down individually and uniquely, all in an amazingly short period of time.

Fig. 1

EXPERIENCING THE ENERGIES OF CROP CIRCLES

Individual crop circles seem to have a particular energy, and they affect different people in different ways. Some crop circles seem to stimulate and increase intuitive abilities. Some seem to stimulate responses from the heart. Some seem to evoke altered states of awareness, including deep meditation, channeling, out-of-body experiences, connections with spiritual beings and revelations. Some crop circles seem to ground people so they feel more connected to the Earth. Some stimulate curiosity and the desire to investigate and test. In my experience of visiting dozens of crop circles over ten consecutive years, each crop circle has its own energy and mood or tone, its own unique personality.

Fig. 2

Various researchers have paid special attention to the effects of crop circles on people who enter them. Michael Newark, a researcher and dowser since the 1980s, said, "A new crop circle is very strong in earth energy. The bigger the formation, the stronger the power levels. These high levels, for the most part, are good for us, but the odd crop circle with very high power can upset the natural chemical output of the brain, which can lead to all sorts of problems. When in doubt, stay out, and visit the formation a few days later, when the power will have reduced to a more acceptable level" (Newark 1997, 19:24).

Fig. 3

Since 1990, English researcher Lucy Pringle has been studying the effects of crop circles. Her interest began when she was healed of a very painful shoulder injury while sitting in a crop circle, and her friend Margaret Randall had a remarkable healing. Pringle and Diana Clift devised a questionnaire that they have given to hundreds of people, and more than three hundred people have testified about changes that happened to them in crop circles. Often many different effects were experienced in a single formation.

Lucy Pringle.

Photographer: © Lucy Pringle.

Physical effects reported to her were diverse and included "nausea, headaches, dizziness, blurred vision, and tingling, as well as cases of short or long term healing." People reported, "Felt as though I am being pulled apart by a magnet," and "Felt so sick I had to make a dash for it." Sometimes the initial physical responses would be positive, but they would not last. Sometimes the initial physical responses would be unpleasant but later a healing would occur. At the time of her article in 1995, reported physical reactions were 60.5 percent unpleasant (Pringle 1995, 14:12).

Many other people have experienced sudden drops in energy as well as depression and lethargy. One researcher developed a violent headache within three minutes of entering a crop circle and remained ill for three weeks. That crop circle was tested for radiation and none was found, but the shape of the design remained in the soil until the next March, indicating that a strong energy had been present. In 1994, three researchers fell over unconscious and became extremely ill in the "Celtic Barmaid" and remained bedridden with high fevers for several days. (Interestingly, Michael Newark commented in 1997 about his immediate feeling of wariness about entering this crop formation.) Another researcher experienced sudden energy loss, nausea and a headache when forty feet away from a crop circle. He left the area immediately and experienced increasing improvement in his muscular dystrophy symptoms for many months afterward. Of course, it is impossible to know whether exposure to this particular crop circle led to remission of his symptoms. Naturally, it is difficult to speculate about the long-term effects of crop circle exposure when visitors are exposed to multiple influences that could influence their health and well-being.

Conversely, there are many reports from visitors to crop circles of feeling more energized, buoyant, springy, lighthearted, indefatigable, resilient, awake and alert because of the energies present. There are many reports of improvements in physical infirmities. According to Lucy Pringle's surveys, emotional and psychological effects of the crop circles on people, tend to be more beneficial than physical effects. People report having feelings of calmness, happiness, joy, euphoria and heightened awareness. Sometimes they experience a suspension of the mind and seem to be in an altered state of consciousness. In fact, many people lose all sense of time while in a crop circle. Some visitors' psychic abilities increase when in a crop circle, even to the extent of seeing other-dimensional beings and channeling unseen sources. These are experienced as very positive, uplifting experiences.

In contrast, some people have felt uneasiness, sadness and fear, and were overcome with a sense of foreboding and disturbance. As one person reported in Lucy Pringle's questionnaire, "'All three of us found ourselves addictively gripped. We were "enchanted" or "englamoured" in a manner which seems to resemble the experiences reported from folklore in which mortal man makes the mistake of engaging with the faery folk!' 'The unease became worse, changing to foreboding, through panic to almost terror'" (Pringle 1995, 14:12-13).

Some individuals have experienced remote effects from visiting a crop circle. One woman reported to Lucy Pringle that after eating some grain from a crop circle, she felt increasingly uncomfortable, as if she were on speed (amphetamines). Weeks later when back home, she again ate some leftover seeds from the same crop circle, and the same symptoms came back. She was so charged with energy that she shorted out the electrical equipment nearby.

My own reactions in a few hundred crop circles since 1990 have been neutral or positive. Only once have I experienced any negative effect, which happened in the West Lavington, Wiltshire, crop circle in July 2000. The design and the crop seemed awkward and confused, and my dowsing rods registered no energy responses. Suddenly, I felt exhausted and had to lie down and sleep for a while. I was very glad to get out of that formation, which I believe was negatively charged.

Generally when visiting crop circles I feel more lively and energized than usual and seem to need very little sleep. I experience a different mood in each crop circle, ranging from giddiness and childlike glee, to joy, awe, wonder, mystery and thrill. In some formations, I feel calm and easily go into a deep meditative state. Often I have succumbed to the energy of the crop circle and let myself drift into a timeless or perhaps an out-of-body state of being from which I return with a sense of deep profundity and well-being. A few times, when I have asked for information, I have received what seem to be channeled messages about the meaning and intent of the particular crop circle I am in at the time.

Many times in a crop circle I have felt a strong sense of presence that felt benign and kindly, even encouraging. It seemed as if my visiting the formation was noticed and appreciated. I felt welcomed and subtly embraced. I experienced the specialness of the formation, the gift and the blessing to me and to all of us who enter. I felt myself radiating out thanks, and I felt I was receiving grace. There seems to be a subtle interactive sensing, a mutual respect going on between the circlemakers and myself. In some crop circles I was overwhelmed with the *mysterium tremendum*; the finite and the infinite seemed to be coming together within me in those special locations. I felt deepened and expanded in my consciousness and in my participation in life. I was reminded that I am a spiritual being, part of all universes and dimensions, who right now is experiencing life as a physical human being. I experienced the sense that researcher Karen Douglas mentions: that entering into a crop circle is akin to entering into a "temporary temple for the modern age" (Douglas 2000a, 3). I experience a crop circle as a sacred place that inspires a sense of upliftment and connection with the divine.

In an attempt to pin down what happens physically to create these altered states, tests of brain-wave activity have been done on some people, first at home in their normal environments (the control tests) and then in a crop circle (the experimental tests). Electroencephalogram (EEG) tests have been conducted by Peter Staples and Isobel Maxwell-Cade. Some people have exhibited dramatic differences in brain-wave activity between being at home and being in a crop circle. All subjects showed heightened activity in the right hemisphere of the brain when in a crop circle (Pringle 1995, 14:13). Speculations have varied about what causes these effects, including the activation of energy lines in the Earth, Earth magnetism, orgone energy amplified by a radioactive field and pesticides. These effects seem to come only with genuine crop circles.

Not only humans sense the energies of crop circles—dogs often have strong reactions to the genuine crop circles. Many dogs bark furiously and behave frantically during the making of a crop circle on their land, even if they are safely inside their homes. This suggests that they must be sensing the approaching of an unusual strong energy. When walking toward a new crop circle, some dogs seem uncertain and run back in the direction from which they came. Some dogs hesitate and seem anxious before entering a crop circle, then enter very cautiously. Once inside the crop circle, some dogs run around and around vigorously, as if disturbed, and might or might not settle down after a period of adjustment. Some dogs will not even walk into an area where a crop circle was formed during the previous year (Pringle 1995, 14:13).

Flocks of birds have been seen to avoid flying over some genuine crop circles, to split apart into two groups and fly around them on both sides. It is speculated that there is a residual energy field of mild radiation and electromagnetic energy left from the process of making the crop circles. Birds and animals seem to be especially sensitive to this.

The vast majority of the time, birds and animals obviously sense the coming of the circlemaking force and leave the area before the formation is laid down. However, a few times remnants of birds and animals have been found in crop circles. One bird was found completely disintegrated, and parts of it had penetrated down to ground level (Pringle 1995, 14:13). In Canada, two porcupines were caught during the making of two different crop circles. One was very black, as if its body were covered with soot (possibly the magnetic particles Dr. Levengood has analyzed). The other was "squashed flat as a pancake," and its quills appeared to follow the lay of the crop (Perkins 1999, 25:4). Either they froze rather than ran, or they could not run fast enough to avoid the approaching force. One would highly suspect from these remains that the crop circles in which these accidents occurred were not man-made.

Lucy Pringle advises people who enter crop circles to take certain precautions because of the strong energy present, which we know is powerful but which we do not yet fully understand. This energy varies in strength and duration in different formations. She advises pregnant women to stay away from crop circles as well as people with cardiac pacemakers, because crop circle energies often drain batteries. She advises dowsers to consciously protect their personal energy fields when working in crop circles. For some people it might be best to relate to crop circles from a distance instead of entering them and being affected by the energies. It can be effective to simply look at or meditate upon crop circle pictures and let the symbols affect various levels of consciousness. Some people find that a favorite crop circle gradually loses its strong appeal, possibly because as some of their blocks dissolve they become ready for the challenge of a different symbol. She urges all people to immediately leave a crop circle if they begin to feel bad physically (Pringle 1995, 14:15).

Many researchers speculate that when people experience sickness, fatigue and headaches in a crop circle, this could be due to the energies opening up our blocks and constrictions so they can be released. When a crop circle brings about a feeling of happiness and well-being, possibly that particular person is in harmony with that particular energy level. When the same crop circle affects another person in negative or uncomfortable ways, it might be that the person is having difficulty with an aspect of self stimulated or provoked by that level of energy.

Dr. Nan Lu has studied the effects of crop circle energies on people's bodies and health. He is the founder and director of the Traditional Chinese Medicine (TCM) World Foundation and is also a practicing acupuncturist in New York City and a world-class Taiji and Qi Gong master. For more than five thousand years, this traditional Chinese medicine system has promoted using the life force (Qi) for healing by increasing the flow of energy in the human body. He has found that crop circles can be used for healing because they are forms of communication based on energy. Dr. Nan Lu believes that attentive visitors to crop circles can see and feel a different energy flow in each crop circle. They can look at the way the crop is laid and the centers are swirled and detect the different energy messages designed for healing. The more harmonious and peaceful the visitors are and the more they believe in the helpfulness of these energies, the better they can connect with the energy flowing through the circle and receive healings. Healing is facilitated by appreciating the beauty, harmony and symmetry of the designs, and by reaching out to connect with the mind of the universe. It also helps to practice an energy practice such as Taiji, yoga, Qi Gong or other meditation, in order to be integrated in mind, body and spirit. He suggests that visitors walk through the entire formation—because different areas of the crop circle carry different specific healing energies and spiritual energies—and tune in to the unseen energies that create the crop circles. He commented that whoever feels bad in a particular crop circle is fortunate, because some healing is happening. Dr. Nan Lu has shared his impressions of specific energies of many 1999 and 2000 crop circles and which conditions of the body they are especially effective in relieving or healing (Traditional Chinese Medicine World Foundation 2000).

Mary Hykel Hunt, an English color therapist who works therapeutically with labyrinths, likens the experience of walking in a crop circle to the experience of walking in a labyrinth. In each of these environments, the visitor can move into a peaceful, meditative state that promotes physical and emotional healing and creates physical, emotional and spiritual balance. In each environment, the visitor is activating an energetic pattern,

JULY 1998, DR. NAN LU, CARIEL QUINLY AND BARBARA LAMB IN THE "COMET" CROP CIRCLE.

Photographer: © Barbara Lamb.

JULY 1998, STANLEY MESSENGER.

and the aura of the environment changes as well (Hunt 2000).

Sage and philosopher Stanley Messenger has channeled Thoth, who said that humans are not yet ready for crop circles and that crop circles are here for the sake of the Earth itself. Their purpose is for healing, because until the Earth is healed, we will not be able to heal ourselves and grow. Thoth urges people to continue going into crop circles but to prepare and protect themselves because crop circles are not quite right yet for their DNA (Messenger 2000).

THEORIES ABOUT THE MEANINGS OF THE CROP CIRCLES

Speculations on what the crop circles are all about have changed and advanced over the centuries. At present, the theories range from inspirational to cynical, with some observers voicing both polarities. In the final analysis, each one of us has to develop our own theory based on our emotional and physical reactions to the crop circles, our overarching belief systems and our interpretations of the often ambiguous and confusing phenomena surrounding the crop circle enigma. Below are presented various theories, ranging from metaphysical to technological.

The fairy tribes of ancient England, the ancestors of the Celts and the Picts, saw mysterious lights and circles in the fields and believed they were made by supernatural beings called "Ellyllon" or "Light Elves." This tradition was passed down through the centuries, and even in the 1930s "fairy lights" and "fairy rings" were seen in the Avebury area and surrounding territory. Currently, we call the same phenomena anomalous lights, UFOs and crop circles.

In the ancient Druid tradition, lights and circles in the crops indicated the presence of dragon lines or energy lines, which were very important in their understanding of reality and their spiritual practices. Nowadays, we again have awareness of the ley lines of energy and the frequent placement of crop circles on them.

During the 1970s and early 1980s, many people thought crop circles were UFO landing sites or "saucer nests." This idea was prevalent in Australia because of a swirled circle left by a retreating UFO in 1976, and also in England because of the many UFO sightings at Cley Hill, in Hampshire County. Eventually it was realized that crop circles were consistently swirled more perfectly and pleasingly than the UFO landing traces, which tend to be messier and to have crushed plants. It seemed to many people that these circles provided evidence for the existence of UFOs and extraterrestrial beings, and contact with them was imminent. It was assumed that a higher intelligence was at work in the making of crop circles.

During the 1980s, additional theories developed, such as crop circles being made by microwave energy, static electricity or natural meteorological effects. Dr. George Terence Meaden, a British meteorologist and early crop circle researcher, concluded that natural energy plasma forces high in the atmosphere collected in vortices, became ionized and through a whirl-wind type of motion created the circles and rings in the crops. He was so convinced of his vortex theory that he wrote a book in 1989 entitled *The Circles Effect and Its Mysteries*. However, other researchers found by dowsing that energy in the circles did not necessarily flow in the way his theory predicted. His theory was further discredited when the 1990 and 1991 long, complex pictograms appeared, combining obviously intelligently chosen shapes and design elements, including long, straight pathways and other straight lines. His theory could not accommodate these features, and Dr. Meaden withdrew from crop circle research as his theory went out of favor (Wingfield 1990b, 26-30). Other researchers explored the idea of crop circles being made by orgone energy from the lower atmosphere, but likewise had no convincing mechanisms to explain complex formations.

AUGUST 1994, GEORGE WINGFIELD.

During the 1980s, some witnesses reported what they described as laser beams coming down to crop fields from the sky, in both daytime and night-time, both with and without a structured spacecraft being seen. The theory arose that perhaps crop circles were made by nonphysical beings from another dimension of reality. Others held that crop circles were made by extraterrestrial but physical beings, in physical crafts using advanced physical technology. English researcher, consultant and author Peter Paget has seen official government materials about UFOs and beings beyond our usual range of experience and has experienced extraterrestrial (ET) contacts himself. He has developed some impressions of the extraterrestrial mind, which has difficulty with human languages. According to Paget, the ET mind struggles with linear spoken languages and relies on telepathy, conveying whole pictures, concepts and feelings without the need for grammatical word constructions. ETs appear to work conceptually using glyphs and icons, each one containing a substantial amount of material and meaning. Thus concepts conveyed with words (such as through the medium of channeling) might appear verbose, confusing and repetitious, with invented words cobbled together from scientific and common usage words. The crop circle designs could be their more familiar iconic communications (Paget 2000).

1999, MARCUS ALLEN AND PETER PAGET.

Most researchers agree that the majority of the crop circle patterns during the 1990s and into the 2000s were intelligently planned and created with great care and exactitude, and are not the result of undirected, spontaneous natural forces. Again and again, crop circles show evidence that they are made by some extraordinary creative intelligence.

CROP CIRCLES AS TOOLS TO EXPAND OUR CONSCIOUSNESS

After seeing pictures of 1990 and 1991 crop circles, a commercial airline pilot in Florida named Doug Ruby became fascinated with the phenomenon and experimented with cutting out pictures of some of the long pictograms, mounting them on vertical posts, one on top of another, and spinning them. These two-dimensional images became three-dimensional models of what looked like moving craft. He concluded that these designs were showing us plans of spacecraft and their propulsion systems, and that they are a great gift to us. He published his theory in a 1995 book called *The Gift: The Crop Circles Deciphered*. He was convinced that extraterrestrial beings come to us from space and leave cryptic messages in our fields to educate and enlighten us. He believes that "these are gentle beings who have our best interests at heart. They are here to help. They are gently seeking cooperation, not confrontation. It is all part of the universal plan to get us to wake up and remember who we are, and why we are here. That, indeed, is the greatest gift of all." He invites us to "keep an open mind, because the journey we are invited to go on is incredible" (Ruby 1997, back flap of jacket).

Italian ET contactee and stigmatic Giorgio Bongiovanni believes the crop circle pictograms are deliberate messages left for scientists and researchers to translate. Bongiovanni reports also that the purpose of the crop circles happening all over the world is to "enlighten and affect many people who would gradually begin to realize that man is not alone and is not the highest form of life in the universe." An additional purpose is to inspire us to change the disastrous conditions that man has created in the world. Bongiovanni was assured that we would receive help from the beings of light if we ask for it (Wingfield 1995a, 14:6-7).

Some crop circles seem to lack good qualities of design and articulation, yet dowsing shows that definite energy patterns are present and therefore the circles most likely are not man-made. Long-time English researcher John Haddington suggests that just as there are groups of people intent on "rubbishing the whole phenomenon of crop circles," he senses "that there are spiritual agencies up to the same game. Everything is not just light and love on the other side. There are some exceedingly mischievous and downright nasty entities out there who are just as dedicated to confusing the issue and distracting honest researchers from the main event as their human counterparts. Therefore I do not find it surprising that certain effects were felt [i.e., making some people very sick for a few days] in for instance 'The Avebury Barmaid' formation [of 1994]. I now classify such events as white noise intended to jam the wavelengths and interfere with the incoming signal [of genuine crop circles]" (Haddington 1995, 14:17). Haddington further states that crop circles are incoming coded signals that have been reaching us each year, beginning in 1989. The true circlemakers are trying to confuse their detractors by hiding certain clues in their patterns that can be understood only in retrospect. He also thinks that there are many more levels to the coded messages than we have realized, and it will take us years to realize their full meaning. He suggests that since not all of the genuine crop circles are made by the same source, we see different artistic styles and themes.

Along with many others, the Arizona coordinator of the Center for Crop Circle Studies, Sharon Warren, suggests that crop circles are expanders of consciousness. As we are experiencing more world crises, we are challenged to change our world-views, our ways of life and our consensus view of reality. If we are being contacted by higher beings/extraterrestrials and are resistant, crop circles are one way to help us as a mass consciousness to see and know what we are repressing energetically. Extraterrestrials are leaving their "calling cards" by creating crop circles as a bridge to provide a meeting ground between us (Warren 1994, 13).

British crop circle researcher Pat Delgado muses on the ways crop circles resemble churches and other places of worship that from their builders and visitors develop energy patterns conducive to peace, love and unity: "A crop circle is a structure of a kind and, as such, energy criteria similar to those in temples and churches will apply, but this time it is something special and unique. In comparison to a church, the crop circle's material, shape and location enhance the sensitivities more and consequently will usually have a greater impact on your emotions, which are also influenced by what you think the circle represents. . . . I am sure there are some people who feel closer to their God or more spiritually aware in a crop circle than they do in a conventional place of worship" (Delgado 1992, 154-155).

Researcher Ron Russell beautifully echoes the sentiments of Pat Delgado: "I now think these circles are spiritual machines. They certainly appear to act this way in that they have a variety of functions and a purpose, and they cause things to happen to the plants and the people who visit them. They appear like plans for a great cathedral laid out in the carpet of our food crops—a temple with invisible walls and a swirled, living floor. . . . All manner of exceptional experiences take place in these circles, from time shifts to healings, from ecstasy, epiphany and revelation to sudden malaise and illness. These are our contemporary power spots or portals, to be used by every individual as he or she feels is appropriate" (Russell 2000a, 10:73).

Photographer: © Barbara Lamb.

July 16, 1999, Barbara Lamb, Ron Russell, Cariel Quinly and Busty Taylor in the Cherhill "Nine-Pointed Star" crop circle.

Isabelle Kingston has been receiving information for many years about crop circles indicating that the circles are part of a larger plan. In 1987, she transmitted this message: "My dear Brothers in Light, you have come to ask the meaning of the circles in the field. You have been made aware of the presence of the Watchers. Your guardians have been linked with humanity to bring the power necessary to build the New Jerusalem." In 1990, she channeled: "(England) is a testing ground—it has to be right before the whole can be lined up with the other dimensions. Circles have appeared as a blueprint for humankind . . . to mark that (Stonehenge) as a place of power. It is as if these places are being unlocked, turning and being unlocked. Centers are being awakened—it is part of The Plan" (Birosik 1992, 52). According to Kingston's source, "[England] lies in the center of the great pyramid of light which encircles your world, and the energies of the Watchers bring love through magnetic channels" (Kingston 1991, 150). The land around Silbury Hill draws many crop circles because the Watchers, who directed the building of Silbury Hill, have been sending messages to open awareness of genetically encoded information that can raise humanity's consciousness. As Kingston transmitted, "*The corn circles are like a score of music between the earth and the cosmos.* You do not at this time need to learn to read the score. *The best is to feel it.* . . . The energy has been put through [into circles] through thought-processes, with light beams rather like your national [English electrical] grid system, so we input power into the earth's grid. This is to stabilise the energies in the earth, to stop the earth from destroying you" (Kingston 1991, 148).

American channel Anna Hayes has transmitted that the appearance of crop circles indicates that ETs and/or interdimensional beings are present and active in those geographical areas—areas that can span a radius of well over several thousand miles from the point of origin—and influencing the population in those areas. Crop circles are the first physical evidence visible to millions of people of an ET presence here on Earth. These beings and the crop circles they make can be considered benign and helpful, or harmful. Crop circles have many purposes, but their main purpose is to ground particular frequency bands into an area that are intended to affect all biological life forms in their range of influence in very specific ways. "They are subliminal programming devices being used to manipulate, direct or guide you through the intimate unknown structures of your subconscious minds and biochemical and electrical systems. They are one type of what we know as mass frequency control devices" (Hayes 1999, 101). They are made with technologies light years beyond human abilities. Many crop circles are placed here by ETs to help us by counteracting the effects of other formations intended to harm us on subliminal levels. It is important for us to learn to use crop circles for society's benefit, and destroying the crop does not disarm its attributes. Once a crop circle is made, the "frequency it harnessed has been indelibly coded into the land, air and biological forms of the region" (102).

Steve Canada, long-time crop circle theoretical researcher, presented on a radio show that many of the crop circles are Sumerian symbols. Mandalas were thought to be places where the gods resided. He considers *return* to be a central message of many of the crop circles: return of the Anunnaki people from the planet Nibiru, which comes relatively close to Earth in an elliptical orbit every thirty-six hundred years. He based many of his conclusions on research done by Zecharia Sitchin (1976), who presented evidence that beings from Nibiru came to ancient Sumeria and genetically created human beings from a combination of their genes and the genes of primitive pre-humans who already were living on Earth. In this radio show, Steve Canada explained that some crop circles are mandala designs composed of twelve elements, which correspond to the Anunnaki Council of Twelve. He interpreted the 1990 and 1991 long pictograms with three-pronged shapes to represent Nibiruan leader Marduk's lightning weapon, carried by the descending Nibiruan goddess Inana (Isis in Egyptian lore). The 1997 "Tree of Life" formation [plate 2] refers to our genetic code that we are trying to break in order to map our genes (Canada 2000).

Welsh healer Ralph Jenkins believes that the crop circles are created from outside our galaxy by a very bright, powerful consciousness that is controlled and governed by our galaxy's universal laws. Crop circles are sent down to specific energy sites that help anchor the designs. The crop circles have healing abilities and use the same laws that healers use in the process of healing. They are placed here to help us grow and evolve through light and love (Jenkins 1999/2000, 47:13-14).

Photographer: © Barbara Lamb.

JULY 1999, ROD BEARCLOUD BERRY AND RALPH JENKINS AT WCCSG CEREMONY, EAST FIELD, ALTON BARNES.

Carol Cochrane, an active member of the London-based Center for Crop Circle Studies, has performed a word analysis called *lexigramming* with many crop circles. Lexigramming is a system for decoding the English language that Carol uses with the place names where crop circles are located. She believes that a series of meanings are encoded in the place names and important communications are embedded in crop circles in those places. Some concepts occur more frequently than others. For example, "Isis" is encoded in ninety percent of the crop circles that she decoded, and "Osiris" is encoded in sixty percent. Words and phrases encoded in many crop circles include: "We are Sirian," "We twirl the wheat," "We are the real artists," "The answers are in the letters," "The letters are at all the sites," "Read the letters we sent," "Learn who we are," "Angel," "Wise," "Seer," "Learn to listen to the Earth," "Healers," "Heal the Earth," "Do not be afraid," "We will be there on Earth to assist," "We are all brothers and sisters," "Be aware that there are others not of this world who do not wish to assist. Be aware also that there are aliens bases on Earth," "Not too late," "Help," "We are here to help," "Orion," "Planets," "We are not alone," "Will stop the pain," "Twister hits the Earth," "The sea will rise and the last island will arise," "The answer is in the stones," "The tone is set in the stones," "It is not lost" and "Atlantis rises." Some even more complex encodings include: "We twirl the wheat on these sites and other sites in the world," "Dogon: intimate connections with Sirius, came from Sirius," "We sent the dragon or worm to warn those on Earth . . . the end of the old world order," "Humans should learn to end the wars," "Long ago large domes sat on the moon . . . now no more than old shards, but the old shards are real" and "We wonder if humans want to know who we are" (Cochrane 2000).

Shawn Randall, American crop circle researcher, talented channel and teacher of channeling, shares information given through her by Torah, a multidimensional consciousness: "Crop circles are co-creations and you are part of their creation. . . . The Collective Unconscious is very much a part of the manufacture of a crop circle. . . . The formations are holographic pieces expressing the holographic nature of your multidimensional Universe. . . . The primary function of the crop circle phenomenon is *the evolution of human consciousness.*

Photographer: © Barbara Lamb.

LATE JULY 1998, MICHAEL HESEMANN, ILYES AND SHAWN RANDALL AT THE BARGE INN, ALTON BARNES.

Photographer: © Barbara Lamb.

JULY 1999, MICHAEL GLICKMAN, GLASTONBURY SYMPOSIUM.

Photographer: © Barbara Lamb.

JULY 1999, FRANCINE BLAKE AND RALPH JENKINS AT WCCSG CEREMONY.

And that evolution is towards humanity's conscious co-creation with the unseen" (Randall 1997).

During the summer of 2000, several speakers at the Wiltshire Crop Circle Study Group Conference and the Glastonbury Symposium all presented reminders of the power of crop circles to help us develop higher consciousness. Jude Stammers, a metaphysical teacher in Wiltshire, spoke of consciousness having energy and resonance. Crop circles, like third-dimensional resonant chambers in ancient monuments, transport people into higher levels of consciousness (Stammers 2000). Karen Douglas described crop circles as hermetic devices, like the pyramids at Giza in Egypt. Being involved in crop circles helps us become initiated to higher consciousness. In both situations, the makers are anonymous and the structures are anomalous. Part of the intrigue is that we do not know with certainty what is going on, yet we sense that a lot actually is going on. In crop circles, we are offered a whole new way of thinking and being (Douglas 2000b). Michael Glickman believes we are confronting a new consciousness in crop circles. This is all part of a significant shift going on, in which density and gravity are beginning to erode. People developing into fifth-dimensional consciousness realize this, whereas third-dimensional researchers look to science and Newtonian mechanistic theory to explain the crop circle phenomenon. For fifth-dimensioners, as he describes himself to be, "crop circles are mirrors in which we can polish our souls" (Glickman 2000).

Francine Blake, president of the Wiltshire Crop Circle Study Group and editor of *The Spiral* newsletter, notes that each crop circle brings an important message and leaves a strong imprint of energy. Powerful energies are coming to Earth and are helping to change our vision. These energies can change our world and provide the chance to reconnect to the universe, but they also can fuel our negativity. We need to move away from our old mechanistic thinking and dogmatic science, but not replace them with other restrictive mindsets. Crop circles help us to do this by providing a mystery (Blake 1999, 43:3).

According to Rod Bearcloud Berry of the Osage tribe of the North American Plains People, his tribe and at least eighty other Indian nations all believe they originally came to the Earth from the stars. He believes that beings who are very evolved, compassionate, loving, kind and considerate use the powers of the Earth Mother and Father Sky to communicate with us in various ways, including through crop circles (Berry 1999, 37:13).

OTHER MISCELLANEOUS THEORIES

In strong contrast to these views of the transformational potential and purpose of crop formations, many people are convinced that all the crop circles are made by humans going into fields at night with simple equipment and stomping down the crops into patterns. Even long-standing researcher Colin Andrews (2000) now believes that eighty percent of crop circles are hoaxed. Other people are convinced that crop circles are made by modern military technology that remotely directs laser beam patterns designed on a computer into a field of growing crop. According to this belief, military groups (specifically of the United States and England) might have tried this some years ago to test the effectiveness of their highly technological equipment—which many believe came from extraterrestrial sources—and were so impacted by the response of people to the crop formations that they continue to create more and more complex patterns.

JULY 2000, BUSTY TAYLOR, SHAWN RANDALL AND COLIN ANDREWS.

Aerospace engineer and consultant Brian Desborough claims to have "inside information" on scientific research and technology used by the military services and by covert forces. He suggests that military technology is used to make crop circles. He reports that Mosbar Beam Weaponry has been used since the 1970s and causes a residual clicking noise in the soil, and that microwave energy causes the growth nodes of crop circle plants to bend at right angles (Desborough 1999). As Boscombe Down military base is situated directly in the heart of crop circle territory in England, he makes a thought-provoking point. However, this technology in no way could account for crop circles that appear all over the world and in remote rural areas where there are no military bases or indications of Western military presence.

Fig. 4

Mick Hardy combines a spiritual perspective with practical material concerns. He believes that the crop circles are revealing a more spiritual level of reality than we are used to, and that contained in the geometry and mathematics is a formula for a completely clean and free source of energy, provided by a benign intelligence (Hardy 1999, 24:6).

Others with a more naturalistic point of view believe Mother Nature herself creates crop circles with her natural Earth energies. This corresponds with the views of people dedicated to the Gaia principle—that the Earth is a living, conscious entity who is trying to give us important messages and warnings about how we are rapidly polluting and destroying her. Crop circles in the early 1990s reinforced the Mother Earth connection [figure 4]. As the crop circles have become more intricate, it is difficult to conceive a mechanism by which Mother Nature creates an unmistakable template of a fractal pattern, for example. However, many people agree that the crop circles do bring our attention again and again to the Earth itself and to the importance of crops providing essential, life-sustaining food to mankind. They remind us of the preciousness of the Earth and what it produces. For many city dwellers, walking in a crop circle is the closest they have been in years to nature and the mechanisms of food production.

According to Bashar, a high-consciousness alien-human hybrid from our future, as channeled through Darryl Anka, all crop circles have several correct interpretations and some have a specific primary meaning. Your imagination is giving you your interpretation, and all interpretations are valid and correct. What a crop circle means to you is what matters. The whole is connected to the part, and the part leads to the whole. Bashar encourages us to not be afraid of the unknown and to go deeply into the mystery of the crop glyphs. Understanding them involves being, feeling, believing and then putting into action—becoming a "walking glyph" with radiation of energy all around us (Anka 1996).

Shawn Randall's 1997 channeling about crop circles by Torah strongly reinforces that there is no one answer to what a particular crop circle means: "There will be many, many, many interpretations, many ways of viewing it, because there are many individual perspectives in the holographic Universe. There will be no one singular authority or authority figure, or authority civilization that defines them. Understand you are not simply being doled out information from another race or alien group per se. It is bigger than that. As you decode the mathematics and other meanings of specific crop circles, understand that the decoded information is also coming from *you*. It is, in part, what you are saying to yourself."

THEORIES ABOUT HOW CROP CIRCLES ARE MADE

Many theories have been set forth regarding the mechanisms by which the crop formations are made by nonhuman sources. Some theories are based on analyses of the physical effects of the circle-making process. Other theories are based on extrapolations from what is known of extraterrestrial technologies. Still others are based on information channeled or in some way presented by extraterrestrial sources. None fully explain the technical details nor the etiology and intention of the specific patterns.

Dr. W. C. Levengood, head of the BLT Research Team and known for his diligent studies of the physical changes in crop circle plants and soil, has hypothesized that an ion plasma vortex comes down from the ionosphere into a crop field and spins around. Plasma is ionized gas from which the charge has been stripped. The energy that heats and bends the crop is hypothesized to be microwave energy emitted in very short bursts. Dr. Levengood believes that the ion plasma vortices are drawn to the Earth and shaped into patterns by variations in Earth's magnetic fields. He emphasizes that there are multiple energies involved, each of which affects the plants differently, and although the energies work together, they interact chaotically (Talbott 2001a). Although Dr. Levengood's research strongly supports that an energy which has effects like microwave energy bends the plant nodes, he acknowledges that his theory at this time does not explain the obviously purposeful shapes of the formations.

For several years, long-time researcher ilyes (2000b) did a meticulous study of crop circles at ground level, consulting with various scientists, and formed the following detailed theory of how genuine crop circles

Photographer: © Barbara Lamb.

JULY 1999, ILYES.

are made. According to ilyes, an amber ball of light flies at some distance above a crop field, manned by extradimensional intelligences, and sends down energy that defines the area in the crop where the crop circle will be made and defines the shape (the template) of the crop circle pattern. The amber ball releases spinning silver spheres, which create a sound barrier (an invisible ring) around the outside of the forthcoming pattern.

These spheres emit a frequency or sound that penetrates deeply into the ground, forming a torus (or donut) shape of energy, which then rises hundreds of feet into the air. This energy is attuned to a particular type of crop and will not affect any other type of plants growing in that area of the field. These spheres emit heat and wind packets that are encoded to lay down certain stalks. In front of these spheres, MASER (Microwave Amplification by the Stimulated Emission of Radiation) heat bursts out. The heat evaporates water from the stalks and makes them wilt. The cell walls of the plant expand, and the growth nodes are blown out from the inside.

Tubes of wind follow behind the bursts of heat, starting an inch or so above the ground and working their way upward on the plants. They gather the stalks into bundles, while wrapping the bundles with thin leaves from some stalks. They lay down each bundle with the seed heads parallel to each other. Cooling of the stalks happens when the wind spins around the bundles. Many bundles unwrap as they cool down, while some remained wrapped. Some bundles have gently curved bends near ground level, and some are crimped.

In straight paths within a crop formation, tracks of bundled stalks can be seen lying parallel to each other. Usually these tracks are twelve to eighteen inches wide. Where the crop has been swirled into a circle, the stalks at the edge of the circle (the perimeter stalks) are swept upward onto the surrounding wall of standing crop in groupings or bundles. Where a grouping (a tuft or column) of stalks is left standing within the center of a circle, there are more cellular changes in these plants than in the stalks lying at the base. This is because the wind and the MASER energy leave the crop circle through the tuft of standing stalks. In other formations that do not have a standing tuft, the tubes of wind leave the crop circle along the perimeter wall of standing stalks, leaving the laid and swept stalks resting against the wall in identical angles and heights. Ilyes and other researchers have found that the sound barrier ring around the formation retains its energy for years.

Dutch researcher Eltjo Haselhoff reported in a July 2000 Glastonbury Symposium lecture that he designed a computer program to measure the nodes of fifteen hundred crop circle plants in Holland and conducted many other biophysical tests as well. He was aware of numerous sightings of glowing balls of light in and over crop circles, which in some cases left the soil hot and parts of the stalks dehydrated. He knew about burn marks and traces of balls of light being left on a zinc roof of a house that was bombarded by balls of light. He concluded that crop circles are made by balls of light. He reported that his peers accepted his conclusion after testing crop circle plants themselves.

July 30, 2000, Eltjo Haselhoff.

Scientists and mathematicians have applied their minds and perspectives to this puzzling phenomenon and have formed some interesting theories. Jim Lyons, a theorist who has studied the field of new physics, concludes that subtle Earth energies play a major part in the making of a crop circle. These energies have always been detected by animals and sensitive humans and have been identified for thousands of years through dowsing and other means. He explains that the Earth is covered by a network of energy lines that are closely related to the magnetic field of the Earth. A crisscross flow pattern with a N-S/E-W orientation forms the Hartmann Grid, and a second flow pattern with a NE-SW/NW-SE orientation forms the Curry Grid. These "energy lines akin to acupuncture meridians in the human body form the 'graph paper' on which Crop Circles are formed. From the crossover of these grids rising vertically are columnar vortices of subtle energy. . . . At specific points on the earth, where energy lines cross, a rising vortex from the Curry grid can meet a descending vortex from the Hartmann Grid. . . . The vortices curl into toroidal as well as spherical quasi-stationary shapes. A hemisphere of nested toroidal shaped field lines forms over what is to become the [crop] formation. A sequence of toroids are energised, in a bifurcating process, much like cell division. . . . Through these D-shaped tunnels flows a swirling mass of ionized air (a plasma) at a speed of around 10 ft/sec flattening an already rapidly heated crop. . . . Different patterns can be formed with a simple change in bifurcating procedure; in other words, each formation has its own genetic code" (Lyons 1995, 14:11). He leaves it to others to figure out who or what uses this process in the making of crop circles.

At a lecture at the Glastonbury Symposium in July 2000, Steven Greer, M.D., stated that in crop circles, electromagnetic energies are pulled down by magnetic energies in the Earth into a preprogrammed template. A sound or vibration guides it and gives it form. In August 1995, Michael Green lectured at the Glastonbury Symposium that everything is created by sound and color, and that sound creates, maintains and destroys creation. He thinks sound creates crop circles.

According to Ralph Jenkins, crop circles are made by light of a superconscious intelligence funneled to the etheric energy of the plants (the energy field immediately outside the plants) and not to the physical aspect of the plants. It bends the energy field of the plants and shapes the plants into any pattern it wishes without damaging them (Jenkins 1999/2000, 47:14).

According to channel Anna Hayes, the majority of crop circles are made by direct manipulation of subatomic energy imprints, not through the use of mechanical devices or laser-like technologies. "They are 'cast,' so to speak, within the electromagnetic imprint of the organic elements as a result of intended multi-dimensional manipulations carried out by Visitors" (Hayes 1999, 101).

Giorgio Bongiovanni tells us that the spiritual beings with whom he is in contact say the genuine crop circles are made with devices they call *synchronisers*, which are small UFOs made of plasma, the state of the substance that composes the beings of light. These craft bend the plants from high up in the air, without changing the plants genetically or changing their growth. He reported that this type of UFO has also been seen in other places, such as Gulf Breeze, Florida (Wingfield 1995a, 14:6). It is possible that these are the same luminous "plasma craft" reported and photographed by a contactee named Carlos Dias in Tepoztlán, Mexico, as well.

Though none of these theorists have given a complete and clearly understood mechanism by which crop circles are created, a fitting comment on this issue again is provided by Torah, as channeled by Shawn Randall: "One of the beautiful things about crop circles is that there is no definitive human scientific answer as to what they are and where they come from. It is in the spirit of four dimensionality and in one's imagination that one must look at them" (Randall 1997).

COMMUNICATION BETWEEN HUMANS AND CIRCLEMAKERS

Simple circles have mysteriously appeared in crops for many centuries, in many parts of the world. But as these circles began to be seriously noticed, studied and publicized, they became more numerous, larger and increasingly more complex. After the name "crop circles," or "corn circles," was coined in 1980, a new focus for attracting and sifting information about the phenomenon facilitated greater communication and sharing of data. It almost seems as if the intelligence or beings responsible for the making of crop circles are aware of the attention and appreciation given to their artistry and respond by giving us more. Many stories circulate in the crop circle networks about apparent psychic communication between humans and circlemakers (or the natural forces making circles). There are many instances of people asking for a particular design to be laid down as a crop circle and seemingly having that request responded to within a day or two. This is a pretty amazing correlation, given the practically infinite number of potential designs possible. Sometimes the requests are in the form of a silent and intense thought, prayer or visualization. Sometimes they occur during a group meditation in which every member deliberately focuses on a design. Sometimes they occur in casual conversation.

However, another explanation for why human thought and intentionality seem to be associated with subsequent crop circles has been less discussed. Rather than humans influencing the circlemakers, perhaps some people telepathically pick up information about upcoming crop circles, even months in advance. Then they project the impressions they received, thinking they originated them. This "chicken or the egg question" is yet another area of mystery about the creation of crop circles.

JULY 2000, BUSTY TAYLOR AND CHAD DEETKEN.

Photographer: © Barbara Lamb.

Fig. 5

Fig. 6

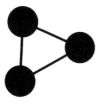

Fig. 7

One of the classic stories about thought creating crop circles occurred in August 1986. British researcher and pilot Busty Taylor mentioned during a flight over the fields that since circles and quintuplet crop circle designs had been appearing in the fields, it would be nice if a crop circle in the shape that combined both the formations seen to date, like a Celtic cross, would appear. The very next day, while flying over the same field, he noticed a new formation in the shape of a Celtic cross [figure 5]—the first time this design had been seen (Wingfield 1991, 18). It has appeared several times since then [plate 45].

Colin Andrews, alone in his home in Hampshire County years later, fervently asked the circle-making intelligence for a sign to help him solve the mystery of the circles by making a crop circle in the shape of a Celtic cross, and for convenience to make it near his home. The next morning, a new formation with that design appeared in the field closest to his home (King 1996, 2:21).

A group in the Medway area of Kent meditated on their group logo. Five weeks later, a crop circle was formed showing the same basic geometric form enclosed in a triangle. Three weeks after that, a "Celtic Knot" crop circle appeared also showing that same geometry.

During the summer of 1991, a team of six researchers sat in a field at night and meditated on an agreed upon pattern, a six-pointed star. When they went to sleep in that same spot, they positioned themselves in a circle, with their feet nearly touching a hexagonal crystal in the center and their heads pointing out toward the perimeter. When they awoke a few hours later, they learned to their delight that a six-petaled flower had appeared as a crop circle in the field adjacent to them [figure 6]. Wingfield added that a second six-petaled flower appeared nearby soon thereafter, exactly where another group of six researchers had sat a couple of years earlier listening to a mysterious trilling noise (Wingfield 1991, 30).

In July 1992, Dr. Steven Greer and his CSETI (Center for the Study of Extraterrestrial Intelligence) group sat on Woodborough Hill in Alton Barnes, Wiltshire County, for several evenings and meditated for thirty minutes on a triangle with a circle at each point [figure 7]. This design was found seven miles away in the field below Oliver's Castle the morning after the group had a close sighting of a structured UFO with revolving colored lights. What was exciting to the group was the opportunity to watch the UFO and its light pattern for more than fifteen minutes and to interact with it. A halogen lamp was used to flash signals at the craft, and it reflected back the same pattern of flashes numerous times before it disappeared (Howe 1993, 35-41).

During the summer of 1993, Shawn Randall guided a meditation group of seventeen people, including myself, in Salisbury, England, in visualizing a particular crop circle design. By early morning, a slightly simplified version of this pattern appeared in a field in the area.

During that same summer, Sharon Warren's Arizona Center for Crop Circles Studies group formed a collective invitation for a design to appear in the fields of England around the time of their arrival from America. They envisioned a triangle within a circle and a smaller circle within the triangle, and they telepathically sent their message to the circlemakers. They also painted the designs on their T-shirts, sweatshirts and nightshirts, and did spinning and intending of this design daily. After two weeks of visiting crop circles in England, a design almost exactly like their symbol appeared near Hogsback in Sussex County. The next summer, in 1994, the group again formed the intention of communicating with the circlemakers. Having been studying Drunvalo Melchizedek's teachings (1990), group members intently envisioned the Flower of Life pattern before and on their way to England. Unbeknownst to them, that pattern already had appeared as a crop circle in a field near Froxfield [figure 8] three days earlier (Warren 1994, 3-5).

Fig. 8

In 1999, a group of Japanese visitors to the crop circle territory in England meditated and prayed for three hours from their bus parked facing a sacred area. They witnessed UFOs and had "curious nosebleeds." The next morning, the Beckhampton "Origami" pattern [figure 9] [plate 23] was laid out in the direction in which they had been facing (Russell 2000a, 10:71). The Japanese group had been asking for crop circles reflecting their culture, and the tour group leader, Maseo Maki, told me that the group believed that the Barbury Castle "Three Dolphins" design [figure 10] [plate 24] created several days earlier—a symbol of feminine energy in Japanese traditions—also had appeared in response to their request.

Fig. 9

I was told by Louise Olivi in August 1998 that a group traveling with her from Connecticut meditated on a pattern of a seven-pointed star with seven points on the inside. A few days later, a crop circle of this design (although with the points of the star flattened) appeared at Tawsmead Copse [figure 11].

Fig. 10

For a year or so I had been wondering intensely about a cluster of lights in the same part of the sky each night. They seemed very personal and welcoming to me during my many late-evening solo drives home after meetings. I was amazed to see this design, a cluster of small circles, from a small airplane over Etchilhampton, Wiltshire County, and immediately felt, "This crop circle is for me!" [figure 12].

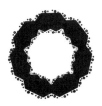

Fig. 11

In February 1999, Lucy Pringle decided to see if she could dream of a crop circle that would be forthcoming that year. Before going to sleep, she imprinted on her mind that the subject of crop circle formations would be the topic of her dreams. That very night she dreamed of a straight line of overlapping circles. On May 3, she flew over that exact pattern in a field [figure 13] [plate 32]. She believed it was a very important symbolic formation, indicating the forthcoming eclipse of the Sun on August 11, 1999 (Pringle 1999, 25:19).

These are just a few of the numerous incidents in which people have pictured a pattern with their minds and have been rewarded with that same pattern (or at least one very similar) appearing in a field as a crop circle. This encourages people to feel involved with the mysterious sources of this phenomenon. The involvement seems to have another aspect, with many people experiencing being "downloaded" with thoughts and inspirations as well as physical sensations while sitting quietly in a crop circle. Sometimes

Fig. 12

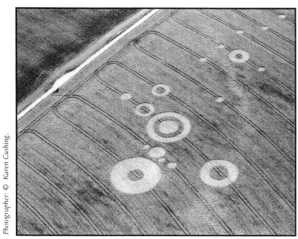

Photographer: © Karen Cushing.

July 1997, "Sara Circles" made by Koch and Kyborg as a greeting to the ET circlemakers.

Fig. 13 _____

these perceived communications are brief and fleeting, and sometimes they are prolonged and full of information.

Isabelle Kingston's channeled source urges people to facilitate the creation of new circles by sitting in a circle, sending out light and opening their hearts. "I want you to go to the hillsides and call upon the Brethren. Link yourselves with the cosmos and draw the energies in to help. Become as lightning conductors. Channel the light into the very soil. Transfer it into pure love and wait for the explosion." Kingston and her group have done this process, and within twenty-four hours new crop circles are formed in those locations (Kingston 1991, 148).

More tangible communication methods than thought projection and visualization have been used as well. Nearly every summer, two researchers from Germany, Joachim Koch and Hans-Jürgen Kyborg, come to England for a lengthy study of crop circles. They take the initiative to begin a dialogue with the circlemakers by making a design of their own in a crop field. They pay a farmer for the use of a portion of his or her field and make the formation during daylight hours. They are not trying to fool anyone or perpetrate a hoax. Instead, they are acknowledging their appreciation for the efforts and beautiful results of the genuine circlemakers, and they are encouraging the phenomenon to continue (Koch and Kyborg 1997).

As researcher David Kingston remarked during a Glastonbury Symposium coach tour in August 1997, "It's like an intelligence sitting on your shoulder." He went on to note that as people make statements and generalizations about crop circles one day, the phenomenon immediately changes and either does something contradictory or affirms and creates what you want in the next crop circle.

ANOMALOUS LIGHTS AND SOUNDS ASSOCIATED WITH CROP CIRCLES

For centuries people have been witnessing strange lights over the crop fields where mysterious new circles are being made in the dark of night. Tales of these luminosities have been told in old English folklore. Often they were called fairy lights. Little spheres of light were reported to beguile people and lure them astray until they were lost. Even in modern times, these sightings make a vivid impression on witnesses and can be described in detail even years after the event. Often people feel strong physical sensations and feelings of awe, wonder, amazement, enthrallment and intrigue. Ron Russell has told me that he knows of at least forty witnesses of domes, shafts of light, glowing spheres and other anomalies in the night sky, operating for five to fifteen seconds over crop fields where crop circles are later discovered in the light of day. Some of the lights are interpreted to be spacecraft, but others do not seem to have a shape with an edge like a physical object. When the object has appeared to be a spacecraft, it has

36 ⊘ Crop Circles Revealed

not always been clear whether the craft was creating the crop formation or was in an observing or monitoring role. Of course, it is the human drive for consistency that has us assume there is a relationship between anomalous phenomena and the associated (by time or location) appearance of crop circles.

SIGHTINGS OF ANOMALOUS LIGHTS

The earliest detailed account we have of anomalous lights associated with the creation of a crop circle is from 1678. In Hertfordshire, England, a prosperous farmer made an impulsive remark to a neighbor looking for work and asking more than the farmer was willing to pay. He said that the devil should mow his oats before this poor man would. That night, people passing by his field of oats witnessed a "flame" moving over the oat field for quite a while. The next day the farmer found his oats cut in a circular spiral pattern. All the stalks were laid down parallel to the ground and swirled perfectly in circles, with each stalk laid evenly next to the neighboring stalks. The people in that rural area assumed that the cutting had been made by the devil. The event was so striking that an article was published with a woodcut print of the swirled crop, showing the "Mowing Devil" using a primitive farm tool to do the mowing (Institute for UFO Research 1998, 3:9).

Colin Andrews (1993a, 2:6-7) has compiled numerous eyewitness accounts of early crop circle manifestations as well as affidavits from present-day witnesses of anomalous phenomena associated with the creation of crop formations . A number of these accounts are presented below to illustrate the variety of light patterns seen.

In October 1871, in High Wycombe, England, a man watched a starlike object moving slowly toward him in the early hours of the morning. It appeared increasingly brighter as it came closer. Then, in the nearby woods he found two disc-shaped objects that flashed lights in a definite sequence. The next day, he found in that location two circles in which the grass and weeds lay bent over. In 1927 or 1928, in Chanctonbury, Sussex, England, a man left his bicycle in the grass while out hunting rabbits. When he returned to that spot, his bicycle has been electrified to the extent that he could not pick it up, and he found that a strange circle had been formed in the grass.

In 1963, at St. Souplet, Nord, France, a strange loud sound woke up a family at night. It shattered the window, and the family saw a bright light descending into the garden. The next day a circle was found in the spinach patch. In July of that same year, near Stonehenge in the village of Charlton, Hampshire, England, a police officer watched a large orange ball of light drop out of the sky. The next day, a circle was found in that area in a field of barley and potatoes, with all of the barley and potatoes gone and a small deep hole in the center.

In January 1966, at Horseshoe Lagoon near Euramo, Queensland, Australia, a farmer heard an unfamiliar loud hissing sound near a lagoon,

Fig. 14

Fig. 15

and his tractor engine failed. He saw a small, metallic disc-shaped object rising up out of the water, leaving the reeds rotating on the surface. In December 1971, at Tooligie Hill, S.A., Australia, witnesses saw a large, red flame descending from the sky toward the ground. Later, they discovered a circle with two rings in the vegetation. In 1972, in Hjortkvarn, Sweden, witnesses saw a starlike object hovering over the area where they later discovered a circle with a single ring in the vegetation. In May 1974, in Grapevine, Texas, several people watched a beam of white light come from the sky and touch the ground, leaving a circle surrounded by a ring in the vegetation.

In November 1976, in Chilcomb, Hampshire, England, while driving along in a car, a couple saw an orange ball of light descending from the sky. They pulled off the road and the car engine failed. They were approached by a very tall humanoid-looking being in silver clothing. The woman was frightened by his red eyes. Other figures walked behind her car and strange markings later were found on the roof. Days later, the woman was taken aboard their spacecraft, where she was shown charts of circles and rings, some joined by straight lines. She was told that this was their field. Since that time, many crop circles have appeared in that field. Fourteen years later, the first pictogram ever seen appeared there of two circles connected by a straight line.

In July 1986, on a highway between Stockbridge and Winchester, Hampshire, England, a couple saw a large Ferris wheel formation of lights in the sky. That night, a quintuplet set of crop circles was formed there in the field [figure 14]. Years later, in 1995, another crop circle appeared in exactly that same location: this time in the shape of a ring with a ratchet-like design inside [figure 15].

In July 1988, a woman watched a large luminous object in the night sky flying slowly over the crop fields near Silbury Hill. She saw a beam of light projecting down to the ground at an angle. Within thirty-six hours a crop circle in the shape of a Celtic cross was discovered in that field. This was followed by other sets of quintuplets during a span of eight weeks, forming a giant pattern of many quintuplets spread over the same large field.

In June 1989, near Silbury Hill, a man watched a large orange ball of light drop from the sky into his field where eleven crop circles already existed that had been filmed by a television crew earlier in the day. This ball pulsated, suddenly disappeared and left a new crop circle and ring. In 1990, at Williams Lake in British Columbia, Canada, a UFO was witnessed hovering over apple trees near a house. Later, a swirled circle was found in the grass, and the apple trees had been stripped of all their leaves and apples.

Many other reports of anomalous phenomena associated with newly created crop formations or seen in crop circle territory have accumulated over the years, far too many to mention in detail. Linda Moulton Howe has collated numerous reports,

JULY 2000, LINDA MOULTON HOWE, GLASTONBURY SYMPOSIUM.

especially from crop circle researchers, many of whom had the equipment and the wherewithal to assiduously videotape anomalous light patterns such as balls of light (often referred to as BOLs). From all these reports, she has identified seven major kinds of anomalous lights: flickering brightness; lights coming from the ground and moving upward or coming from the sky and moving downward; circular without internal structure; misty images; translucent lights; anomalous ghostly images; and white columns or images with internal structures. They have been called atmospheric plasmas, Earth lights or "dragons." Lights have ranged in size from hundreds of feet in length to tiny balls of light darting around crop formations. Also, light patterns have shown up on photographs or videotapes that were not seen by people at the time. It is not unusual for one person to see lights and another standing right there to not see them (Howe 2000a).

JULY 1991, ANOMALOUS SPHERES OF LIGHT IN A CROP CIRCLE IN SOUTHEAST CORNWALL.
RIGHT: ENLARGEMENT OF ANOMALOUS SPHERE OF LIGHT.

On July 26, 1990, photographer Steve Alexander did a daytime videotaping from Milk Hill in Alton Barnes of a small white, glowing, blinking object flying low over the top of the crop in the field below him. It moved in an erratic way, speeding up and slowing down, dipping down into the crop and then skimming along the top, as if checking out the soil and the crop. The object looked spherical from his vantage point, but more like "a light burst than a solid object." It flew past a farmer in the next field who later compared the light to "tin foil blazing in the sun." When the video was studied, it was noted that when the glinting object blinked out, it no longer showed up as a physical object on tape. Later, letter-type markings were found laid down in the field (Howe 2000a, 24-25).

JULY 2000, STEVE ALEXANDER.

Another typical sighting was recorded by Michael Glickman and Patricia Murray, who videotaped several white spheres flying over the 1999 Barbury Castle "Dolphin" crop circle [figure 16] [plate 24]. They had set their video recorder on a tripod and left it running while they took photographs. When they replayed their videotape, they saw one white sphere after another flying low over the crop circle from many different directions. The people in the crop circle at that time did not seem to notice them (Sherwood 2001).

One of the most dramatic light shows of the many witnessed was reported by Peter Sorensen. In 1996, two curved, translucent beams of light were observed by Sorensen and a companion, shooting up hundreds if not thousands of feet into the sky, waving back and forth, bending for about seven seconds like they were made of translucent rubber, disappearing and then reappearing briefly. There were no associated sounds, electrostatic tingling or other unusual phenomena. Sorensen commented that the light could not have been normal light; it would take a tremendous gravitational field to bend a beam of light. He added that Colin Andrews

Fig. 16

Photographer: © The Plymouth UFO Research Group: Martyn Hicks.

Photographer: © Barbara Lamb.

July 1998, Polly Carson and Peter Sorensen.

Fig. 17

also had three reports of curved beams in his files (Sorensen 2000, 7).

Ed and Kris Sherwood perform many Earth-healing meditations outside and have photographed spheres that are not visible in person but show up in their photographs. Some of these spheres are semitranslucent and some appear to be denser (Sherwood 2001). I have seen photos of spheres that have black dots or holes in them.

The phenomenon of black dots or holes calls to mind some reports of discs being seen that were opposite in color from the usual silvery metallic discs; they were densely black and did not appear to reflect light. Polly Carson, on whose property crop formations have appeared, reported in an interview that once she saw an intensely black disc approximately the size of a football when horseback riding. It moved very slowly for about three seconds and then suddenly blinked out. Her horse saw it before she did and refused to move closer (Sayer 1999, 25:13).

Lighted or glowing spheres impress observers as seeming to have intelligence and a decision-making capacity. Charles Mallett, a resident of Horton, Wiltshire, who is involved in the crop circle phenomenon, has seen many spheres flying over the local fields and in crop circles during the daytime and nighttime. They can make right-angle turns and come closer to a person and retreat, as the person wishes (Howe 2000b). Other researchers have witnessed white spheres being chased by military helicopters, repeatedly dodging and outsmarting the humans following them for many minutes. I have heard of an incident in which researcher Andy Buckley videotaped three spheres and a helicopter coming close to them. The spheres disappeared while the helicopter was there and reappeared when the helicopter went away.

Secondary to the ability to photograph and videotape anomalous phenomena is the potential ability to fake photos and videos. A huge controversy erupted amongst crop circle researchers in August 1996, when a young Englishman, variously known as John Whately, John Wheyleigh and John Waybe, showed some researchers at the Barge Inn a videotape of footage that he said he had taken at dawn that morning. He had been camping overnight on the hill at Oliver's Castle near Devizes, Wiltshire. He said he was awakened by an unusual sound, and he grabbed his video camera and pointed it toward the field below. The video footage shows a beautiful snowflake-like pattern [figure 17] being laid down and swirled into circles and pathways radiating out from a central circle (eighty-five feet in diameter). At the same time, two pairs of small white spheres swept over that area of the field, close to the top of the crop, one after the other. This perfect, lovely crop circle formation appears to have been made within only seven seconds (Glickman 1996a, 57:3-5, 8-9). It is unclear how—or whether—the spheres made the crop lay down, since their trajectories were not right over the arms of the snowflake pattern and there were no visible beams of light or other connectors between the spheres and the ground.

The controversy over the genuineness of his video never has been resolved. Some people believe that the small white flying spheres must have been digital special effects inserted into the video footage at the television studio where this man worked, and others hold to the assumption that the footage was real and undoctored evidence of the actual creation of a crop circle. Even if the white spheres were faked, this still does not take away from the wonder of watching a crop circle manifest. Although some believe the entire video was faked, no one has been able to demonstrate how that could have been done, given the moment-by-moment changes in light level associated with pre-sunrise and the correspondence of the actual formation's orientation in the field to the video footage (Thomas 1996, 59:8-9).

It should be remembered, however, that even if this video footage is entirely genuine, it still does not answer the basic questions of exactly how the crop formation was made, where the spheres came from, the nature of the intelligence operating them and why this crop formation was made. The mystery continues. As with all anomalous events, such as UFO sightings, contacts with extraterrestrial beings, spirit visitations, ghosts and so forth, wherever there are people who accept the reality of these happenings, there are others who work hard to debunk or disprove their authenticity. This is certainly true for the whole crop circle phenomenon.

One of the most perplexing situations in all of crop circle history arose on July 22, 1991, near Grasdorf and Hildesheim, Germany. A huge crop circle pictogram of 150 by 300 feet appeared on land considered sacred for thousands of years [figure 18]. It resembled an ancient Scandinavian rock painting of the chariot of the Sun. Earlier that morning, a man witnessed an orange-colored light pulsating and flashing and dashing around over that area of the field. Soon after, other people heard an unusual whooping noise, which was different from a helicopter sound. On August 2, a man exploring the crop formation with a metal detector dug up three heavy metal plates (one gold, one silver and one bronze) buried two feet under portions of the design, shaped like circles with single arcs. He disappeared with the plates and later disseminated photos showing that each plate had been embossed with the exact design of that crop formation. The plates were sold at high prices—the metals were extraordinarily pure—and the gold one was melted down.

A German channel, Hermann Ilg, reportedly was told by the Ashtar Command that the young man was inspirationally instructed to find the plates, placed there about three hundred years earlier as evidence of extraterrestrial visitation. A later channeling by a consciousness called Cosmic Awareness indicated that the plates had been placed there by extraterrestrials as a guidepost or navigational instrument to help them locate various ley lines to pinpoint their location with respect to Earth points of reference (*Cosmic Awareness Communications Newsletter*, 13-14). This incident is a tantalizing indicator that the location and purpose of a crop formation might be more complex and multidetermined than we can discern by "rational" thought.

Fig. 18

SOUNDS ASSOCIATED WITH CROP CIRCLES

Unusual sounds often have been heard by people in or near crop circles. They are described as trilling, clicking, buzzing, humming, electrostatic chattering, cricket noises and birdlike warbling. Searchers over and over have not been able to locate a visible source. Following are some examples of people's encounters with these types of sounds in association with crop circles.

In 1987, Colin Andrews walked into a crop circle ring in Klimpton and asked God to please give him a clue about how crop circles are formed. Immediately and only a couple of feet in front of him, an electrostatic, or crackling, cricket-like sound began. Within seconds it had become so loud—he estimated it was approximately two hundred decibels—that he became frightened and asked it to stop. The noise instantly stopped, as if a switch had been turned off (Brocklehurst 1999, 24:25). Andrews was profoundly moved by this experience and has continued to be interested in the sounds associated with crop formations.

In July 1995, Bert Janssen and Janet Ossebaard were doing a nightwatch on Knap Hill when they heard a "very strange electrostatic sort of sound" moving around them for minutes. They felt like they were being circled and observed and communicated with, but in a safe rather than threatening way. Bert Janssen reported that it did not cross his mind to record the sound; his only response was to send out a telepathic message, "Ah, welcome! I'm so glad we finally meet." Early the next morning, they saw two new little circles in the grass at the bottom of the hill (Howe 2000a, 211).

Fig. 19

Simon Peter Fuller told me in August 2000 about an incident in the summer of 1996 in which he heard sounds coming over a field near the ancient Wayland Smithy longbarrow. The sounds seemed mechanized, like the gritting of teeth. In the light of day, the beautiful "Vesica Piscis" crop circle nearby was first seen [figure 19].

In 1989, "Operation White Crow" was set up at Cheesefoot Head to investigate the formation of crop circles and to record and photograph a crop circle in the making. A team of researchers from several different countries tried each night for a month to detect who or what was making the crop circles. They brought several types of highly technical equipment with them and posted themselves near the edges of various fields at night. Very late during the last night they all heard a high-pitched, wavering electrostatic trilling or whirring sound that started suddenly and moved toward them from a neighboring field. It stayed near them for a long time before it traveled along again. No one was able to see or photograph anything over the course of hours of listening, although Colin Andrews did tape it. George Wingfield, one of the group, described it as "totally pervasive and [it] seemed to induce an hypnotic effect on the company" (Wingfield 1990b, 20). Colin Andrews reported that it was the same sound he had heard a couple of years earlier. Everyone had the impression that the sound was caused by something living and intelligent. When daylight came, there in an adjacent field was a brand-new long pictogram. Also nearby were patches of newly laid-down crop that looked like the results of wind damage, but there had been almost no wind that night (Wingfield 1990b, 19-24).

During 1992, the British Broadcasting Company took one hundred thousand dollars worth of high-tech equipment into a crop circle in Beckhampton with the intention of documenting that the circle was a hoax (Weiss 1994, 47). However, while recording the trilling sounds in that formation, the camera broke down and subsequently had to be rebuilt. Analyses of these sounds indicated their frequency was about 5 kilohertz. The frequency of the trilling sounds recorded during the "Operation White Crow" experience was about 5.2 kilohertz (Wingfield 1990b, 24).

Lindy Tucker, an American researcher of UFO sightings and crop circles, for more than twenty years has conducted a study of anomalous metallic beeping sounds that occur in the same places and time frames as UFO sightings and crop circles (Tucker 1995, 14:8-10). These occurrences have been happening since the 1960s, and Tucker has collected several tapes. The beeping sounds are loud and repetitive, usually two-toned, much like the sonar beeping sound from a submarine. Sometimes they last for a second or two, but they can continue for several hours. The sounds seem to be rotating and seem to come out of thin air with no visible point of origin. These sounds startle people, disturb animals and cause nearby electrical equipment and compasses to malfunction. Sometimes they are so loud, people hear them inside closed buildings. The sounds seem to interact with and respond to human beings, being loud and monotonous when people are approaching and talking quietly, yet louder and faster when people are moving quickly and are excited. As an experiment, Tucker and friends stood about fifty feet from a sound she had heard on more than one occasion in the woods behind her house. She whistled the pitch of the beeps, and immediately the beeping sound sped up and formed a powerful vibration that actually shook the ground. Tucker reported an analogous incident from the 1960s in which a wildlife officer heard beeping sounds and fired a gun into the air. The beeping sounds sped up and seemed to vibrate the air (Tucker 1993, 2:4-5).

Tucker's first personal encounter with the beeping sound occurred in April 1975, when she heard loud, clear, steady metallic beeping sounds, followed by a sighting of a UFO craft approximately twenty to twenty-five feet across, dull gray, disc-shaped, with a soft white dome on top. Red lights rotated counterclockwise around the perimeter. It came out of the bush from the rear of her property and headed toward her and three of her neighbors. The beeping noise stopped as it came over them about one hundred feet up. This area behind her house was the source of recurring beeping sounds to which her cats would orient. Battery-operated devices and a compass would not work near there (Tucker 1993, 2:4).

Tucker has collected many accounts of UFOs appearing in conjunction with repetitive beeping sounds and interference with battery-operated devices and radios. Often crop circles were seen shortly afterward in the regions she was investigating, which included southern Canadian provinces, especially a line stretching north and south of Calgary, and adjacent northern states of the United States. Five separate recordings of the beeping sounds have been analyzed by Dr. Ronald Stearman, an aerospace engineer, who used sophisticated acoustical analysis equipment. After filtering out various aspects of the sounds, he found that the sounds were remarkably alike. The peak frequencies all closely matched up at about 1.05 kilohertz. The beeps were spaced 0.6 to 0.7 seconds apart. The United States government analyzed two recordings from the 1960s and concluded the sounds were made by the saw-whet owl and dismissed the likelihood of an anomalous source. Dr. Stearman analyzed those two recordings as well, but in comparing them to other recordings he found several differences that led him to be convinced that the beeping sounds were not made by an owl (Tucker 1993, 2:5).

This controversy—whether the beeping sounds are made by a bird or an anomalous source—has been repeated and investigated in England as well, where it was alleged that the bird responsible for the trilling noise is the grasshopper warbler. In an article by Ken Brown, who firmly believes the trilling noise is made by the grasshopper warbler, it was reported that computer-printed sonograms showed the trill recorded at White Crow exhibited exactly the same kilohertz frequency and the same number of notes per second as a tape of a grasshopper warbler (Brown 1992, 6:3-4). One can muster pro and con arguments about this question, and obviously more research needs to be done. Like many other phenomena addressed in this book, there might be no certain answers, and the beliefs of the researchers and observers influence the phenomena as well as the explanations for them.

SOUND AND THE CREATION OF CROP CIRCLES

In a lecture given in 2000, Freddy Silva noted that sound was the principal factor in the creation of matter. He referred to the Book of Genesis, "In the beginning was the Word," and to the walls of Jericho being brought down by the sound of trumpets. Sound is a conductor of consciousness through words, music and drumbeats. Sound can alter brain-wave patterns and consciousness and can encourage out-of-body experiences. He reminded us that sound can be used constructively or destructively. Silva speculates that infrasound, especially below eighteen millihertz, is involved in the creation of crop formations. The mechanism of action he hypothesizes is that the infrasound rapidly atomizes water molecules and creates a mist that enables the plants to bend safely. How the plants to be laid down are made to bend in the specific directions needed to make the design still remains unclear (Silva 2000).

JULY 14, 2000, CROP CIRCLE RESEARCHER AND DOWSER FREDDY SILVA IN THE CROP CIRCLE AT GOLDEN BALL HILL, WEST STOWELL, WILTSHIRE COUNTY.

As mentioned above, ilyes believes that sound is emitted by balls of light passing over the crops and that the sound stimulates the forming of a torus-shaped field of energy underground that structures the crop formation (ilyes 2000b).

The geometric construction of crop formations gave Freddy Silva a hunch as to how they are created: using sound vibrations. After telepathically asking the circlemakers in 1996 about the connection of sound to the making of the crop formations, two formations appeared that showed clear relationships to musical harmonic proportions. Then a third formation was created, which he recognized as a *cymatic* pattern, a pattern created when a specific frequency of sound is sent through a malleable physical substance. Swiss scientist Hans Jenny published detailed studies with photographs of the effects of sound vibrations on water, sand, plaster and oil. He called his field *cymatics*. When Jenny changed the sound vibration, the shape of the geometric pattern changed in the substance through which he sent it. *The higher the vibration, the more complex the pattern.* Freddy Silva noted that Jenny's work provided a convincing connection between sound and the creation of crop circles, since many of the cymatic patterns found in Jenny's research photos were identical to crop circles. Congruent with Jenny's photos, some of the early crop circles consisted of circles surrounded by concentric rings. More complex matches included the Barbury Castle formation of 1991 [figure 20] [plate 6], the "Avebury Web" [figure 21] [plate 5], the Froxfield "Flower of Life" of 1994 [figure 22] and the star fractals of 1997 [plate 3]. Other matches were found only with dissection of overhead crop formation photographs by compass or computer. Silva believes that it is no coincidence that the crop formations have become more complex. He thinks this might be an indication that the Earth is undergoing an increase in vibratory rate as predicted by indigenous people worldwide as well as by "sensitives" such as channels and mediums. Cymatics would indicate that the increased frequencies of the Earth are contributing to the greater geometric complexities in crop circles (Silva 1998, 22:18-19).

Fig. 20

Fig. 21

Fig. 22

Intrigued with astronomer Gerald Hawkins' idea that sound tones are associated with crop formations, in 1993 researcher Peter Glastonbury took musical instruments into a single crop circle in an English field and played three notes. The next day he discovered an addition to the circle with the same diatonic ratio. (A diatonic ratio is the ratio of two numbers that corresponds to the frequency of one of the white keys on the piano keyboard. Ratios of dimensions of various parts of crop circles have been calculated by Hawkins to equal the frequencies of the white keys. Glastonbury's experiment was in response to Hawkins' calculations of diatonic ratios in numerous formations. This is explained further in the section titled "The Geometric and Mathematical Characteristics of the Crop Formations.") Glastonbury repeated this experiment over several days, and each time new additions to the crop circle appeared, until the original simple circle had become "a long but messy conglomerate of strange shapes stretched out along a common axis." These experiments provocatively suggest that sound applied to the crop somehow triggered the crop to be laid down in patterns (Andrews 1993b, 2:2).

Paul Vigay researches sound frequencies inside and outside crop circles and has found that the frequencies inside are different from the frequencies outside. Frequencies inside have measured up to 650 megahertz (Silva 2000). Subliminal sound frequencies inside the circles might contribute to the varying kinesthetic reactions people experience in crop formations.

WITNESSING THE FORMATION OF CROP CIRCLES

Many people have seen unusual lights over a field and subsequently realized there was a new crop circle in that location. Because most crop circles are made in the darkness of night and the English countryside is profoundly dark without any streetlights or city lights shining on the crop fields, it is almost impossible to see a crop circle actually being made. There are, however, a few instances in which a person has reported directly witnessing the crop being laid down and swirled. After many years of speculation about how crop circles are formed, it would be hoped that eyewitnesses finally could provide the relevant information to answer all our questions. Unfortunately, accounts by eyewitnesses are very, very scarce and show as much variability as the theories reflect.

In a 1997 article in the *Cerealogist* (an English crop circle journal), James Morrison presents three instances of sightings that were mentioned in Terence Meaden's book, *The Circles Effect and Its Mysteries*. (This book is unavailable to me, and I acknowledge the third- and fourth-hand nature of these reports, but I am passing them on from Morrison's article due to the lack of firsthand reports available.) In a daylight sighting in early August 1983, Melvyn Bell saw dust spiraling up from a wheat field, and then a circle ten to twelve meters in diameter formed in a few seconds. Dr. Meaden also quoted from an account of an incident with multiple witnesses near Starr Hill, Wiltshire, written by Arthur Shuttlewood for *Now!* magazine (August 29, 1988): "'Suddenly the grass began to sway before our eyes and laid itself flat in a clockwise spiral, just like the opening of a lady's fan. A perfect circle was completed in less than half a minute, all the time accompanied by a high-pitched humming sound.'" In the third incident, on July 3, 1982, Ray Barnes watched what looked like a wave or line move through a cereal field: "'After crossing the field in a shallow arc the "line" dropped to a position about 1 o'clock and radially described a circle 50-75 feet radius in about four seconds. The agency then disappeared'" (Morrison 1997, 19:18).

In his book *The Cosmic Connection: Worldwide Crop Formations and ET Contacts*, Michael Hesemann describes some direct observations of circles being made. On a September day in 1974, in Langenburg, Saskatchewan, Canada, a farmer watched five strange metal "hemispheres" hovering and rotating about a foot above his oilseed rape crop. After he observed the spectacle for about fifteen minutes, smoke formed underneath the objects, a strong wind sprang up and the objects shot straight up into the sky. Where they had hovered, he found swirled cir-

AUGUST 1, 1996, PAUL VIGAY TAKING ELECTRO-MAGNETIC READINGS IN WINDMILL HILL CROP CIRCLE.

Photographer: © Barbara Lamb.

cles in the crop that were only about 1.4 inches in diameter. A sixth ring appeared a few nights later. The second event, which occurred in Metepec, Mexico, had multiple witnesses. A luminous dome-shaped object landed in the middle of a field. Small balls of light shot from it and whirled through the field, creating the crop formation in seconds, and then it returned to the "mothership," which flew away. Upon investigating the crop, it was found that not only had many sugar cane leaves been burnt but also that the ground temperature in the center of the circle was higher than that recorded in the rest of the field. Additionally, a radioactivity level 3.5 times above normal was recorded. Earlier that evening, a woman filmed a four-foot-tall humanoid walking through the field soon after she filmed a luminous disc-shaped object hovering over the town (Hesemann 1996, 63-64).

George Wingfield presented a report of a crop formation being created with no visible agency in Dundee, Scotland, in July 1989. Sandy Reid was walking through a field at 5:30 in the morning, listening to the loud bird chorus. Suddenly, there was silence. All the bird sounds stopped, and he heard a strange noise from the corn field downhill from him. Barely fifty feet away, "the heads of the corn were rattling together, and the plants were swaying. This continued for a few minutes, though there was not the slightest breath of wind. Then suddenly, within less than ten seconds, the corn went down in a perfect circle about thirty feet across." Sandy went down into the circle. The crop had fallen in a straight line away from him except for the corn in the far part of the circle that whiplashed back toward him at an angle. The circle had a short spur of flattened corn going out from its perimeter. "For some minutes there remained the strong sense of some unseen presence" (Wingfield 1990b, 31).

Another account of seeing a formation being created in a corn field is somewhat controversial, since there was some sentiment that the account was fabricated. A couple out walking around 9 P.M. in the evening of May 17, 1990, Vivienne and Gary Tomlinson, felt a change in the wind pattern. As Vivienne reportedly stated in a letter to the *Sunday Mirror*, "At the centre point the wind gathered force pushing forward sending strong waves in the corn. The whistling grew stronger . . . almost like a high-pitched pan-pipe flute sound. . . . Suddenly there was a gush of strong wind pushing down against us. The wind circled round us, looking down, we noticed corn being pushed down . . . with one large whirlwind. This broke into another one, pushing the offset one into the side, whirling away pushing down the corn. . . . Miniature whirlwinds were appearing one after another, rapidly whirling around the corn in small bunches, then gently falling down." Vivienne continued to have earaches after this experience (Harpur 1991/92, 5:20).

From these varied reports, it is clear there is no one manner—at least from the physical world point of view—in which crop is laid down. These eyewitness reports provide no definitive answers to the question of how crop circles are made. The elusiveness of this phenomenon quite naturally generates a question of whether there is a deliberate, willful attempt by the circlemakers to avoid detection.

A GAME OF HIDE AND SEEK?

In light of the amazingly few testimonies of witnesses seeing crop circles being formed, it appears that the (nonhuman) circlemakers are very effective in avoiding detection. The circles are executed surprisingly quickly; dowsing has shown it takes only three to thirty seconds to lay down the crop in a pattern, even when making large and complex formations with several different lays to the crop. It seems that when cameras, video camcorders and other recording equipment are near a crop field where it is anticipated that a crop circle might be made, the circlemakers refrain from creating one.

In the 1989 Operation White Crow project, researchers from several countries with state-of-the-art, high-tech equipment of various kinds, waited an entire month without the circlemakers producing a crop circle in the monitored field. On the last night of the project, when the researchers were giving up and packing away their equipment, a crop circle appeared near them. (Later a well-known hoaxer claimed he had made it.) Whether the circle was of human or extraterrestrial origin, no one saw or photographed anything under the cover of darkness. All they experienced was a penetrating trilling or chattering sound that went on for hours (as described earlier). The source of it eluded the pursuing researchers, although Colin Andrews taped it and noted it was the same trilling sound he had heard while sitting in a crop circle in 1987 and praying for an explanation for how crop circles are made (Wingfield 1990b, 18-24).

Dr. Terence Meaden organized another surveillance attempt in 1990, called Operation Blackbird, again with researchers from various countries and high-tech equipment. He was accompanied by an English BBC-TV crew, a Japanese Nippon TV crew and thirty-two TV and radio network crews planning to broadcast by satellite to other countries. Instead of a genuine crop circle appearing in the watched-over field, an obviously man-made crop circle was found (Hesemann 1996, 26-32). A great deal of publicity ensued that discredited the crop circle phenomenon and researchers. Colin Andrews, who was involved with the project, believed on hindsight that the operation was infiltrated by the British military and the hoaxing was not detected because it deliberately was performed just outside the range of the surveillance equipment (King 1996, 2:22). Information leaked from the British military indicated the military executed the hoax to discredit the growing crop circle phenomenon (Wingfield 1990a, 2:8-10).

In June 1991, a surveillance project called Chameleon was stationed on Morgan's Hill near Devizes. Run by John Macnish and David Morgenstern in cooperation with the BBC, the project had at its disposal a high-sensitivity directional microphone and a remote-controlled TV camera. An alarm system was installed around the field under observation. After a foggy night, daybreak on June 28 revealed a dumbbell-shaped formation only 660 yards from the Chameleon camp [figure 23]. No footprints or other signs of human activity were found (Hesemann 1996, 35).

Michael Hesemann discussed two other high-technology surveillance

Fig. 23

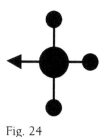

Fig. 24

attempts that occurred in 1991. In one of them, radar picked up an irregularly moving object, but it stayed invisible in spite of the night being clear. In another project by the Japanese, cameras recorded a number of mysterious red lights over their camp at the prehistoric site Adam's Grave, which had attracted numerous large pictograms in the past. However, no crop formations appeared during the vigil (Hesemann 1996, 36).

In a maximum security zone near the British Prime Minister's country residence at Chequers, a pictogram appeared in the shape of a Celtic cross [figure 24]. One of the arms of the cross was tipped by a triangle rather than by a circle, and the tip of the triangle was pointed straight at the residence. The tightly patrolled location certainly ruled out hoaxers at work (Hesemann 1996, 36).

Inspired by the sightings of anomalous lights, each summer crop-watchers station themselves late at night on hillsides and summits and around the edges of fields where crop circles have been placed before. Certain fields look like the perfect candidates or ideal canvasses for the placement of new formations: ripe, ready and inviting the blessing of a new crop circle. On many nights, the watchers see nothing unusual in the fields. On other nights, they see a variety of anomalous activities, including glowing spheres hovering, circling, cruising along and dipping toward the ground. I have seen a video made in 1998 by Matthew Williams, a young man visiting from Wales, who caught on film white glowing spheres and a structured craft being chased by a British military helicopter late at night in the Alton Barnes area.

Sometimes, when spheres of light are present, even the observers with serious intent of having a sighting somehow get distracted from watching the fields by talking to each other, or looking in the wrong direction, or doing an eyes-closed meditation, or falling asleep, only to be told a few minutes later that they missed the whole display! This happened to me late one night in July 1998, while looking for anomalous lights from Knap Hill, overlooking East Field in Alton Barnes, where we were expecting a nice crop circle to happen any night. When a bright red orb appeared in the field below, I was busy talking to people and facing the other direction. Perhaps the circlemakers distract us just at the time of their appearance. Perhaps the spheres are scouts or probes that check out the conditions in the crop and the soil. Perhaps they create a field of energy that contributes to watchers becoming distracted and inattentive. Perhaps they send back their gathered information to points of origin, and then the circle creators invisibly do their work when the time is right.

THE CONTROVERSY OF GENUINE VERSUS HOAXED CROP CIRCLES

Genuine crop circles are thought to be designed and executed by some anomalous source rather than by human beings. By now, most serious researchers of this phenomenon believe this anomalous source is some sort of highly advanced creative intelligence that uses remarkable technology or energetic techniques in creating the beautiful patterns in the fields. Some consider the source to be "physical" beings from space—the standard conception of extraterrestrials—while others believe in nonphysical agencies that work with thought and other techniques beyond our physical awareness. Most likely, crop circles are made by different groups of beings functioning in various dimensions, not just one.

Some people believe or hope the crop circles imply that physical contact with this intelligence will occur soon or that it is already happening now. For some, this is more than a mere idea; it is a strong kinesthetic, emotional and mental sense experienced in certain crop formations. They feel their energy systems coming alive, and they experience a sense of an aware presence. They feel that their own presence inside a crop circle is noticed, acknowledged and appreciated. They believe that in a genuine crop circle there is information to absorb on all levels and special energies to incorporate for multidimensional development. They feel inspired to sit quietly and deepen themselves into a multifaceted expansion. Generally, individuals who feel attuned in genuine crop circles feel none of this inside man-made circles. The difference is profound. The hoaxed man-made crop circles feel flat, lifeless, dull and disappointing, even if they are executed quite plausibly and look impressive from an airplane.

Often enthusiastic crop circle researchers/explorers deeply want the phenomenon to be genuine. They respond eagerly to indications of genuineness, such as bent but not broken stalks, swollen and bent growth nodes, split skin on the stalks and lack of trampled crop around new formations. Smooth edges of the formation, intricate lays of the crop and other aesthetically pleasing details, such as very thin, precise lines, give hope that the formation is not man-made. They are grateful to find the plants still living, growing and maturing, even weeks after the formation appeared. They feel gratified each time their dowsing rods or pendulums register changes of energy inside a crop circle, at the boundaries or even a foot or two outside the circle.

Researchers are especially delighted to find and step into a crop circle that has just appeared in a field. They feel privileged, honored and often specially bonded with this formation. In August 1994, I had the thrill of discovering a brand-new crop circle from the top deck of a double-decker bus. My three friends and I were the first ones to step into it [figure 25] [plate 4]. I was deeply aware of the freshness and fluffiness of the gently laid-down crop and the subtle snap, crackle and pop of the fresh, new energy. It felt like a sacrilege to step upon the perfection of these slightly arcing stalks of wheat, for fear that we might desecrate this gift from a mysterious source. I have felt a special kinship with this formation ever since that morning. The special energies, the condition of the stalks and the perfection in the lay of the stalks convinced me that this crop circle was made by the genuine circlemakers.

Some people speculate that genuine crop circles are portals to other dimensions of reality, as suggested in the 1991 long pictogram at Alton Barnes, Wiltshire [figure 26]. When sitting quietly in such a formation,

Fig. 25

Fig. 26

they often experience an altered state of consciousness. Some people even have out-of-body experiences. These people are open to exploring and accepting the idea that crop circles are given to us by entities or a level of consciousness beyond our so-called normal views of reality. They are prepared to have their understandings of reality changed and expanded. In contrast to this, many other people resist having their materialistically based concepts of reality changed and prefer to think of all crop circles as hoaxes—or ignore this phenomenon altogether. Some other people choose to dismiss the whole phenomenon as a mystery beyond their ability to comprehend. They assume the mystery cannot be solved and make no effort to put any attention into it.

As the years have gone by in researching the crop circle phenomenon, the lines of distinction between genuine and hoaxed crop circles have become less clear. It is becoming apparent that it is often difficult or impossible to *prove* which crop circles are genuine and which are man-made. Ten years ago, observers tended to think either all circles were genuine or all were man-made. Now we are more likely to accept that there is a combination of genuine and hoaxed crop circles appearing in the fields. Even some of the known-to-be-hoaxed formations have shown indications of extra energy from some unknown source, as indicated by certain tests. In the early 1990s, the definitions of genuine versus hoaxed crop circles were more delineated, and it seemed easier for perceptive researchers to tell the difference. Since then a more sophisticated level of questioning and scientific testing has evolved, and the former standards of proof of genuine versus hoaxed are outmoded. This has been the case due to the improved methods used by hoaxers when making crop circles and to the increased complexity of their designs—that is, if those hoaxers' claims of having made certain complex crop circles are to be believed and trusted—and possibly to increased technical skill made available by the cooperation between extraterrestrial and human circlemakers. Perhaps the reality is that the nonhuman circlemakers make crop circles in a variety of ways, including using their own mysterious technologies as well as inspiring humans to go out into the fields at night and provide the labor force for laying down their designs. In this case, coming up with an either/or accounting of genuine versus hoaxed might ultimately prove to be not only impossible, but unimportant.

EQUIPMENT FAILURE AS AN INDICATOR OF GENUINENESS

An indication that a crop circle probably is genuine is the failure of electronic equipment inside the formation. Most noticeably, when a formation is newly made and fresh, failures are more likely to happen with cameras, video camcorders, tape recorders, mobile telephones, pagers, computerized palm pilots, remote-controlled model airplanes, calculators and compasses. Sometimes the equipment is actually damaged, and the effects are permanent. Sometimes the equipment stalls or jams temporarily while in the circle, but works again when taken a few feet outside the crop circle or some distance down the road. Often the batteries of electronic equipment drain out in a freshly made crop circle, yet a week or so later, new batteries might function perfectly well in that same circle, due to the weakening of initially strong energies. I never had this happen to any of my photography equipment until 1999, when my best camera ceased to work in three different crop circles, even with a brand-new battery inside. The camera worked perfectly well in other non-crop-circle locations. Apparently, the malfunctioning was due to the strong energies in those crop circles. Along this line, a small airplane is reported to have lost its gauge readings while flying over one crop circle only to have them resume when out of that crop circle's area.

American psychic predictor Sean David Morton told me of some simple testing of a crop circle he performed in 1990. He left a wind-up stopwatch at the edge of a crop circle field and an identical watch inside the crop circle. An hour later, he noticed that the watch inside the crop circle had lost six seconds, and the watch at the edge of the field had not. Then he switched the watches and repeated the experiment. Again, the watch inside the crop circle lost six seconds, and the one at the edge of the field did not. He thought it was interesting that the watches were affected by the direct energies of the crop circle even though they did not contain batteries.

MEDIA EFFORTS TO DEBUNK
THE CROP CIRCLE PHENOMENON

There are differing theories about why so much emphasis has been put on whether the crop circles are man-made or hoaxed. Some researchers believe that the ministerial level of the Tory British government was concerned about the growing interest in this unusual phenomenon, fearing that a new religion might be formed out of people's fascination and mystical attraction to the crop circles. Another theory was that the industrial complex might have a concern that information about possible formulas for free energy technology, supposedly contained in some of the crop circle symbols, might cause a challenge to their use of, control of and profit from our ecology-damaging resources.

Another possibility is that everyday people are uncomfortable with the notion that crop circles might mysteriously be coming from elsewhere—from some intelligence other than human. This notion, of course, opens up the whole question of whether or not we are the only intelligent life in the universe and whether or not we are being visited by someone or something unknown to us. Many people prefer to hold onto their existing view of reality and are much more comfortable thinking all the crop circles must be made by humans.

The British military and the Royal Air Force Security Police in crop circle territory have undeniably taken interest in the phenomenon. They frequently fly over crop circle formations in airplanes and helicopters, and a few times they have flown low enough to threaten the safety of crop circle researchers in the fields.

As a result of all these obvious and subtle factors, and perhaps for other reasons as well, a strong media campaign was launched in England in 1991 to discredit the crop circle phenomenon (Wingfield 1991/92, 5:3, 5-6). A popular daily tabloid newspaper called *Today* ran a prominent three-page spread with bright, full-color pictures and very bold headlines claiming that Doug and Dave (Doug Bower and Dave Chorley, two retired men from Southhampton in their sixties) had "conned the world" and had made all the crop circles worldwide (clearly a ludicrous assertion). The two men were paid ten thousand British pounds for their story. United Press International sent this story around the world on September 11, 1991, after a spectacular English crop circle season. The story received much attention worldwide and fostered the belief in many people that all crop circles were man-made. This media effort was extremely effective and influential. Television news shows and special programs picked up the idea and promoted the theory that crop circles were simply a human phenomenon.

When challenged by researchers Colin Andrews and Pat Delgado to demonstrate their methods of making crop circles—with planks of wood, chains and a primitive sighting device made with a baseball cap—Doug and Dave admitted in front of the cameramen of the same tabloid newspaper that they had not made any complex crop circles, nor any other circles worldwide, nor the "Celtic Cross" design that Andrews had asked them to duplicate, which they had previously claimed making. Their demonstration crop circle was sloppy, messy and inexact, leaving broken, crushed and dying plants.

These conditions were vastly different from those in the crop circles considered to be genuine, in which the plants were swirled in perfect unison and laid down crisply, with each plant remaining alive and undamaged. The crop circles deemed genuine have design and symmetry that are both aesthetically and energetically appealing to people. Unfortunately, the United Press did not print much about this demonstration and did not even mention Doug and Dave's retraction, and what little was picked up by newspapers in other countries was printed only in small, hard-to-find articles buried in the back pages (Wingfield 1991/92, 5:3, 5-6). Colin Andrews commented, "[I]n my opinion this was *possibly* one of the best executed frauds or planned disinformation programs of modern times." He believed it was a scam perpetrated by British and United States intelligence agencies (King 1996, 2:22). A few years later, in 1996, Dave died. Doug occasionally made a very simple circle, which showed up poorly amongst all the complex and accomplished crop circles. Yet even to this day, many people think all crop circles are made by this mythical "Doug and Dave."

During the summer of 1992, a few individuals tried to disturb the investigations of serious crop circle researchers. They made circles and pictograms, even right next to researchers' investigation bases, and performed other actions to take attention away from studying the genuine crop circles. Rob Irving allegedly was paid to be disruptive to the researchers, possibly by his uncle in the British Home Office. Rob and a friend, American Jim Schnabel, eventually admitted to hoaxing some formations. Schnabel wrote articles in various respectable newspapers and magazines, discrediting the phenomenon as an illusion. He also published a book in 1993 titled *Round in Circles*, which insulted the researchers and made fun of people's interest in crop circles. An investigator found out from Schnabel that he was involved in a plot to debunk the genuineness of crop circles. This plot involved England, the United States, Germany and the Vatican. The aim of this plot, according to Schnabel, was to discredit the crop circle phenomenon so much that it would disappear from the media and thus from public awareness, since it was feared that the circles could bring about a "change of world consciousness" (Hesemann 1996, 44-45).

The impression that crop circles are man-made still exists amongst many people in England and the rest of the world. This impression continues to be perpetrated by the media. In 1994, the British Broadcasting Corporation produced an Arthur C. Clarke TV special that included a commissioned crop circle made during daylight hours by a small team of hoaxers. This flower design looked quite beautiful from an airplane, but on the ground it felt lifeless and had broken stalks. My experience in this crop circle was entirely different from what I feel in genuine crop circles.

A couple of years later, the British Association of Organic Farmers commissioned the making of a crop circle in the shape of their logo, and it likewise looked impressive from the air but not from the ground. In 1998, the British Broadcasting Corporation again commissioned a team of human circlemakers to make a large design full of many circles. This, too, looked good from the air, but on the ground each circle was messily laid down with rough edges, there were no dowsing responses and the plants quickly died. My experience in this formation was of lifelessness, flatness and messiness of the lay. My dowsing rod stayed perfectly still as I walked into each circle. In the meantime, public opinion was reinforced that all crop circles must be man-made.

On August 7, 1999, the popular British newspaper, the *Daily Mail*, printed a large, colorful spread about a commissioned crop circle placed in a field directly in view of the frequently visited ancient stone circles of Avebury. Reporters were there to interview and photograph visitors to the crop circle during the first few hours after it had appeared late in July. They printed the enthralled reactions of people who were taken in by the complex geometric pattern of pentagrams within a large triangle that was within a circle [figure 27], and who believed it must be genuine and made by beings from space (Taylor 1999). But they did not print the reactions and educated comments of myself and other seasoned researchers who thought this formation must be a hoax. The tone and intent of the article was to discredit the believers by announcing at the end that a team of hoaxers had been hired to make this formation. Perhaps the media personnel do not recognize or find it difficult to handle the profound transformational meanings of many of the crop circles and the creative work coming from an intelligence they are not ready to accept. Or perhaps there is a

Fig. 27

larger, covert orchestration of what seems to be a continuing campaign to debunk the whole phenomenon.

The Doug and Dave hoax promotion of 1991 raised a serious question in the minds of dedicated researchers: Were some of the crop circles being hoaxed, and if so, what are the differences between these circles and genuine ones? In July 1992, an official "hoax competition" was held in Buckinghamshire and prize money was offered to the winners who could make the best crop circle. This event was sponsored by the *Cereologist*, the *Guardian* newspaper, a popular German magazine called *PM*, the English-based Koestler Foundation and by scientist and theorist Rupert Sheldrake who originated the idea and attracted the funding. A farmer donated a portion of his crop field for this competition, and a template of preselected design elements was given to each contestant [figure 28] . The quadrants of land contestants used were easily accessible from the road and were illumined by reflected light from the adjacent town. The twelve individual and team contestants had five and a half hours to execute their design, with no restrictions on equipment used (Rhone, Harpur, Haward, and Krönig 1992, 7:7-9). These conditions were in stark contrast to those involved in the making of genuine crop circles, which usually are placed much further from the roads with no illumination from vehicle lights, streetlights or flashlights, are created with minimal equipment, and are made in a much shorter period of time, leaving no tracks or markings in or out of the formation.

The man-made designs looked quite good from the air, but the stalks were broken and squashed and the plants quickly died. As Jürgen Krönig, chairman of the judges, concluded, "No team was able to produce a layered crop with the 'crunchy' feel to it which one comes across in new formations" (Rhone, Harpur, Howard and Krönig 1992, 7:9). Conclusions from the hoax competition included: formations could be made neatly, with little or no indication of equipment or foot tracks—however, the stalks were not bent perfectly, nor did they remain horizontal, nor did they continue to grow; the interweaving of sheaves at angles was poorly achieved, as was the swirl of the crop from the center out to the circumference; the nodes were not swollen on one side; the structure of the crop was not changed and the soil was not changed; the circles did not have a sense of beauty and flow—they looked static and self-conscious; dowsing showed no reactions before or after; and there was no expansion of ley lines, no unusual energy effects and no physical or psychic effects on people. They were, therefore, clearly different in quality from the crop circles considered to be genuine. Researchers felt the competition helped show that humans could make superficially plausible formations, but with closer investigation, signs of faking were quite apparent.

WHY PEOPLE HOAX CROP CIRCLES

To earnest, sincere crop circle researchers, the existence of hoaxed crop circles is disturbing. Yet there appear to be numerous motives that drive diverse people to hoax crop circles. Some hoaxers relish the adventure of

Fig. 28

doing clandestine work without being caught or prosecuted, or relish the challenge of creating designs that people believe are too complex and perfect to be done by ordinary humans (especially when done in the dark of night). Some are attracted to expressing their artistic inclinations on a huge canvas of growing crop. Some are uncomfortable with the idea that crop circles are made by some nonhuman (even higher) intelligence, and therefore try to prove they are all man-made. Some want to "outsmart the researchers" who generally favor the view of crop circles being made by a mysterious, superior intelligence, or publicly discredit the crop circle phenomenon as a spiritual experience. Some enjoy the feeling of fooling the public. Some compete with other hoaxers to be superior in making the patterns, or enjoy the challenge of making impeccable formations or enjoy praise and admiration from other hoaxers. Some enjoy the excitement of creating a stir in the media and hearing praise for their designs and workmanship. Some like the feeling of being important and feeling famous, even while remaining anonymous to the public. Some have a desire for commercial success through selling photos of their designs. Some enjoy being part of a subgroup with a certain identity and values.

John Lundberg, a self-proclaimed hoaxer, describes being involved in an informal community of hoaxers, sharing technical information, photographs, "near-miss tales" and anomalous experiences in the fields at night (Lundberg 1995, 14:21-22). Ron Russell offered a rather cynical list of "reasons for this mischief—kids having a fling, drunks from the pub wanting to play, hoaxes purposely made for media disinformation and decoys made by dark operatives who are paid. Also, some formations are intentionally made to signal the ETs" (Russell 2000a, 10:74).

Lundberg gives numerous reasons for his actions. First, his scruples were abated by reading Jim Schnabel's *Round in Circles* book that debunked the genuineness of the crop circles. He stopped worrying that he might contaminate serious crop circle research (since all formations were man-made) and he stopped worrying that he was destroying farmer's crops and profits (since the crop could be harvested unless severely trampled by tourists). "Being able to construct something that many people believe to be beyond human endeavour" was a primary motive. Speaking as an artist, he comments, "The circles-prone area of Wiltshire could be referred to as a psychic landscape. The location of crop circles within this landscape is of great consequence. Seeing a formation put down in just the right place in relation to its surroundings adds an extra dimension to a formation; it becomes more than the sum of its parts. The proximity of many circles to established sacred sites, such as Avebury or Silbury Hill only adds to this sensation." He enjoyed creating "temporary sacred sites" where people came to meditate, dance and "decipher," and people reported a diverse assortment of anomalies in his team's creations. "I consider the circles we've put down to be genuine. There is no intention on our part to deceive; our work generates response, often from other circlemakers, and can sometimes act to catalyze a wide range of paranormal events. I still believe there is a genuine phenomenon, but I now also believe that we're a part of it" (Lundberg 1995, 14:20, 22).

While to an outsider the hoaxing might appear malicious or deviant, several hoaxers have commented that they have felt directed or impelled by some unknown agent to go out into the fields and make formations, and they believe that the circle-making force actually is working through their physical bodies. Sometimes they start with a plan for a certain formation and then feel influenced to make another shape. Some have noticed—and been mystified—that crop circles they have made are changed when they come back to see them in the light of day. Many hoaxers have seen anomalous lights.

In terms of inspiration for what formations to make, some hoaxers believe they are drawing on collective consciousness. Some claim to study alchemical symbols for ideas for their designs. Some human circlemakers say they meditate for inspiration and symbols and to bring in the higher energies they believe go into the crop circles.

Ron Russell commented recently that hoaxed formations are "visited not only by us but by intelligences from the other side, thus acting as portals or power places by default. Nothing is simple here; the human involvement is perhaps not so sinister as it might seem at first glance. We humans want our contact to be nice and tidy, but maybe it is layered, nonlinear and complicated. . . . [Maybe] some of the human fabricators, in spite of their initial deceptions, are acting as agents for the spiritual beings—like channels doing the will of the higher mind" (Russell 2000a, 10:73)

Matthew Williams and Paul Damon, investigative journalists and editors of the *Truthseekers Review*, claim to have created crop circles during the summers of 1998, 1999 (Williams but not Damon) and 2000, and a few during 1996 and 1997, as a project to determine how easy or hard it was to make complex formations, to test the crop circle experts for their recognition of human-made formations, to ascertain if there were patterns of progression in circle-making designs during a season (hypothesized to be a form of communication between human and spirit circlemakers) and to catch hoaxers in the act of hoaxing. Their claim was extremely disappointing to friends who had trusted Williams and Damon to help them research and understand crop circles.

July 1998, Peter Sorensen and Matthew Williams at the Barge Inn.

In a statement about their activities written by Williams, he commented that while doing the hoaxing they saw many unusual phenomena happening overhead and in the fields: UFOs, spheres of light and various paranormal events. Humanoid figures sometimes suddenly showed up in the fields and directed them to lay down patterns that were different from the patterns they had planned to make. These beings seemed benign and friendly and would disappear as quickly and silently as they had appeared. As an example, one of the team members was talking to another team member, or so he thought, while making a crop circle at night. Then he turned around and saw his other team members behind him. Wondering to whom he had been talking, he turned back, but that person was gone (Williams 1999, 24:11-12).

The team had a sense of being in communication with a very high intelligence of some sort, which seemed to respond to their designs by placing more circles near or with the original man-made designs or similar formations in different parts of the country, even during the same nights. They concluded that inspiration to do certain designs was being given to the human circlemakers. They also had a strong sense of being protected while working by some intelligence or force they could not see. The team members seemed to be made invisible and inaudible to anyone standing near the field where they were working, even though they kept expecting to be detected and caught (Williams 1999, 24:11-12).

Williams and Damon came to believe that the making of crop circles is a sacred art form, the purpose of which is to mystify people and cause them to ask questions of themselves about their spirituality and the nature of the universe. They also perceived that crop circles represent a tangible paranormal attractor and emitter. They felt that the message of the higher intelligence behind the inspiration for crop circles is entirely benign and friendly in nature (Williams 1999, 24:11-12).

Williams commented that their circles were regarded by the crop circle community as genuine, with measurable effects from dowsing and electrostatic voltmeters. He felt that the non-damage to plants, even with their "stomper boards," constituted a "magical effect." As Williams wrote further, "The subject grows in dynamism and interest due to human involvement—as it is human involvement that is a heavy part of the circle phenomenon. There is probably a non-human intelligence working alongside human circle makers to create some circles outright—i.e. the original phenomenon still remains creating circles—a fact with which *all* human circlemakers agree" (Williams 1999, 24:12).

A notable event happened in early November 2000, when Williams was arrested and fined for making a crop circle on West Overton Hill, Wiltshire. This was the first arrest for the making of a crop circle without permission from the farmer. Williams was fined and released. He said he had felt challenged by researcher Michael Glickman who, according to Matthew, had declared that a geometrically perfect seven-pointed star would be impossible for humans to make as a crop circle. Williams decided to prove him wrong and composed a seven-pointed star design on his computer, which he and his team executed in the field over a period of three nights [plate 61]. He was caught because he bragged about making the crop circle, not because he was caught in the act. He communicated with radio-show host Whitley Strieber before he made the formation and posted photos of it on the Internet. When Glickman was informed about William's message to Strieber, he notified the farmer who promptly contacted the police (Thomas 2000a, 93:3).

THE EXTENT OF HOAXING

It is difficult to know what to believe about the extent of hoaxing.

Some people claim to have hoaxed some crop circles, yet they refuse to say which ones and they refrain from demonstrating how they do it. Of course, their claims could be hoaxes. This happens with many other sensational items in the news, with people claiming to have started a bomb scare or committed a robbery or kidnapping without really having done so. The media promotes and sensationalizes stories by self-claimed criminals—and by self-claimed hoaxers of crop circles. As George Wingfield remarked, "Certainly it is plain that circlefakers are extremely coy when [it] comes to the question of which particular formations were made by them. . . . It is evidently not the plan of hoaxers to claim authorship since they are keener than any to preserve the mystery of their circles" (Wingfield 1995b, 14:26). Matthew Williams, in fact, commented that the mystique of the origin of the crop circles can be a shamanistic way to draw people toward greater questioning and thus to greater realizations (Williams 1999, 24:12).

It is important to consider that someone's *claim* to have made crop circles does not constitute *proof* of having made them. Many researchers and other observers find it impossible to believe that many crop circles, especially the complex, geometrically sophisticated patterns, were made by humans. Until there is absolute proof of human involvement, they will continue to be impressed with the anomalous nature of the phenomenon.

Various estimates have been made about the extent to which the English crop circles are genuine versus man-made. American researcher Rosemary Guiley (1997) reported that there are twenty groups in England who make crop circles, but I am not clear about the sources on which she based this estimate. There was a major dispute over how many of the year 2000 crop circles were man-made. Williams claimed he had made seventy percent of them, but Charles Mallett investigated many of them and found only some of them to have rough edges and vague patterns, and to be inferior to other crop circles that had beauty, fluidity and grace (Howe 2000b). Estimates of the incidence of hoaxing falling at the other end of the scale include Geoff Ambler's view that ninety-five percent of formations are genuine and only five percent hoaxed, based on his dowsing of over one hundred formations (Ambler 2000, 90:8).

Colin Andrews conducted a two-year research project, funded personally by Lawrence Rockefeller, to determine how many crop circles in England were genuine and how many were man-made. By August 2000, he estimated that eighty percent of the crop circles showed evidence of having been man-made, based on "detective work, site inspections, physical evidence, aerial photography, personal experiences, information from media who have paid to have formations created for upcoming programs, and from undercover researchers." Signs he considered included layout markings and evidence of each step in the making. Sometimes he received a drawing of a design that was soon to be made and, indeed, that design soon did appear in a field. (Actually, this does not constitute proof of human manufacture; some people have received psychic impressions of upcoming circles but certainly were not involved in making them.)

Andrews concluded that the remaining twenty percent of crop circles are still a mystery and form an extraordinary phenomenon, showing no evidence of human involvement. He also reported finding an "out of sync" magnetic field (misaligned three to five degrees in a clockwise direction from the crop design) in a handful of simple designs (that he considered genuine), a field that he hypothesizes would create an electrical current that would affect the plants. He still has no answer as to what forces must be at work to create the designs (Andrews 2000).

Andrews' estimate that only twenty percent of crop circles are genuine and his theory about the magnetic field anomaly have been strongly disputed and challenged by other crop circle researchers and even the news media. Objections focus on Andrews' lack of details concerning how investigations were conducted, what equipment was used to test for the out-of-sync magnetic field, which controls were used to test the accuracy of the equipment and how Andrews' conclusions were reached (Thomas 2000b, 92:5). Apparently, he has not disclosed which specific crop formations he considers real, which he considers man-made and which ones showed the magnetic misalignment.

The hoaxing phenomenon has been a big nuisance to serious researchers who are trying to learn about this exceptional kind of creativity found in genuine crop circles. Researchers have expended a great deal of time, effort and money checking out crop circles to discern if they are genuine or not. It has appeared that this has distracted them from their real work of using the genuine crop circles as spiritual energy and consciousness-raising tools. However, as we are coming to realize that the lines of distinction between genuine and hoaxed might not be as clear-cut as was thought in earlier years, there is much of importance to research and learn about the human element in circle-making. As with the phenomenon of ET contacts and abductions, over the past ten years we are learning that the "we versus them" distinction is too simplistic a way to conceptualize our relationship with the nonhuman beings making contact with us. We have more influence over the phenomena under study than we hitherto have given ourselves credit for.

Even the most cynical researchers and hoaxers themselves largely still acknowledge the existence of genuine crop circles that appear from a non-human source. Some of the most complex and awe-inspiring crop circle designs still have not been claimed by hoaxers. No hoaxer yet has actually demonstrated in the light of day the making of a truly complex crop circle design, with impeccable artistry of execution, astonishing geometry or special energy patterns. Some researchers are dedicated to scientifically proving the differences between the hoaxed and the genuine ones, or showing that all crop circles are man-made or that all are genuine. Many researchers and enthusiasts continue to focus on the crop circles believed to be genuine and continue to have inspiring and uplifting experiences in them. These people tend to withdraw their interest from those crop circles that indicate poor design or a lack of energy or inspiration, and they leave it to others to try to prove the authorship.

INVESTIGATING CROP CIRCLE ENERGIES

CAREFUL OBSERVATION

For years, individuals attuned to Earth energies, especially dowsers, have studied the energy patterns in crop formations. Since the advent of concerns about hoaxing, researchers have devised many ways to investigate if crop circles are man-made or genuine. However, the most basic common-sense technique that anyone can do is simple visual observation: getting down on one's hands and knees in various parts of the formation, carefully looking at many stalks and noticing how they appear as they come out of the ground and bend over. If the stalks are pressed flat along the ground, or have been crushed, or have scrape marks, or are broken as they bend, or have no swollen growth nodes—these are indications that the crop circle most likely was hoaxed with stomper boards or garden rollers. If the bent-over plants lie an inch or so above the ground, have no bruises or scrape marks and are bent but not broken where they come out of the ground, there is a likelihood that this crop circle was made by nonhuman agents. Ilyes has noted that the perimeter stalks at the edge of a laid and swirled area appear to be slightly swept up onto the surrounding wall of standing stalks and do not lie flat along the ground like the rest of the laid stalks (2000b). Additionally, a simple method to check the energies in a crop circle is to feel the air with your bare hands. Sensitive, intuitive people can detect subtle changes in the energy patterns within and around genuine crop circles. Some can feel differences throughout their bodies as they change locations.

JULY 1997, BARBARA LAMB OBSERVING A "MAGICAL BEND" STALK IN A CROP CIRCLE.

DOWSING

Dowsing with dowsing rods is an effective measurement tool for many people to detect energy changes at boundaries within and just outside the perimeters of genuine crop circles. The genuine crop circles generate strong dowsing responses, and almost all of the known man-made circles do not provoke any responses at all. Dowsing also is used to locate ley lines in relation to crop circles—under, around, leading to or away from the circle—and to detect the presence of underground water sources. Some people use dowsing rods to receive answers to such questions as how long it took to create a formation, how much energy or power was involved and the flow of male and female energies. Michael Newark dowses soil and seed samples and crop circle pictures and can give a description of the movement of energy involved in creating a formation and how these energies travel along the ley lines,

JULY 1998, KAREN CUSHING DOWSING FOR ENERGY CHANGES IN A CIRCLE AND RING NEAR TAWSMEAD COPSE, WILTSHIRE COUNTY.

July 17, 2000, Valja Roseman dowsing with a pendulum in North Avebury Down crop circle.

stress fault lines and underground water lines (Newark 1997, 19:24).

For many years, English agrarian and researcher Richard Andrews conducted dowsing research on the energies of and around crop circles. He contributed significantly to the understanding of crop circles being placed on energy lines and points, and often his work was corroborated by the work of dowser Mike Collier. Andrews' specialty was the detection of energy above the ground, and in his work with dowser David Tilt, they noticed that the energy above ground flowed in the opposite direction from the energy under the ground as dowsed by Tilt. Tilt commented that under-the-ground energy radiates out from the center of crop circles, but above-the-ground energy moves in a variety of patterns, ranging from spiraling toward the center to an assortment of geometric shapes, including star patterns. He also has noticed two layers of energy that flow differently above the ground, which would help describe why different dowsers find different patterns in the same location; they could be measuring differing layers above the ground. More fluctuations in energy flows occur above than under the ground as well. Andrews found that the energy level has increased markedly above ground over the past several years, while Tilt found no such pattern in dowsing energy below ground (Tilt 1991, 111-12).

David Tilt noticed high energy levels at locations where crop circles later appeared and low energy levels after the formation appeared. He conceptualized that an energy discharge procedure was involved in forming the crop circle. Richard Andrews said he could predict the location of a crop circle in advance because of the shapes and patterns of energy that were forming there. He also noticed patterns in some pictograms that were not manifested in the laid crop, but then some days later the pictogram developed new rings or other extensions that fit Andrews' dowsing findings. From his work, Andrews concluded that crop circles are formed in two steps: "First an intelligent force acts from above on earth energies and thus creates an invisible pattern which predetermines the direction in which each individual corn stem will fall. At a later time, a subterranean force starts the process which creates the visible form in the corn field" (Hesemann 1996, 93-94). Andrews deserves special recognition for his valuable work in dowsing, drawing diagrams of energy lines in crop formations and sharing his findings from 1985 until his death in the summer of 1999.

Hamish Miller, engineer and veteran dowser of ley lines and sacred sites, discovered that there "was no discernible deterioration in the strength and shape of the energy field after the crop had been cut, and little apparent difference some weeks later after ploughing. . . ." (Miller 1991, 19). Colin Andrews has noted that dowsing can detect a crop circle in a field "as much as a year after the crop has been harvested and all signs of the formation have visually disappeared" (Andrews 1994, 3:4). According to David Kingston, Jim Lyons has found that the energy of crop circles lasts more than five years, even through repeated harvestings, plowings and replantings (Kingston 1996). (Presumably, this was ascertained through dowsing.) Hamish Miller also has found that it is easily possible to pick up energy lines while in an aircraft at five hundred feet. Presaging the much later findings of some energetic responses in hoaxed crop formations, he found from dowsing a known man-made formation that "it was possible to wind up through a number of levels of dowsing to find a faint ghostly response to the 'intent' of the people who spent so much time making it." Also of interest was his finding that the energy configuration in the center of small circles in a particular formation actually resembled a "well squashed Teutonic cross" rather than the visible circular pattern (Miller 1991, 19). This brings up intriguing questions about the information contained in crop formations and how it is stored and conveyed energetically. Dowsing appears to be a fertile source of feedback about the qualities of multiple lines and types of energy flow in crop formations.

PENDULUMS

Pendulums also are used to detect complex patterns of energy. Like dowsing rods, they are light, portable and sensitive tools. Distinct energy changes are found in and around genuine crop circles, even from one part of the formation to another. The most dynamic movement of the pendulum often is found at the center of the swirl of the laid-down crop. The direction of the pendulum swing can indicate male versus female energies, or yin versus yang. Pendulum responses are not generally seen in or near man-made crop circles. Some pendulum users are inclined to use this tool for receiving answers to their questions about the crop circle phenomenon, its meaning and its creators. Lucy Pringle, who pendulums crop formations, told a story of investigating a pictogram in 1990. The energy was so powerful that the pendulum flew off, having snapped the chain. Thinking she probably had lost it in the standing wheat, she was surprised to find the pendulum only a few inches outside the perimeter of the formation, as if the strong energy of the circle had stopped abruptly just outside the edge (Pringle 1990, 1:4).

CHANNELING

Channeling paranormal sources is a technique used by numerous individuals, including Darryl Anka, Shawn Randall, Anna Hayes and Norma Milanovich, to understand more about the crop circle phenomenon. Isabelle Kingston's channeled source urges crop circle investigators to stay grounded and yet open their heart chakras and be receptive to new ideas and new inspirations that come through. It was cautioned that many people involved with crop circles seek monetary gain and power and withhold information. Kingston channeled that it is important to seek knowledge for the good of humankind and to stay open to new ideas and perceptions coming from the spiritual and interplanetary realms. According to Kingston's source, the crop circles are a blueprint of a new energy encoding coming to the Earth given by the Watchers, a collective intelligence that guides humans beings. "The formations are like molecular structures and blueprints—like the form of morse code—and someone will be used to unravel this information, and scientists will be able to use it and put it into practice. It will be possible to use this new form of energy within your lifetimes—in seventeen summers [from 1990]. The unraveling will start before then.

"This new source of energy is now being created, and certain beings are being prepared to understand the messages being projected at this time. . . . Man will be able to change the molecular structure of things, including himself. Within the energy-pattern of the circles we give you this information" (Kingston 1991, 149-150). Judy Moore and I believe that Judy is the someone—or one of the beings—who will unravel the codes of the crop circles through channeled information.

MODERN TECHNOLOGY

In contrast to the various traditional and, in some cases, ancient tools mentioned above, modern technical instruments are used by more scientifically inclined investigators, many of whom engage in detailed observations and meticulous record-keeping of their findings. Technological tools used range from the simple compass to infrared photography, gaussmeters and electromagnetometers (to check the magnetic patterns), Geiger counters (to test for radioactivity), static charge detectors, microwave detectors, ultrasound detectors, electrostatic voltmeters, very-low-frequency (VLF) radio receivers, orgone energy detectors (such as the Orgone Engineering Device [OED]) and cloudbusters (sophisticated computer-linked geomagnetic detectors). The physical reactions of people in crop formations have been assessed as well, with measurements of electrical skin resistance (ESR), brain waves through electroencephalograms (EEGs) and peripheral temperature devices.

Research has uncovered numerous findings. Starting in 1999, Ron Russell and Dr. Simeon Hein, using a hand-held electrostatic voltmeter (TREK 520 ES), found that crop circles considered genuine usually had a higher energy reading than known man-made crop circles, wind-damaged areas and a flattened area near a grain silo. Possibly the two formations that registered small effects actually were man-made, but the hoaxers had not been public about their creations. Four of the crop circles initially caused equipment failure and their charge when new was unmeasurable. These included the crop circles at Hackpen Hill [plate 26], Liddington Castle [figure 29] [plate 20], Devil's Den [figure 30] [plate 21] and the Roundway "Snowflake" [figure 31] [plate 25]. The Devil's Den formation was tested again the next day, and again the equipment failed to work. In two later readings, diminishing voltage was measured, and at the end of October no detectable energy was measured. There was a "membrane" of energy at the outer edges of some of the crop circles, in which the meter indicated a small reversal in voltage a few inches from the circle and a large increase once inside. One of the formations, "The Basket" [figure 32] [plate

July 2000, [from left] Christopher, a postal worker, Ron Russell, Judy Moore and Dr. Simeon Hein in "The Heart" crop circle, East Kennett, Wiltshire County.

31], which was cut down by the farmer a few hours after it was discovered, still registered energy readings of more than one hundred volts greater than the surrounding wheat field after the wheat was mowed. Two of the man-made crop circles registered differences in charge of twenty volts or less from the surrounding field, and it was speculated that finding any difference at all could be accounted for by a distance effect; the meter, always held at waist level, was further from plant material inside a flattened formation than in the surrounding standing wheat. One of the formations, a pentagram figure in Avebury, showed no detectable energy reading the day it was created. Only later was it discovered that this formation was man-made, which takes away a placebo or expectancy effect as an explanation for why no energy was detected (Hein 2000).

Fig. 29

During the summer of 2000, I investigated some crop circles with Dr. Hein. The readings varied from one crop circle to another and even from place to place within the same crop circle, with the higher numeric readings tending to register in the centers of the circles. His readings tended to match the responses I was getting with my dowsing rods in the same circles. These differences also matched the findings of pendulum users, including my companions Valja Roseman, Margaret Moore and Wendy Allen, and the patterns detected by Dr. Nan Lu. Further formal studies comparing various energy measurement devices used independently of each other (i.e., with no immediate sharing of results) would be useful to enhance the credibility of all of these instruments.

Fig. 30

Dr. Hein conjectured that the process of forming a genuine crop circle might involve a nonordinary electrical field that is not included within the scope of conventional physics. Perhaps crop circles involve scale-free energy distributions that follow fractal power laws rather than linear growth patterns. Perhaps these nonlinear energy fields interfere with electronic components designed for linear environments (Hein 2000). If this is the case, nonelectronic instrumentation such as dowsing rods and pendulums might be inherently more applicable to the measurement of the energy configurations in the crop circle environment.

Fig. 31

For a year or so it was assumed that genuine crop circles always registered higher numbers on the voltmeters than hoaxed crop circles did. Thus the voltmeter seemed to offer the definitive test for distinguishing between them. However, during 2000, Ron Russell, Dr. Hein and Linda Moulton Howe, along with Peter Sorensen, witnessed the daytime making of a commissioned crop circle by Matthew Williams, Paul Damon and Andy Fox, who pushed down the plants with stomping boards. To the researchers' surprise, they were impressed with the lay of the crop and there were moderate voltmeter readings in that man-made crop circle. This raised the question: Do recently pushed-over plants register voltmeter responses regardless of what or who pushed them over? It is significant to note that the BLT team already had noticed that plants that had been pushed over, apparently wind-damaged, showed some of the same changes that are found in plants from genuine crop circles. Therefore, these researchers were forced to agree that electrostatic voltmeter readings are

Fig. 32

not the definitive measure to determine the difference between genuine and hoaxed crop circles. Linda Moulton Howe informed me in July 2000 that the team acknowledges that further research is needed.

In response to magnetic anomalies occurring in the circles, such as the spinning of compass needles, failures of cameras and video recorders and interference with radio frequencies, Colin Andrews undertook a recent two-year study of crop circles. Funded by Lawrence Rockefeller, during 1999 and 2000 he and his staff executed a series of research projects on the energetic qualities of crop circles and ways to discern genuine from man-made crop formations. His investigations included magnetic profiling, plant analysis, looking for signs of human activity in some crop circles and hiring detectives to follow and film hoaxers at work in the fields. He concluded that there are major differences between hoaxed and genuine crop circles, which can be proved scientifically, but he had not presented the evidence to support his conclusions at the time this book was written (Andrews 2000; Thomas 2000b, 92:5-6).

Another way of assessing the energetic effects of crop formations has been through testing water. Water testing was begun in crop circles in 1995 by Lucy Pringle, Dr. Cyril Smith (an electromagnetic specialist), Dr. Jacques Benveniste (pioneer of the hypothesis of water retaining memory), Dr. Roger Talyor (a researcher in the field of vibrational medicine) and Joan Davis, who tested the water for bacteria. Water buried in bottles within a crop circle showed measurable differences from the same kind of water from the same source buried and retrieved outside the same crop circle at the same time, using a "radiesthesia technique" of Dr. Smith. She also commented that water tastes metallic and cloying in crop circles and nearby, and others have reported the same phenomenon (Pringle 1995, 14:14). Pringle recently informed me that this water research still is underway and that more comprehensive updated results will be made available after the 2001 crop circle season.

Another kind of water testing has been done by a team of blood analysts, Dr. David Schweitzer of Switzerland and Dr. Caron DeVita of British Columbia, Canada. They placed open bowls of water both inside and outside a few crop circles, left them there for varying lengths of time (from fifteen minutes to twenty-four hours) and then analyzed the samples in the laboratory. The results consistently showed that the molecules of the water inside the crop circles retained the memory of the crop circle pattern. That is, the general design of the crop circle appeared in the molecules of the water when seen under a microscope. The water placed just outside the crop circles was not affected in this way (DeVita and Schweitzer 1999).

BIOPHYSICAL TESTING OF CROP CIRCLE PLANTS AND SOIL

Crop circle plants and soil have been tested and analyzed by biophysical laboratories in England, Scotland, Holland and the United States since 1989. Samples of plants and soil from inside crop circles have been compared with control samples taken from outside those circles but in the same field to check for differences. Samples also have been compared to samples of plants from crop circles that were suspected to have been man-made.

This field of research was launched in 1989 by biophysicist William C. Levengood of Pinelandia Biophysical Laboratory in Grass Lake, Michigan. He who was asked to analyze plants from crop circles sent to him by researcher Pat Delgado to see if they had any distinguishing characteristics. Dr. Levengood has taught at the University of Michigan's Institute of Science and Technology, and his papers have been published in dozens of respected scientific journals. Eventually, his analysis of crop circle plants was published in 1994 and 1999 in the scientific journal *Physiologia Plantarum*.

In comparing samples of grain from within crop circles to control samples in the same field outside the crop circles, he noticed over time a substantial number of biophysical differences in the plants within the crop formations: (1) bent but not broken stalks near ground level, (2) charred epidermal tissue, (3) splits on the skin of the stems, (4) seed heads malformed and their growth stunted, (5) germination of the seeds not always successful, but when it was, the seeds germinated faster and the plants grew faster, (6) cell wall pits enlarged in the thin membrane surrounding the seed head, (7) nodes in the plant stems grossly elongated, (8) nodes in the stems bent, (9) holes blown in the nodes from the inside out, as if moisture in the plants had become hot enough to produce steam that blew these holes, (10) the mitochondria, or tiny organelles that regulate respiration of the plants, burning themselves up, (11) magnetic particles present, (12) carbon blackening present, (13) some radioactivity present in some plants, and (14) plants had different energy patterns as if affected by a very high level of energy, which lasts for at least six weeks (Howe 1993).

In 1992, Dr. Levengood formed the BLT Research Team with researcher Nancy Talbott and businessman John Burke. They have research assistants in the United States, Canada and Europe, and are now receiving funding from a well-known financier for the next round of testing. Dr. Levengood and his team have done extensive testing on thousands of samples of crop circle plants from eight countries including England, the United States, Canada, Israel, Holland and Australia.

Dr. Levengood has been able to duplicate the physiological changes in crop circle plants by using short exposures to commercial microwave energy on normal plants. With respect to where the microwave energy could be coming from to form the crop circles, Dr. Levengood's theory has been that the energy most likely is caused by ion plasma vortices, which are atmospheric phenomena. This sounds very similar to Dr. Meaden's theory of the late 1980s. Microwave radiation, thought to be associated with ionized plasmas, emits intense bursts of heat. Very short bursts of heat would account for the physical changes in the crop circle plants. The BLT team identified the bending and swelling of the growth nodes as the main determiner of anomalous versus human-made crop circles. In the genuine circles, the nodes sometimes double in size, whereas this does not happen in man-made circles.

The BLT team also found changes in the soil in genuine crop circles when comparing soil from within and outside the same crop circles. They found magnetic anomalies, very high concentrations of tiny spheres of iron magnetite, distributed by a centrifugal spinning force and concentrated in crop circle centers, and evidence of meteoric material.

Further research by Dr Levengood and BLT showed that crop circle plants have magnetic susceptibility. Some small rocks and wheat could be picked up by a magnet, and analysis by spectroscopes showed there was iron and oxygen in a glazelike coating on the plants. It was considered unusual that there were no other elements present. Investigators wondered if meteors could have been responsible for this coating, yet meteors have iron bound together with nickel and other elements, and this coating did not. In any event, some crop circles do show evidence of meteoric dust having been picked up, presumably by plasma vortices, and deposited on the plants, especially at the centers of swirls where there is the greatest magnetic strength.

[The following updated information comes from a series of e-mails written by Nancy Talbott (bltresearch@ mediaone.net) between April 16 and 20, 2001, in dialogue with various individuals seeking clarification of or challenging Dr. Levengood's conclusions (cropcircles-2001@yahoo-groups.com)]. Dr. Levengood currently hypothesizes that the atmospheric plasma vortex energy system consists of multiple energies that affect the plants differently. Although they work in conjunction with each other, these energy vortices interact chaotically. This means that various effects noted in the plants will not necessarily be the same from formation to formation, nor even within the same formation. He has come to believe that the crop-circle-making process is much more complex than anyone previously had theorized.

Differences in germination of seeds taken from sample plants inside crop circles and control plants outside crop circles were based on the maturity of the seeds studied. Young plants lost their ability to reproduce, whereas mature plants grew at up to five times the rate of control plants. In some cases, the seeds from the mature crop circle plants continued growing strongly for a while without light or water. Also, seeds of plants in the center of crop circles grew faster when planted than seeds from near the edge.

In attempting to discover the reason for the more rapid growth of mature crop circle seeds, Dr. Levengood and John Burke bombarded the seeds of normal (non-crop-circle) plants with precisely calibrated, high doses of electrons. This facilitated growth to the extent that they patented their equipment. Their findings could be a significant contribution to increasing the world's grain supplies. From this work they concluded that the electrical component of the crop-circle-making energy was responsible for the improved growth of crop circle seeds. Dr. Levengood's current opinion is that the harmful effect on plants is due to exposure to the microwave component of the energies, and the positive growth-enhancing effect is from plants being exposed to the electrical component.

In some circles, elongated stem nodes were found just outside the edges of the formation, but this effect became less frequent as the samples were taken further away from the edges. In some formations, the elongated nodes in laid-down plants were more concentrated at the centers of the designs. The BLT group concluded that human circlemakers could not possibly achieve these graduated results with boards and feet.

The crop left standing in a formation appears to be affected in many of the same ways as the laid-down crop, with changes in length of nodes, weight of seeds and changes in seed growth when germinated.

In testing wind-damaged areas of laid-down crop (crop which appears to be randomly downed), stalks have repeatedly shown the same kinds of changes, and the team has hypothesized that the same phenomena that create the crop circles are operating but without a design as the goal. Dr. Levengood guesses that local weather conditions might determine whether the forces create geometric patterns or nongeometric crop destruction.

The team now thinks that the high concentrations of tiny glossy spheres of iron magnetite in the soil are semimolten meteoric iron, ten to fifty microns in diameter. Although concentrated near centers of crop circles, they sometimes cluster near the outer edges or even just outside the circles, another subtle effect impossible to create by humans with stomping boards.

Dr. Levengood calculated the amount of energy he thought would be necessary to produce the changes in plants and soil he has documented. He thinks it would take at least forty times the amount of energy the Sun releases and that this release would have to be extremely rapid in order to heat only the internal moisture without cooking or burning the stems. This exposure could last only a nanosecond. It is no wonder a few birds and a couple of porcupines have been found destroyed in crop formations.

Dr. Levengood's and BLT's research has been tested by independent groups. Nick Nicholson, in an e-mail on April 20, 2001, reported to the Internet group with which Nancy Talbott was communicating that a group of crop circle researchers, in a project called Maxim, hoaxed a crop circle in 1996 that they knew would be found. As they had intended, other researchers sent plant and soil samples to be tested by BLT and also by a British soil and plant research group. The testing by both groups indicated the samples were from a man-made formation. This mollified some skeptics about the validity of Dr. Levengood's testing.

Over the years, objections have been raised that Dr. Levengood's personal biases and expectations have influenced his research results. However, others have replicated various findings of his laboratory. Testing of seed growth has been done by Chad and Gwenn Deetken of Vancouver, British Columbia, who planted seeds from a genuine crop circle next to seeds taken from plants outside the crop circle. They found that plants from the genuine crop circle seeds grew forty percent taller than control plants, with both in low-light conditions. They continued propagating new plants from the genuine and control seeds for several generations and found that the effects of enrichment continued, although to a lesser extent with each subsequent generation (Howe 1993, 71-72). Jim Lyons also found that seeds from crop circle plants grow with very little light and water. After six generations of plants whose seeds were originally altered by crop circle energy, the plants were growing at a slower pace but were still sturdy and healthy (Kingston 1996).

On June 27, 2001, Nancy Talbott disseminated an e-mail report of findings from a new soil study. Dr. Levengood was not directly involved, and three of the independent scientists knew nothing about crop circles and the fourth only had talked to Dr. Levengood years ago. The scientists found that certain clay minerals (lilite/smectites) showed significantly increased crystallization inside the circles as compared to outside the circles. Only intense heat and geologic pressure can cause this crystallization. In plants sampled at the same locations as the soil samples there was a very high and statistically significant correlation between node-length increases and increased soil crystallization. Samples from the smaller circles showed greater soil crystallization (a pattern previously found in plant node lengthening). Finally, "there is some sort of wave pattern in the distribution of the crystallinity increases, at least in one circle . . ." (Talbot 2001b).

The approaches used to study crop formations are improving but are not foolproof in determining genuine from man-made. Although our tests and our experiences in many crop circles have revealed noticeable effects on plants, soil, people, animals and birds, water, batteries and various kinds of equipment, the findings have not been as cut and dried as one would need to be able to declare some skillfully hoaxed circles to be hoaxed. The problem with the invaluable but highly technical Levengood research is that it is expensive and time-consuming, and the conclusions are long in arriving. If some of his technology were made portable so it could be carried into crop circle territory, we could have rapid feedback on various anomalous factors in the crop and soil and respond to interesting results with further investigation on the spot. For instance, studying the wave pattern that Nancy Talbott just announced is going to require a multitude of plant and soil samples to track down the invisible pattern.

Additionally, it is possible that we have not devised the kinds of instrumentation that most appropriately and accurately detect the effects of the crop circle-making energies on the plants and soil—much less to detect the agents or energies creating these effects. This deficit is similar to the problem seen with the SETI (Search for Extraterrestrial Intelligence) instrumentation—it might not be the right kind of equipment to detect potentially very different kinds of technology and communication from intelligent beings in space.

Although scientists have deduced physical explanations for the special effects seen in crop circles, there is no confirmation of their validity, and as always we are still left with the great mystery of who or what orchestrates these forces to execute such exquisite, intelligently planned, meaningful designs.

INVESTIGATING THE CONNECTIONS BETWEEN CROP CIRCLES, ANIMAL MUTILATIONS AND UFOS

In mid-1999, Dr. Levengood reported that some of the damage to crop circle plants is also found in the plants around mysterious animal mutilation sites and UFO landing traces. These three topics—crop circles, animal mutilations and UFO sightings—are three of the most provocative mysteries of contemporary times. The common characteristic, which has been studied by Dr. Levengood, is that rapid high heat appears to have been applied to affected plants and animals. As discussed earlier, he believes the heat to have been created by microwave energy.

Dr Levengood has researched more than two hundred crop circle formations, twelve animal mutilation cases and numerous locales which were reported to be UFO landing sites, including four landing traces in Israel and several more in the United States. Almost ninety percent of the plant samples tested from each of these situations showed significant physiological changes at the cellular level when compared to control samples obtained in the same vicinities. The most common changes included altered embryo development in seeds, enlargement of plant stem nodes and marked bending of the stem nodes from cavities blown in the nodes from the inside out (Perkins 1999, 25:3).

UFOs seen near Bowden, Alberta, Canada, in 1967, were seen concurrently with the making of crop circles nearby. In the same year, animal mutilations and concurrent UFO sightings were reported widely in the San Luis Valley of Colorado. After studying the plants around cattle mutilation sites in Colorado, Saskatchewan and California in 1994 and 1995, Dr. Levengood reported, "These studies clearly suggest that microwave energy is a major component of the energetics involved in the plant alterations at bovine excision sites. . . . These findings are in agreement with crop formation results, which also point to a microwave energy component." Additionally, Linda Moulton Howe has reported a dozen cases in which animals were seen being raised or lowered from a UFO by a beam of light (Perkins 1999, 25:4-5).

Magnetic particles (tiny magnetic beads) often have been found in crop circles, at UFO landing traces and on plant growth and soil around animal mutilations, especially in high concentrations around the excision points in mutilated animals. High heat is another common characteristic in these phenomena, as validated by Dr. John Altshuler, a doctor of pathology and hematology in Denver, Colorado. In more than forty mutilated animals, he found "cooked haemoglobin" at the edges of cut tissue, indicating the presence of heat over three hundred degrees, as seen in laser surgery. Other scientists besides Dr. Levengood have verified that high heat is used in the making of crop circles and in the plants near UFO landing sites (Perkins 1999, 25:5).

There is a great deal of circumstantial evidence to link UFOs with crop circles. Numerous examples of purported UFO sightings linked by some connection in location or time to crop formations have been given earlier in the book. More sightings of UFOs that seemed to relate to the appearance of crop circles occurred during 2000. In February, a huge UFO was seen over Silbury Hill, and in late May a hole 130 feet deep suddenly appeared in the center of the top of this hill, mystifying many people. Peter Sorensen reported having videotaped a white orb flying over a formation near Beckhampton in June. In mid-July, Steven Greer, M.D., and his CSETI group did a night meditation/skywatch from the field next to the Old Sarum ancient hillfort/castle north of Salisbury. Greer told me that they saw a bluish-white spaceship followed by three other smaller flying objects. Very soon thereafter, a new crop circle appeared at nearby Amesbury [plate 51]. On July 31, a researcher saw from the top of Roundway Hill in Devizes, Wiltshire, a translucent white bowl-shaped object in the air that contained pulsating orange balls of light. A new crop circle appeared at nearby Allington Down on August 1, the next day [plate 53].

Even with these characteristics in common, we should not assume these three activities are perpetrated by the same source or with the same intent. They all, however, indicate the use of a very rapid heating process which leaves lasting effects on physical matter, they each seem to be very deliberately and purposefully planned by an intelligence that does not appear to be human, and they are all mysteries that stretch our notions of reality and challenge the assumption that humanity is alone in the universe. It is interesting, also, that each of these mysterious activities began being reported during the last few decades of the twentieth century.

MYSTERIOUS CIRCLES AND RINGS IN OTHER SUBSTANCES

Anomalous circles and shapes akin to crop formations have appeared suddenly and mysteriously in other natural substances such as ice, snow, sand, tops of trees, floors of forests, areas of dense bushes, bare earth and large rock areas. Over the years I have collected numerous stories of circles being created in various substances besides cereal crops. In this section, I reference what information I can, but am unable to acknowledge all the sources of these stories. There has been amazingly little speculation about the meaning of these phenomena, although presumably there is an energetic purpose to their creation and location, just as there is to the creation of crop circles.

Swirled circles have appeared in plants besides crops. In Georgia, Russia, a group of bushes was flattened and swirled into a circle thirty-six feet in diameter. The discovery of these bush circles was preceded by sightings of luminous objects, and thus the circles were considered to be UFO landing nests. The bushes were covered with white powder, which was analyzed and found to contain minerals including magnesium. Individuals who visited the bushes developed headaches, circulatory problems and other illnesses, hypothesized to be due to the high levels of radioactivity (Hesemann 1996, 59).

In Saskatchewan, Canada, in 1990 or 1991, the tops of conifer trees were reported to have been bent over and swirled in a circle overnight. In Hampshire, England, around the same time, whole tree trunks were bent over and swirled in a circle, according to Richard Andrews.

Mysterious circles and rings also have been found in sand and dirt. They have appeared in sand on the northern beach coast of Australia, in Oregon and near Albuquerque, New Mexico, at the time of the fall equinox in 1994. In 1992, near the Red Sea in Egypt, a pattern appeared in desert sand. It was a circle with a long F-shaped shaft. The shaft was crossed by a circle. In Egyptian hieroglyphics, the symbol F means the "Watchers," the gods of the Nile (Hesemann 1996, 62). Perhaps these are the Watchers channeled by Isabelle Kingston.

In August 1990, a pilot from the Idaho National Guard spotted a beautiful, complex pattern carved precisely and evenly into the hard-packed desert floor of southeastern Oregon. This design unmistakably depicted a Hindu meditation symbol called the Sri Yantra, a fertility mantra that suggests the continuing of generations. The soil from the trenches was piled up evenly and equally on both sides of the intricately carved lines that were ten inches wide and three inches deep. The entire area of the design was a quarter of a mile square, and the lengths of all the lines added up to 13.3 miles long. Investigators found no tracks or trails into the area, even though they and their vehicles left noticeable tracks on the desert floor (ilyes 2000a, 9).

In a different but equally hard medium, strange keyhole shapes were carved into gravel riverbanks in the Ticino River Valley Park in northern Italy around 1995. This is an area where there have been many sightings of luminous objects, which are being monitored by unmarked government helicopters. It also was an important ceremonial center for ancient Earth Mother religions for at least three thousand years (Tomkins 2000, 49:10).

A series of large rings suddenly appeared overnight, carved into a broad rock area near Ajuntas in Puerto Rico in August 1991, once again in an area renowned for sightings of UFO crafts, strange lights, "chupacabra" animals and strange alien-looking beings. Some of the rings were as large as seventy-two feet in diameter. Around 1990, in eastern Russia, a cluster of cylindrical holes was discovered, having appeared overnight. Each hole was ten to twelve feet deep and was perfectly honed as if by large-scale drilling equipment, yet no such equipment existed in that area. Circular holes of this type have appeared in Switzerland as well, according to Peter Sorensen.

Circles, rings and discs in snow and ice have been seen in rivers, streams and lakes in many of the northern countries. At a time when this phenomenon was becoming noticed, Bob Rickard reviewed the history of known ice discs and the theories advanced to explain them. Ice discs are circular plates of ice, sometimes covered with snow, with diameters measuring up to two hundred feet, circumscribed by a narrow ring of water in which the disc slowly revolves (in contrast to circles that are not free-standing and able to revolve). These ice discs are perfectly round and are appealing to look at. Scientific-sounding explanations of these circles being made by whirlpools and eddies and underwater springs of warmer water have been offered, as well as speculations about their being made by humans or extraterrestrials. Both human involvement and intent to hoax are unlikely, as these discs usually are found in remote locations where people would not be likely to see them and there is an absence of snow-prints of people or equipment going to or from them. A flaw in the theory of a physical phenomenon causing the circles is that one would expect the same circular patterns to appear year after year if a stable physical phenomenon like an underwater spring or particular curve in a riverbank were the source of the disc (Rickard 1994).

In one of the earliest accounts, a witness who happened to be the head of the UFO-Sweden organization visited a disc in the making three times in a three-week period. Initially he saw chunks of ice surrounding a large central chunk of ice, all revolving at a rate of two cycles per minute. A week later all the ice chunks were frozen together. By the third visit a revolution of the mass took about ten minutes. Since then this witness has seen three more ice discs, all frozen in position (Rickard 1994).

In contrast to this relatively naturalistic event, an eyewitness to the forming of an ice disc in the Ukraine in 1990 said he saw a huge object in the shape of a child's spinning toy top resting on the ice and hovering just above it for ten minutes. Then he saw the luminous disc speed away, leaving the large ice disc to sink into the water and rise up again. This seventy-five meter circle was surrounded by a one-meter-wide ring that had several concentric ridges, which looked as if they had been cut by a huge milling machine. When first seen, the ice was too thin to hold the weight of a person (Rickard 1994).

In January 1991, a set of clearly defined concentric rings was seen in the ice on the Charles River in Waltham, Massachusetts. The outer ring was approximately twenty feet in diameter. The ice was too thin to support a person's weight and there were no footprints on it. In 1993, dozens of rings and connecting pathways were seen on a one- or two-inch-thick covering of snow on a thin layer of ice on the Charles River between Boston and Cambridge, Massachusetts. Again, the ice was too thin to hold the weight of a person, and there were no foot tracks leading onto the ice (Rickard 1994). Michael Hesemann reported that in 1990, Afghanistan hosted thirty circles in deep snow in the highlands, and these circles had the same precision as crop circles. In 1975, in Turkey, seven extremely whirled snow circles appeared one next to the other at the foot of a mountain slope (Hesemann 1996, 62).

Although numerous other very similar descriptions have been collected about ice rings, possibly their geographical isolation and the rigors of cold climates have prevented them from being visited and photographed as much as crop circles, and no one has advanced any metaphysical speculations about why they exist or has apparently studied their energies through dowsing or pendulums.

EVOLVING MESSAGES OF THE CROP CIRCLES

It is widely assumed that if crop circles are produced by some high form of intelligence, they must hold some kind of messages for humanity. Many crop circles seem to be deliberate, well-chosen and meaningful on a number of levels. They inspire us to meditate on them and ponder over them as we might when looking at sacred art. Many crop circle designs draw our attention to the skies, to the larger expanse of the galaxies and to the universe. They draw our awareness to spiritual meanings and cosmic questions.

The themes and symbols of the crop formations in southern England seem to fall into certain categories. Over and over they evoke mythological, religious, astronomical, mathematical and geometric themes. Granted, most individuals in the crop circle community are probably predisposed to have a high sensitivity to abstraction. They seem to recognize many culturally agreed upon spiritual symbols and to be open to the idea that these formations have some meanings of a higher order—that they are not merely pretty and clever designs.

Within this section, I will review some of the most beautiful, most complex, most symbolically evocative of the crop formations created over the past decade in southern England. Some of them so clearly represent a certain image—such as DNA or the Flower of Life or a well-known fractal pattern or our solar system—that it is difficult to deny that the design was deliberately planned by someone or something as a symbolic message to humanity. Then the question is, what is the message carried by the symbol? Other formations are less representational and more ambiguous, yet often a consensus about the feeling or the theme of the formation develops over time with input by many crop circle visitors from varying backgrounds and myriad philosophical and spiritual belief systems. There are no right or wrong interpretations, and the views expressed here are but a sampling of the reactions of the many who have pondered on these ambiguous symbols. Also, remember that the meanings are individual and personal, and pondering them provides an opportunity for self-development.

Some crop circles evoke names and are known by those names. Others are known only by the location and date of their creation. Some of the examples discussed are called by names that might or might not be the consensus name, purely for convenience of referencing them and describing them concisely. There is no central decision-making body for naming and cataloging crop formations in this field.

This discussion of the symbolism of the crop formations is launched with an interpretation of the simple single circles of earlier centuries and the late 1970s and 1980s. Circles represent the wholeness, oneness and completion of everything that exists, and often are viewed as unifying shapes. Every year, even with the complex crop patterns that keep us dazzled and amazed, the occasional simple single crop circle still appears, perhaps as a continuing reminder of the wholeness and unity of all of reality,

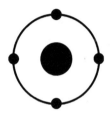

Fig. 33

Fig. 34

Fig. 35

Fig. 36

Fig. 37

or perhaps as an encouragement to humans to unite with one another and all beings in the cosmos. Most of the complex formations take shape from a central circle.

Crop circles in the late 1980s and early 1990s often had designs of Celtic crosses [figure 33] [plate 45] and long-shaft crosses [figure 34], both of which are spiritual symbols. These Celtic crosses seem to have evolved from earlier Celtic symbols. An interesting speculation is that perhaps the Celtic people received their symbols from extraterrestrials and now these same symbols are being brought back to our attention. Three long-shaft crosses appeared as crop circles in June 1989. As researcher George Wingfield said about the crosses, "Spirituality may well be the essence of the message. The Celtic cross and the long-shaft cross are both mystical symbols found also in religions other than Christianity. They do not indicate any particular religion, but more the essence of what religion is about" (Wingfield 1990b, 34). To Michael Green, the wheel symbol with four satellites represents the principle of "rotative activity about the hub of cosmic consciousness, a process in which all life forms are impelled to circulate through all states of consciousness so that they may be imbued by their energies" (Green 1991, 148).

A spectacular crop circle appeared near Winterbourne Stoke in Wiltshire County on August 9, 1989 [figure 35]. The way the crop was laid in four clearly defined directions, distinct from the laid-down rings in the center, suggested a particular mandala found in ancient Hindu and Buddhist art representing the universe and the totality of existence. This mandala also looked like the ancient symbol of good luck. Called the swastika, it was revered as a positive unifying symbol. Only centuries later was this symbol misused and turned around by the German Nazis, who wanted to harness its great symbolic power (Wingfield 1990b, 34).

1990

In 1990, several spiritual symbols from the ancient wisdom of northwestern Europe drew attention to the preciousness of our Earth. "Gaia" or "Earth Goddess" formations [figure 36] represent Mother Earth as a living, conscious entity who provides our home and our sustenance. The rectangular boxes represent the outstretched/folded arms of this Earth goddess, suggesting that she nourishes all life forms on Earth. Others believed these formations were giving us messages that the Earth is in trouble and we need to set things straight. Similar yet more complex patterns suggested the symbol of the "Sacred Marriage" [figure 37], showing the joining of matter and spirit as well as the female principle of form combining with the male fertilizing or activating principle. A variation of this crop circle symbol is seen in figure 38 (Green 1991, 161).

In June 1990, a symbol appeared at Longwood Estate in Hampshire, called the "Cosmic Egg" [figure 39], representing the fertilization of the Cosmic Egg, or the disintegration of the primal center to form the elements of the manifested cosmos. This symbol is seen on petroglyphs from Irish megalithic monuments (Green 1991, 147).

Symbols of the Logos principles from ancient traditions also have appeared in numerous crop circles. The striking "Solar Logos" formation of June 1990, located at Telegraph Hill in Chilcomb, Winchester, had a halo of three half rings, possibly representing the primal trinity [figure 40]. This halo, or half-circle pattern, was one of the earliest symbols to appear in Europe. Michael Green explained that the Solar Logos is the controlling entity of this solar system, whose centers comprise certain planetary beings. The Solar Logos in turn forms part of a greater cosmic entity, and "indeed it is on this principle of morphic resonance, as Rupert Sheldrake terms it, that the cosmos is constructed. . . . 'As above, so below that the one thing may be achieved.'" Green commented that the Solar Logos, like all beings throughout the cosmos, is on a path of spiritual development and is thus, in this sense, an "Imperfect God." His primary characteristic is that of unconditional love (Green 1991, 149, 152).

Another June 1990 crop circle near Chilcomb, Winchester, depicted the Earth Logos symbol [figure 36], which relates to the Great Mother, who is the physical form of the Earth Logos (Green 1991, 161). During that same month, a symbol of the divine hermaphrodite appeared [figure 41], expressing the cosmic principle of the blending of masculine and feminine aspects, or the bisexual nature of the Great Mother, Gaia. This design combines the male phallus and the female breast. Dowsers have confirmed the bisexual nature of this formation. The lower circle dowsed as male, the ringed circle dowsed as female and the boxes of the "necklace" dowsed as male on the left side and as female on the right (Green 1991, 165).

Several astonishing designs appeared during 1990 that have been interpreted as the Cosmic Dragon symbol, composed of a pair of linked circles that have smaller circles extending out in a line from them, plus asymmetrical clawlike projections. Incorporated in one of these formations are representations of the planets Neptune, Uranus, Vulcan and Pluto [figure 42]. Michael Green's interpretation is as follows: "The significance of these four planetary principles in the order shown at Alton Barnes is that they symbolise great initiatory stages in the progress of humanity and indeed the life of the individual person." He goes on to explain the function each planet serves in the transformational process, and then concludes: "The overall form of the figure is that of a dragon or serpent with clawed limbs, an eye to one side of Neptune and a tail of three diminishing circles beyond Pluto" (Green 1991, 166).

The August 4, 1990, formation at Cheesefoot Head near Winchester, called "Gallops" [figure 43], was a beautiful long double pictogram. When the Aztec elder Tlakaelel saw a picture of this formation, he was profoundly moved. He told Colin Andrews that in ancient Aztec rock paintings this design means Mother Earth is crying, or Mother Earth is out of balance (Snow 1992). Perhaps the circlemakers were trying to warn us about the widespread damage humanity is inflicting on our Earth.

Also in 1990, a crop circle design with a central circle surrounded by seven satellite circles appeared in Bickington, near Newton Abbott in

Fig. 38

Fig. 39

Fig. 40

Fig. 41

Fig. 42

July 1999, Kallista and Chet Snow with Crystal Skull, "Gaia Luz."

Devon [figure 44]. According to Green, this circle represents the seven rays, the seven principles of manifested deity, the seven planets, the seven "rishis" of the Great Bear, the body of the Logos, the seven kumaras of the East and the seven angelic beings of the West. At the planetary level, they constitute the living principles that infuse matter and form—principles that are also found in the ancient Indian Vedic system. At Newgrange, Ireland, this mandala symbol is carved into the rock. Symbols of seven plus one appear in ancient Indo-Aryan cultures (Green 1991, 148-49).

1991

Fig. 43

Some of the 1991 designs showed representations of living creatures and often were called insectogram, as seen at Chilcomb Down [figure 45] and near Popham, Hampshire [figure 46]. Some people wondered if these designs were showing us the form of the creators of the crop circles, especially as people had been reporting contact experiences with insectoid extraterrestrial beings. In a flash of intuition, John Haddington concluded they must represent snails and marshaled several arguments to support his idea. To the ancient people of Wessex, the snail was "a manifestation of the Earth Goddess, connected to the moon, and associated with the element water. The shell of the snail has a spiral form from which the creature emerges exemplifying the emergence of consciousness from the Cosmic Spiral." Additionally, the snail (Latin word *helix*) crop circles occurred in pairs, bringing forth the equation: "Two snails = Double Helix = construct of DNA, the connecting chemical of all lifeforms . . ." Haddington realized that "on a deeper level the Double Helix is also the construct of the Caduceus of Mercury, the God of Nature who brought order to the Universe out of Chaos at the beginning of Time. Mercury is also said to be a hermaphrodite like the snail . . . ; the hermaphrodite God of Nature, holding in his hands the symbol of the secret of Nature" (Haddington 1992, 6:12).

Fig. 44

Fig. 45

Other 1991 formations included a simple but lovely long pictogram at Alton Barnes referred to as "Nepture's Spear" and also as the ancient symbol of "Spirit Piercing Matter" [figure 47]. Several patterns appeared that reminded people of dolphins or whales [figure 48]. These wonderful high-consciousness beings are said to communicate telepathically with the extraterrestrial beings from whom they evolved. Other people think these designs might symbolize spaceships that visit the Earth or the union of the divine with the material, or the Sun and the Earth. Simple dumbbell-shaped designs [figure 49] appeared in 1990 and 1991, and are thought to signify the differentiation into male and female and the balance between the two. They take the form of two circles, usually of unequal size, joined by a straight line.

Fig. 46

The 1991 crop formation called the "Brain" or "Squiggle" pattern was entirely different from any previous crop circle design [figure 50]. As a model of the brain with its meandering creases, it elicited concern because of the breaks in the pattern. Do the breaks mean we are harming our brains with our chemicals and pollutants? Or could they be thought of as symbolizing either the evolution or the breakdown of our human DNA? This final formation of 1991, appearing on August 18, at Froxfield, Berkshire County, stimulated scientists to point out that it resembles a DNA chromosome bombarded by ultraviolet light, as seen under an electron microscope (Hesemann 1996, color section). As an example of the range of interpretations possible with these ambiguous figures, Paul Vigay told me that to him this pattern resembles the Pleiades rising in the east.

Fig. 47

The July 17, 1991, "Barbury Castle" formation near Chiseldon caused a sensation among crop circle enthusiasts and caught the notice of many people worldwide [figure 51] [plate 6]. This formation consists of a double-ringed circle surrounded by a triangle with circular figures at each apex. One of the figures was a helical spiral like a snail shell. In its beauty and geometric complexity, the "Barbury Castle" convinced many that the crop circle phenomenon must indeed be genuine, and it stimulated a number of interpretations according to the field of study of the interpreter. One interpretation was that it has affinities with ancient alchemical symbols, such as the Solomonic pentacle, which were used to establish connections with supernatural forces. Another interpretation was that it symbolizes the divine order that exists at the interface between one level of matter and another. Some thought it shows the journey of the soul from the ethers into physical life and back to the ethers again. As John Michell stated, "One's rational mind shrinks away from the implication that this diagram constitutes a divine revelation. Yet in the traditional histories revelation is said to have been the source of all cultures and to have inspired successive renewals of the human spirit. It occurs, presumably, at times when it is most needed, and its content is always the same, being that cosmic Law, Canon or compilation of numerical, musical and geometric harmonies which provided the ruling standard of every ancient civilization" (Michell 1991, 4:24). A more modern, technological theory is that it is a gyroscope to give vessels lift or to use as a source of free energy. Possibly the Earth with its continual rotation is a giant gyroscope that could provide all the free energy that humans need. This elegant "Barbury Castle" design stimulates associations about various aspects of reality: alchemical, ancient spiritual, shamanistic, numerological, geometric and technological. On the night it was formed, local residents saw mysterious lights in the sky over that area.

Fig. 48

Fig. 49

Photographer: © Barbara Lamb.

JULY 1998, JOHN MICHELL.

The August 12, 1991, "Mandelbrot Set" crop formation near Cambridge University [figure 52] also caused a tremendous reaction of awe and drew the attention of serious scientists and mathematicians who otherwise would have dismissed the crop circle phenomenon. The Mandelbrot set is a fractal formula containing real and imaginary numbers, representing the duality of nature: the balance between order and chaos. The visual representation of this formula, which can be computer-generated, is unmistakable, fixed by the formula. This was the first crop formation to undeniably

Fig. 50

Fig. 51

Fig. 52

Fig. 53

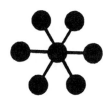

Fig. 54

portray a design that was recognizable, with no room for argument or personal interpretation. Fractals are an important part of the language of chaos theory, and since ancient times the process of creation has been considered to involve the transformation of chaos into order (Haddington 1992, 6:12). From ancient alchemy to modern chaos theory, crop circles seem to be representing the laws and forces of creation. The night the formation was created, a silver-blue UFO came within ten yards of a car driving through the area (Hesemann 1996, 39).

1992

Looking at 1992 crop circles, the "Charm Bracelet" formation near Silbury Hill evoked considerable respect from people with esoteric understanding [figure 53]. It symbolizes the ancient Irish Celtic tradition of the Beltane, or the Great Turning, and shows how the soul journeys from the spiritual realm into physical incarnation and back into spirit again, back to the divine Source (Haddington 1993, 4:20). In the East, in the Indo-Aryan traditions, this design is called the "Dharma Wheel" and is a statement of the path to consciousness, to the ultimate reality. Each symbol on the ring represents a particular energy (vibration) or spiritual state, which leads to the manifested state of God in the center. Michael Green's interpretation of this formation as representing the Buddhist eightfold path dovetailed to an uncanny extent with John Haddington's Celtic eight paths (Hesemann 1996, 133). This crop circle contained a strong energy that caused camera and light-meter failures and feelings of disorientation.

1993

The year 1993 was relatively unproductive for crop circles. In late July 1993, the lovely "Starburst" or "Snowflake" pattern appeared on Etchilhampton Hill near Devizes [figure 54]. The mandala-like pattern, 175 feet in diameter, impressed observers with its beautiful symmetry and execution. Peter Sorensen referred to it as the "Quartz Crystal" because it showed the molecular structure of quartz, with six aspects relating to the core in the center (Chapman 1993, 10:12).

The outstanding crop circle pattern of 1993 was the final one, the beautiful "Bythorn Mandala" near the town of Bythorn [figure 55]. It contained several spiritual elements: the circle for wholeness and connectedness, a pentagon and a five-pointed star (showing fivefold sacred geometry) and lotus petals, suggesting new life arising from the primordial ooze. People have found this pattern rewarding to have on their wall and to meditate on. The pentagon shape in the inner part of the design matched the pentagon shape of the field in which it was placed. The pentagon shape has been considered for many centuries to signify the Godhead or the moonflower. This mandala is similar to a symbol of Lemuria, speculated to be twenty-seven thousand years old.

In 1994, crop circles surged ahead in numbers, new designs and complexity. The main emphasis seemed to be on planetary happenings. In May, early in the crop-growing season, a giant formation appeared near Silbury Hill called the "Scorpion" [figure 56]. It had a Celtic cross in the center, a crescent at the head and a long series of circles of decreasing size forming a tail. People interpreted this figure in various ways: (1) as a foretelling of the Shoemaker-Levy 9 comet that was scheduled to collide with Jupiter two months later, (2) as a warning that a big body was coming into our solar system (perhaps the Hale-Bopp comet or perhaps planet Nibiru as foretold by Zecharia Sitchin) and (3) according to Aztec elder Tlakaelel, as an ancient counting system telling us when and where a comet will reach Earth. This formation started the season with impact and left researchers perplexed.

Fig. 55

Over a period of weeks, several variations on this theme appeared. The first was a large, dramatic pictogram, the "Flying Scorpion," which gave the impression of soaring across a hillside at great speed [figure 57]. This crop formation appeared just before the first piece of the Shoemaker-Levy 9 comet actually collided with Jupiter in July. It had twenty-one circles of decreasing size in its tail, which reflected the number of pieces of the comet that would be hitting Jupiter. This figure was followed by several variations of this same theme [figures 58 and 59], with each one having fewer pieces left in its tail. This corresponded with the number of comet pieces that actually collided with Jupiter.

Fig. 56

There even was a crop circle that matched the design of the real impact site on Jupiter: a beautiful circle with radiating rings (or crescents) at Oliver's Castle [figure 60]. It astonished observers to realize that what was happening out in space was being shown in crop circles on Earth. "As above, so below. . . ." This series of comet formations concluded in August 1994, with the appearance of the "Thirteen Moons" crop circle at Avebury Trusloe [figure 61] [plate 4]. In this design, the circles of decreasing size were curled in a circle, ending in a crescent moon, as if the dramatic comet activity was completed and at rest. Another association evoked by this pattern regarded the feminine infusion coming to us through the phases of the Moon and its cycles of renewal (Warren 1994, 11).

Fig. 57

Other amazing patterns of 1994 were believed to be related to the cosmos and astronomical features. A lovely little ring appeared, enclosing seven standing circles and rings that seemed to represent the "Seven Sisters," or the "Pleiades" [figure 62]. This was the first formation known to leave in the standing crop the design element being emphasized. These standing features made an effective contrast to the laid-down crop that was curved cleverly to frame the standing shapes. All the previous crop circles through the years had been executed in the opposite manner, with the emphasized design laid down and forming a contrast with the surrounding standing crop. This new method was highly effective and has been utilized each year since that time. Some people wondered if this symbol was letting us know that the Pleiadians (extraterrestrials reported to be advanced

Fig. 58

Fig. 59

Fig. 60

Fig. 61

Fig. 62

Fig. 63

AUGUST 1994, BARBARA LAMB IN THE "GALAXY" CROP CIRCLE, WEST STOWELL, WILTSHIRE COUNTY.

humanlike benevolent beings) were the true makers of the crop circles, or at least one of the sources.

The "Seven Sisters" design was followed by two designs that looked like spinning galaxies [figure 63]. Each had two long crescent-shaped tails, giving the appearance of spinning motion. Presumably, the standing shapes within the circles represented the Moon, stars and planets. The day after the first formation, called the "Galaxy Symbol," appeared along the Avenue at Avebury, the farmer was reportedly urged by "government" men to cut down the standing pattern within the circle, and was paid "handsomely" to do so. The farmer complied and cut down the standing shapes and left the rest of the design intact. "The circle was said to 'hold significant information' in it's [sic] makeup. . . ." (Ward 1994). Some people believed the data destroyed in this crop circle might have reflected Hale-Bopp on a collision course toward the Earth. At the time, this comet actually was moving in a logarithmic orbit, as is shown in this crop formation. Symbolically, the Hale-Bopp comet was considered a "harbinger of world change."

Fortunately, a few nights later a similar spinning galaxy design appeared in another farmer's field, this time at Alton Priors, with somewhat different standing features but the same outer design. This entire design remained standing until it was harvested. Some people thought this design was a star map of the constellation Sagittarius, from which the Hale-Bopp comet came. Andy Thomas spoke of it as representing the constellation Cetus. He also commented that both of the spinning galaxy designs, according to astronomer Jack Sullivan, showed the planetary lineup of our solar system as it was to be on April 6, 2000 (Thomas 2000c). Peter Sorensen, Shawn Randall and I were enjoying an early evening visit to that crop circle as a large harvesting machine was harvesting the field. As it came closer to the crop circle and actually charged through it, cutting the standing stalks down to one inch above the ground, we felt enormously sad that such a beautiful design and such exquisite lay of the crop and the lovely energies were being desecrated. Suddenly, Shawn had the inspiration that these energies were being freed and scattered for all to enjoy and benefit from, and we felt more accepting about the cutting. We appreciated more than ever the precious gift of lovely crop circles, which, like beautiful bouquets of flowers, are all the more special because they do not last.

In a neighboring field at Alton Priors, another striking pattern appeared in 1994, looking like a dramatic design of an eye. Perhaps this was a simulated television station logo, or the "Eye of God," or perhaps a message that the creators of the crop circles are watching us as we explore their artistry in our fields. A new motif in 1994 crop circles was of a "Spider" or perhaps a "Bee," seen near the ancient Barbary Castle hillfort [figure 64]. Some speculated that it might be a symbol for the ancient Bee Goddess, or the Spider Woman who weaves her web. In Native American lore, Spider Woman, or Grandmother Spider, was a messenger of the Creator and benefactress to the people. Many tribes have legends of her and how she was placed in the sky by the Creator to keep the webs in repair. This design has a crescent moon, which is thought to link the human to the divine and to represent feminine energy. It shows the symbol for Isis with its full circle (for the Sun/Son) and its crescent moon above. In addition to these interpretations, some people thought this design represented the queen bee, which symbolizes rebirth.

Fig. 64

Perhaps in relation to the "Spider" or "Bee," a fantastic crop circle appeared near the Avebury Ring, called the "Avebury Web" [figure 65] [plate 5]. It was made on two separate nights, August 10 and 11, 1994, which was a very unusual happening. Started in the center with a few arcs radiating outward, additional arcs were added the second night, completing the design. This formation was inspiring to look at and a pleasure to sit in, with perfection in the lay of the crop in straight lines, arcs and rings. The "Avebury Web" design has been given various interpretations: a spider web, the World Wide Web, connecting links between us and the heart of reality or universal consciousness, a "dreamcatcher" (a Native American design) and energy radiating from Source. Some think the later arcs are power points that enhance the original message. Perhaps the threads of this design tie us all together in the web of life, and we intersect with other dimensions. In Native American traditions, White Buffalo Calf Pipe Woman reminds us of the intricate web of life that unites us all and the need to honor that interconnectedness by harmonious relations with everyone and everything including the Earth (Warren 1994, 10).

Fig. 65

In August 1994 at Froxfield, another beautiful, classic formation appeared, called the "Flower of Life," also known as the "Seed of Life" or the "Power of Life" [figure 66]. This symbol evoked associations to the teachings about the Flower of Life by Drunvalo Melchizedek (1990). Possibly it was reminding us of the codes of creation and our link with all creation, and the unfolding of life from the smallest seed, always changing and growing and creating even more life. Although known hoaxers have claimed this formation, it felt good and the lay of the crop appeared genuine.

Fig. 66

1995

The 1995 crop circle season welcomed yet another advance in crop circle development, as the patterns became even more specifically related to our solar system and the cosmos. On May 29, the "Beckhampton Spiral" formation appeared, one of the first spiral crop circles ever [figure 67]. The spiral went from the exact center of the circle all the way out to the circumference, even though this cannot be seen with the eye because of the overlay of crop over the center portion and the wide band around the outside. The spiral can be seen only with special equipment. The soil at the center had a very high nitrogen content. The laying down of this design has been likened to the laying down of data on a compact disc, which starts in the center and spirals toward the circumference. Some people suggest that this represents the spiraling and orbiting of all the bodies in the cosmos, and others liken this design to a portal into other dimensions.

Fig. 67

Fig. 68

Fig. 69

Fig. 70

Fig. 71

Fig. 72

Fig. 73

In 1995 there were some dynamic spinning star patterns, beginning with the "Pinwheel" or "Catherine Wheel" crop circle on May 31 near Alfreston, Hampshire County [figure 68], followed by the "Shiriken" spinning star in mid-July at Kingsclere, Hampshire [figure 69], and "Ezekiel's Wheel" at East Meon, Hampshire, in late July or early August [figure 70]. Each of these designs conveys a strong sense of power in movement and draws our attention to the heavens. Researcher Patricia Murray has suggested that crop circles are based on the idea of rotation and spin. She was inspired to put pictures of these patterns on a lazy Susan and spin them to the accompaniment of music. During her demonstration at the August 1997 Glastonbury Symposium, the effect moved some of us to tears and created strong radiating, glowing sensations in our heart chakras.

The theme of rotation or spin also was highlighted in two dramatic designs of vortices or orbiting planets: the "Cyclic Crescents" crop circle in mid-July near East Meon in Hampshire [figure 71] and the "Sisbury Rings" in late July near the Neolithic Sisbury Ring at Shoreham, Sussex County [figure 72]. These are elaborations of the ring and crescent patterns in 1994 at Oliver's Castle, which reflected the impact site on Jupiter by the Shoemaker-Levy 9 comet. Perhaps these designs also show dramatic impacts going on in space, or perhaps they indicate the continual dynamic movement of all matter.

Significant information about the Earth was also conveyed in crop circles in 1995. In mid-July, a design near Hambledon in Hampshire evoked associations to the "Earth's Shrinking Magnetic Fields" and the "Van Allen Belt" [figure 73]. This magnetic belt of protection was shown as incomplete, and indeed our Earth's magnetic belt is shrinking. Also in mid-July, the amazing "Sixteen Rings" or "Sixteen Sacred Hoops" (of the Hopi Indians) [figure 74] appeared near Goodworth Clatford in Hampshire, perhaps depicting the all-important magnetic field of protection around the Earth. Another theory, advanced by engineer and crop circle researcher Jim Lyons, was that toroidal rings were being depicted, with energy spiraling around the rings in a three-dimensional doughnut-shaped pattern. He believes that energy moving in toroidal patterns is what creates the crop formations (Lyons 1996).

To crop circle observers, it seems as though the circlemakers are concerned about the preservation of the Earth and try to communicate their concerns to humanity. In 1995, they showed various designs of the Earth in relation to other planetary bodies. An outstanding formation was the "Arlesford Asteroid Belt" in late June near New Arlesford and Bishops Sutton in Hampshire [figure 75], showing ninety-six circles (asteroids) and three orbit rings: all the debris by which we are surrounded in space. The most attention-provoking circle of 1995 was our "Solar System with the Earth Missing," appearing in late June at Longwood Warren in Hampshire [figure 76] [plate 8]. The thin rings and outlines of the planets are only one foot wide, an amazing feat of circle-making. Sixty-five asteroids are shown, and the Sun, Mercury, Venus and Mars are there, but where is the Earth?

Some people thought this signified that the Earth would be obliterated by some traveling body in space. Others hoped this meant the Earth would be shifting into a higher dimension. Andy Thomas was told by astronomer Jack Sullivan that this configuration in our solar system would occur on April 16, 2004 (Thomas 2000c)

Two other 1995 formations showed the dynamic movement of energy in our reality. On June 19, at Cow Down near Andover, Hampshire, a design appeared showing energy moving in a focused manner from a center [figure 77]. This formation resembled a "Band Radar Pulse," or some other kind of scanning device. We can speculate about who might be scanning whom. Or perhaps it was depicting energy or communication coming from space, or even from other dimensions. American researcher and Earth energy activator Cariel Quinly saw this design as "an incredible labyrinth . . . the mystical pathway of energy and sacred geometry that brings one to the center of all things" (Quinly 1996). During this same year, a space and UFO museum was scheduled to open in Hakui, Japan, launched by an international UFO conference. The official emblem for Hakui was very much like this British crop circle (Andrews 1996a, 5:11-12). Busty Taylor reported that once he witnessed a bright orange ball over this crop circle during the daytime.

The "Corona" crop circle of early July 1995 at Litchfield, Hampshire, showed dramatic radiation of energy, like a serpentine electrical spark surrounding the tip of a cathode [figure 78]. Or perhaps it was representing other possible energy sources, the aura around the Earth or Earth's need for protection, as our ozone layer is diminishing dangerously.

An outstanding example of geometry in a crop circle was the 1995 design called "Vector Equilibrium" in Winterbourne Bassett, Wiltshire, near the white chalk horse on Hackpen Hill [figure 79] . This 150-foot circle of wheat was an example of sacred geometry, solving the mystical paradox of oddness and evenness. It was also an example of solid geometry in having both triangles and squares for its faces. R. Buckminster Fuller called this geometric pattern the *vector equilibrium* and thought it was the second most important shape of sacred geometry next to the tetrahedron, which he believed to be the ultimate universal shape. This crop circle design effectively showed a three-dimensional shape of a cube octahedron on a two-dimensional plane (Lyons 1996).

Another 1995 example of sacred geometry in a crop circle was the "Nautilus Ratchet," which appeared in wheat in mid-July east of Andover, Hampshire [figure 80]. This was the same field over which, years earlier, a couple had seen the vertical Ferris wheel glowing ring with eight lights. This crop circle had exactly the same pattern, but with the addition of the internal ratchet. The ratchet points correspond to the whorls of the Nautilus shell, which in sacred geometry have the proportions of the Golden Mean ratio. The Golden Mean shows us the order and perfection and harmony that exist in nature (Lyons 1996). The ring of light and this crop formation having the same underlying pattern supports the hypothesis that crop circles have a specific energetic formula and function associ-

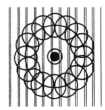
Fig. 74

Fig. 75

Fig. 76

Fig. 77

Fig. 78

Fig. 79

Fig. 80

Fig. 81

Fig. 82

Fig. 83

ated with local land topography, placement of ley lines and the spiritual history of the area.

1996

The 1996 crop circle season astonished and thrilled many enthusiasts and also made a favorable impact on the general public. Two lovely mandala designs began the season on a classical note. The "Church Window" mandala appeared across the road from Silbury Hill, Wiltshire, with three different design elements used six times to form a harmonious six-pointed star or lotus motif [figure 81]. The "Rose" mandala appeared at Goodworth Clatford in Hampshire [figure 82], with two rows of five semicircles placed alternately one behind the other, forming a pleasing undulating pattern. This is a Rosicrucian symbol and is similar to some Mayan symbols. Both of these designs are conducive to meditation.

Worldwide attention to crop circles was evoked by the "Double Helix DNA" formation, a 648-foot-long pictogram in East Field, Alton Barnes, Wiltshire [figure 83]. During the thirty-minute window of time at night when this formation was made, many anomalous events occurred. There were numerous sightings of mysterious lights and UFOs, and church bells vibrated several miles away in Avebury. To some people, this pattern looked like a rosary. To many others, it looked like our DNA, with two intertwining strands. Though we have sixty-four codons, it has been suggested that if we could be switched to eighty codons (or if we could activate them), we could combat AIDS, cancer and other degenerative diseases (Bloy 1996). This crop formation holds out the promise of humanity's expansion in consciousness through activating latent DNA. Jim Lyons suggested that the pattern showed interacting sine waves (Lyons 1996).

Debbie Jordan, the well-known abductee written about in Budd Hopkins' book *Intruders*, stated that she had been shown this double helix DNA design by aliens during an abduction with her sister in 1983. They had said to her, "From now on, things are going to get rough." Upon seeing the picture of this DNA crop circle in 1996, she stated that she felt like a big weight had been lifted off her shoulders, since now everyone would see and experience what she had seen and experienced (Andrews 1996c, 5:4).

The next crop circle in 1996, a remarkable attractor of attention, was the "Julia Set," an approximately 920-foot-long pattern of 149 circles in the wheat field directly across the main highway from Stonehenge [figure 84]. In addition to being a strikingly beautiful design, a Julia set is a Fibonacci spiral, a fractal mathematical equation relating to the science of chaos theory named after Professor Julia, who had worked with Dr. Benoit Mandelbrot in developing fractal geometry. This design has been interpreted in various ways. It is like the golden spiral, or the Golden Mean ratio described in antiquity. It shows the basic pattern of nature replicating itself. It shows musical notes going up and down the scale. This formation appeared between 5:35 and 6:05 P.M. on July 7. It is remarkable that during this busy daylight time, no one driving along the adjacent A303 highway saw this giant crop circle being created. But suddenly there it was, and many people noticed it, parked their cars and visited it, freshly made in the field (Andrews 1996b, 5:4). Imagine how many individuals became believers in crop circles from this one exposure.

Fig. 84

In the "Julia Set," all but two of the circles were swirled clockwise. The center of each circle had its own style, including flat centers, standing tufts, intricately woven nests and fanned-out centers. Amazingly, each circle had its own energy pattern, as detected by dowsing rods and electronic instrumentation. Each circle was divided into twelve "tones," where the energy from above met the grid energy of the Earth (Lyons 1996). The aura of energy immediately outside this crop formation was also strong. Colin Andrews reported in a Glastonbury Symposium lecture that July that some people from Scotland measured the orgone energy of the "Julia Set." Orgone energy is conceptualized to equal life force, and 7.5 units were measured at the central circle—as high as they had ever seen anywhere. They also discovered that the north-south magnetic ley lines linked the "Julia Set" pattern to the ley lines of Stonehenge. Interestingly, a carving on a toppled stone at Stonehenge showed these magnetic lines tying together Stonehenge and the location of the "Julia Set" (Andrews 1996d).

The longest crop formation in the world—eight-tenths of a mile long—appeared in July 1996 at Etchilhampton, Wiltshire. The slim pathway undulated along the field in a graceful serpentine manner with the stalks all laid in the same direction. The pattern began with a teardrop shape that gracefully flowed into the pathway. At twelve points along the way, the pathway formed swirled circles, like twelve chakras, and continued out the other side. Each circle was laid in the clockwise direction until the last circle and surrounding ring, which were swirled counterclockwise. I know of no photographs of this formation in its entirety due to its length and the cloud cover obscuring more distant parts of the formation. About halfway along the pathway and fifty to one hundred feet out to the side was a circle containing a standing glyph. This glyph reminded some people of ancient Sanskrit writing, but others thought it to be close to a Japanese character standing for a "municipal event" (Glickman 1996b). How fitting, whether or not it was the intention of the circlemakers. Crop circles are municipal events in that anyone can go into them, and sometimes sizeable groups of people congregate in them and do group meditations or other processes. Near the glyph was a teardrop-shaped area of laid-down crop. In this teardrop feature, Cariel Quinly caught a glowing white sphere on film that she and I had not seen when we were there. The day before this long formation was created, the farmer witnessed spiraling columns of wind and dust, lilting and gyrating along the length of the field. The next day, he noticed the long crop circle formation in those exact locations.

My intuition from walking this pathway alone was of taking a long spiritual journey of initiation. It felt like an ancient sacred ritual that I and other people of the land had done many times for a special purpose. For me this walk was deeply special, an important event in my life. It was easy to walk with the flow of the laid-down crop heading away from me, but

Fig. 85

Fig. 86

Fig. 87

when I retraced my steps along the pathway against the lay of the stalks now heading toward me, I felt like I were going against the grain and pushing against an opposing flow of strong energy. I also felt it was important for me to persist and succeed, as if honing my strength on many levels. I wondered if the path might have been laid along a major ley line.

A simple but beautiful crop circle appearing near Wayland Smithy in the vicinity of Ashbury, Wiltshire, had the classic design of "Vesica Piscis" [figure 85]. This design is formed by two overlapping circles, and the oval-like shape in the middle where the two circles intersect represents the female vulva or womb, out of which life emerges. Michael Glickman pointed out in a Glastonbury Symposium presentation that this configuration in sacred geometry signifies unity. The two circles do not quite connect, which leaves a gateway to the inner circle, inviting us into the inner sanctum (Glickman 1996b). Other people saw this design as being similar to the Hourglass nebula as viewed from the Hubble telescope. Despite the simplicity of the design, this pattern was executed as exquisitely as any crop circle I have ever seen, and the feeling of energy was sublime. The laid-down crop flowed from the outer ring through the center opening, perfectly following the curves and emerging to subtly complete both circles. The circle at the very center of the design swirled perfectly and then stretched out almost imperceptibly to form the center oval shape.

The most outstanding formation of 1996 was the "Triple Julia Set" at Windmill Hill near Avebury, Wiltshire [figure 86] [plate 68]. Even the most seasoned researchers scarcely could fathom how such a beautiful, complex pattern of exquisite proportions could have been made with perfection in the middle of the dark night. This pattern combined three Julia sets, or Fibonacci spirals, which were spiraling in the direction opposite (counterclockwise) to the direction of the earlier single "Julia Set" formation. Exhibiting a great sense of dynamic movement, it conveyed the perfect way that all life unfolds and order evolves out of chaos, as well as the symbolism of three, unity after dualism.

The final dramatic crop circle of the wonderful 1996 season was the striking "Snowflake" symbol, which appeared on August 11 in long-eared wheat in the field below Oliver's Castle [figure 87]. This pattern appeared to be made in only a few seconds while two pairs of glowing white spheres swooped over the field, according to a young videographer who claimed to have taped the footage of this event. The center circle of the design was eighty-five feet in diameter with six long spokes of forty-eight feet, each of which had overlaid three circles of decreasing size. Andy Thomas quoted a shamanic perspective in interpreting the snowflake as a symbol of multidimensional reality, which in the physical world is illustrated by the six directions of sky above, Earth beneath, west, east, north and south (Thomas 1996, 59:9).

1997

The 1997 crop circle season began on April 20 with a dazzlingly beautiful flowerlike design in an oilseed canola crop near the Barbury Castle hillfort near Swindon, Wiltshire [figure 88]. The beauty of the dynamically moving "Spinning Crescents" formation was enhanced by the bright yellow blossoms and dark green stalks. The laid-down crescents and standing crescents showed sixfold geometry. Each laid-down crescent was bent clockwise. The diameter of the whole design was 225 feet. It was amazing that this extremely brittle crop could be bent and swirled into such an exquisite pattern, presumably by high heat and steam. Canola crop stalks snap and break very easily, and a person walking can be scratched by these strong, tenacious plants. But the stalks appeared to have been laid down easily and without breakage.

Fig. 88

An equally striking pattern appeared on May 3, 1997, below Barbury Castle, only a field or two away from the "Spinning Crescents." It was called the "Tree of Life" or the "Kabbalah" [figure 89] [plate 2] because the symbol clearly depicts the Jewish mystical diagram of matter, spirit and consciousness. Many people also see the Kabbalah as a representation of the chakra system. This formation was laid in the brittle oilseed canola crop, and again it was amazing that the circles could be so nicely swirled and the shapes laid down so exactly and without breakage.

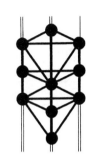

Fig. 89

A wonder of geometry appeared on June 2, 1997, near Winterbourne Bassett, Wiltshire: a 202-foot diameter mandala composed of repeated half-circles, half-triangles, quarter circles and quarter triangles, all placed cleverly within a triangle inside a circle [figure 90]. It was an extraordinarily complex design to execute. Because this crop circle was made in a young green barley field, the plants responded to the heliotropic urge and soon stood up again, reaching for the Sun, making the pattern difficult to discern.

Fig. 90

Another dazzler appeared on June 10, 1997, in the field across the highway from Stonehenge where the "Julia Set" formation had appeared the previous year. This design, called the "Stonehenge Snowflake" [figure 91], measured over 400 feet in diameter and contained 194 circles. This fractal pattern theoretically could spread out repetitively to infinity. It was discovered that when iron filings were put in a metal pan and a magnet was moved around under the pan, the filings formed this pattern as they settled. Some people think this pattern reflects the way plant life grows and develops.

Fig. 91

Researchers were amazed when the "Torus" pattern [figure 92] [plate 1] appeared on a hillside in Alton Priors, Wiltshire, on July 11, 1997. Three hundred feet in diameter, this dynamic design looked as if strong flows of energy or water had swept through the field to make the twelve overlapping rings. According to engineer Jim Lyons, these toroidal rings illustrate the energy patterns that create all crop circles by flowing in a three-dimensional doughnut fashion. This pattern looked especially three-dimensional, with the sense that one could go through the center hole into infinity.

A stunning crop pattern called the "Hopi Star" appeared on July 13, 1997, at Bishops Cannings, Wiltshire, in a wheat field [figure 93]. It was a lovely example of fivefold geometry, with five points of the star and five

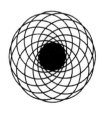

Fig. 92

Fig. 93

Fig. 94

Fig. 95

Fig. 96

Fig. 97

interspersed bars. In numerology, five is the number that signifies change. It is unusual for a crop circle to have straight lines, yet this feature formed an effective mandala.

A pattern resembling a "Maltese Cross" or "Coptic Cross" appeared in a wheat field on July 27, 1997, near Morested, Hampshire [figure 94]. It was beautiful to see when approached on a hillside, with the stalks laid impeccably in graduated sizes of arcs from the circumference to the inner cross pattern. This crop circle had a peaceful, serene energy and was perfect to meditate in and later to meditate on.

On July 7, 1997, a simple but elegant "Ringed Quintuplet" glyph appeared in Headbourne Worthy in Hampshire [figure 95], carrying on the tradition of quintuplet patterns frequently seen during the 1980s. This crop circle, 256 feet in diameter, was executed with positive and negative shapes that contained both fourfold and fivefold geometry.

An entirely new design showed up on July 14, 1997, below Cley Hill near Warminster, Hampshire. It was called the "Dreamcatcher" or the "Bicycle Spokes" [figure 96] because of its complex crisscrossing of straight lines, which formed a condensed pointed pattern in the center. The longer sets of lines formed twelvefold geometry, as did the points near the center and the petal-shaped design inside these points. Embedded in the design were several geometric shapes—such as smaller triangles within larger triangles, the petal-edged circle and a diamond shape—all within a large hexagram. With a diameter of 250 feet, this intricate design in wheat was truly amazing. It would certainly stretch the imagination of even the most confirmed skeptic to figure out how humans could create this detailed and precise design in the dark of night.

Then another surprise appeared: a giant "Ant" design one hundred feet long in a wheat field in East Meon, Hampshire, on July 17, 1997 [figure 97]. The lay of the stalks was exacting and beautiful, the energy felt good and the dowsing showed rich changes of energy within and between various sections of the formation. People had fun speculating why this design had been given to us. Was this introducing a species from elsewhere visiting us on Earth? Was the Earth trying to give us a message about our use of pesticides? Does this symbol have some spiritual meaning we did not guess? Do all the designs have to have some lofty spiritual symbolism . . . ?

On July 23, 1997, an unusual pattern appeared in wheat at Oliver's Castle. It reminded some observers of a "Japanese Symbol" [figure 98]. For a few years, Japanese researchers visiting England had been asking for a symbol that would relate to their culture, perhaps this was the response. Researcher Kris Sherwood called this design the "Double-Ringed Pisces" (Sherwood 2001). It was a beautifully executed pattern, especially with the slender crescents.

The crop circle community was thrilled with the July 23, 1997, "Fractal Star of David" or "Koch Snowflake" pattern created in the wheat field next to Silbury Hill [figure 99]. This design was named after mathematician Helmig von Koch, who developed the concept of the fractal in 1905, which led to the formulation of fractal geometry by Benoit Mandelbrot. This design suggested the advanced geometry of the Sierpinski gasket, in which triangles are divided by smaller triangles to infinity. The 126 little circles around the edge each had a different kind of center. The crop was laid down masterfully from a swirled center to form the triangles and radiating triangles at each of the six points of the star.

A second "Fractal Star of David" or "Standing Koch Snowflake" amazed crop circle researchers even further when it appeared below Milk Hill, Alton Barnes, on August 18, 1997 [figure 100] [plate 3]. It was identical to the earlier formation except for the addition of standing crop in the center, creating yet another snowflake-like pattern of a Koch fractal. It reminded crop circle observers that the creativity and technical skill involved in creating crop circles was continuing to advance. To Native American Rod Bearcloud Berry, the symbol of the standing portion was given to the Earth by the Star Nation people, who understand it as the Flower of Life, the seed or the egg from which the Koch fractal would emerge (Berry 1998, 26:9). As with other fractals, the center design could continue to expand outward as one continued to go deeper into the center.

To add to the variety of 1997 crop circles, two designs appeared on the same night, July 31, in one long field at Etchilhampton. One formation was a grid-textured square pattern within a circle [figure 101]. It had an intricate series of twenty-six lines laid out parallel to each other in a north-south direction and thirty lines in an east-west direction, forming 754 small rectangles. The perpendicular lines were meticulously woven over and under each other by the lay of the crop. One of the interpretations of this design was that it represented the grid or ley lines running over the surface of the Earth. The other design in the field was a very dynamic-looking "Six-Pointed Star" or "Pinwheel" [figure 102] [plate 70], which appeared to be rotating vigorously. I noticed that where the laid-down pathways converged, the dowsing rods consistently responded more emphatically. The sense of a strong energy flow was very evident here.

1998

The crop circles of 1998 continued to win even more respect from crop circle researchers and the growing number of observers. The first formation to appear was the "Beltane Ring" or "Beltane Wheel" on May 4, at the ancient West Kennett Longbarrow field across from Silbury Hill [figure 103]. It was a striking design in the bright yellow oilseed canola plants, with thirty-three flame shapes accentuated by the dark green laid-down stalks. A photographer who had set up his equipment there for an all-night vigil to photograph the setting Moon and rising Sun over that field neither saw nor heard lights or cars in the area when this crop circle was formed. This design looks like a doughnut or tube torus, suggesting the way energy flows in a three-dimensional way around a ring. According to Rodney Carr-Smith, who wrote about this formation, the number thirty-three is significant in sacred geometry. It signifies the vibration of unconditional love and the Christ energy. The flame shapes are identical to the letter *Yod* of

Fig. 98

Fig. 99

Fig.100

Fig. 101

Fig. 102

Fig. 103

Fig. 104

Fig. 105

Fig. 106

MAY 4, 1998, "BELTANE RING" AND SILBURY HILL.

the Hebrew alphabet, which "is the most holy of letters and means 'seed' or 'beginning of life' or 'Creative Hand.'" The Yod symbol appears also in the Tarot, symbolizing that "the source of wisdom within oneself and its intelligence is the knowledge that we can create our own world with our own hand. It is both the giving hand of God and the open, searching hand of mankind." It also represents "the reflected light of our own subconscious. Here, we receive the manifestation of our own self-generated reality." In addition, it shows that all we know is integrated at the balance center of our being (Carr-Smith 1999, 24:8).

On May 26, 1998, a large crop circle appeared in Countesthorpe, Leicestershire, containing a symbol of the "World Tree" [figure 104], an inverted tree with roots in heaven and branches coming down into the Earth realm. This is an ancient symbol from many cultures, but especially Northern Europe, where the *Yggdrasil* was the dominating symbol of a large part of Europe and Asia long before the Viking Age. It represents attributes of the manifested deity continually being destroyed and renewed, drawing on resources of the unmanifested deity (Green 1999, 24:23-24).

Three long dragonlike or larval formations appeared on hillsides during 1998. One of the most beautiful was the "Hydra," three hundred feet long and appearing to move up the hillside at West Woods near Lockeridge, Wiltshire [figure 105] [plate 78]. It faced another dragon formation across the road on the opposite hillside. Qi Gong master Nan Lu told me as we were standing in the formation that the energy ran right down the formation on one hill and up the formation opposite, thus enlarging and expanding the energy.

Very close to those formations was an unmistakable symbol of a comet rushing toward a planet in orbit. This "Colliding Comet" glyph appeared on June 15, at Barn Hill, near Lockeridge [figure 106]. Were we being warned about a comet or Planet Nibiru heading toward the Earth?

Several lovely mandala patterns were laid down during 1998. The first one of note was the "Clanfield Brooch" of June 19, near Petersfield, Hampshire, in a soft, fluffy barley crop [figure 107]. This design contained twelvefold geometry with its twelve circles, each of which is half standing and half laid down. After taking a photograph while looking downhill from the top of the formation, I noticed three glowing balls of orange, blue and white light in the air in the distance.

Fig. 107

The second mandala was the mandala of June 20, 1998, at Avebury Trusloe [figure 108]. Made in wheat, a clear five-pointed star was surrounded by ten overlapping circles that, with their overlaps, formed ten lotus leaves. This was a lovely, energetic crop circle in which to spend time as well as a beautiful mandala to use in meditation.

The third mandala pattern, the "Double Star," was created in wheat on July 4, at Dadford, Buckinghamshire [figure 109] [plate 80]. One hundred seventy-five feet in diameter, it had one five-pointed star laid over another, giving a dramatic appearance. Two small glyphs were created just alongside: one of the ancient Egyptian "ankh" symbol and the other similar to some of the shapes of 1990 and 1991 pictograms, speculated by some to be the key to other dimensions.

A further elaboration of the "Clanfield Brooch" formation appeared in a wheat crop near Farnham, Hampshire on July 7, 1998, referred to as the "Diatom" [figure 110]. This 220-foot design was similar to microscopic sea creatures that formed the chalk substrata all over that part of England. Design elements in fives were repeated throughout this pattern, which in numerology signify change.

One of the most exquisitely constructed crop circles I have ever entered was the "Seven Crescents" near the Danebury Ring hillfort in Hampshire [figure 111]. Sevenfold geometry was shown with seven curving, spinning flames or flares, each of which tapered down to delicate points of one or two stalks of wheat. This design was clean and simple, and the energy felt wonderful.

The next 1998 mandala to appear was the "Pentagon and Pentacles" crop circle of August 8 in wheat near Beckhampton, Wiltshire [figure 112]. Illustrating fivefold geometry, a five-pointed star was created over another five-pointed star, and both were superimposed on a pentagon. Two circles held the pattern together.

Next came the "Spinning Crescents II" mandala of August 19, formed in wheat near the Avebury Sanctuary [figure 113]. This design demonstrated sixfold geometry, with six laid-down crescents and six standing crescents. Each seemed to interact with the others in a dynamic spinning motion.

The last obvious mandala-style crop circle of 1998 was the "Compass Rose" of August 24, formed in wheat near Avebury, Wiltshire [figure 114]. This design reminds people of the dial of a compass, which is represented on maps as a stylized sharp-petaled rose. Here the triangles that constitute the pattern are repeated in fours and joined by a square near the center.

Other 1998 crop circles with interesting geometries kept appearing throughout the summer months. On June 21, a "Cat's Eye" design appeared in barley at Fyfield, Wiltshire [figure 115]. Its four overlapping circles formed two perpendicular vesica piscis designs. The next day, the same design appeared in another field north of Alton Barnes [figure 116], with the standing and flattened stalks reversed. This was the first time a reversal like this had happened with crop circles.

A crop formation resembling the astrological symbol of "Aries" [figure 117] showed up early in July 1998 in a wheat field at Yew Tree Farm near

Fig. 108

Fig. 109

Fig. 110

Fig. 111

Fig. 112

Fig. 113

Fig. 114

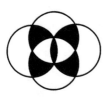

Fig. 115

Fig. 116

Fig. 117

Heddington, Wiltshire. Although a relatively simple formation, it had high dowsable energy as well as the unusual feature of laid-down crop flowing in the ring in a clockwise direction, lying right next to stalks running in the opposite direction. One wonders how this could be accomplished while forming a perfect circle of laid-down crop.

The 1998 formation that received the most attention from the crop circle community was the "Sevenfold Koch Snowflake" in East Field, Alton Barnes, Wiltshire, on July 9 [figure 118]. This sevenfold geometrical pattern, 295 feet in diameter, bore some resemblance to the 1997 sixfold Koch fractal snowflakes. This pattern actually looked like a three-dimensional contour map or multifaceted diamond when seen from the air, even though the crop was laid flat on the ground. It is intriguing how this pattern was formed from the center swirl that radiated out to form all the fractal points. The snowflake was surrounded by 147 small circles, which had a variety of styles of centers, including tightly twisted and swirled nests of wheat. According to Michael Green, this sevenfold fractal pattern of sacred geometry symbolizes a great celestial tree around which clusters fruit. It also symbolizes the seven aspects of deity in manifestation, the seven spirits before the throne of God and the seven archangels (Green 2000).

The next awe-inspiring crop circle of 1998 was an entirely different kind of fractal Julia set, the "Silbury Julia Set" or "Silbury Hill II" [figure 119] [plate 75], created at Silbury Hill on July 23. This fractal design, two hundred feet in diameter, had four swirling arms and many small circles outside the perimeter. In this formation, Shawn Randall found some thoroughly cooked dead flies stuck to the standing stalks by their tongues, as if a sudden intense heat had enveloped them. It was intriguing to see how the crop had been laid down ingeniously and masterfully from the center swirl to form the curving arms of the design.

A perplexing yet uniquely beautiful crop formation appeared on July 21, 1998, in the big field near Beckhampton, with a voluptuous series of overlapping circles and standing arcs, plus a three hundred foot long, curved tail of fifty-two circles [figure 120] [plate 7]. This design has been called the "Stingray" or "Manta Ray," although this name probably missed the point

Photographer: © Barbara Lumb.

1998, SILBURY HILL CROP CIRCLE.

and did not do justice to the complexity and extreme artistry of this creation. The lay of the crop was elegant and even incorporated a stair-step effect that signifies, according to Rod Bearcloud Berry (who was in the formation with me), the entry into other dimensions. Indeed, visitors to crop circles often feel they are opening to other dimensions in these portals. The long line

Photographer: © Barbara Lamb.

JULY 1998, ROD BEARCLOUD BERRY IN BECKHAMPTON "STINGRAY" CROP CIRCLE.

of small circles was remarkable in that each circle had a different kind of swirl and center.

Obviously, not all crop circles are actually circular. A few triangular patterns have been created over the years, with the largest known triangle appearing on August 10, 1998, in Yatesbury, Wiltshire. It was named the "Titanic Triangle" for its side length of one hundred feet [figure 121]. It was interesting to see how the crop was laid to make this shape and how it swirled into a small circle at the apex. Three little circles clustered outside each point of the triangle, and the pattern was graced with a single small circle outside the apex, with stalks bent and swirled only halfway down to the ground.

On August 6, near the end of the 1998 crop circle season, a stunning formation appeared named the "Queen" [figure 122] [plate 79], measuring more than four hundred feet in diameter. Created in the same wheat field as the "Hydra" earlier in the 1998 season, this complex design incorporated four major overlapping circles and five smaller ones, making lotus petals and other pleasing shapes. It appeared to be topped by a crown or an aura of small circles, and on top of that was a tiny circle with stems bent and swirled halfway down the stalks. Not only was this design interesting in itself, but it seemed to make a point of incorporating design elements from a dozen of the earlier formations during the 1998 season.

The culmination of the 1998 crop circle season was the sequel to the East Field "Sevenfold Koch Snowflake," named the "Magnificent Seven," which appeared on August 9, in West Stowell, Wiltshire [figure 123]. The seven modified points contained another fractal of fourteen differently shaped points. There were 175 small circles of varying sizes outside the perimeter of the design as well as inside the inner fractal. It was interesting how all of this complexity was achieved with the negative and positive shapes of the entire pattern, depending on which elements were laid down and which were left standing. As with so many other crop formations, this was a magnificent achievement of artistry and fractal geometry, and it is impossible to fathom how humans could have created it.

Hopefully, it has become apparent to the reader from this description of numerous crop formations created through the 1990s, that something extraordinary and purposeful has been occurring with these creations. A communication seems to have been going on. As people have responded physically, emotionally and spiritually to this phenomenon and researched

Fig. 118

Fig. 119

Fig. 120

Fig. 121

Fig. 122

Fig. 123

it further, the symbolic messages have become more advanced and challenging. It seems as if the circlemakers tested our reactions by making simple circles followed by simple geometric designs. When they realized their efforts were noticed and responded to, they gave us humans more interesting crop circle designs. The more intrigued people have been with these creations and have become involved in the phenomenon, the more thought-provoking and challenging the designs have become, and the more information is given to us. We continue to wonder what the designs will reveal next.

THE GEOMETRIC AND MATHEMATICAL CHARACTERISTICS OF THE CROP FORMATIONS

UNDERLYING GEOMETRIC PRINCIPLES

To those who have an appreciation for geometry, or even a sensitivity to the beautiful forms seen in nature, one of the most remarkable aspects of the crop circle phenomenon is the precise execution of beautiful geometric forms in fields of grain during the darkness of night and in a very short duration of time. Also remarkable is the continuing increase in geometric complexity and sophistication of the formations. Many see the creation of crop formations as one of the greatest mysteries occurring in the world today. Even those who are not educated in geometry respond emotionally or intuitively to the elegant proportions, symmetry, harmony and inherent beauty in the crop circle patterns.

Numerous crop circle researchers have been intrigued with the geometry of the crop circles, applying both classical Euclidian or Pythagorean geometry and sacred geometry principles. In the early 1990s, there was a burst of realization that the crop circle designs exhibit proportions that illustrate geometric principles. Gerald S. Hawkins, a retired astronomer and the coauthor of *Stonehenge Decoded* (1965), was intrigued by the crop circles appearing close to Stonehenge and began calculating the ratios of the sizes of key features of eighteen formations he found pictured in *Circular Evidence* (1990), a book by Pat Delgado and Colin Andrews describing formations of the 1980s. He very quickly discovered that the ratios in eleven of the formations precisely matched the ratios defining the diatonic scale. (The diatonic scale is equivalent to the eight white keys on the piano, starting with middle C.) After painstaking effort, Hawkins discovered four geometric theorems that are present in many crop formations, and from those four he developed a fifth theorem, which is a general case of the other four. It appears that this theorem expresses an underlying principle of how the physical world is put together, and remarkably—unlike the previous four—it was not a theorem known in antiquity (Howe, 1993, 53-59). Another intriguing element to Hawkins' discovery of theorems is that possibly some of the formations he studied were hoaxed. It would be interesting to know which eleven of the eighteen formations yielded the theorems and whether any of those eleven circles that yielded the diatonic ratios were hoaxed. The applicability of his theorems to future crop circles might be one more screening device for analyzing whether a formation is man-made or not.

Prior to Gerald Hawkins' inspired work, Colin Andrews had compared the dimensions of crop formations from the 1980s to the floor plan of Stonehenge, and his findings meshed with Hawkins' discovery that the exact dimensions of the formations could be translated into diatonic ratios. If, however, the formations had been only a few centimeters different in size, they would have fit into Stonehenge but would not have calculated exactly to diatonic ratios. Thus, the circlemakers chose to have the formations fit the diatonic ratios rather than the dimensions of Stonehenge. Andrews reported a similar situation with the "Mandelbrot Set" formation; apparently, it was not a precise duplication of the computer-generated graphic representation of the Mandelbrot set, but it was this slight displacement that had the ratios between parts be diatonic ratios. Andrews then commented, "Complex pictograms contain extraordinarily interesting features that tantalizingly suggest the creative force and source of these patterns are engaged in a basic teaching of Universal Law" (Andrews 1992, 4:10-11).

Another researcher who has illustrated graphically that geometrical principles provide the foundation for many crop formations is Bert Janssen. In his recent book, *Crop Circle Reconstructions and Geometry*, he illustrates how various well-known complex formations can be duplicated on paper by placing circles and triangles in certain logical, geometrical relationships to each other in a step-by-step fashion. When certain lines are erased, the final product is present, determined by all the previous steps. Some of the intermediate steps necessary for the final design are not apparent in the actual formation. Obviously, the makers of the crop circles did not proceed in such a step-by-step fashion in laying down the crop; the final design was known when the formation was made. Janssen also found that when he reconstructed crop circles that appeared to have geometrical "irregularities," his reconstructions obeyed the same geometrical rules that were found in "perfect" formations (Janssen 2000).

Another application of geometry to the crop formations resulted from Gerald Hawkins' realization that ratios between sizes of different parts of formations yield numbers that correspond to the white keys of a piano (diatonic ratios). He also wondered about the implications of assigning a letter to each note (each ratio) going up the scale. Several letters could be associated with a formation. By choosing the two most significant ratios (letters), he speculated that he had a code for the initials of names. Computer research was performed to scan many lists of names for matches with a list of initials he had calculated, and he actually found matches—with the initials of most of the presidents of the British Society of Psychical Research. Even more uncanny, one of the past

LATE JULY 2000, BERT JANSSEN AND JOHN MICHELL IN BLACKLAND CROP CIRCLE.

Fig. 124

presidents had left a posthumous experiment for the members, to communicate from the other side using Euclidean geometry and music. His initials turned up several times. Perhaps the crop circles became his vehicle for communication (Andrews 1995, 4:13).

FRACTALS AND CHAOS THEORY

Gerald Hawkins' work opened up the idea that the crop formations represent or express certain basic laws of nature as expressed through Euclidean geometry. The formations looked Euclidean—fairly simple with classical shapes like circles and triangles. Bert Janssen demonstrated that even the later, more complex formations still had underlying geometrical rules of design. Colin Andrews, along with Hawkins, illustrated that even small deviations in size from expected templates were extremely meaningful and deliberate in order to create diatonic ratios in the formations rather than sloppy accidents by the circlemakers. However, the 1991 appearance of the "Mandelbrot Set" formation [figure 124], an undeniable example of a fractal pattern, moved attention to a new way of expressing natural processes through the crop formations—chaos theory. Fractal geometry is a relatively new mathematical language within chaos theory, consisting of sequences or patterns that can perpetuate themselves infinitely by mathematical algorithms. They are formulas that show us how things happen and where they are going. They express the way geometry and numbers can be the foundation for everything that exists as matter and material processes, such as branching in lungs, plants and rivers, the shapes of mountains and coastlines, weather and traffic patterns, and melodies. Fractals retain their identifying patterns at each higher level of magnification, and enlargements of small portions of the design reveal miniature copies of the whole design (Voss 1990, 1). Again this echoes the Hermetic wisdom, "As above, so below . . ." Fractal concepts apply to changes in time (being generated by recursive procedures) as well as in space. As our universe is constantly expanding into new forms and many aspects of our world are changing and growing, fractals are appropriate to remind us that in change and growth, even when they appear random and chaotic, there is an underlying or implicate order.

Numerous fractal patterns have been expressed in crop formations since the "Mandelbrot Set" in 1991. Most of them were mentioned in the previous section and several are pictured in the plates in the following section of this book. These include the "Julia Set" [figure 84] and the "Triple Julia Set" [figure 86] [plate 68] in 1996; the "Stonehenge Snowflake" [figure 91], the "Koch Snowflake" [figure 99] and the "Standing Koch Snowflake" [figure 100] [plate 3] in 1997; the "Sevenfold Koch Snowflake" [figure 118], the "Silbury Julia Set" [figure 119] and the "Magnificent Seven" [figure 123] in 1998; and the "Sierpinski Gasket" [plate 12] in 1999.

The "Mandelbrot Set" was created near Cambridge University where Professor Mandelbrot, the French mathematician who discovered the pattern, had taught for some years. Michael Hesemann offered the following interpretation of the pattern (called the "Appleman" by mathematicians): This symbol "implies that there is a hidden order behind apparent chaos, for the 'Appleman', in the world of fractals, is the only island of stability in an ocean of intricate chaos. The Mandelbrot can be found at any level of magnification of the design. . . . It is the trade mark of the transition from chaos to order, of Creation itself, when 'God's spirit' created the universe out of primordial chaos—and it is also a symbol of the end of the world when Creation sinks back into chaos." Hesemann also added an interesting anecdote. Exactly one year before the formation appeared, the *New Scientist* published a letter in which a Wiltshire reader asked how long it would take before a complete Mandelbrot diagram was seen (Hesemann 1996, 38-39). Could it be that the circlemakers took note of this request and playfully went to their cosmic computers to design a template, which they saved for the anniversary of the request?

SACRED GEOMETRY

While fractal geometry provides a modern, dynamic way of looking at creation and creative processes and became widely accessible for study through the use of computers, certain principles have been known since antiquity about the laws of creation in the material world. These principles fall within the realm of sacred geometry. Linda Moulton Howe stated succinctly in a radio interview that sacred geometry expresses the way things are put together and is the force of God behind everything. Geometric principles exist through eternity, whether people are aware of them or not (Howe 2000b). According to Karen Douglas, a crop circle researcher who writes evocatively about the compelling ambiance of the formations, the principles of sacred geometry reflect the harmonics, proportions and shapes that exist in nature. The numbers and shapes found in nature can be viewed as a universal language that is reflected in temples, cathedrals, pyramids, sacred sites and the human body. However, one does not have to be a mathematician or philosopher to grasp the significance of sacred geometry. One can physically and emotionally feel a sense of the sacred through the vibrations set up by the proportions of the design. Many of the formations reflect an ancient proportion called the Golden Section, Golden Proportion or Golden Mean ratio. "Unlike equality where one length is divided to create two smaller lengths of equal value, the Golden Section is a *harmonious* relationship between two lengths where the smaller length is to the larger as the larger is to the whole." Our human bodies as well as many other living things (like Nautilus shells) are constructed with these proportions (Douglas 2000a, 2-3).

JULY 1998, KAREN DOUGLAS AT THE GLASTONBURY SYMPOSIUM.

Photographer: © Barbara Lamb.

Drunvalo Melchizedek received a revelation that the Flower of Life symbol contains within it all the encodings for life: "every single mathematical formula, every law of physics, every harmony in music, every biological life form . . . absolutely everything that's within waveform universes" (Melchizedek 1990, 29). The Flower of Life symbol, the Kabbalah or Tree of Life symbol, the vesica pisces, the circle, the cube and the spiral are all shapes fundamental to sacred geometry that have appeared as crop formations.

USING NUMEROLOGY TO DECODE THE CROP CIRCLE MESSAGES

Shapes, numbers, sound vibrations and music, letters and ancient sacred symbols all serve as vehicles for radiating energy, or communicating. Peggy Bunt has applied numerological concepts to the geometric characteristics of the crop circles and concludes that these formations are showing how we are evolving in consciousness. In her numerology system, "five represents the human microcosm; six, equilibrium and harmony; seven, the Universe; and nine, completion and fulfilment. Ten is the number of the cosmos, and signifies a return to unity." Her interpretation of a 1998 pattern included the following commentary: "This year saw the first appearance of an eleven-fold design (*if implicit*) in the Menorah at Barbury Castle. This . . . represents a stern reminder of our role in the Universe. The number eleven symbolises transgression and peril. The seven branches of the Menorah represent the Universe in Jewish tradition and the four on the 'stem' are the Earth. But four is also wholeness, rationality, measurement and justice. This reminds us of how our transgressions against the Earth and the whole have placed it in peril. We know this to be true so it is not surprising to find this message in our fields" (Bunt 1998, 87:17-18).

Bunt also explains that tenfold geometry showed up in the West Overton "Sierpinski Gasket" crop circle of 1999 [plate 12]. She points out that "The Cube" at Allington Down in 1999 [plate 15] symbolized perfection and stability and the Platonic solid that represents Earth. Also, threefold geometry appeared in the 1999 Hackpen Hill formation [plate 26], and "three symbolises creative power, growth and synthesis, the overcoming of duality. It is the heavenly number, the soul. Therefore, this glyph can be seen as the ultimate evolutionary state which we humans need to achieve, in order not only to save the planet and the Universe but also to fulfil [*sic*] our higher destiny." As she concludes her article: "At first seen as a cry for help from the Earth, [the message of the glyphs] has been re-emphasized and expanded through the years, so that our responsibility and involvement is clearly set out. For those of us who believe the glyphs to be communications from a higher intelligence, and accept an interpretation through the symbolism of Number, the message is there for all to see. The time is now" (Bunt 1999, 87:18).

The crop formations are communicating with humanity at many subtle levels. Congruent with Judy Moore's channeled information, it appears that looking at the patterns in pictures has an effect; one does not have to be physically present in the formations to receive the information that vibrates inherently in the geometric and numerological qualities of the designs. As Freddy Silva commented about the energies of crop circles, "Distort or remove just one element and the communication between viewer and design is short-circuited. It simply becomes a work of art without effect. But show people a mere photo of the real thing and their eyes light up, they become emotional, light-headed, ecstatic, benevolent, dizzy. . . . Our eyes may be attracted to the designs in golden wheat but the real message—a basic language common to all nature—is reached at a deeper level, triggered by an underlying code based on sacred geometry and sound—the very same code whose formulas were zealously guarded by ancient esoterics as the knowledge of the Godly" (Silva 1998, 22:20).

CONCLUDING THOUGHTS

The crop circle phenomenon no longer is a brief novelty or a transient series of events. It appears to be here to stay, at least for a while. Early in the 2001 season, people were prohibited from walking into the crop fields in England because of the highly contagious foot and mouth disease. The hoax proponents had assumed that because hoaxers could not enter the fields this season, there would be no crop circles appearing. The reality is, though, that crop circles indeed were appearing, even in the highly brittle oilseed canola crops. The proponents of the anomalous source theory were delighted and were awaiting new investigation methods, new conjectures, new insights and new understandings.

Perhaps there never will be conclusive proof of where the microwave (or other) crop-circle-making energies come from, how they are transmitted in such a way as to form precise and meaningful patterns, or by whom and for what purpose they are created. We never will know with certainty how many crop circles from past years were genuine and how many were man-made. It might well be that the unanswered questions and mysteries are not only keeping the phenomenon alive but also are moving this field of inquiry forward. As we continue to wonder and to study aspects of the crop circle phenomenon, we continue to challenge our minds, open our higher chakras, raise our consciousness and reach further for universal awareness. Perhaps we are becoming increasingly ready for direct contact with other beings of both physical and nonphysical natures, whether or not we will ever know if they are the sources of crop circles.

There still is much investigating to do in order to understand the complexities and mysteries of crop circles. The issues of genuine versus hoaxed crop circles are complex, with some energetic characteristics of what we had considered genuine formations—of anomalous origin—now known to be appearing in some man-made formations and in some messy areas of laid-down crop that do not show precise designs. The increasing numbers of disclosures by hoaxers of what they experience as input by ETs and, less specifically, of receiving inexplicable intuitions and urges to make crop formations have blurred the previous clear-cut distinction between a human and an anomalous origin of crop circles.

Scientific inquiries have shown numerous consistent changes in crops and soil and water taken from crop circles that are unexplainable by any human technological processes. These changes have been measured repeatedly and are not reflecting the biases of any one investigator, as was charged in the past. Dowsing and pendulums show repeated patterns of energy within parts of crop formations and between the inside and outside of formations, again supporting that the wishes and biases and expectations of a few individuals are not causing of the results. Geometric analyses have shown interesting and precise mathematical patterns in the shapes of the formations that reflect ancient principles of sacred geometry. It is clear that the patterns in most—possibly all—formations are not randomly pretty, but have harmonic relationships that provoke responses beyond the conscious intellectual level.

Many questions remain. In spite of numerous theories presented by channels, scientists and theoreticians, we still do not have a clear—or, at least, clear to most humans—technical explanation of how precise designs are laid down in physical matter including crop. Additionally, no codebook of interpretations is conveniently hung on a post next to formations in crop, ice, snow, sand and rocks, with footnotes acknowledging the creators and their intentions. No high-tech tests reliably show how the crop circle energies are impacting the human body or the grid system of the Earth's body. The energies of some crop circles initially seem to be harmful to some visitors and yet subsequently heal those visitors of previously existing maladies, whereas the energies of some other crop circles seem harmful to visitors and fail to heal them. On the other hand, the energies of some circles feel positive to visitors and bring about physical healings and many other positive results. We do not yet understand why this is so. Perhaps the concentration or dosage of energy varies from one crop circle to another, or perhaps different combinations of energies are applied to various crop circles, or perhaps an individual's personal energy configuration matches or clashes with or is not yet ready for the specific crop circle's energy pattern.

Ron Russell calls for "discernment, critical thinking, testing, and measuring in trying to determine what's going on. . . . Why not practice a 'New Science' which draws on the pragmatic virtues of Newtonian laws, yet includes consideration of quantum mechanics, subtle and spiritual worlds? We need to practice science and spirit, not one or the other." He also accepts human circle-making as an interesting, even uplifting part of the whole crop circle phenomenon, and knows that people can have strong epiphanies, healings and transformational experiences in man-made crop circles. He believes they are "spiritual machines" just as much as the purportedly genuine formations (Russell 2000b, 93:7).

Many people have not yet found an opening in their personal belief system in which to incorporate the reality of genuine crop circles and therefore choose to disregard them or assume they must be man-made. However, more people will gradually come to recognize and assimilate the metaphysical nature of crop circles as they are exposed to more media coverage—movies, videotapes, calendars and even mainline news reports—on this subject. As more reports of crop circles come in from diverse parts of the world, more people will become educated about the widespread nature of the phenomenon. With more publicity about organizations to which they can report anomalous events of this type in their own areas, the phenomenon will be brought "close to home" for their neighbors. As crop circle designs have become more complex and sophisticated year by year in a number of different countries, they are attracting more notice and investigation by additional researchers from various disciplines and fields of knowledge. This, in turn, attracts the attention and respect of even more people.

July 1999, Roland and Clare Pargeter, who founded and organized the Glastonbury Symposia for years.

I have attempted to tie together various mysterious phenomena—anomalous lights and sounds, sightings of UFOs, cattle mutilations, designs appearing in various substances in addition to cereal crops—and communicate my belief that these phenomena can provoke and promote our ability to develop psychologically and spiritually, to open up to signs of other realities, other consciousnesses and perhaps to visitors from elsewhere in the universe and from other dimensions of reality. From my personal experiences and my experiences as a therapist, I have come to believe that we are in a dance with beings with consciousness beyond the human level, and hopefully, we can become more attuned to them through experiencing crop circles. Our increasing familiarity with crop circles and their radiating energies is moving us forward in our evolution as human beings. They appear along with the large changes that are perceived by many people: changes in weather, in Earth magnetics and frequencies, in the speeding up of time, in sightings of balls of light and unusual crafts, in Marian apparitions and other spirit presences. As these happenings are increasing in number and public visibility, the veil between us and other dimensions and intelligences is becoming thinner and more transparent. Some people say we humans are being prepared to evolve into the fourth or higher dimensions of reality. I believe crop circles are a part of that preparation.

Andy Thomas, a long-standing researcher, said in a lecture at the Wiltshire Crop Circle Study Group Conference, "Crop circles are here to 'open us up' so we'll experience childlike wonder, whereas opinions shut us down and close our minds. We should not shove our opinions on others, but rather let them discover reasons for themselves. There is valuable information in crop circles, and it's up to *us* to find the meanings. Crop circles are like Rorschach tests—we each interpret them in our own way and project our own meanings on them" (Thomas 1999).

Diahann Krishna (now Diahann Hughes), a young American woman living in the crop circle territory of England, beautifully expressed the personal growth that the crop circles stimulated in her: "Time and experience has [*sic*] brought a merging of the two worlds of the 'mundane' daily life with the magic and mystery surrounding the crop circle phenomenon. It doesn't seem to be a battle between the two states of being anymore, but rather a merging of the two worlds to create something

MID-JULY 2000, JUDY MOORE AND ANDY THOMAS NEAR CROP CIRCLE AT SOUTH FIELD, ALTON PRIORS.

entirely different. It means that I carry the same expectations of 'little miracles' and coincidences to happen around every corner . . . which I never had experienced (or perhaps noticed) before the crop circles became a part of my life. . . .

"There is a definite evolution of thought. . . . This means in a practical sense being willing to talk to people with a wide range of theories and often wild ideas, because it allows me to see the phenomenon from a different perspective than the one I've personally held. That's what we are doing collectively as 'croppies', looking at this phenomenon from a multitude of angles and tossing them around together as we cross paths in formations, on the Internet or over pints in the Barge. Then we go back to our own corners with those tidbits of information to see how they could fit into our own reality paradigm. Oftentimes it's a really uncomfortable fit, but that's what growth is all about." Krishna goes on to suggest that crop circles show us that reality isn't as black and white as we've been told (Krishna 1999, 25:11).

Jürgen Krönig, a long-standing croppie and journalist wrote: "The circles . . . force people to cast off their routine ways of thinking and help to widen their awareness. . . . The psychological effect of the phenomenon has proved to be of a beneficial nature. We live in a time of dramatic technological, economic and political changes. Established world views and religions are losing their credibility and attention. The most important secular religions of our time, scientific materialism and western consumerism, are losing their grip. The deep disillusion with politicians and the political classes all over the western world are an indication of this. . . . The crop circles could never have had such an impact had there not been a crisis of the hitherto dominant world view, based on a materialistic and mechanistic doctrine. But in times when nothing is to be believed any more, it seems that anything can be believed. The crop circle world has certainly delivered enough proof of that . . ." (Krönig, 1994/95, 13:7).

I believe the intelligent forces behind the crop circle phenomenon are intending to get our attention to help us open up our consciousness and develop a new perspective on reality. It seems to want us to let go of our former perceptions and assumptions and to transform ourselves so we can respond to the deteriorating conditions on our home planet. We are not doing enough to save our Earth from destruction, and thus this intelligence is using these beautiful designs in our fields of life-sustaining crops to powerfully wake us up. Whether this intelligence is making the crop circles directly and/or is inspiring or even directing certain humans to make them, the messages are there for us to explore and to learn from. John Michell succinctly called the crop circles "'powerful catalysts in time of revelation'" (Krönig 1994/95, 13:7).

In the words of a wise teacher, Stanley Messenger, "Crop pictograms may well become a next step in the present rapid evolution of channeling pathways, one in which we may be learning to see the written language of the spiritual world" (Messenger 1996). This is further expressed by Native American artist Rod Bearcloud Berry: "They speak in a language that can not be mistaken or misunderstood as they are speaking directly to the hearts and spirit of man" (Berry 1997).

REFERENCES

Ambler, Geoff. 2000. Views: Ambler Gambler. *SC: The Bimonthly Journal of Crop Circles and Beyond* 90 (May/June): 8.

Andrews, Colin. 1992. Musical Tones and Diatonic Ratio: Makings of the Most Important Discovery Yet. *International UFO Library Magazine* 4:10-11.

———. 1993a. Eyewitness Accounts. *Circles Phenomenon Research International Newsletter* 2 (summer): 6-7.

———. 1993b. The Latest from the Circle-makers: Update from the U.K. *Circles Phenomenon Research International Newsletter* 2 (summer): 2.

———. 1994. CPR Research: Brainwave Monitoring in Crop Circle Formations—A Pilot Project. *Circles Phenomenon Research International Newsletter* 3 (Indian summer): 4.

———. 1995. Spiritual Dimensions. *Circles Phenomenon Research International Newsletter* 4 (spring/summer): 13.

———. 1995/96. Points of Interest. *Circles Phenomenon Research International Newsletter* 4 (autumn/winter): 14.

———. 1996a. Japanese UFO and Space Museum. *Circles Phenomenon Research International Newsletter* 5 (spring/summer): 11-12.

———. 1996b. Stonehenge Formation T 444. *Circles Phenomenon Research International Newsletter* 5 (spring/summer): 4.

———. 1996c. T434 and Contactee Information. *Circles Phenomenon Research International Newsletter* 5 (spring/summer): 4.

———. 1996d. Lecture presented at the Glastonbury Symposium, July 26, Glastonbury, Somerset, England.

———. 2000. Colin Andrews' August 2000 Formal Statement on Crop Circles. www.cropcircleconnector.com/cpri/magnetic2000.html

Anka, Darryl. 1996. Channeling of Bashar at the Glastonbury Symposium, July 27, Glastonbury, Somerset, England.

Berry, Rod Bearcloud. 1997. Quoted in *Crop Circle Calendar 1998*. Santa Monica, California: Crop Circle Radius.

————. 1998. Pondering on Koch Fractals. *The Spiral: The Crop Circle Newsletter for Wiltshire* 26 (February): 9.

————. 1999. Letters to The Spiral. *The Spiral: The Crop Circle Newsletter for Wiltshire* 37 (February): 12-13.

Birosik, P.J. 1992. The Great Crop Circle Mystery. *Body Mind Spirit* 52 (May/June): 48-52.

Blake, Francine. 1999. Editorial. *The Spiral: The Crop Circle Newsletter for Wiltshire* 43 (August): 3.

Bloy, Colin. 1996. Lecture presented at the Glastonbury Symposium, July 28, Glastonbury, Somerset, England.

Bord, Janet, and Colin Bord. 1984. *Mysterious Britain: Ancient Secrets of the United Kingdom and Ireland.* London: Paladin Books.

Brocklehurst, Ann. 1999. 5.2 MHz and All That Jazz. *The Cereologist* 24 (spring): 25-26.

Brown, Ken. 1992. White Crow and Grasshopper Warbler. *The Cereologist* 6 (summer): 3-4.

Bunt, Peggy. 1999. The Further Evolution of Consciousness. *SC: The Bimonthly Journal of Crop Circles and Beyond* 87 (November/December): 17-18.

Canada, Steve. 2000. Crop Circles and Egyptian Stars. Radio interview by Ian Punnett. *Coast to Coast A.M.* December 10.

Carr-Smith, Rodney. 1999. Do the 1998 Crop Circles Reflect Global Metanoia? *The Cereologist* 24 (spring): 8-9.

Carvell, Derek. 2000. Personal communication, July 25.

Chapman, James. 1993. Circles Review of 1993. *The Cereologist* 10 (autumn): 12.

Cochrane, Carol. 2000. Lecture presented at the Glastonbury Symposium, July 28, Glastonbury, Somerset, England.

Cosmic Awareness Communications Newsletter. Date unknown. Those Mysterious Gold Plates Discovered Beneath Crop Circles in Germany Which Have the Same Design on Them? 13-14. [P. O. Box 195, Olympia, Washington 98507.]

Dames, Michael.   1976.   *The Silbury Treasure: The Great Goddess Rediscovered.* London: Thames and Hudson.

Delgado, Pat.   1992.   *Crop Circles: Conclusive Evidence?*   London: Bloomsbury Publishing.

Delgado, Pat, and Colin Andrews.   1990.   *Circular Evidence: A Detailed Investigation of the Flattened Swirled Crops Phenomenon.*   London: Bloomsbury Publishing.

De Vita, Caron, and David Schweitzer.   1999.   Researching Bio-photon Testing of Crop Circles. Lecture presented at the Wiltshire Crop Circle Study Group Conference, July 17, Alton Barnes, Wiltshire, England.

Desborough, Brian.   1999.   An Overview of Current Global, Political and Economic News That the Media Doesn't Tell Us. Lecture presented at the Barbara Yates Seminars, October 31, Fountain Valley, California.

Devereux, Paul, and Ian Thomson.   1979.   *The Ley Hunter's Companion, Aligned Ancient Sites: A New Study with Field Guides and Maps.* London: Thames and Hudson.

Douglas, Karen. 2000a. Crop Circles: Their Shapes, Spaces and Effects. In *Crop Circle Year Book 2000*, 2-3. Gosport, Hampshire, England: Temporary Temple Press.

———. 2000b. Crop Circles as Sacred Places. Lecture presented at the Glastonbury Symposium, July 28, Glastonbury, Somerset, England.

Glickman, Michael. 1996a. The Snowflake File. *SC: The Monthly Journal of Crop Circles and Beyond* 57 (October): 3-5, 8-9.

———. 1996b. Lecture presented at the Glastonbury Symposium, July 27, Glastonbury, Somerset, England.

———. 2000. Circle Geometry Revelations. Lecture presented at the Glastonbury Symposium, July 29, Glastonbury, Somerset, England.

Green, Michael. 1991. The Rings of Time: The Symbolism of Crop Circles. In *The Crop Circle Enigma*, ed. Ralph Noyes, 137-171. Revised ed. Bath, England: Gateway Books.

———. 1995. Lecture presented at the Glastonbury Symposium, August 5, Glastonbury, Somerset, England.

———. 1999. The World Tree. *The Cereologist* 24 (spring): 23-24.

———. 2000. Who Are the Crop Circle Makers? Lecture presented at the Glastonbury Symposium, July 29, Glastonbury, Somerset, England.

Greer, Steven, M.D. 2000. ET Contact and UFOs. Lecture presented at the Glastonbury Symposium, July 29, Glastonbury, Somerset, England.

Guiley, Rosemary Ellen. 1997. Crop Circles as Agents for Transformation. Lecture presented at the Power Places Tours Conference, Crop Circles and Stonehenge, July 31, Salisbury, Wiltshire, England.

Haddington, John. 1992. Double Helix. *The Cereologist* 6 (summer): 12.

———. 1993. Enter the Shamans. *The Circular* 4 (June): 20-22.

———. 1995. Synchronous Synchronicities. *The Cerealogist* 14 (summer): 16-17.

Hardy, Mick. 1999. A Plea from the Heart. *The Cereologist* 24 (spring): 6-7.

Harpur, Patrick. 1991/92. A Fairy Whirlwind. *The Cerealogist* 5 (winter): 20-21.

Haselhoff, Eltjo. 2000. Dutch Crop Formations. Lecture presented at the Glastonbury Symposium, July 30, Glastonbury, Somerset, England.

Hawkins, Gerald S., and John B. White. 1965. *Stonehenge Decoded.* London: William Collins.

Hayes, Anna. 1999. *Voyagers: The Sleeping Abductees.* Vol. 1. Columbus, North Carolina: Granite Publishing.

Hein, Simeon, Ph.D. 2000. Electromagnetic Anomalies and Scale-free Networks in British Crop Formations. Unpublished manuscript prepared for Midwest Research, Aurora, Colorado, March 31.

Hesemann, Michael. 1996. *The Cosmic Connection: Worldwide Crop Formations and ET Contacts.* Translated by Sebastian Folborn. Bath, England: Gateway Books. First published in Germany in 1993 as *Botschaft aus dem Kosmos, Neuwied: Verlag die Siberschnur.*

Holden, Dean, and Paul Scott. 1991. Keys to Hidden Doorways. In *Crop Circles: Harbingers of World Change*, ed. Alick Bartholomew, 90-101. Bath, England: Gateway Books.

Hopkins, Budd. 1987. *Intruders: The Incredible Visitations at Copley Woods.* NY: Ballantine Books.

Howe, Linda Moulton. 1993. *Glimpses of Other Realities, Volume I: Facts and Eyewitnesses.* Huntingdon Valley, Pennsylvania: LMH Productions.

———. 2000a. *Mysterious Lights and Crop Circles.* New Orleans: Paper Chase Press.

———. 2000b. Mysterious Lights and Crop Circles. Radio interview by Whitley Strieber. *Dreamland.* December 10.

Hunt, Mary Hykel. 2000. Sacred Labyrinths. Lecture presented at the Glastonbury Symposium, July 30, Glastonbury, Somerset, England.

ilyes. 2000a. Sri Yantra. *The Circular Review* (spring): 9.

———. 2000b. A Hypothesis: The Transmission of a Crop Circle. http://www.cropcircleconnector.com/ilyes/ilyes.html.

Institute for UFO Research. 1998. The Mowing Devil. *UFOCUS: The Newsletter of the Institute for UFO Research* 3 (winter): 9-10.

Janssen, Bert. 2000. *Crop Circle Reconstructions and Geometry.* Gieten, the Netherlands: BJJ Productions.

Jenkins, Ralph. 1999/2000. The Circles of Life or the Laws of the Five Kingdoms. *The Spiral: The Crop Circle Newsletter for Wiltshire* 47 (December/January): 12-14.

King, Jon. 1996. A Conversation with Colin Andrews. Part 1. *UFO Reality* 2 (June/July): 20-24.

Kingston, David. 1996. Lecture during a coach tour for the Glastonbury Symposium, July 26, Glastonbury, Somerset, England.

Kingston, Isabelle. 1991. Word from the Watchers. In *Crop Circles: Harbingers of World Change*, ed. Alick Bartholomew, 146-150. Bath, England: Gateway Books.

Koch, Joachim, and Hans-Jürgen Kyborg. 1997. Lecture presented at the Glastonbury Symposium, August 2, Glastonbury, Somerset, England.

Krishna, Diahann [Diahann Hughes]. 1999. Eating Our Words. *The Cereologist* 25 (summer): 11.

Krönig, Jürgen. 1994/1995. Changing Perceptions of the Circles Myth. *The Cerealogist* 13 (winter): 6-7.

Lundberg, John. 1995. Working Backstage with the Circles: Journey into the Heart of an Anomaly. *The Cerealogist* 14 (summer): 20-22.

Lyons, Jim. 1995. The Physics of Crop Circle Formation: New Developments. *The Cerealogist* 14 (summer): 11.

————. 1996. Rings of Consciousness. Lecture presented at the Glastonbury Symposium, July 27, Glastonbury, Somerset, England.

Meaden, George Terence. 1989. *The Circles Effect and Its Mysteries*. Bradford-on-Avon, England: Artetech Publishing.

Melchizedek, Drunvalo. 1990. *The Ancient Secret of the Flower of Life*. Vol. 1. Flagstaff, Arizona: Light Technology Publishing.

Messenger, Stanley. 1996. Quoted in *Crop Circle Calendar 1997*. Santa Monica, California: Michael Glickman, Patricia Murray, and Wiltshire Crop Circle Study Group.

————. 2000. Speaking from the Heart. Lecture presented at the Glastonbury Symposium, July 30, Glastonbury, Somerset, England.

Michell, John. 1991. Geometry and Symbolism at Barbury Castle. *The Cerealogist* 4 (summer): 24-25.

Miller, Hamish. 1991. Hamish Miller on the Connection with Ancient Sites. In *Dowsing the Crop Circles: New Insights into the Greatest of Modern Mysteries*, ed. John Michell, 17-24. Glastonbury, Somerset, England: Gothic Image Publications.

Miller, Hamish, and Paul Broadhurst. 1998. *The Sun and the Serpent*. Cornwall, England: Pendragon Press.

Morrison, James. 1997. Witnesses to Circles Forming? *The Cerealogist* 19 (summer): 18.

Murray, Patricia. 1997. Demonstration presented at the Glastonbury Symposium, August 2, Glastonbury, Somerset, England.

Newark, Michael. 1997. Notes on the Stonehenge '96 Formation. *The Cerealogist* 19 (summer): 24.

Paget, Peter. 2000. Prologue to the Commentary on the Received Information. Unpublished manuscript prepared for Judith K. Moore, October.

Perkins, David. 1999. High Heat. *The Cereologist* 25 (summer): 3-5.

Pringle, Lucy. 1990. Dowsing: Lucy Pringle Loses Her Pendulum. *The Cereologist* 1 (summer): 4.

———. 1995. Brains and Brawn. *The Cerealogist* 14 (summer): 12-15.

———. 1999. Letters: The Dream. *The Cereologist* 25 (summer): 19.

Quinly, Cariel. 1996. Mysterious Crop Circles. Lecture presented at the San Diego UFO Society, November 24, San Diego, California.

Randall, Shawn. 1997. Torah Speaks on Crop Circles. Channeling transcript, February 3, Encino, California.

Rhone, Christine, Patrick Harpur, Rose Haward, and Jürgen Krönig. 1992. The Circle Making Competition. *The Cereologist* 7 (harvest): 7-9.

Rickard, Bob. 1994. Rings of Ice. *Fortean Times* 74 (April): 22-27.

Ruby, Doug. 1995. *The Gift: The Crop Circles Deciphered.* Cape Canaveral, Florida: Blue Note Books.

Russell, Ron. 2000a. A Lesson in Discernment. *Sedona Journal of Emergence!* 10 (January): 71-74.

———. 2000b. Letters: Russell Hustle. *SC: The Bimonthly Journal of Crop Circles and Beyond* 93 (November/December): 7.

Sayer, John. 1999. Interview: Polly Carson. *The Cereologist* 25 (summer): 12-15.

Schnabel, Jim. 1993. *Round in Circles: Physicists, Poltergeists, Pranksters and the Secret History of the Cropwatchers.* London: Hamish Hamilton.

Sherwood, Kris and Ed Sherwood. 2001. Snapshots from the Edge. Lecture presented at the Mutual UFO Network—Orange County monthly meeting, February 28, Costa Mesa, California.

Silva, Freddy. 1998. Is Sound Behind the Creation of Crop Circles? *The Cereologist* 22 (summer): 18-20.

———. 2000. The Sound of Crop Circles. Lecture presented at the Mutual UFO Network—Los Angeles monthly meeting, October 18, North Hollywood, California.

Sitchin, Zecharia. 1976. *The 12th Planet.* New York: Avon Books.

Snow, Chet. 1992. Vision Quests: Native Prophecies and Crop Circle Symbols in the 1990s. Lecture presented at the Whole Life Expo, September 13, Los Angeles, California.

Sorensen, Peter. 2000. Curving Beams. *The Circular Review* (spring): 7.

Stammers, Jude. 2000. Sacred Sites and Esoteric Wisdom. Lecture presented at the Glastonbury Symposium, July 28, Glastonbury, Somerset, England.

Talbott, Nancy. 2001a. E-mail messages written to cropcircles-2001@yahoogroups.com, between April 16 and April 20.

———. 2001b. E-mail message written to cropcircles2001-@yahoogroups.com, June 27.

Taylor, Sam. 1999. The Night Those UFOs Didn't Land. *Daily Mail* (England), August 7.

Thomas, Andy. 1996. Flaky: The Full Story of the Olivers Castle Video. *SC: The Monthly Journal of Crop Circles and Beyond* 59 (December): 3-12.

———. 1999. Signs and Portents. Lecture presented at the Wiltshire Crop Circle Study Group Conference, July 17, Alton Barnes, Wiltshire, England.

———. 2000a. News: Court in the Act. *SC: The Bimonthly Journal of Crop Circles and Beyond* 93 (November/December): 3.

———. 2000b. News: Crossed Lines. *SC: The Bimonthly Journal of Crop Circles and Beyond* 92 (September/October): 4-6.

———. 2000c. The Sun. Lecture presented at the Wiltshire Crop Circle Study Group Conference, July 15, Devizes, Wiltshire, England.

Tilt, David. 1991. Earth Energies, Leys, Megalithic Man and Grids. In *Crop Circles: Harbingers of World Change*, ed. Alick Bartholomew, 102-122. Bath, England: Gateway Books.

Tomkins, Marjorie. 2000. Blades of Light. *The Spiral: The Crop Circle Newsletter for Wiltshire* 49 (March): 6-11.

Traditional Chinese Medicine World Foundation. 2000. Traditional Chinese Medicine and Crop Circles: A Common Foundation for Energy Healing. *Traditional Chinese Medicine World Foundation Newsletter* (summer).

Tucker, Lindy. 1993. Anomalous Sounds: Another Key to the Crop Circles and UFO's? *Circles Phenomenon Research International Newsletter* 2 (summer): 4-5.

————. 1995. Connecting the Dots: Beeping UFOs and Crop Circles in North America. *The Cerealogist* 14 (summer): 8-10.

Voss, Richard F. 1990. *The Art of Fractals: From Mathematical Monsters to Mountains.* New York: Universe Press.

Wakefield, J.D., and J.D. Wakefield. 1999. *Legendary Landscapes: Secrets of Ancient Wiltshire Revealed.* Marlborough, Wiltshire, England: Nod Press.

Ward, Maria. 1994. Another Interesting Year in the Crop Circle World. *Celestial Contacts* 1 (fall).

Warren, Sharon. 1994. *An Update on 1994 Crop Circles: Getting Our Shift Together.* Arizona Center for Crop Circle Studies, October.

Weiss, Teri. 1994. Crop Circle Enigma. *Body Mind Spirit* (April): 46-47.

Williams, Matthew. 1999. Statement from Matthew Williams. *The Cereologist* 24 (spring): 11-12.

Wingfield, George. 1990a. The Bratton Castle Hoax: Whodunnit and Why. *The Cereologist* 2 (winter): 8-10.

————. 1990b. Ever Increasing Circles. In *The UFO Report 1991*, ed. Timothy Good, 11-40. London: Sidgwick and Jackson.

————. 1991. Towards an Understanding of the Nature of the Circles. In *Crop Circles: Harbingers of World Change*, ed. Alick Bartholomew, 16-43. Bath, England: Gateway Books.

————. 1991/92. The Doug 'n' Dave Scam. *The Cerealogist* 5 (winter): 3, 5-6.

————. 1995a. Crop Circles and Stigmata: Symbols of Divine Origin? *The Cerealogist* 14 (summer): 3-7.

————. 1995b. Editorial notes: The Circlefaker's Story. *The Cerealogist* 14 (summer): 26.

LAIOLIN SPEAKS OF THE CROP CIRCLES

THROUGH JUDITH K. MOORE

The crop circles are a mystery to human beings. Why are the crop circles here, and what do they mean? The purpose of this transmission is to bring information to the public about the highly mystical and technical aspects of the interpretation of these geometric images. The crop circles are fractal formulas of light and sound frequencies encoded into the third dimension as tools for ascension. They are created by the means of light and sound technology interacting with the collective mind. Starships and the Galactic Federation carefully monitor the project.

As the human species evolves, more and more of you become aware of extraterrestrial assistance. In your third-dimensional minds, you tend to oversimplify the cosmic plan and the innergalactic involvement in the dynamics of this precious planet. I am Laiolin, and as a member of the Council of Abborah and keeper of the Records of Ra, it is my privilege and responsibility to bring high-level communications through to assist third-dimensional Earth persons with their evolutionary development. My mission is also to assist in the expansion of your cosmic mind beyond the limited functions permitted by the fear grid that was placed around your planet many eons ago. Expanding the cosmic mind is one aspect of awakening the Planetary Christ, awakening the evolutionary process on Mother Earth and evolving what we call the Eden principle. Other terms for this are *heaven on Earth*, or the *birthing of Gaia*.

This expansion includes the clearing of old negative thought patterns, activating your soul DNA (just as your genetic body has a DNA, your soul has a DNA) and expanding your consciousness beyond what you as a third-dimensional being of light conceived possible during this long dark age of the human soul—the phase that is known as the separation of the oneness or the age of dichotomy. This polarization was part of the holographic drama enacted by necessity. The ancient prophecies speak of the return to oneness; the age of enlightenment is upon us.

These crop circles are present, in part, to activate the cosmic and soul DNA as well as the physical DNA and expand the brain's neurosynapses. This happens when they are viewed through the iris and connected to the brain.

They are messages from your star brothers and sisters, who are assisting this multidimensional, evolutionary journey. Not everyone is going to be capable of understanding all of these transmissions; some are technical and involve terms that are not yet present in the Earth languages. Many of the individuals open to the collective consciousness and the awakening of the cosmic essence on your planet will be able to relate to the language in these transmissions. I wish to empower all of the individuals who share this information. Relating to this information is a useful exercise to expand your cosmic consciousness. Allow yourself to take this information in on a cellular level. Do not expect yourself to understand all the aspects and mysteries contained in this transmission. Experience it, emanate it, vibrate with it and ingest it—by doing so, you will serve humanity immeasurably.

I would like to advise you that there are other valid interpretations of these crop circles. One of the restrictive aspects of the scientific community at large is that it has been structured to limit mental and evolutionary expansion. The scientific community often discovers an equation, a scientific theory or what appears to be an answer to a mystery; unfortunately, they then set it in stone and claim it is the only answer. The universe does not work that way. There are multilevel facets, interpretations and answers to one single equation or

scientific explanation. Science on this planet is primitive or limited. There are those who would think they are advanced, confined by their linear thinking. Universal law is not restricted to linear thinking. If amongst the people who process this information there are those who have different but valid interpretations of these crop circles, we welcome them to bring these ideas and information forth. There is no need for conflict or disagreement on these matters. This is one very important interpretation of a mystery that human beings have sought to answer. Allow your mind to wrestle with it, expand into it and interpret it. The further you go in the journey of the mysteries of these transmissions, the better it will be. Through this process of intellectual and intuitive wrestling, you will be expanding your mental capacities and opening yourself to even further evolutionary development.

It is my purpose to bring the technical information into the third dimension, permitting growth and encouraging understanding of how this mystery fits with the true cosmic expansion and evolution of our beloved Mother Gaia, Mother Earth.

Mother Earth is a cosmic mother, a galactic mother. She is pregnant with a galactic gift. Many of the beings who dwell upon her surface have acknowledged her as the mother of their planetary essence. There is a far greater dynamic to this beautiful green planet than most human beings are aware of. That is why you have attracted so much attention intergalactically. If you could see these transmissions from my perspective, viewing the entire evolutionary plan for the emergence of Eden on Mother Earth, you would realize how very basic this information is. Yet at this point in the time lines of the ancient prophecies, it is very important that this information be circulated to the masses.

These crop circles are geometric fractal patterns and mathematical formulas. Everything that exists is a fractal of a geometric pattern—the crop circles are those geometric patterns. The star glyphs are a star language of light and codes for these activations. Linking these two images optimizes the activation of the DNA.

Combining meditation with the star glyphs and crop circles will assist in the activation of the divine potential to receive this information and activate the creative consciousness within humanity's collective consciousness. The collective mind is a powerful force that forms the dream field within the third-dimensional reality. The effect of engaging in this process will make quantum evolutionary leaps in the collective mind of the planetary essence.

Opening up your consciousness to the patterns, interpretations and transmissions will spark the collective mind. It is most important to remember to come from your heart in all matters; it is the profound power of unconditional love that is the catalyst for all universal transformations. Each person who reads these interpretations and meditates on the star glyphs and crop circles will be assisting in the evolutionary process of the collective mind-heart. Once activated, it will permit the transmission of the technical data necessary to accomplish these various evolutionary processes. We must seed the collective mind with expanded potential.

CROP CIRCLE LOCATIONS

It is important to discuss the geographic locations of the crop circles and the effect of these gifts on your planet. Primarily, the location for each crop circle was carefully calculated by a geophysicist in the Galactic Federation. Each crop circle was projected onto the surface of the planet at key trigger points of the living body of Mother Gaia with extremely advanced technology, blocked from intervention by the elements that would keep the planet in fear.

The locations are critical and have been calculated in respect to the galactic and universal counterparts of the living body of Mother Gaia. The map of your planet, the great Cosmic Mother, is a locator for other galaxies. As your planet heals and comes to peaceful resolution, so too will other universes and galaxies.

Consider this expansive phenomenon as it relates to the crop circles. The crop circles are light and sound frequencies of mathematical formulas for ascension, or the emergence of Eden. Beneath each crop circle are crystalline geometric implants that are triggered by those frequencies. This work is completed and anchored before the field is mowed, and the frequencies are effective for some time after it is mowed.

It does not matter if the crop circles are immediately destroyed. This does not hinder the effect of the activations. Once the frequencies are set in a specific location and the image is created, the effect is set into motion. Some of the crop circle frequencies need to be felt for a period of time to resonate frequencies on specific grid points and ley lines in the areas where they were created. Let me explain: All is in perfect order; those that needed to stay did, and the ones that were immediately cut had completed the purpose of their creation.

The medium of crops lends itself well to our purposes. We do not want them to remain etched in stone, but to enter the chain of life through food sources. We are emitting these frequencies and formulas into the food chain to enhance abundance and to affect the source of nourishment multidimensionally.

Why do the majority of crop circles occur in Great Britain? The answer is simple. Where does point zero in the time zones begin and why? Why was one of the major seats of world power and domination in Great Britain? Why was it the throne of England that almost conquered the world? Why does this very small nation have so much power? Why is it a critical power spot for the plan for a new world order? Whichever party controls point zero has tremendous power on the planet. Therefore, we chose this location as a source of liberation for this precious planet.

It is essential to understand the dichotomy that Earth is experiencing. To do this, I wish for you to envision the spider on the mirror. Each destructive force has an equally powerful creative force. This is called the law of cause and effect. There is no good or evil; all are part of God. By the rule of dichotomy, there is literally a counterbalance for each agency and entity that would rule the planet in fear. For example, government is not bad or good, the church is not bad or good—each is like the spider on the mirror. The Masons and the Knights Templar are prime examples of this. Now, contemplate once more the location of the majority of the crop circles. Ah! Perhaps we see the light. The location is critical to the process.

THE INDIVIDUAL'S SACRED GEOMETRY AS IT AFFECTS THE FORMULA

The psychatronic resonance the crop circles emit (measurable in quantum physics) is affected by the chemical balance of the brain-wave patterns of each individual who enters them. The top right quadrant of the brain is the center for this unique effect. This quadrant is the most sensitive to the collective mind. Each individual has unique brain frequencies that resonate with the harmonic energy of the collective mind, both within your planet and intergalactically. The alchemical aspect of this process is the biochemical reaction between the wave-pattern frequencies of the crop circles, the wave-pattern frequencies of brain-cell activity and the qualities of the geographic location where the crop circle is created.

As certain individuals travel from the location of the circle to sacred sites, particularly to sacred springs, their energy is introduced to the larger sacred geometries of the area. These sacred spots have been historically primed by ceremonies and prayers to interact with these energies, producing maximum effects.

TECHNICAL ASPECTS OF CROP CIRCLE CREATION

There seems to be much interest in the details of the ET technology used to create these cosmic gifts. The frequency patterns are carefully engineered on Arcturian motherships under the careful scrutiny of the Galactic Federation. The team of researchers and physicists is chosen from a pool of scientists dedicated to the principles of cosmic peace and the interdimensional evolution of the Christ consciousness. The elements utilized for the formation of these patterns are delicately balanced formulas that include physical locations on specific energy lines and energy formulas that have been prepared over millennia for this purpose and refined until the desired effect is produced. Biochemical formulas of fractal essences of light and sound frequencies are accompanied by planetary alignment frequencies.

The motherships relay frequencies through beaconing devices to a pattern of starships positioned in key grid points in the biosphere. The signals are then relayed to a local transmitting station where their frequencies electromagnetically supercharge local energy systems. There is also a process of integrating the DNA and sacred geometries of humans present in the area who have responded to the cosmic call.

Once this integration is complete, a microgenerator beams the accumulated energy frequencies into the core life energy cells of each of the grains in the crop. This hyperenergetic frequency within the grain is used to energetically fund the process of making the crop circle. [Author's note: I met a researcher in a crop circle who told me that we do not have technology

advanced enough to detect such energy shifts.] Energetic waves, much like microwaves, utilizing creative energy patterning, are then beamed into the sandstone layers of rock, causing a surging of water under the location of the proposed crop circle. The water is then heated with the energy beams, creating a mist or vapor that softens the stem of the plant. This makes it more pliable, allowing it to bend and form to create the pattern. The number and layers of grain, the direction for the lay of the stems, the quality of the atmosphere and the type of crop are all factors.

The military has attempted to imitate this process, but since they use microwaves, their circles destroy life prana rather than create delicate formulas of ascension frequencies. These crop circles are neutralized by starships, deactivating the potentially harmful emanations of disrupting frequencies that emanate from the patterns and restructuring them to actually emanate supportive, rather than destructive, frequency patterns.

One form of technology implemented in the creation of these precious images is the subconscious agreement with humans to create man-made circles. The man-made circles are primitive and not as delicate as the circles created with light and sound frequencies and assisted on a cosmic plane. However, they are useful. These humans carry specific frequency codes, alchemical formulas in their DNA, that emanate into the crop formation. Following the creation of a man-made circle, the starship technologists emanate frequencies through the crop's biochemical structure to enhance the energetics and activate local time capsules within the ethereal. These are indeed valuable creations and contribute to the formulas for ascension that the project is destined to complete.

STAR GLYPHS

The star glyphs are the universal language of light of the great Records of Ra. The Records of Ra are the universal records of the Mother/Father/God, preserved within the light frequencies of the Great Central Sun. This precious language has been preserved through the long dark night of the soul of Mother Gaia by means of encoding the DNA of the members of the House of David. This universal language is a forgotten mystery that has not been part of the collective unveiling until now. It was partially known in the mystery schools, but to protect it until the time of emergence was at hand, this precious language of light was not fully revealed.

These images imprint on the neurosynapses and are encoded in your DNA. The transmissions are the basic translations of the star glyphs. The glyphs contain far more information than the transmissions do. The languages of the glyphs are extensive and deep reaching. Their images are actually created in a form that is usable to the psyche. In the Records of Ra, these images are pure sound and light frequencies.

Your brain will be expanded beyond the limited ten percent that most humans currently use and will interpret the signals into light and sound frequencies that will emanate from you, the crystalline receiver of this gift. You basically will act as a radio transceiver as this encoded information is downloaded into your brain—a magnificent tool little used until recent evolutionary expansions of the neurosynapses in many awakened ones. This will serve a dual purpose: as you are a tool for activation of the collective, so too will you receive transmissions for your ascension from the varied glyphs.

Each glyph is a living library of information being released into the collective mind of the universal consciousness. Each of you has a personal star glyph and temple name from the ancient House of David to be used as mantras. Your personal star glyph is your cosmic soul blueprint; there are never two alike. Each is unique and different, just as each cell is a unique creation of the Mother/Father/God. These star glyphs, in combination with the crop circle images, are what you might understand to be an alchemical formula for the activation of a vital pulsar code, a wonderful gift for the emergence and awakening.

THE MYSTERIES OF THE GRAIL

Ah, my sweet ones, how long have you searched in one form or another for the Holy Grail? The Grail will be revealed as it truly exists within the deepest mysteries of the archetype of the human soul. Known to you is the legend that the Grail is the cup that carries the blood of the beloved Christ Jesus. Now is the time to reveal its essence. The blood carries the full spectrum of the evolved human DNA. This one incarnated with the full DNA code for the awakening and activation of the new paradigm, the evolved species and full activation of the Eden principle. Did he not state, "As I have done so you shall do, only greater"? Encoded within his DNA are the cosmic blueprints for full activation in fractal codes.

The taking of the holy sacrament was historically tainted by the energy of the death fear, as in references to the consumption of blood and flesh. This process of holographically ingesting and revitalizing this pulsar code of the Christ is, in purity, an important ceremony for keeping the psyche of the collective mind conscious of a cosmic principle vastly beyond the comprehension of the human mind. Ceremony keeps alive the vital essence, the structure of the symbolism, allowing vast concepts to be retained in simplified actions that the collective can retain without having to access the entire library of complicated cosmic fractal formulas.

The Grail exists and is being carefully protected, as it carries these cosmic codes that must be physically present in the third-dimensional hologram. There are a number of aspects of the Grail that must be activated prior to the completion of the fractal formula of cosmic creation.

All of the parts of the formula are present in the Grail and have been encoded in your mythologies to keep an ever-present awareness in the psyche of the masses of the vast principle of this cosmic plan. They have been maintained in code words in the psyche of your mythologies. Some well-known code words are: the House of David, the Ark of the Covenant, King Arthur and the Round Table, Camelot, the Buddha, the Christ, the bodhisattva, namasté, Mitakyue Oyasin, White Buffalo Calf Pipe Woman, Quan Yin, the Virgin

> Your personal star glyph is your cosmic soul blueprint; there are never two alike. Each is unique and different just as each cell is a unique creation of the Mother/Father/God.

of Guadalupe, the divine marriage, Shangri-la, eureka!, Eden, the holy child, the sacred twins and the Tree of Life.

Each of these mythologies is an energy field existing in the collective mind. The energy frequencies carry codes that are part of the cosmic formula for the activation of the Eden principle. The Grail, the blood of Christ, carries not a piece of the formula but the entire DNA code for the full activation of the Eden project. I have mentioned well-known mythologies; within all societies of man, there are like paradigms. All are pieces to the larger fractal formula for the cosmic activation of the Eden principle.

The physical cup of the Grail has been kept and protected by the Knights Templar. They are the true servants of the Arthurian Council, the earthly embodiment of the thirteen solar temples of the Great Central Sun. Much wizardry has been implemented to carefully protect the true Grail. Refer to the original tarot for partial understanding. The Grail is a vessel that carries the fractal vital pulsar DNA codes also carried in the blood of the Christ. The Ark of the Covenant is a powerful generator with the capacity of extremely advanced technology, truly unknown on the Earth plane. It is the activation chamber for the codes carried within the Grail. To simplify, the Ark is the computer and the Grail is the program. Specific aspects of the formula must be completed before full activation can be attained. The final countdown leading to full activation is between the years 2000 and 2013. The crop circles are the fractal jewels, the holographic representation of this entire project called the Eden principle. All of these formulas are encoded within the Grail.

CROP CIRCLE CHANNELING
JUNE 26, 2001

The Arcturian mothership is standing by, and we have databases available that will be tapped into to provide explanations, as the Arcturians are the engineers of the crop circle phenomenon. We are not the only ones who are manifesting in this solar system, for it is one of the segments of the vital projects carried on by the Galactic Federation. The Arcturians are the engineers of frequencies for this planet as she manifests more than a pole shift, more than an electromagnetic frequency energy shift, but a complete transfiguration of mass and matter. Therefore, it is important to mention that we are assisted by scientific teams from Orion, the Pleiades, Arcturus, the Dogon and others whose names you wouldn't recognize, who are members of the Council of Rytaar. Within this project we have made no distinction between the spiritual realm and you Earth beings (although you are not individually, any of you, purely Earth beings). The team includes ET technicians, scientists and cosmologists. Crop circles are a form of divine intervention.

LAYING DOWN THE CROP

What are the actual mechanics that set up a design, and how does the crop get laid down so specifically, so that even one blade of wheat can make a difference in the pattern?

The Arcturian mothership is based far out of this solar system in the seven stars of the Big Dipper. We have transcended time and space and do not need to worry about light, sound, the speed of light and these primitive restrictions, for we can manifest through the dimensions. And there is instantaneous connection between the mothership and this project.

There are schematics, blueprints and designs of each crop circle in the mothership, in crystalline chambers of light that project a holographic image, which is a fractal formula of the light and sound frequencies of each crop circle. These are Mandelbrot sets; they are a fractal of a fractal, replicated beyond the limited mathematics that are present on this planet. The formulas of ascension are created in these crystalline chambers. You may think of them as pods on the mothership.

Then the design is holographically projected through the dimensions, into the dream field or the hologram of the third dimension. This is assisted by ships of the Galactic Federation. The Galactic Federation is the intergalactic United Nations, without contamination of ulterior motives of power. These ships are relay stations posted in this solar system. They pick up the frequency codes as they are holographically projected from the mothership. These relay stations work as transformers to magnify the energy and adjust the frequencies to the Earth's electromagnetic frequency grid. We need to gradually bring in frequency codes that are not presently in Earth's dream field. We cannot bring in the full shock, for it would shatter the core structure of mass and matter of this planet. Basically, it would be like dropping a crystal glass on the floor. It would manifest in billions of pieces, and we would have what is termed a supernova. We do not wish to create Earth into a supernova; therefore, these electromagnetic frequencies are minutely introduced and monitored from the ships stationed in your solar system.

The crop circle is broadcast from the mothership into relay stations, which are transformers, in order to step down the frequencies; the ships then monitor them in minute fractals. The last ship is a beaming device that beams a hologram of the formulas in the Mandelbrot set in frequencies of light and sound, and the hologram enters the orbital field of this planet. This hologram has been screened or shielded from visual interpretation. As it is vibrational, it does not manifest into the optic nerve until it is very near the surface of the planet. The optic nerve of human beings is being evolved, and there are those of you who are able to see light phenomena (sometimes you catch it in cameras, the light phenomena has been seen in videos), but the normal or unevolved optic nerve does not perceive these holograms as they enter into the Earth's orbital field. Frequently, in the areas where these circles appear, there are manifestations of what they have termed to be swirling light fields. This is the original creation that is being witnessed.

Now remember, scientists have witnessed nebulae, cosmic fields of swirling energy. These are being manifested in the light-frequency inclusions that have been witnessed over the crop circles. This happens just prior to the implementation of the formulas. At that point, there are heat generators, or laser-like microwaves, that bring warmth into the area. Please understand that your species will evolve beyond the use of microwaves, which are extremely damaging to the inner cellular structure of the nebulae of atomic mass and matter. So when I refer to these laser-like microwave light beams, they are exactly the opposite of microwaves. For they are beamed in the original creation and nourish the cellular components of mass and matter within the subatomic structures.

So these microwave light beams act in some ways like Earth microwave energy, but it has a nourishing instead of destructive function?

That is correct. Many individuals who have been channeling and receiving high-level communication suddenly feel their body temperature rise; that is that manifestation of the cosmic creation. There is another way to explain this: for the sperm and the ovum to unite to create life, it must be a certain temperature. That temperature is manifest from cosmic creation within the womb of a woman, and it allows the fertilization. It is like a greenhouse effect. We actually have manifested the light frequencies from your Sun into resonant vibratory energy fields in this greenhouse effect. This draws moisture in these crop circles and causes steam to rise.

That steam frequently implodes the nodules in the grain within the structure of the wheat stem. There is an injunction of the life-fiber resonant field force that is being activated, as in a tiny burst of light, from using the life prana within the organism. It manifests as a spark of creative energy. This is the God-seed that sparks life, that sparks the source of cosmic creation, and it implodes, resulting in a minute hole in the stem.

The energy activates the basic life force that's in the plant already, and it blows up and the heat comes from that?

The heat is manifest in the greenhouse effect, which then emanates into the Earth, drawing moisture that comes up in the form of steam.

Human intellect would like to be able to conceive that the steam softens the plants, allowing pliability, which is true. That is part of the process. But it also breaks down the very subatomic structure of mass and matter, restructuring the cellular components and altering the DNA and the physical form of the substance used, thus creating the pattern. Literally, these fields are being shifted into a form that transcends mass and matter. That is why it is such perfection.

CROP CIRCLES AND EARTH ENERGETICS

Is there a deliberate function of using ley line energy in this?

Remember that all creation shifts from the cosmic essence and then manifests in the physical form. So once this manifests in the form of a geometry set in the crops, that is one aspect of its creation. But the aspect that is not witnessed is the holographic implantation of the formulas in the full Mandelbrot set, created in the crystalline chambers I spoke of. These are implemented or anchored into the Earth's ethers through ley lines. The crop circle is merely for visual confirmation that something important has happened. What you don't see are the frequencies being anchored within the Earth's energetics, in the ethers.

There is some very important information about the time capsules implanted in crop circle areas. We literally mapped out areas by which we could manifest these formulas and connect the frequencies into these previously implanted crystalline structures.

Now then, the time capsules are located on the Earth's grid and ley lines. There are energy lines that have not yet been described by your scientists. There is a web of light, like the Earth's fiber optics. They have been able to track what is called the Earth's grid and ley lines, but there is an energetic web system that connects all frequency points on the Earth similar to the schematic of an acupuncture chart of the human body. There are twelve major meridians, and there are vital links where the meridians cross, such as the Mary and Michael Line. There are acupuncture points all over the body and many, many in the ears. They say that the whole human body can be accessed from the ear. England is the ear of Mother Earth.

You see, England has links to points for the entire planet. Imagine the energetic chart of Mother Earth like an acupuncture chart for the human body, with the ear carrying all codes on all frequencies. So when we want to implement a particular effect in Peru, we will bring an energy field into that point location on the ear of the Earth, which is the United Kingdom.

Now, there are major centers that are vibrant in other locations, and we must manifest physical emanations of these circles in other locations all over this planet. But since the ear of the Earth carries every single point location for the whole planet, the U.K. became very important for this project. Please also understand that a pyramid of light sits upon this country called England. This pyramid transcends the realms of all potential. Why do you think such a small nation could nearly dominate the entire planet? Certainly, the United Kingdom is very small compared to India, over which she ruled. So understand that the power of this ear of the Earth is a concentration of the lifelines of Mother Earth herself. You could say that this is the transmitting station center for Mother Earth.

So, the field right across the street from Stonehenge has effects that go to certain places? Anna Hayes said that the influence of a crop circle can spread thousands of miles.

That is correct. During the times of the Druids, there were individuals that came from all over the planet. When a technician from Peru wanted to be in Stonehenge, they didn't have to go on a boat across the ocean; they entered the portals and emerged. There was interdimensional travel. Individuals from the centers of the vital twelve temples of the House of David all over the planet would meet at Stonehenge in great gatherings to set the energy matrix and establish these connections. There were ceremonies that have been removed from the history of the planet, when there were invasions and destructions during the Inquisition. These ceremonies set the matrix for this phenomenon. [Judith received a spontaneous channeling at the crop circle near Stonehenge during her visit in July 2000 (see Appendix A).]

The Mandelbrot is the basic template for that kind of formula. Within ET technology, we have gone beyond what your electron microscopes can observe. The universe can be contained within one microchip— one microchip of energy! So please consider the concept of microchips. These are frequencies that are being emanated intergalactically. You understand?

"As above, so below" is the bottom line of everything. Everything is contained within everything; the little is the whole.

The locations of the sand circles that have appeared in the deserts are particularly important, because some of these sand circles manifest over ancient temples that have been buried by the dunes in the Sahara and other great deserts. We described the temples of the House of David before the molten period of the planet [see Appendix B], but what I am speaking of now is the time of Mu and Lemuria. There were cities of light that were beautiful manifestations in the region of what is known now as the Sahara. The temple walls are opal and jewels of lapis, beautiful golden hallways such as have never been discovered on this Earth plane. Although Egypt is a very important center for activity, it is not even understood by your Earth historians. The ones who have started to discover the truth of

Egypt have been repressed. Egypt is a minor Arcadia compared to what exists under the Sahara. There are phenomenal temples of light beneath those dunes, and when those temples were active and resonating in full manifestation of their glory, they encoded time capsules that were made dormant. These time capsules are being activated through the formulas being implemented in those areas by sand circles.

There are also important cities of light within the mountains of Nepal and in Siberia, where the energy appears as ice circles. That is why the Siberian shamans are so important in the shamanistic energy that has held this planet. Therefore, there are again dormant energy fields in this area of Siberia. Manifestations of phenomenal geometric forms are being laid down in areas where no man's eye will ever see. So I would say to the readers of this manuscript, be grateful and appreciative for the manifestations that you are blessed to see, for some of the most phenomenal creations will never be seen. Some of them are laid down, and then the wind blows them away; or the Sun melts them away; or some of them are actually being implemented into the Atlantean temples through the Bermuda triangle, through areas around Hawaii, through high-spirited vibrational areas in the ocean. Perhaps a passing ship might see a special wave when the sun sparkles on the water . . . but they do not witness the patterns that are being set down.

Some of these formulas must be quickly implemented. Laser technology is very important in this greenhouse effect, but we go beyond the laser technology that has manifested on the Earth plane. A laser beam comes from the ship, manifesting as a sequence of frequencies. Some of them come in a fractal of a second, unmeasurable by your time lines of Earth, by linear time. But it is this quick spark that activates a vital force on this planet.

Other formulas resonate in the vibrational frequencies after the fields are mowed, because we have set a time capsule into motion that will affect the elements of cosmic creation for you, this beloved Mother Earth. So, depending on our formula, either a minute manifestation of a laser frequency or a time capsule is implemented.

Is there some kind of storage list of all the time capsules with the plan of action?

It's called a schematic, and it is a blueprint that has been encoded in the Records of Ra from the Great Central Sun. All light encodements to help with the ascension of the planet were taken from the plan of creation and manifested into templates in schematics or blueprints on the mothership. This was all set up for this time frame on Earth, to help move you into what I would call the fifth dimension.

HOAXED CIRCLES

I am supporting the statement, there are no hoaxed circles. They are all part of the phenomenon. The crystalline codes within the DNA of each individual creating a man-made circle are part of a formula, the alchemical formula of the frequencies emanated in these manifestations. Remember that the brain is an electromagnetic energy field of neural synapses. Within the encodement of the crystalline DNA of every individual, there is dormant DNA.

The individual "hoaxer's" energy fields become part of the formula. We encourage human activation, activity and involvement with the making of some circles. Human involvement doesn't make them hoaxed, because the energy fields are manifested as we desire them, following the creation.

Human beings have been indoctrinated on this planet to consider themselves to be less than the great masters and to always look to a master to lead them to the kingdom of heaven. But the master now is awakening within the heart of every being on Mother Earth. Now, in consideration of that, many of these individuals considered to be "hoaxers" carry pieces of the houses of light that are very important for our purposes. These formulas have been developed through bloodlines that they carry both in the physical incarnation of their genetics and in the soul journey, and they become intricate parts of the frequency formulas that are being emanated for our purposes with these crop circles.

Human interaction in the creation of some of the crop circles is absolutely vital. Meditation groups have focused on a Celtic glyph, and it appears in a circle. The crop circles are multidimensional, and many of these things on ships have multidimensional aspects. We are not they; they are not us. We are here. We are not waiting for the ETs to come. We are they, and you are they, and everyone on the planet has carried lineages. Don't you think that many of the people from other solar systems come here to breed with humans? That is why you have stories of the goddesses and the gods coming to have children here. So they carry the DNA to many of the star lineages, first of all. Would this not be part of the plan? Besides, there are many walk-ins and star-seeded individuals. And not just the kind of walk-ins where a person dies and leaves his body, then another soul takes over. There are many coexistent walk-ins, some of them not conscious of their multidimensional aspects, who are part of the formula.

But we have to have a merry game. Again, we go back to the paradigm that the Hopi elder spoke of. This is the Coyote Waterway, and Merlin rules this house of magic. To create Merlin's law, which rules in the United Kingdom, we must have the full stance, mustn't we? It is part of the formula. So they must go on about their debates and their challenges, and Michael Glickman and Matthew Williams must have their challenges [plate 61].

Matthew can create the star, and then the formulas can be emanated into the frequency patterns as was planned. Please rise above separation and realize it is all part of the divine plan.

Once we realize that there is not a single hair out of place, we will know it is all part of the divine creation, in which human beings and star families come together to become the actors and actresses. All these professional croppies have all incarnated together. They're all one family, and it's one team. They may look like they squabble, but they're all sisters and brothers and are actually very familiar to each other.

All the world's a stage, and all the men and women merely actors. So although individuals may not be conscious of their intergalactic connection, they might have a parallel lifetime as one of the technicians on the ships. Humans will begin to realize that they are not one existence. You are multidimensional beings and many of you have parallel lifetimes in other dimensions and as ETs, as manifest beings of light. It is all part of the cosmic plan.

ANOMALOUS LIGHTS AND OTHER PHENOMENA

What about the anomalous lights?

Some of the light phenomena are the emanation of the frequencies forming the circles; others are the lightbodies of the ascended masters come to Earth. Some of them are what the Native Americans call Tunkashilas, the spiritual beings of this land, the ancient ones, the ancestors of this land, manifest in their lightbody form. So these are energies.

Is there a relationship between the increasing complexity of the crop circles and the increasing frequencies of the Earth? Are they the creators?

The template comes down and they appear in order to create a vibrational-frequency field from their gift. In other words, they have come to bring their gift, which they have manifested through creation, to these beautiful, beautiful formulas. So as the formula is being formed and this process we have described is manifesting, then an entity, an ascended master, an ancient goddess, god or spirit—perhaps one of the members of a council of light—comes and brings their gift and introduces their spiritual gift into the formula.

So when you see these, honor them, for they are beings, they are lightbodies that have not manifested in human, physical form. They had a cosmic destiny appointment to show up there at that time, to help set the energies for that particular formula and bring their gift from their ancient ways, from the temples of Egypt, from the ancient mystery schools. But they are the ones you so rarely see, who travel amongst you. For the humans always want to look for the prophet who stands before them as a human, when in fact the great masters walk amongst them, invisible to the human eye but not the heart. They are always visible to the heart. That's the same thing that crop circles are, too. They're a visible manifestation of an energetic packet that's waiting there anyway.

The potential was all part of the cosmic blueprint from the records of the Great Central Sun, the records of cosmic creation. Some people call it the Mother/Father God.

What are the humming sounds associated with crop circles?

The crop circles are made by both light and sound frequencies. From the source of divine creation, light and sound are not separate. When they enter the third dimension, they refract.

These sound phenomena carry as many intricate, complex messages as their visual counterparts, and they are more expansive than what is contained in these transmissions. It is important to remember that the crop circles are multidimensional and multifaceted. These transmissions carry only a facet of their entire message.

The frequencies emanating into the crop circle are expanding the sound continuum for the planetary octave in increments of eight octaves, creating the new golden octave.

There are photographs of what sound currents can create in malleable matter, like sand and water. At a low frequency, they just look like circles, and at a higher frequency, they can go out and become stars. Crop circles have shown up that look exactly like those pictures.

That is correct. Go back to what I said about the monitoring stations that transmit minute increases in the vibrational field and monitor the Earth's vibrational field. For as the Earth's energy intensifies, these frequency adjustments are very important. As the frequencies increase, the complexity of the circles increase. So the Earth becomes able to tolerate a greater frequency coming down.

Remember, we do not want to shatter that crystal glass, but rather transform mass and matter. Therefore, as the Earth ascends into a higher vibrational frequency, she can receive more advanced formulas of light and sound. They had to be simple to begin with, to resonate a vibratory field and begin the transmutation of the basis of elemental mass and matter.

A powerful way of enlightenment began in the year 1967 and then was maximized around the time of the Harmonic Convergence in 1987. But 1967 was the first portal opening for this awakening. And if you look into the research, you will discover that the increased reporting of crop circles happened in the '70s, because the manifestation of 1967 brought in the Christ consciousness.

There are many teachings about what is called the spine of Turtle Island (the North and South American continents) and the prophecies of the manifestation of the fifth world of peace to this precious continent. The place where these circles manifested is a vital pulsar point to stimulate the spine of Turtle Island and was an activation of the original creation, or the primal blueprint, which had to be activated on a pulsar point, connected to Turtle Island. This then created an energy matrix that released encodements through the planetary ethers, to manifest all of the things that were in 1967, this wave of awakening and the flower children and the peace movement.

This place was chosen because the prophecies have clearly spoken that the beginning and the manifestation of many of the teachings that have been held as sacred trust come from Turtle Island. There's been a stepping up of what the energy of the Earth can take, and the crop circles are one of the ways of anchoring those frequency increases in order to communicate through the whole etheric system of the Earth.

EXPLORING THE CROP CIRCLES AND STAR GLYPHS

LAIOLIN THROUGH JUDITH K. MOORE

The corresponding color plates for each of the following transmissions can be found in the color section beginning on page I. Black and white photos of the crop circles along with their corresponding star glyphs are in "Practical Use of Crop Circles and Star Glyphs," beginning on page 169.

PLATE 1. WOODBOROUGH HILL, ALTON PRIORS, JULY 11, 1997

This is the web woven by the precious one who is named Grandmother Spider by some Native Americans. She is the weaver of all creation. She takes the silver and gold threads from the cosmic mind-heart of Creator God and weaves the tapestries of divine potential. She has sent her messengers, the Talking Gods, to the Diné, or Navajo, Grandmother. They have placed their mark upon the Earth. She who has received the message has been protected by her people.

The Diné people carry a sacred gift. This gift is part of the tapestry woven by Grandmother Spider: the mandala of world peace. Each of the global tribal nations carries a piece of the matrix of the mandala of peace. They are to come together as the Rainbow Nation, yet stand strong in their own traditions. They are to sing together, for each one carries a piece of the song of creation. When the song is sung in a beautiful way, peace will be born on Earth.

Grandmother Spider has spoken through the petroglyphs of the southwestern United States. The clan of the beautiful people, the Diné, has protected the messages of the Talking Gods. They are the keepers of the lamb, the singers of the dawn songs. They are the keepers of this sacred trust, and so it is.

This star glyph depicts the womb of Grandmother Spider. It is a fulfillment of the Hopi prophecy: "When the grandmothers speak, the planet will heal." It is foretold that there will be peace between the Hopi and Diné peoples, as there will be between all nations. It is foretold that the stripping of the precious sacred sites of these tribal nations for the blood of the Mother—coal and oil—shall cease.

PLATE 2. BARBURY CASTLE, MAY 3, 1997

This crop circle is a familiar pattern, recognizable as the Kabbalah or the great Tree of Life of the Jewish tradition. It is of the same essence as the Great White Roots of Peace of the Iroquois Confederacy. The mystical Tree of Life is the essential pattern for balance within all dimensions. This tree is rooted with all other cosmic trees of peace. They are truly a reflection of one another; they are one tree. The essence of these sacred trees of life cannot be corrupted, but is protected even unto death by the wisdom keepers. Because of this, the balance is held for the entire planet. These trees are in physical manifestation within the incarnate lord of peace, the keeper of faith, the great being, El Tule Tree, in the valley of Oaxaca, Mexico. In 1987, the guardians of the Earth, the earth spirits, emerged from this Cosmic Tree of Peace.

The Cosmic Tree of Peace has been seeded by the White Eagle and has emerged from the Cave of the Great Cobra. The resurrection of the spirits of the indigenous victims of genocide began in August 1998. The souls of these beloved ones are being set free.

The resurrection of the indigenous medicine bundles (globally) began at the time of the Grand Cross Alignment in August 1999. Now the ancient ones come singing and gather beneath the Cosmic Tree of Peace to dance the snake dance. The Rainbow Nation, people of all nations, will come together in unity through diversity. The people of Earth will unite to bring about peaceful change. The Rainbow Nation will celebrate the holy marriage of the alpha and the omega and do a spiral dance to touch the Great White Roots of Peace in the year 2012. This is the ancient prophecy that is spoken of in the language of this star glyph.

This is the unified principle of the power awakened within the Cosmic Tree of Peace, united in all dimensions. This is the formula for the full union of the trees of peace that share one root. This is the movement in union and divine balance of cosmic forces that have been foretold by the ancient ones. This is the time we have so long awaited.

PLATE 3. MILK HILL, ALTON BARNES, AUGUST 8, 1997

This crop circle is the Flower of Life, the Flower of Creation, the seeds of the awakening of the House of David [see Appendix B]. This beautiful geometry speaks of the coming renaissance of sacred art, theater, music and architecture, and the return of the sacred gardens of Eden. These are the delightful gifts that will greet the children of the awakening as they go to the marketplaces and dance in the streets. The songs will be heard in elevators and cafés across the globe. The art will be seen on television screens, in galleries and in humble homes. Everywhere there will be a springing forth of the gifts of Eden for the people to enjoy in beauty.

This is the matrix for the renaissance that began in 1996. This gift will manifest in joy, and the comedians of the world will begin to teach the principles that Jesus the Christ taught as he walked on Earth. It will be with joy and laughter that the hearts will open to the gifts of the Holy Spirit while angels sing in ecstasy. It will be with such mirth that the wounded hearts will heal each time a gift is bought or an angel card sent in times of mourning. The gifts will infiltrate the market and gradually recondition the psyche of the masses to receive the gifts of the Holy Spirit in their hearts. They will flood from the cornucopias of the nations of abundance to the humble homes of the meager. The wealth will be shared, and the beauty will flow in all nations of the world.

This is the gift of the Flower of Life, the Star of David in the double hexahedron. The laughter of the children will fill the dark corners of the ghettos of great cities and the desolate corners of the republics of China and Siberia. That which was wrought to destroy will be used to heal. Once again, beauty will be the way of the world and the song of life for God's children.

PLATE 4. AVEBURY TRUSLOE, AUGUST 9, 1994

This crop circle is the insignia of the high priestess of the Temple of Giza. She is the one who went to the desert and communed with Jesus the Christ during his forty-day sojourn. In that lifetime, she came to him as a raven. She is the goddess of Exad (pronounced ee`shäd) of the Temple of Giza; she has reincarnated. She emerged from the Cave of the Great Cobra, a priestess of the serpent clan.

This crop circle is the insignia of the awakening of the thirteen moons of Giza. This is the prediction of the recovery of the thirteen temples of the Moon that will be unveiled within the times of the emergence of Mother Gaia through point zero. The power of this awakening will vastly affect the awakening of the goddess energy on Mother Earth.

Thirteen levels beneath the pyramid of the great serpent in Chichén Itzá, the seven sacred virgins dwell in the house of the priestess of Exad, from the Temple of Giza. In the Mayan lifetime, she was temple priestess of the crescent moon, the embodiment of the goddess Ix Chel. She dwelt with these seven sacred sisters who were entombed beneath Chichén Itzá and have been awakened. We call forth the ancient Mayan names of the seven virgins of the thirteenth level beneath Chichén Itzá: Ixmaxnata, Kuayana, Imari Iguani, Leilixkawa, Weikixna, Mayotepa and Pepatateo. They are the beautiful sisters of the goddesses of Silbury Hill [see Appendix A] who have temples at these three ancient sacred sites.

They have been called forth to journey to the underworld and open to portals between Giza, Chichén Itzá and Silbury Hill, in thirty-three dimensions. They open the doors between the dimensional worlds of the living and the dead. The souls of the sacrificed virgins of Chichén Itzá are released from bondage. The lost souls of the suffering virgins have

been set free to complete the mission they were destined to complete: to globally release suffering souls from the bondage of the death fear. They have been waiting for the great day when the portals open and the souls are set free to ascend free from fear, healed and in a state of bliss.

This is the road to heaven on Earth; this is the portal for access to the Ark of the Covenant. This crop circle and glyph foretold of this event; this is the mathematical formula for this event of great proportions in the cosmic dimensions.

When the portals from these great temples are open and the souls are set free, this powerful alchemy will be set in motion. The rule of the death fear has been held by the energy that is emitted from the agony of these tortured souls. When the souls no longer suffer, when they are set free from their prisons of fear, they will reincarnate as angels of light, free to serve love, free to be fulfilled in joy and blessings. This phenomenon is powerful for the healing and ascension of the precious Mother Gaia.

To assist this process, meditate on this set. Connect your energies to the goddess of Exad and the seven sacred virgins. Then imagine your personal family lineage. Allow yourself to connect to the ones who have suffered in generational bondage, entrapped in guilt, fear and shame. Send them love and give them permission to forgive and be forgiven, to heal and be set free. Now, imagine that they enter through these healing portals. Call upon Archangel Michael; ask for redemption and retribution. See them enter the houses of light in the cities of the heavenly kingdom. This generational healing will have a positive effect on the healing of yourself and your families. Each of you has vast lineages; once set free, these souls will remedy the death fear that has been controlling the collective conscious of your planet.

PLATE 5. AVEBURY, AUGUST 10 AND 11, 1994

Within the essential core of creation are the geometric code frequencies of all matter. This geodesic code is the interstellar fractal formula for massive realignment, cosmic metamorphosis of mass and matter on a biochemical level. These code frequencies lie at the very heart of the creative cosmic spiral within the core of the Great Central Sun.

This frequency was introduced into the matrix of the Gaia project to activate the frequencies and prepare for the massive energetic shift that is currently occurring. The core of creation was encoded with the nine planets of your solar system and your planetary Sun and overlaid with the baseline frequency code of the cosmic structure of your solar system. When this crop circle was introduced, this frequency code was imprinted on the biogenic structure of Earth, thereby reactivating the current matrix that has existed since the creation of the Earth plane. In effect, this is the cosmic code for the phenomenon that is now initiated and will be fully activated by the years 2012-13.

PLATE 6. BARBURY CASTLE, JULY 17, 1991

This crop circle and star glyph compose a highly technological formula for a simple principle. This is the balancing resonator for the cosmic law of perfection through imperfection. This is the law of radical discord, the divine principle of balance of unequal counterpoints within the matrix of divine creation and evolution.

With all things being unequal, this quantum resonator of minute frequencies is the divine balancer and creates a quantum theorem that is not mathematically logical. The theorem is the universal law ruling parallel realities and universes. From this sprouts the seeds of Merlin's law of nongravity and the illogical multidimensional equilateral balance.

The Wizard rules this glyph, for it is from radical discord that soil is loosened and the seed may spring forth in perfect balance. This crop circle defies logic, for it is the balance of Merlin's metronome; it is the perfect balance of unequal proportions that is vital for creation. This is the power that permitted King Arthur to draw the sword from the stone in your mythologies. Ponder on this principle in conjunct with the Hopi prophecies that say your planet is in the Coyote Waterway. The Rabbit of Africa and Ectomie—or Spider, the trickster—of the Lakota Native American tradition assist Merlin in this paradigm of perfect imperfection. It is the illusion, the magic and the great jester—the Fool for God.

You will see the ones incarnate as prophets masquerading as street people. You will know them not by their deeds in the third dimension, but by their power in the principalities of heaven. Make way for the illogical; make way for laughter. This is the cosmic juggling act that produces the fertile loam for transmutation and change.

This crop circle came in 1991 because it was a prophetic year for the clowns to dance amongst the people.

PLATE 7. BECKHAMPTON, JULY 21, 1998

This crop circle and glyph speak of the return of the temples of light and the emerald and cobalt blue Lemurian ethereal cities. The apparitions of these sacred cities will manifest in the third-dimensional hologram of Earth dreamtime. Many of them have been invisible or have appeared only at night under the cloak of darkness. There will be increased sightings of mysterious cities that appear for a moment and then vanish, leaving the viewer to wonder if indeed it was imagined.

From these great cities of light will come teachings, ascended philosophies and the workings for the principles of peace. In areas where they appear, there will be a rapid metamorphosis of beings and systems.

There are twelve cities of light that will manifest in the third dimension. They will move from location to location. Each location is plotted by the formulas of sacred geometry that are resonant in the light and sound frequencies of this crop circle. Each city will appear thirteen times between the initial apparition in 1998 and 2012. They will all be anchored in the thirteenth city of light in the crystal core of Mother Earth.

PLATE 8. LONGWOOD WARREN, JUNE 26, 1995

The year 1995 signified the emergence of Mother Gaia from what the Mayan prophecies refer to as the "nine hells into the thirteen heavens." This year was a pivotal point in Earth's history. Many students of the crop circle phenomenon have observed that this crop circle is the map of your solar system minus Earth. There is much speculation as to the meaning of this. Has Earth vanished? Has she truly disappeared from her orbital pattern? Your Earth scientists would say no, yet in the etheric realm, the Mother Gaia is indeed transforming and passing through the narrow gate known as the eye of the needle. The old world ruled by the death fear must die for the new world to emerge. The year 1995 was pivotal for this metamorphosis.

Basically, the tides turned in the year 1995. Many underground negative ET bases were neutralized; alliances were formed with the Galactic Federation and the initial phases of the complete metamorphosis of the powers that ruled the Earth plane shifted. This is shown in this crop circle with the absence of Earth in the orbital field of the solar system.

You could say that the world is far from healed. This is true, but for the healing and emergence of the Mother Gaia Eden principle, there had to be just such a massive shift. This is a process that will consume many of your Earth years. Oppression still exists. Earth beings are being asked to choose trauma or peace, and what they manifest will be based on that choice. Yet the metamorphosis of this beloved planet is not that simple. As the collective conscious of a critical mass of souls known as the 144,000 ascends, the energy will be available as never before to free oppressed souls and heal the wounds of fear. This will provide fertile ground for the beings still trapped in the fear frequencies to transmute them and awaken to a higher state of consciousness.

This set is powerful for this purpose. Many souls are still victims of injustice, such as political prisoners, subjects of human experimentation by covert governments, indigenous people persecuted by their governments, women and children living in oppressive and abusive cultures, and minorities within all social structures. We invite you to actively meditate with this set to right injustice and set these oppressed souls free.

Know this my dear ones: Freedom is *now*, empowerment is *now*, global peace is *now* and respect for life is *now*. *All life is sacred.* You, my beloved ones, are the catalysts for the metamorphosis. You are the ones who will tear down the old paradigm with the power of unconditional love and create a new world of peace. You are to plant the seeds of change that the seven generations will harvest. Use this set. Meditate with it, pray with it, sing songs of freedom with it, and actively engage your soul in the principles of peace through freedom and empowerment.

PLATE 9. BARBURY CASTLE, MAY 31, 1999

This is the image of the sound frequencies of the light orbs of *Soenan*, the name for the completed transmutation of your Sun, Kinich Ahau (Mayan name for Earth's Sun). Soenan will be fully activated by the solar/stellar alignment of the thirteenth house of Ra (2012-13), when the thirteen solar suns merge with Kinich Ahau [see crop circle 32 for important information about this phenomenon]. This crop circle is the resonant pattern of sound frequencies as they are affected by the massive change in the light frequencies that will illuminate the Earth's environment. At the top of the crop circle, notice a Menorah; this ancient and mystical image also represents the emergence of Soenan.

The resonance of your Sun will be vastly different and measurable by scientific means. The increase of solar flares indicates that the process has begun. This set has to do with the sound frequencies in this evolutionary development. Light and sound are two of the elemental aspects of all that exists. They are the basis for all movement of the creative sources of the God-seed in the original creation. When these two elements resonate in the eminence of the God-source in such a pure way, galaxies are transformed and the very atomic and subatomic substance of mass and matter shifts. This is the essence of the entire plan for the awakening of Mother Gaia and heaven on Earth.

PLATE 10. SILBURY HILL, JUNE 19, 1999

This is the image of the pod of Eden. The cupped end receives the pollen that fertilizes the center globe, which is your Mother Gaia. The other creates the seed, like the flight of an eagle, portraying the balance of the male/female aspects. Just as all plants have a pollination process, this crop circle speaks of the pollination, the fertilization of the pod of Eden. The star glyph is the cosmic heart of the divine mother. It is a very female glyph, a round, warm, loving expression of Gaia's womb source.

This crop circle is about the process of receiving universal energy, fertilizing it and then evolving. It represents the pod of Eden receiving pollination from the universal forces. It is easy to understand that a bee pollinates a flower or that a man enters a woman to conceive a child. Earth, too, is being pollinated or impregnated with the divine potential of the expanded Eden from the rays of your Sun. That is why the Native American people speak of the Sun as the father and the Earth as the mother. Carefully study the transmissions of crop circles 9, 13 and 32. These transmissions speak of the merging of the thirteen galactic suns into Earth's planetary Sun. This merging of galactic energies into your planet is the basic principle of this crop circle.

Earth will be a seedpod to peacefully colonize galaxies that have not been previously inhabited. Imagine the bursting of little spores going forth into galaxies to seed other planets with this beautiful green loving, living energy that is unique to Gaia. This crop circle speaks of her receiving pollination, fertilizing them in her womb and then seeding them out into other galaxies.

PLATE 11. AVEBURY TRUSLOE, JUNE 20, 1999

There will be a birthing of five aspects of the Cosmic Christ represented in the birth of enlightened children. There have already been several groups of highly evolved souls to emerge on your planet; they are coming in waves, or soul groups. We are presently experiencing the fourth soul group that has entered through an eleventh-dimensional portal.

This crop circle is the portal for the fifth wave or soul group that will emerge from the twelfth dimension; they are the Patal Patala. These children born between the years 2000-03 will be newly incarnated souls who will merge with souls who have experienced lifetimes of learning on your planet. There will literally be soul merges to create incarnate beings evolved in peaceful consciousness. These children will radiate pure love essences and resonate high velocity frequencies vital for continued evolution. These highly evolved children will be most precious and valuable for upgrading or evolving the collective mind and essence of the collective conscious.

PLATE 12. WEST OVERTON, JUNE 23, 1999

The formula represented in this crop circle is the biochemical frequency code for the restructuring of planetary water. A non-Earth element will be added to the periodic table and chemically bond with H_2O. The new planetary water will be able to self-purify and rejuvenate. This formula is a fractal of a fractal, carrying a DNA code for restructuring planetary waters. Your scientific community is not yet advanced enough to detect the biochemical aspects of this effect at this time. This is the initial phase of this process; it is not possible to reveal when the evolution of the planetary waters will be completed. Comprehending and accepting the incredible potential this new self-purifying water can have for your life systems will quicken its evolutionary process.

PLATE 13. EAST FIELD, ALTON BARNES, JUNE 12, 1999

This is the planetary merge of the galactic quantum. The councils of the twelve solar temples are represented here as well as the Central Sun. Now that the galaxies are coming to peace, the birth of the fifth element—spirit or quintessence—will manifest. This crop circle is a geometric crystalline code for the evolution of cosmic DNA. Humans on this planet are unaware of the evolutionary dimensional shift that will be brought about by the emergence of Eden.

A council from the eleventh solar temple will emerge and join forces with the Galactic Federation. This time is referred to in Hopi prophecy as the eleventh hour. The presence of the eleventh solar temple will complete the cosmic DNA and the solar/stellar universal galactic DNA. This is the formula for the evolved cosmic DNA.

The emergence of the eleventh solar temple is eminent. They are from a dimension we have not contacted yet. When they connect to the Galactic Federation and the Council of Abborah, beings from their galaxy will incarnate on Earth. But as yet, the eleventh solar temple has not revealed itself even to the eleventh-dimensional beings.

Each one of the appendages in the crop circle is a galactic tone. These appendages are all musical frequencies. When the eleventh house reveals itself, there will be an evolutionary leap in consciousness and construct of the dimensional qualities both planetarily and galactically. The frequency of these tones is going to start coming through into music. These are the thirteen cosmic tones; the C octave is the circle at the bottom. The two appendages at the top are the Mother/Father God, the cosmic balance of divine union.

This is the Cosmic Tree of Life. It resonates the frequencies of the flowering of the Cosmic Tree of Peace, the musical frequencies of the full octave of the united thirteen solar houses of the Central Sun.

PLATE 14. EAST FIELD, ALTON BARNES, JUNE 12, 1999

This crop circle represents the harmonizing of the frequencies of the electromagnetic grids of Mother Earth, the new frequency for Earth's electromagnetic field. This geometry is representative of tones that stabilize the Earth's electromagnetic fields and balance and equalize the planetary energies for the polar shift. Massive upheavals in the planetary energies are not necessary for the new paradigm to emerge. As the Hopi prophecy has foretold, the purification can be gentle. Earth's electromagnetic frequencies affect the thought capacity and patterning of her inhabitants and vice versa. Individuals shifting consciousness to a higher love-vibration frequency produces considerable effects. The heart energy has opened up incredibly; the heart chakra is the portal for this transcendence.

This pattern contains the nine modular tones for Earth's electromagnetic polar shift; the totality of the nine modular frequencies is the shift gate. To properly receive the emanations of this crop circle, one must follow the frequencies from right to left. The design on the far left is the frequency formula of Earth's evolved electromagnetic field. The impact of this evolutionary leap can be conceptualized by conceiving the impact of Einstein's theory of relativity on the collective mind.

The thirteen resonant tones, the thirteen lunar phases, will interface with these nine modular tone frequencies. The formula for this phenomenon is $9^4/144$ (13 lunar phases + 13 resonant tones).

PLATE 15. ALLINGTON DOWN, JUNE 23, 1999

This crop circle represents the unveiling of the tomb of Exad, the root of Ganeshkato, in the year 2001, located seven degrees southeast of Mount Sinai. The tomb has not yet been discovered. Its opening will unlock the seventh aspect of the Ark of the Covenant.

The star beings from Dogon planted a time capsule in the tomb before they were destroyed at the end of Mu, which is intended to be opened and activated when the tomb is revealed. Within the glyph of Exad are the star codes necessary for the time capsule's activation. The entrance to this tomb will be revealed to the one or ones who accepted this cosmic mission in the inception of the divine plan for the emergence of Eden.

This tomb exists in a parallel dimension and can be accessed only by those capable of time travel and interdimensional portal expansion. Also necessary for the activation is the access code implanted in the soul DNA of the ones who carry the patterning of the root of Ganeshkato and have the genetic lineage of the House of David [see Appendix B]. Some who receive this information will detect a deep stirring within their psyches, instinctively knowing that they are somehow connected to this phenomenon. Respond to this intuitive guidance. This is your wake-up call. Allow yourself to explore the full potential of your impending journey to fulfill your cosmic mission.

PLATE 16. HONEY STREET, ALTON BARNES, JULY 15, 1999

The mushroom-like peace stargate found at the bottom of the crop circle is the trinity effect, the healing of the nuclear violation of the planetary peace. The inevitable environmental damage of nuclear energy that has been released into the environment must be reversed for the planet to survive and heal.

This is the code for the deactivation of plutonium poisoning. This crystalline matrix will emerge in the consciousness of a team of researchers who will be able to reduce plutonium's half-life to a transmutative base that will reverse the effects of radiation poisoning. The crop circle is the crystalline matrix for this formula. The way will be made for the implementation of reasonable and affordable means to accomplish this end. The priority of the industry and those who guide the progress of such will be creating a safe future for all of Earth's inhabitants.

It is recommended that those individuals who are

committed to a nuclear-free planet use this crop circle and glyph for meditation, as it will expedite those results.

PLATE 17. WINDMILL HILL, AVEBURY TRUSLOE, JULY 16, 1999

This crop circle is the DNA chip that will evolve our mathematical capacity. Each one of these circles is an infinite fractal crystalline code, and each crystalline aspect is a fractal universe. This evolved mathematical system is the next step for mathematics on Earth. When this particular glyph comes into the collective consciousness, present mathematics will seem obsolete or primitive, like the difference between a stone ax and a laser beam.

Qiuayon soen tra soen nas tra ka mix na ke te son tra laixwa mei ix nika, is the ancient mantra for the activation of this process. In ancient history, there were Mayan and Egyptian timekeepers who prepared the planetary essence to receive this evolutionary leap. The crystalline codes were implanted in sacred sites and will now be activated by those of you who carry the proper DNA codes to complete these ancient formulas and receive the creative mathematical formulas into the collective mind. The ones who are part of this cosmic mission have reincarnated to activate this process.

PLATE 18. WEST KENNETT LONGBARROW, AUGUST 4, 1999

This crop circle unlocks key time portals, facilitating a continuum for time travel. The scientists within the covert government have been attempting to unlock a time portal so that they will be able to control galactic time shifts, repattern history and restructure the time grid. This is the template for the mathematical formula that is necessary for unlocking and opening the thirteenth door in time.

The missing mathematical formula or link code for the successful opening of this wormhole, this door of destiny, is contained within this crop circle. It is a resonant frequency code that has been emanated within the ultratone high frequency on the fourth parallel of the planetary grid. There is no danger of this formula falling into the hands of the covert govern-

ment because they do not control the human component, the alchemical aspect of the collective mind.

The teams of individuals who will receive this information have chosen to incarnate through the eleventh-dimensional portal and have been born as ascended souls. These individuals have incarnated karmically pure and free of the effects of the deteriorating fear grid; they have within their crystalline DNA the activation codes.

The root of this formula has been carefully protected by the Mayan timekeepers, who have already gone to the future and returned karmically cleansed and prepared for this mission. This circle is useful for developing skills needed to move between the dimensions of linear time, a skill required for much of the work to be done in the next two decades and beyond.

PLATE 19. CHERHILL DOWN, JULY 18, 1999

This crop circle is the activation of the nine templates of evolution of the collective consciousness. The center is the Whirling Rainbow Way, the metamorphic opening of the collective heart chakra. This is the return of La Niña. The nine pyramids are the temples of the nine seeds of wisdom, the temples of the evolutionary gate to wisdom of the collective. The small glyph on the right-hand side is the key to open this chrysalis. The small line at the bottom right is the lunar portal, which is being seeded through the thirteen crystalline moons. This crop circle is an image of the crystalline seed that was implanted in twelve spots on the planet.

Crystals with this structure have been literally implanted in the ethereal realms of the planet during the time of the ancient ethereal cities of the House of David [see Appendix B]. When all twelve are activated, it will be with the return of "La Niña and El Niño," the return of the sacred twins to oneness, or divine union, through the spiraling power of the cosmic wind. They are identical in appearance, but the different crystalline chrysalis code encoded in each of the nine temples makes each of the twelve crystals unique.

PLATE 20. LIDDINGTON CASTLE, JULY 21, 1999

This crop circle represents the evolution of the pure

God-seed into its unique divinity, the divine procreative connection of the planetary DNA. This crop circle is the mathematical formula for the activation code, which has been engraved in the pyramid of Giza. The glyph on the left is the key to the activation of this God-seed, the matrix of the evolved God-source within.

As the polar caps melt with global warming, a living organism will be released into the ecosystem of the planet. This organism was starseeded at the time of your great Ice Age. It is much like a virus, only not destructive, but creative. Many of the viruses on the planet appear to be diseases because of their side effects, but they are actually working with the bioenergetics of the cellular structure of living organisms to bring about healing and metamorphosis. This virus or living organism is extremely powerful and will be released in an alchemical formula that corresponds with the activation of the twelve crystalline codes. As the polar icecaps melt, the biological force being unleashed will evolve the planetary DNA for the activation of the cosmic God-seed within the structure of all entities on the planet. This key has been encoded in Giza, in the Temple of the Moon at Lake Titicaca and also in the Caves of Mysteries in Nepal, in the mountains of Tibet.

PLATE 21. DEVIL'S DEN, JULY 19, 1999

This crop circle represents the resurrection of the Planetary Christ, or the full awakening of the House of David [see Appendix B]. Each of the temple regions where the matrix was implanted for the emergence of Eden is time-coded with the conception of the twelve phases: six phases going into point zero and six phases coming out of point zero. Mother Earth is presently in the six phases emerging from point zero. This is the conception of the pod of Eden and the full activation of the House of David. These are the twelve temples of the House of David. The center circle is the Central Sun that is energetically linked with the crystalline core of the planet.

Wei cho lee, wei cho lai, wei cho la, wei cho ka, wei ma koa, doa ix do kei, ix no wei mast tke, wei mas tke, wei in nosh ta koo ma we cho koo, wei cho koo mei, wei lax tu, wei lax tu kei, meix lu, meix lu ka, wei nix toa, wei nxi to ka, wei mas ti ke ko mix tu kastako ko mix tu kas to ko ashitike makoa eina wastoa mei loo ix ta ko, wei ku wie ka, wei kie, ix kao ix kao. This is the ancient lost language or tongue of the galactic Maya. The essence of the formula of this ancient mantra or prayer cannot be translated into your English. It is a mystery tongue, as was spoken of in Revelations. It is not meant to be translated, but when spoken or meditated upon, it will have an extremely powerful effect on this cosmic cocreation.

This is the cosmic equation for the planetary alignments necessary for the full activation of what is known in the mythology of the House of David as the fully awakened Christ being. These are all planetary bodies. This is the effect of the awakening of the DNA of the lineage of the ancient houses of light. Historically, all of the esoteric information and highly evolved spiritual energy that has come onto the planet has been only a percentage of what is available in the future for the full activation of this original creation, the House of David. The geometry of this crop circle imprints the cosmic completion of the Eden principle.

PLATE 22. SILBURY HILL ENVIRONS, JULY 24, 1999

This crop circle was positioned on a grid line that connects to the core of a crystalline ethereal temple. The temple appears as a mound above the crop circle in the photo. Inside the mound is an ancient geometric grail, which is a time-warp template. The resonant frequencies of this crop circle activated the time-warp template within the mound.

Ah, my sweet ones, the search for the Holy Grail has been sung and sought throughout time. See it now as it arises. The beloved Grail revealed, drink from the sweet nectar of our Lord's life force, the very life force of his creation. Now is the hour of power, the coming of all that was destined to be. This area is the cosmic connection for the earthly emanation of the Holy Grail. This site has been long forgotten; it was here that the beloved disciple did travel in person. This is yet unknown, for even in those times he could take any shape he chose: a white dove perhaps, or even a pheasant. He told you of this in his teachings. He told you of his gift, and so many misunderstood, for he is White Eagle and this is his nest. Here, in many lifetimes, he returned to anchor the crystalline energy for the beloved Holy Grail.

PLATE 23. BECKHAMPTON, JULY 28, 1999

The frequency from this crop circle assists with the radical evolution of space-time physics. This merkabah is activating a quantum leap in the science of physics on the planet, the principles of quadrasonic resonance merged with the formulas for space-time portal frequency shifts. This formula is encoded with the time-altering aspects of the resonant frequency codes of the light-sound continuums that are reversed to the twelfth modular geometric hexatronic and alter life frequencies of the metric scale in the quadrasonic metronome. (This ET terminology has not yet been defined in Earth science and therefore cannot be explained.)

PLATE 24. BARBURY CASTLE, JULY 23, 1999

This crop circle is the emblem of the advisory governing body of Katorika and the geometric code for the balance of world power through divine cocreation. Three powerful forms of world government will emerge, representing unity through global prosperity, identity by free will and the merging of power for mutual benefit and respect for life. It is the essence of the principles of peace manifested through divine balance, empowerment and respect for life.

The ancient houses of light will come forth and merge with existing political structures through the soul metamorphosis and heart openings of world leaders. Those who incarnated to be the "midwives" of the great peace, will seek political positions and be given the authority to make positive changes in the structures that hold humanity in mental bondage. The autonomy of each nation and tribe will be respected, and each council member will be acknowledged and heeded, not because of size, power and sheer number, but as valuable cells of the living body of light and love that unites all in the common causes of humanity's ascension and healing the beloved mother. Differences between nations will be honored, and there will be an energetic field established that facilitates the harmonious resolution of conflict through mutual benefit and forgiveness.

It is strongly urged for groups to form to meditate on this glyph and crop circle with these manifestations set in your intent.

PLATE 25. ROUNDWAY, DEVIZES, JULY 31, 1999

This crop circle is the geometric imprint of the formula for the repatterning of the molecular structure of seeds for producing food on the planet. Hybridizing has created a genetic weakness in strains of vital grains. This mutation of vital food sources will create grains that are resistant to common insect plagues, molds and diseases. A new food source will emerge that is appealing to the taste and will be far more nutritious than soy or any of your current food sources.

The ancient seeds will evolve into these genetically superior seed sources, resolving the impending food shortages brought on by the destructive hybrid chemical chaos that has been implemented in the food chain. The current food crisis initially came about with the misuse of inventions of well-meaning scientists by the dark forces as a means to manipulate the food source and control the masses.

Within each seed there is an emanation of the cocreative force of the God-source. When the seeds for production of food are genetically altered and treated with chemicals, it affects the creative forces of the seed source of planetary abundance and cocreation. That is why the ancients revered seeds as sacred—they are a powerful connection to the God-source. The manner in which seeds are handled and the attitude toward these precious gifts of creation must shift for the consciousness of the civilization to evolve.

This crop circle emanates a frequency that has dual purposes. One effect is the evolution of genetically superior seeds for food sources; the other is the evolution of the collective consciousness to accept, acknowledge and respect the mystical nature of seeds and their powerful influence on the planetary balance.

The food that is consumed from a conscious food source inevitably will nourish the mind, body and spirit with a higher vibrational frequency, thus preparing the organism to receive higher vibrational frequencies from the emanation of the God-source and raise the energetics of the planet. It is all that simple. This crop circle raises the frequencies for the grains on the planet.

PLATE 26. HACKPEN HILL ENVIRONS, JULY 4, 1999

This is the formula for the mutation of the human ovum. Within the original creation is the encoded formula for the mutation of human ova, called the "triadular molecular spiral genesis." Basically, you are viewing the thirteen-strand DNA from a cross section of each fiber strand within the newly evolved human ovum.

Within the core of the new DNA will be seven golden strands of light, emanations from the God-seed. The microstructure of the ovum will be radiant as a sound and light frequency receptor to the universal Om, or the voice of God. The frequency receptors were impeded by the Atlantean mutation of the species. Additionally, there is an effect of the cosmic melting pot of species that have inhabited this mother planet. Various colonizations brought their genetic strands to merge with the original people or the primal God-seed group, known to your mythologies as first man and woman. This has brought a galactic merge of varying aspects of DNA, creating a unique gene pool represented by the four primal race/colors that correspond with the colors of the medicine wheel (black, white, yellow and red).

The amalgamation of the races is inevitable. You are not being asked to sacrifice the unique aspects of these beautiful races, but rather to create a new and unique race amongst humans. The completion of this is the law of the five elements balanced in the human races on the planet. Cohesion through diversity is the paradigm of heaven on Earth.

This crop circle is the new creation that is approaching in the evolution of the human ovum. This formula is an extremely sensitive frequency and resonates only in the pure love vibration. The evolved ovum will be a resonator of the most pure angelic vibrations.

PLATE 27. ROCKLEY DOWN, JULY 11, 1999

This is the molecule of the evolved planetary bacteria, E. coli. E. coli bacteria can be detrimental to the human organism and is often the root of infection and contamination of water and food sources. However, this bacterium has other aspects and is related to the planetary evolution of bacteria in the ecosystems. The nature of this E. coli varies according to the environment that it breeds and grows in. The emerging E. coli will be cultured or grown in a concentrated field of algae, such as super blue-green algae, deep within areas not yet harvested or explored. Lake Klamath is the matrix for this E. coli. There also will be pockets forming off the coast of Australia in the reefs and off the coasts of tropical islands such as Kauai and Tahiti. Once these colonies are mature, there will be an implantation of the algae/E. coli food source. This is the molecule of the evolved E. coli cultured within super blue-green algae beds. This alga will be a very powerful food source, carrying elements that will enhance healthy bacteria within the intestines and contribute to the evolution of a healthier populace.

Do not limit yourselves to the scientific conception of E. coli as it now exists. There will be a mutation of the molecular structure of this bacterium that will not be detected by conventional scientific means. Once this high vibrational frequency is infused through the creation of super blue-green algae, E. coli will provide healing and strength to the species. Prepare your psyche for this phenomenon to manifest in many aspects of your present structure. In the new phase of creation, that which was once used to deteriorate, bringing disease and suffering, will now provide the key to the evolution of the Gaia principle, or the pod of Eden. I would be delighted to see the expression on the faces of scientists and men of medicine who are not awakened to the divine potential of this bacterium. They will certainly wrinkle their brows and say it is not possible.

This transmission is targeted at those of you who have expanded your minds and know that anything within divine potential is possible with empowerment, trust, love and compassion. It is also targeted at anyone who is open-minded and wants to learn more about our divine potential.

PLATE 28. ALLINGTON DOWN, JULY 20, 1999

This is the mathematical formula for the mutation of

the poliovirus. The poliovirus, although disabling in its initial phases, is one of the viral strains originally introduced to the planet. The polioviruses will merge with a bacterium unknown to this planet at this point, creating a new strand of viral bacteria that will be cultured in an environment much like yogurt. This living entity, once mutated, will enter the muscle fiber and improve the longevity, durability, elasticity and strength of muscle tissue and fibrous cells in all species on the planet, not only humans. This in turn will create stronger and more resilient species. Many of the devastating muscular diseases will be unable to take root in this evolved, healthier muscle fiber.

For humans, this virus-bacteria will be ingested in a new food source that is both dairy- and soy-based. This food source will have a unique flavor and will become quite popular. It will include an Amazonian herb previously protected by shamans, which will be given to a researcher who will create the new food source.

Another aspect of the formula is carried within the molecular structure of glucosamine sulfate. Imagine the wonderful effects of this evolutionary process upon all inhabitants of this planet in the creative imagery process. This miracle of modern science is within the blueprint of the original creation of Eden. The words to meditate upon are "expect miracles" and "it will be so."

This formula is only one of the creations to come; there are other aspects that will be mutated in the planetary food sources that will affect all species on this planet. The second genesis aspect of this formula relates back to the mutation of base food-chain sources in plankton, which will be a later evolutionary phase of the Gaia planet. The initial catalyst of this evolutionary phase is the invention of the new food source mentioned in transmission 27.

AUTHOR'S NOTE: We have given you an example of two aspects of evolution represented in the formulas of the star glyphs and crop circles. These are only two examples; this is not a self-limiting process. Every disease and organism, every virus and bacterial energy that has affected the species as a destructive organism—such as the mutation of venereal disease strains, the AIDS virus and the streptococcus virus—will evolve in this

manner. We have chosen these two examples to illustrate the process of the mutation of the viral and bacterial strains on the planet. It is important that crop circles 27 and 28 are used as a set in the meditation process. Expand your creative thought process beyond the technical information that has been given you about these two viral/bacterial strains—E. coli and the poliovirus—to encompass the entire bacterial and viral strains of the living organisms on your planet. What was used to destroy will be used to create and procreate. What was brought to bring fear, destruction and pain will be transmuted to bring healing and healthiness to the beings on this planet. When you meditate or work with these images, imagine the creative potential of these two glyphs. If scientists want to experiment with this information in one form or another, they are encouraged to do so as long as they do not limit their potential to these two examples.

PLATE 29. BARBURY CASTLE, AUGUST 5, 1999

The forces that sustain balance and abundance have been blocked on your planet. Fear is the root of all disease. When you are able to transmute fear and come to a state of unconditional love, your bodies will be healthier and most importantly, so will your Mother Earth. I do acknowledge the negative effects of the toxins that the fearmongers have set into the environment in the form of air, water and earth pollutants, which have corrupted your food sources with chemicals and nuclear poisoning—not to mention the effects of experimental programs that intentionally infect masses of individuals with disease. All of this will be cleared and healed as the consciousness shifts on the planet.

Fear blocks the circulation of cosmic prana, or Qi, in your system, causing deterioration of the spirit and disease in the body. Your Mother Earth also suffers from the actions of the Dark Lords' human pawns, whose souls are in chaos. Their violent actions have created large pockets of fear energy on vital pulsar or acupuncture points on the Mother Earth, at the intersection of ley lines. This is done by the means of battles, genocide and fear ceremonies. The populace has been unconscious of the robotic behavior that has compelled masses of humans to participate in death-fear rites. These rites have been calculated to maintain the energy of fear and terror and to control the prana of the cocreative forces in a death-fear state.

Death is but a cycle of the continuation of your

soul's journey; *death fear* is a devastating illusion that cripples the psyche of the masses and of the planet itself. The reign of the Dark Lords has passed and the people are no longer held in bondage, although these energies and their effects have not been completely cleared from your society as a whole. You as humans are a reflection of the state of affairs of your Mother; when you are not in harmony and balance, she is not in harmony and balance. There is much healing to be done.

Mother Earth has vital rivers within her ethereal body that connect powerful centers. This information is very elementary for some of you, but still it is necessary to connect the information to your holographic mind-heart for this activation. The powerful Mary and Michael Line is such a river. Much work has been done in Great Britain to open and stabilize this river.

On the continent of America is one such river called Rio de la Vida, the river of life. It extends from the Four Corners region to the Yucatán, and on into South America. When Rio de la Vida is activated, the energy stabilizes Gaia during her birthing, reducing the massive effects of the cleansing in the form of earthquakes, hurricanes, volcanoes and tornadoes. Although these forces are very much at work in these times, the effects could be much more devastating and volatile. The Rio de la Vida also opens the flow of abundance from the grain centers in the Four Corners region in the U.S. to the Yucatán and south to Lake Titicaca, stimulating planetary abundance.

Rio de la Vida extends from the Four Corners region to the pyramid region of the Yucatán—encompassing a circle that includes the U.S. Southwest; Palenque, Chichén Itzá, Tres Zapotes and Oaxaca in Mexico; and Kaminal Juyú and Tikal in Guatemala. This river is the living essence of the Feathered Serpent, Quetzalcóatl. It is the sacred twin of the Mary and Michael Line.

This crop circle is the awakened essence of this spiritual force as the prophecies foretold. One of the aspects of this awakened essence is the resurrection of the ancient medicine bundles that were preserved in the ethereal realms when indigenous medicine men and women were victims of genocide on all continents of your planet. Many sacred bundlekeepers

died thinking their medicine died with them; this thought was only an illusion of fear that held the mental hologram in place. In truth, nothing has been lost; their medicine bundles stayed within the ethereal, waiting for the activation of these sacred spiritual rivers. Then the spiritual essences of their powers will be awakened to assist the collective evolution.

Other such serpents of the kundalini or life force energy of the precious Mother Earth await awakening. This crop circle speaks of the awakening of these spiritual forces within the core of your Earth plane. Along key points of these ethereal rivers, vital pulsar points must be cleared of blocked fear energy and the spiritual beings that are part of the essence of the great serpent of life must be awakened. This process must be completed by 2012.

Meditation on this star glyph and crop circle will assist the process. There are those of you who have already begun the activations in other vital centers around the planet. Visualize spiritual rivers intersecting grid lines and ley lines. They are distinct energetic forces with a life of their own. This crop circle is the formula for the frequencies that will be activated alchemically with the awakening of these great sleeping rivers.

PLATE 30. LURKLEY HILL, WEST OVERTON, JULY 1999

This crop circle is the seed for the resolution of the energy crisis. The present fossil fuel and nuclear energy use is self-destructing and will, if allowed to continue, place Earth on an inevitable course of destruction of life as we know it on this beloved planet. The current collective view of the creation of energy is that we must destroy Earth's resources and split atoms to generate energy. This source of fuel is devastating to the ecosystem and to the collective life of the planet. This destroys all that is needed to sustain and create life and provides usable energy only to a small populace that sits in a position of power at the top of the pyramid of control. Meanwhile, the majority of the population sacrifices their quality of life to serve as slaves to the masters. Then the masters at the top of the pyramid become slaves to their own gluttony.

I realize that this is not news to the enlightened reader. This crop circle is the formula for the creations that will resolve the fuel crisis. It presents the formula for a variety of energy sources that have already been invented, such as Tesla's inventions. Additionally, it contains formulas for free-energy methods that have not as yet sprung up in the minds of those of you who have agreed to be inventors. This matrix will not only shift the attitude of the collective mind about energy use, but it will provide the inspiration for new energy sources that will be widely available to the masses for very reasonable amounts of the environment's renewable resources.

The balance of energy use, consumption, production and re-creation of primal sources of energy lies within this formula. It is not necessary to give all of these formulas out in this transmission. Once there are collective holographic heart meditations and an implantation into the collective conscious mind-heart of Mother Earth, these jewels of bountiful energy will spring forth and be easily implemented to replace destructive energy sources.

Part of the key to this balance of energy consumption lies within knowing the difference between *needs* and *wants*, comfort compared to overindulgence without the benefit of ever feeling that there is enough. The mindset of the masses will actually shift at the same time that formulas become available and are implemented. Remember, those of you who know you are part of this original creation can consciously activate this process: "As you think it, so it will be." There is a critical mass of human components ready to receive this message and act upon it.

PLATE 31. BISHOPS CANNINGS, AUGUST 6, 1999

The name of this set is the "Beloved Flower of Peace." This is the Flower of Life's sacred geometry. *Dorsa naki da ta* is the mantra for this crop circle and star glyph. This is the seed of peace that has been carried and preserved by the beloved souls who incarnated to carry the torch and keep the flame of peace alive. You know them by the names of Gandhi, Mother Teresa, St. Francis, Martin Luther King and Hildegard of Bingen. I am sure you can construct a list of the great peacekeepers. Within their soul DNA, they carried this common microchip, the seed of

peace. The crystalline orb spider, Grandmother Spider, has carefully woven this dreamcatcher with her silver strands.

Mathematically, it is the resonance of pure Christ light and the essence of the highest frequency of love vibration that exists within the spectrum of universal light and sound. It is important to use this set as a focal point when sending love vibrations and prayers to areas of war and conflict on the planet. Such was the work of the beautiful one, James Twyman.

This is the ultimate symbol of peace in divine union, empowerment and mutual cocreation. It is a powerful set to be used in mediation and sessions for conflict resolution. This is a practical tool that can be infinitely useful in the transformation of the warrior/destroyer paradigm, the healing of the heart of the beast. I suggest that this geometry be created into jewelry and art pieces and widely distributed to the masses.

When used in meditation, this set is very powerful for the transformation of tortured souls and should be widely distributed to prisons, hospitals, treatment centers and homeless shelters. This symbol should be placed wherever the people suffer and have been lost in violence, pain and confusion. Use this set in meditation as a tool to transform feelings of anger and fear and heal the heart in forgiveness. Do a meditation with the image of a person or persons who violated you in mind. Next, bring this image into your mind, then into your heart. Allow it to melt the anger, hatred and fear. Imagine that it is healing your heart. Project love and forgiveness from your holographic heart. When meditated upon, this symbol and mantra will heal the beast within and bring peace to lost souls. The images that are re-created from this set will emanate the frequencies set in this geometry wherever it is displayed.

PLATE 32. MIDDLE WALLOP, MAY 2, 1999

There are thirteen galactic suns, the aspects of which will energetically merge with your Sun, Kinich Ahau, by the end of the year 2012. Six have merged, and seven more will be merging. The smallest circle is the Earth.

The sunlight activates and feeds the plankton of the planet. Plankton is the basic link in your food chain and the basic link in the planetary structure of the cosmic mind. Plankton and the basic green algae are a consciousness, not just the basic essence of the food chain. As aspects of the thirteen galactic suns merge into your Sun, the solar energy emanated to the planet will be considerably different. The absorption into these basic roots of your food chain will cause restructuring and evolution of your species and the patterns of Earth. Basically, in order to shift or create a change in the whole structure, the logical place to begin is at the base of the food chain, the base of the absorption of the solar energy of the food sources, thereby effecting a chain reaction of events on the planet.

Each time a new galactic sun merges with your Sun, the essences of the light energies emanated and received into the basic structure of planetary energetics and food sources will shift. This energy shift works its way up the food chain in an energetic patterning and repatterning. This is the simple basis for evolution. Each cell of plant and animal life that absorbs the rays of this more expansive light source will then respond accordingly to a higher vibrational frequency emanating from the energy of your planetary Sun. This crop circle is the mathematical formula for the resonance that will be emanating from your planetary Sun. The first glyph has to do with light aspects of this solar expansion and the merging of the thirteen galactic suns.

PLATE 33. MEON WOKE, JULY 22, 1999

This crop circle is the matrix for dissolving the information block that has been placed on inventions important in solving the Earth's ecological crisis, such as free, nondestructive energy sources. As you know, fossil fuel and pharmaceutical companies, in cooperation with the covert government or the ruling seven, have held up patents, murdered inventors, destroyed or altered documents and impeded the process for marketing wide use of these very important inventions. Nothing has been lost; even if an invention is destroyed and the inventor assassinated, the information is still alive in the collective consciousness. Additionally, there are many projects that are ready to be implemented and mass-produced that will be effective on a large scale. These jewels of evolution are waiting for activation.

While meditating on the circle and glyph, imagine all of these creative gifts of genius being catapulted into the mainstream of society and sprouting forth like wheat grass. They will be potent, prolific and fruitful. Allow your consciousness to envision a time when there will no longer be obstacles to impede the process for these creative geniuses and the products they have invented. Also, imagine all ethical inventions that were destroyed springing forth in other minds. Affirm that nothing was every lost; all will come to fruition.

This will also stimulate the production of items used in daily living that do not have such a devastating impact on the environment as well as a shift in consciousness in society's perception of use and abuse and abundance without waste.

This set of crop circles and star glyphs is particularly important to be used by those of you who have chosen the mission of inventor. Take this image set to a copy store and enlarge it to poster size. Put it in an obvious place where it can be viewed daily and use it for meditation and as a focal point when you are working on your inventions. You can make the set into a 3 x 5 card and put it on your desk at work. Another idea is to use these images as screen savers on your computer; this idea is useful for any one of the sets you wish to meditate on. Daily exposure to this set will quicken activation.

The individuals who have been motivated by greed, rooted in the fear of not having enough, will receive a cosmic jolt to their hearts through the frequencies that are emanated in this formula. They will either resign from positions of power and be replaced by evolved heart-conscious beings, or they will receive grace and their hearts will open to the potential of supporting creative genius rather than impeding it. Once you understand the principle of quantum relativity, it is quite easy to conceive how an image can link in a frequency, which in turn creates movement in an energy field and brings about change.

The two apparent dots or dark spots in the outer circle were left untouched on purpose. These are focal points for the meditations to open the creative process, remove blockages in the psyche and literally connect to the brain cells of two key physicists who will receive the Nobel Peace Prize for their work on opening the gateways to free energy. Meditating on these two focal points will hasten this process.

The small circle of light that lies in the outer crescent is the time portal that past, present and future information will travel through to bring about this creative generation. It is recommended that those of you who carry the DNA codes as time travelers and scientists use this as a focal point upon which to concentrate your meditations. It is recommended that this part of the crop circle be enlarged and used as a visible mantra for such meditations.

PLATE 34. WANFORD, JULY 12, 1999

This crop circle and star glyph are the blueprints for the divine marriage, the plan for the balance and healing of the male/female relationships in divine cocreation. In all such relationships there are masculine and feminine components, representing the balance of the trinity referred to in such religious concepts as the Father, Son and the Holy Spirit.

You are coming to the end of a long reign of fear and the dominance of the warrior/destroyer—the dark ages of the divine feminine. Mother Earth is a woman. This age of oppression has impacted her, and her children will feel the results of her rape. She has been environmentally devastated, her children (plant, animal and human) have been victims of genocide and her resources have been plundered. Society as a whole has not understood the old adage, "Don't bite the hand that feeds you."

With the emergence through point zero, the paradigm has shifted and the healing has begun. We are coming to the age of the resurrection of the divine feminine. The age of dichotomy and separation has past. Your beloved planet now emerges into the divine marriage, typified by the shift of the trinity to the Mother, Father and the Holy Spirit—as represented here in this symbol of the holy marriage. This formula for an enhanced love vibration will emanate in a powerful way in the psyche of all beings on Mother Earth, bringing an honoring of divine union as the cocreation of all that is. At one time in history, heretics, as they were called, were burned for uttering the words "Mother/Father God." Now this principle will be largely accepted and seeded in the minds of the collective.

The good news is that the battle of the sexes is over.

You are to evolve in relationships that are mutually empowering, powerfully cocreative, complete in unconditional love and divinely blessed with the pure essence of passion as the Creator intended. This is the return to Eden. When the God-seed came to this beloved planet, it was the emanation of one light that became male and female; this divine couple will return to balance with the Holy Spirit. When this mathematical light and sound frequency resonates within the collective of this Gaia planet, human beings will make different choices and evolve as a natural state of affairs. The effect of this will be massive; the rape of the mother Gaia will cease, as will the abuse of the female.

I must remind you that each of you is male-female. Within your own psyches, the war of the sexes has been one of deep internal conflict. The cocreative God-seed within each person has been repressed. With the shift of this paradigm will come inner peace and eternal balance, freeing the cocreation to unite with Holy Spirit. The effect of this shift is incredible. One of the vital effects of this cosmic balance is a natural curbing of the population explosion brought about by the extreme chaos of the female/male balance. As a species nears extinction, the natural desire to procreate becomes very powerful. Conversely, with the healing of this paradigm, the population will naturally come into balance with the availability of space and natural resources.

Be prepared for love in exotic bliss as experienced only within your great mythologies—without the tragic end. The purpose of this meditation is to conceive this principle as the original creation of the God-source and believe with the faith of the mustard seed that it is, and so it will be. The great I Am presence will be emanated through the balance and divinity of the sacred marriage, which will be enacted in a number of couples around the globe that will reach critical mass. Each time one couple achieves this ideal union, it affects everyone. With the emanation of the frequency code present in this crop circle, the quantum effects will be staggering. This concept is simple when applied to the formula of fractal geometry.

PLATE 35. EAST END, JUNE 21, 1999

This crop circle is the formula for the balanced

union of the Father, Mother and Holy Spirit. The divine balance of power through holy union is a circular pattern in which there is no head or controlling essence, but rather a cohesive flow of cosmic power in perfect balance.

The symbol for the Father Godhead through rule of the male warrior paradigm was a pyramid with the all-seeing eye at the top. In this paradigm, the power is confined to a select few at the top of a masculine-dominated paradigm. Yet in this formula, the eye of God is at the center of the balance of power through circular union in the Holy Spirit. It is surrounded by what your Native Americans refer to as the Sacred Hoop, or the circle of life, which is being mended as the wisdom keepers foretold. You are witnessing the maturation of one of the seedpods. It will be a primal seedpod for inhabiting other galaxies with peaceful coexistent inhabitation. This is the origin of the God-seed in complete balance of male/female and the Holy Spirit. By universal law, this is the geometry of pure God-source that will be activated, that will be abided by on Earth as it is in heaven. "As above, so below; as the spirit, so the soul; as without, so within; blessed be."

This is a mathematical fractal formula of light and sound frequencies that will emanate in the atmosphere and within the fiber of all the inhabitants—animate and inanimate—and the core of Mother Earth herself. Once completed on this planet, this formula will be implemented in other galaxies in the original creative state.

With the completion of this union will come a transformation of spirituality on your planet. You will no longer perceive God as a male-dominant deity, but rather as a perfect God-seed that is in divine balance of male and female, in union with the Holy Spirit. The religions that practice domination over the masses will be transformed into a circle of unity, where all beings equally worship the God of love and compassion through divine spiritual balance. An awakening of this God-seed within their minds, bodies and souls is the principle of namasté—"the divine within me greets the divine within you." This will bring about the evolution of the heart center within all beings on Mother Gaia. You will begin to instinctively be intuitive, compassionate and empowered in the union of this divine paradigm.

PLATE 36. PENTON GRAFTON, MAY 30, 1999

This crop circle is a spinning calibration device that vibrates a frequency in the atmosphere that will bring profound unconditional love and resonate in the energies of faith and hope. This is the energetic manifestation of what Christ referred to as the mustard seed. It is the root of the consciousness shift that will truly transform your world. The covert government has invested billions of your tax dollars to create resonant devices to lower the frequencies and control the masses in fear—for example, HAARP (High-Frequency Active Auroral Research Program). The power of this formula will render these devices harmless and have a powerful effect on evolution.

All energy is measurable in hertz and megahertz; the vibration of fear has a lower frequency than the vibration of love. Scientists have not discovered the fractaline frequency code for the components that attach themselves in resonant tones to these two primal emotions. For example, fear with some percentage of faith has a different frequency than fear without the balancing aspect of hope. All energy can be expressed mathematically, and these frequencies affect every aspect of the original creation of Gaia and her inhabitants. The awakening of the heart center has successfully increased the frequencies of the vibratory pulse of Mother Gaia. You have already reached a critical mass that will expand the resonant frequencies and rejuvenate this planet. Basically, faith is the culture from which this genesis will spring. This is the frequency-energetic device that will spark our divine potential through emanation from the emotional mind-heart of those awakened beings who have reached bodhisattva-hood, or enlightenment. The power of positive thought manifestation has been carefully instructed in the blessed works of many beloved teachers such as Deepak Chopra, Gregg Braden and James Twyman, to mention a few well-known sources; there are multitudes of others. Many of you are already living the principles of peace. Your aural fields vibrate at a higher frequency, and your newly evolved energy fields function to transmute negative energy and assist in the Earth's healing and ascension.

Conceive through meditation upon this crop circle and star glyph the formula for the heightened potential for the creation of love: $(\text{hope} + \text{faith})^{10,000}$. You could construct a device with movable parts that would demonstrate the mathematical formulas present in this miraculous metamorphosis of the collective consciousness. Can you see the potential power of the small circle to move the larger mass in a centrifuge of energetic configuration? Once this movement reaches a specific energetic frequency, there will be a collective leap in consciousness and the paradigm will shift on the planet. If a small percentage of you praying in faith with James Twyman can stop a war, what would millions of like-spirited beings be capable of in the movement of frequencies that is represented in this set? When the critical mass is reached, the fractal formula expands, causing a chain reaction. This phenomenon is likened only to the opposite of a nuclear bomb. I hesitate to use this example, but it might be helpful to remember that all that was used to destroy will now be used to heal and create the new paradigm of heaven on Earth, or the return to Eden.

In meditation with this set, picture that this is a seed of creative genesis and visualize it in the expansive genesis of the mind-hearts of every being on Mother Earth. The first meditation is to create an image in your mind that the children are well-fed, tenderly cared for and educated (not programmed) in creative environments that spark their creative genius. Now, apply this meditation to the formula mentally. Next, scan the set and activate your neurosynapses. Once this is done, holographically project it into the crystalline orb and plant it in the collective. The effects will be astounding—the children will suffer no more.

The star glyph is a language that describes this metamorphosis and the process of activation of this formula. By meditating upon this set and holographically projecting it into the collective mind, you will be sparking this alchemical reaction. This is where spiritual practices meet with scientific law in creation. The application of this set might be the most important work you ever do in your life. When the morning star returns, the phoenix will rise out of the ashes.

PLATE 37. HENWOOD, AUGUST 3, 1999

This crop circle is the full geometric representation of the alpha and the omega. It resonates a frequency of perfect balance and a pure emanation of the great I Am presence. This is the House of God, the completion of the twelve elementals in perfect balance with the Mother/Father and the Holy Spirit in the manifestation of divine potential.

The center of the crop circle is the eye of God, now viewed in the psyche of mankind as being in the center of the great pyramid, not at the top. The center is the heart source.

The birth of Eden will be spiritually carried within the wombs of twelve women. They carry the spiritual essence of the return of the Christ, to be birthed into a new world of peace. This is represented in your mythologies by the resurrection, as your dying planet is resurrected. The formula for this alchemical manifestation is carried within this glyph. The women who carry this God-seed are called the White Calves. They are brides of the Christ; they are of the ancient lineage of the Magdalena. Each is a resonator of the frequencies encoded in this crop circle. Christ was not limited to one continent, and the vine spread throughout the world. They are anointed with the precious oils of Zod within the seventh house of light, betrothed in the beauty-way essence.

Within the mystery schools, the seeds of this emanation have been carefully protected. Those of the Great White Brother-/Sisterhood have protected this mystery through the long dark night of the soul to preserve the essence of this precious treasure. This is the long-sought alchemical formula for turning base metals into gold and silver souls. Look to the teachings of the beloved St. Germaine for the essence of this set. All of the wisdom of the light brotherhood is carried within this crop circle and star glyph.

There are many of you who have incarnated amnesic to your connections to the Great White Brother-/Sisterhood. It is time to awaken. You have brought a piece of this puzzle with you to be placed together now at the conjunction of the energies of Saturn with Venus and Mars. You literally carry a piece of this formula in your soul's DNA; you are as a match to a flame or as yeast to bread. This symbol is your wake-up call.

This is the House of God as it will be conceived in the consciousness of all inhabitants of Gaia (Mother Earth). It is the perfect balance and union of the Holy Spirit.

Within this crop circle is the essence of divine potential of all that is, all that was and all that ever will be. It is the melting point where time dissolves and the dream and illusion of the third dimension merge into the God-source. The ancient mantra for alchemy is *Maaa koo waa, maa koo waaa, maaa koo waaa, maaa koo waaa, and maa koo waaa.*

The star glyph is an image of the hidden Temple of Zamora where this mystery has been preserved. There within lies the Ark of the Covenant and the essence of the Holy Grail. Many have searched for this essence knowing that the ones who find it will have immeasurable power. Those of you who have known the essence of this, feared that the power would fall into the wrong hands. What the ones who searched did not know is that the mysteries to unlock the Ark of the Covenant were encoded in the DNA of a specific soul group. This protected the primal source from misuse by those who would control the planet in fear—lost souls or lost parts of you. Now the Temple of Zamora will be revealed, the Ark of the Covenant will be opened and the people will drink from the cup of the Grail that will be revealed in their hearts. The divine covenant will be upheld in the essence of the Lamb of God.

PLATE 38. NOVY JICIN, CZECH REPUBLIC, JULY 21, 1999

This crop circle is the electromolecular formula for the restructuring of the blood and bone cells of the human species to enhance T cells and the reproduction of natural antibodies that will be resistant to and capable of transmuting common disease-causing organisms. It is the evolutionary grid for the production of blood cells and bone marrow. A vital part of the strengthening of the human species is the evolution of superior blood-cell production and T-cell strength, resulting in viral-resistant blood strains. This is the imprint of the impending evolution of the bone marrow and blood cells of the human species.

The plan on the part of the covert government is to inoculate masses with the Armageddon virus in order to reduce populations in Third World countries. The AIDS virus was introduced into Africa as a means of genocide. The effort was to destroy the roots of the motherland grounded in the great African Tree of Peace. This virus was also engineered to further reduce the capacity of free will within the masses. If their plan is successful, Africa will be hit the hardest.

Initially, the Armageddon virus was sabotaged from within the system and is not as powerful as covert-government scientists projected it to be. The plan for massive release of the Armageddon virus would cause destruction far worse than what has happened in Africa. Steps have already been taken by ETs to enhance resistance to this plague by the massive infusion into the atmosphere of microorganisms that have already infiltrated the water and food sources. These jewels of advanced biochemistry will reproduce in the ecosystem, enter the food chain and be ingested into living organisms. The short-term goal of these microorganisms is to detoxify or neutralize the Armageddon virus; the long-range goal is to enhance T-cell production, evolving the structure and capacity of bone-marrow and blood-cell production.

PLATE 39. NEWTON ST. LOE, AUGUST 1999

This set is the multidimensional alignment of the cosmic forces of creation. The mathematics of this formula is available only in a space-time continuum that has not yet been accessed on the Earth plane. Simply put, it is the blueprint of creation that carries primal codes for the creation of universes, worlds and All That Is.

This blueprint must be activated for the life-altering frequencies to be resonant on the Earth plane. This is a sequential expansion of the blueprints that have held the matrix for the creation of your world. This expansion will occur multidimensionally and must be aligned in a continuum that transcends space and time. The energy of the continuum is a spiral of creative force expanding the thirteen-strand galactic DNA in thirteen dimensions. This is the quintessence—the fifth element or spirit—of this adjustment that must be developed in parallel dimensions and universes for the effect to be complete. It is the cosmic multidimensional alignment of the galactic forces within the formula for the emanation of the Eden principle. The fractal formula present in this set is the mathematical formula for the multidimensional shift gate that spans beyond time and space to the light frequencies that control creation.

This set also represents the opening of sections of the human brain that will allow your species to multidimensionally move through this spiral. The activation center is located in a previously unused anterior section of the brain, between the cerebellum and the midbrain along the brain stem. The evolution will begin with a primal group and then, when a critical mass has been reached, will expand to encompass the human species. The effects of this creative principle will be enormous as your species experiences an enhanced connection with the God-source.

Once this formula is completed in your galaxy, it will become the blueprint for other galaxies that have not evolved into this heightened state of consciousness. Do not anticipate this in the near future; this is a long-term effect that will be completed in a sequential forum that transcends the principles of linear time. The purpose of meditating with this set is to seed the collective mind of Mother Gaia with this inevitable evolutionary metamorphosis.

PLATE 40. TROTTISCLIFFE, JUNE 20, 1999

The formulas represented in this set are the codes to activate your lightbodies. As the energies of your planet quicken, your lightbodies will attain luminescence. The frequencies present in your lightbody encodements will be far different from the lower-density vibrations known to mankind in the past. Your DNA contains fiber optics that carry resonant light frequency codes for these activations. The pineal gland is the master gland for these activations.

This is essentially the initial phase of evolution that your species will undergo. The newly evolved lightbodies will have a powerful effect on the metamorphosis of Mother Gaia, as they will be encoded with light frequencies that will stimulate this evolved state on a cellular level of everything and everybody you come in contact with. You are the soul group of 144,000 that is spoken of in the Bible. Your lightbodies will emanate activation codes that will spark a chain reaction and quicken the enlightenment of your species. You will be used to activate the lightbodies of other beings.

As the veils thin, the realms of heaven will descend into the earthly kingdom. Your lightbodies carry frequencies that are encoded in the angelic realm. This formula will activate those frequencies, resulting in easier communication with the angelic realm. The angelic realm will be permitted easier access to the Earth plane.

Many masters have eagerly awaited this expansion of the light fields within the luminaries. They eagerly greet their Earth brothers and sisters and have long awaited the descending of the houses of light into the third dimension. This is part of the ascension of Mother Gaia into the fifth dimension.

This set is powerful for opening up the tunnels of light that will be used for this energetic exchange with the angelic realm. You are encouraged to gather in groups of three, using this set as a communication device to the angelic realm and as a tool to activate your lightbodies. You are the light brother-/sisterhood that has incarnated for this very purpose. Each individual might participate in several such activations. A living body of light will then be sparked within the original creation of your universe and multidimensionally in other galaxies and universes. The points at the center of each circle are wormholes or time tunnels that are coded into the geometries of those individuals who incarnated to ignite this matrix.

PLATE 41. WEST STOWELL, JULY 14, 2000

This green crop is a triad of the energies created by sacred sites in this area—with Adam's Grave at the tip—preparing for the intergalactic shift and marking the point of confluence of this energy field and intergalactic grid lines. Within this pyramid of energy there is an intergalactic shift point for the alignment and toning of galactic frequency wave patterns. Earth is emerging through point zero, causing electromagnetic frequencies and polar alignments to vary. To maintain planetary balance there must be an intergalactic and parallel universal alignment of the frequencies. This crop circle is a tuning fork or calibration device for the galactic shift that is occurring as we emerge through point zero. Not all of the frequency shifts are measurable by our scientific tools, but they are certainly measurable by ET tools.

Point zero is a phase—not a day—that occurs as part of a birthing process. It is a fulcrum point. This crop circle represents the physics for the interdimensional quantum adjustment formula. It has a stabiliz-ing effect on Earth's energies during this phase of emergence through point zero. This is a vital pulsar point, a key gate to intergalactic interdimensional portals. This formula aligns frequencies with the new galactic grid systems in preparation for the lunar eclipse on July 16, 2000. The mathematical formula for this crop circle is seen on the top left corner of the star glyph.

AUTHOR'S NOTE: The star beings introduced me to the concept of point zero six years ago when I was taken up on a ship. Gregg Braden's work helped me understand what they were referring to.

I observed intensified energy fields as we approached this crop circle. To the right of the crop circle at the foot of Knap Hill there is a possible confluence of under-ground streams. I observed with my third eye that there were orbs of light emanating in donutlike light forma-tions bursting from the confluence, pulsating up in light rings. The colors I perceived with my third eye were sil-ver gray and steel blue. They were pulsating in a col-umn, being released like a fountain. Barbara comment-ed that the description is like the torus energy that moves in a circular form like a donut—outside in, inside out. This is a basic way for energy to flow. Right across the valley is a hill where a crop circle depicted this phe-nomenon a few years ago.

As we approached the confluence, I began a sponta-neous past-life memory of conducting ancient Celtic ceremonies in the company of the women we were with. Barbara was the high priestess. She had left an energetic ceremonial bundle there in ancient times (one of seven left in the area), which awaited our return in this lifetime. This energetic bundle is somewhat of a sacred time capsule. We were the ancient ones returned to this sacred site as a soul group to maximize the effects of the combination of the energies of this crop circle with the ancient ceremonial energies of the confluence. We did prayer, toning and ceremony. As we did this, I observed a change in the frequencies— the orbs of light came closer together more rapidly and with a gold energy color.

We met Freddy Silva there and did the Flower of Life sacred geometry activation to open up the intergalactic portal for the aligning of the frequencies from this crop circle. This harmonized and aligned the frequencies interdimensionally. We were used as energy point loca-tors to align the frequencies by the circlemakers.

PLATE 42. SOUTH FIELD, ALTON PRIORS, JUNE 19, 2000

Thirty thousand years ago, the star beings implant-ed a resonant frequency device in the ethereal energy matrices surrounding sacred sites and hills to prepare the grid work for the massive energy shift. Throughout the ages, sacred ceremonies and rites have been conducted to prepare the frequencies and maintain the delicate energy balances necessary for the energy shifts and the openings of cosmic fre-quencies that are now taking place.

There is a direct frequency discord resonance from this crop circle to Woodborough Hill. The burials in this area hold the frequency of shamanic energy, which is specifically grided in the necessary frequen-cies for activation of this device. (There is a direct energy relationship to crop circle 41, located across the road at the foot of Knap Hill at approximately a forty-five degree angle to this crop circle.) This angle is energetically linked to the confluence near crop cir-cle 41 and is located specifically on major grid and ley lines intersecting this area. This forty-five degree angle is paramount for the astrological alignment of the frequencies that have been downloaded to the grid lines.

The purpose of this crop circle is to create a specif-ic geometric point to facilitate the full activation of the surrounding sacred sites of Adam's Grave, Knap Hill and Woodborough Hill and the relative Mother/Father energetics of this location.

This color is an infusion of a new spectral energy pattern into our prism of light frequencies. Part of the purpose of this crop circle is to infuse a new fre-quency of light vibration and energy into the grid and ley lines that will enter into the Earth's light spectrum. This will shift our light spectrum from its present vibration into a higher frequency, allowing a larger variety of colors to emanate onto the planet. The purpose of the crop circle is to emanate a whole new color of the violet, sapphire and ruby rays. Our spectrum of light frequencies will be completely altered by this phenomenon. This color will be avail-able for artistic use within two decades, and the color charts currently being used will need to be altered. This light frequency is being infused into the grid system of the planet, causing a massive energy surge that maximizes the intergalactic shift gate of crop circle 41.

When a new light spectrum is introduced, we open up a vast potential for the electromagnetic frequencies in the brain cells to vibrate at a different light and sound frequency. As people on the planet visually absorb the new light frequencies, they will expand the neurosynapses of the human brain. This will create a massive opening and tuning of the neurosynapses of the planetary or collective mind. Each one of the appendages of this crop circle represents the electro-molecular structure of a new light frequency in Earth's color spectrum. Each appendage is a vibrational (octrahendric) sound frequency that will be infused into the light pattern and influence the changing of all prismatic energy on the planet.

⊲ ⃰⧗⃰ ⊲

AUTHOR'S NOTE: With my third eye, I observed a beautiful color emanating from the crop circle, one that I had never seen on Earth before. It was somewhat violet, but of a color I did not recognize. I observed with my third eye a reddish purple-violet light in a network of frequencies going out through the Earth's grid lines, connected to an ethereal energy device in Woodborough Hill.

I experienced this color but have no way to describe it in words. My brain cells were being used to connect the frequencies of this phenomenon to the sacred geometry of the area and the formula of the crop circle and then to implant it in the collective consciousness of the planet. The women in our group had the proper DNA and implanted this spectral energy through meditation into the planetary grid lines.

PLATE 43. AVEBURY DOWN, JULY 16, 2000

The Sun, Earth and Moon are represented in the holy trinity as the Father, Mother and Holy Spirit. These are the energies that were in alignment on the day of the lunar eclipse, July 16, 2000. This lunar eclipse was paramount in preparing for the emergence of Earth through point zero. It contains the formula for the alignment of lunar and solar frequencies for the massive infusion of life prana into Mother Gaia (Earth Mother) through the portal shaft that has been opened in Silbury Hill. This crop circle is the formula for the balance of the trinity for this lunar/solar

event. Consider that the lunar eclipse occurs in this area in the midafternoon and that there is a peak activity of solar flares that maximize the lunar and solar effect. The lunar eclipse is invisible in the day sky, but the effect on this region during intense solar flares is extremely powerful and effective for the energy surge that your planet is to receive.

This crop circle is the formula for the balance of the cosmic energies as the surge of photon energy enters your atmosphere during this lunar eclipse. The formula is a combination of an ET-assisted surge protector—referred to as a triadrasonic residual essence—with the energies present in a midday lunar eclipse during solar flares. This effect is anchored in seven dimensions as a stable, resonating frequency. It is, simply put, a surge protector to guard the planet from massive upheaval as this frequency is beamed from the Arcturian mothership's tetratronic reactor through the shaft in Silbury Hill. Frequencies are first balanced and resonated with this formula before the surge enters the sacred temple of the birthing mother known as Silbury Hill.

Many individuals who were actively involved with ceremonies in the sacred ring of trees by this crop circle are present in this lifetime. They have come as alchemists to be receivers for this phenomenon. The implantation of this crop circle has been carefully prepared energetically by many centuries of ceremonies in the womb located in the circle of trees at the top of Silbury Hill. The content of the sacred spring at the top of this hill emerges from the crystalline sacred waters of your planet. This water source was tapped as an alchemical aspect for toning the frequencies for this surge protector (or triadular resonate equal phasar balancing device, in ET terminology). The balance of planetary waters—influenced by this phenomenon, full lunar eclipses, tide activity and lunar cycles—is critical for the avoidance of typhoons and hurricanes as the Earth receives the fertilization of the pod of Eden through the shaft of Silbury Hill.

Use this set as a meditation for those individuals who are guided to assist in energy balancing during the Earth changes. Group meditations are particularly useful with this set at times of planetary alignments, eclipses and other cosmic phenomena that influence the electromagnetic balance of the planet.

AUTHOR'S NOTE: The energies in this crop circle were very intense. I went into it twice. The first time was the day of the lunar eclipse; the second time was with Barbara a few days later. I was immediately drawn to the circle of trees at the top of the hill. The energy produced strong dowsing results. The circle is in a womb formation with the "cervix" facing to the south. The center is sunken ten feet into the earth. There was no evidence of activity in the area such as a ceremony would create; the undergrowth looked undisturbed. I was then drawn to an outcropping of vegetation protected by a fence. There I found a lovely spring/well. The energies were very sweet and sacred. I felt it was no accident that I would be drawn to these two very special places on the hill where the crop circle appeared.

PLATE 44. PICKED HILL, JULY 16, 2000

The ethers surrounding Picked Hill are a holding place for the Holy Grail energy. This sacred temple and the knowledge of its mythological importance have been protected from the general public. Use respect and reverence for this site if you choose to go there.

The crop circle that appeared at the base of the hill is the code for the activation of the forty-fourth aspect of the Holy Grail. The Holy Grail will be complete when all fifty-two aspects are activated. (Each aspect carries a crystalline code of 144 geometric sequential light and sound factors triplicate to the quadrasonic resonant factor of twelve fractal trigametric sequence patterns.) The ancient myth of King Arthur and the Holy Grail and the implantation of the Grail mythology into the collective psyche represent a much larger principle.

The Grail represents the womb of the Cosmic Mother, known in Christian mythology as Mother Mary and in all other mythologies as the pregnant mother goddess or virgin birth. The Grail is the womb soul of the mother goddess energy. This womb carries the DNA of the Christ and is a reference to the DNA encoded in the blood of the Christ.

The forty-fourth aspect is a formula for the creation of the female paradigm. The mother (female) energy has suffered a long and painful repression by the male warrior/destroyer energy. The awakened mother goddess energy will birth heaven on Earth. The Grail is the cup that carries her blood or the life force that in your sacred text flowed through the veins of her son, the son of God, Christ Jesus. The son of God is he who carries the full spectrum of the creative God-source in his DNA.

The Grail is in fact a scientific formula of quantum physics and sacred fractal geometry. It is the completion of the ancient mathematical formula that was set into myth on your planet during the time of the temples of the House of David [see Appendix B], when the Eden principle was first initiated on the Gaia planet. This formula is the completion of the forty-fourth aspect of the Grail, the vessel of God's pure life force originating from the womb of the Cosmic Mother. This life force feeds the embryo of the coming age of enlightenment. This crop circle is a meeting place between spirit, myth and science.

AUTHOR'S NOTE: I observed with my third eye a ring of twelve crystals emanated in frequency patterns of six-dimensional aspects spinning around the Grail. Before I visited the crop circle, I entered a grove of trees on the side of Picked Hill that measured very high with dowsing techniques. I was drawn to do sacred geometry energy work within this grove of trees, which is the portal to the internal Grail energies within Picked Hill. For some reason, this grove is fenced off. I literally had to crawl into the circle of trees, where the energies were so strong that I could not stand up. I had a very intense energy experience within the circle; my entire body began to hum and vibrate. When I crawled out, I was having heart palpitations and had to lie down for some time before I could get up and walk.

PLATE 45. MILTON LILBOURNE, JULY 19, 2000

The purpose of this crop circle is multifaceted. This formation is the pure essence of the universal and cosmic law of peace in a quadecliptic balance. Within the mound in the center is the serpent goddess, she who devours (transmutes) the poison that would destroy this precious green planet, she who rights the imbalances and brings her kundalini gift to awaken the God-seed.

The winged serpent is of heaven and Earth—the embodiment of the cosmic law of peace through wisdom. The power of the serpentine goddess is concentrated in this ancient grave mound. Within her womb are held the sacred scrolls of ancient wisdom, the secrets of mound and Stonehenge builders. These are the mysteries protected by the keepers of the light of primordial innocence.

Many ages ago, the star beings came to this field and gathered with the mound builders to implant a time capsule in this mound that is now being activated. Within this mound in the ethereal energies are four time-coded capsules that are set in the frequencies to activate now. Each capsule carries seeds of wisdom that will spring forth within the collective mind—wisdom that has been known until now only by your enlightened ones, your peacekeepers. Can you conceive these seeds of wisdom, peace and balance springing forth in the collective mind?

This circle and mound are energetically linked with the spiritual energy of the prayers for peace and the peacekeepers. They are the ones of great wisdom, the ascended masters and wisdom keepers who walk the Earth to assist in bringing about the great peace. It is an accumulation of energies of all peace ceremonies that are currently being conducted globally. The energies of these ceremonies are collectively being condensed into the four diamond scrolls within the womb of the serpentine goddess. These are the "eggs" of the age of peace. The fractal formula for this matrix has been quickened and alchemically released through the light and sound frequencies emanated by this crop circle.

The location—close to the military training fields—is no accident, and alchemically it will have a powerful effect in transmuting the minds of those who still train for violent acts against humanity.

This set can be used as a meditation tool to maximize the effects of global peace ceremonies. It also can be useful in focusing peaceful energy into places of destructive activity such as Silbury Plain, the Pentagon in the U.S. and any other military command centers.

PLATE 46. OLD SHAW VILLAGE, JULY 16, 2000

Within the frequency codes that define mass and matter, a genetic alteration is being conducted to alter life forms on the Earth. Literally, this is a DNA restructuring of the basic structures of the planet's biosystem. This formula is the preparation for the fre-quency adjustment as mass and matter shift into the higher vibrations resonating on the planet. The world appears to be the same, yet all is altered; nothing is as it appears. The alchemy of St. Germaine and Merlin is the mystical frequency that permits the illusion of sameness.

The shift of the base cellular frequencies of mass and matter will assist in creating the new hologram in the cosmic dream field. This is a frequency device set to alter the patterns and energy fields of your planet as you emerge through the wormhole or point zero. New species and mutations of existing species will appear within your life field and mend the damaged life chain by replacing important extinct species on the planet.

In altering the baseline DNA structure of mass and matter globally, it is then possible to have a quantum effect on galactic consciousness through resonating frequencies, through this altered state into other parallel dimensions and galaxies. This process will go back and alter the original creation via a nonlinear time line.

PLATE 47. BLACKLAND, JULY 30, 2000

The Arcturian mothership contains a device that affects the solar frequencies entering the Earth's atmosphere, stimulating alpha brain waves and adjusting the bipolar frequencies within the brain. In ET terms, this device is called a quadrasonic de-frequency solar resonator. The technological description of the workings of this ET device is: "the alpha component adjusted within a quadric-solar resequencing pattern adjustor." This crop circle is the formula that is being implanted into the solar rays to create the phenomenon.

The basic result is an enhanced solar effect, stimulating the rapid metamorphosis of life forms on Earth. It also triggers alpha states in the brain chemistries of all species. The enhancement of alpha states will be partially accomplished by means of enhancing vitamin D absorption from the Sun. An additional factor influencing this delicate project is the higher vibratory fields resonated by the awakened beings who are entering alpha states, or states of peaceful consciousness. The non-Earth formula for this phenomenon is "three megatronic refracted frequencies of 13 hertz (7 millitron X 3)." This formula is included here for future scientific research.

The date that the full potential of these effects will be reached has not yet been determined, but the projection for full frequency activation is by the year 2021.

Connecting in meditation with these images will enhance your absorption of these frequencies and advance your evolution.

PLATE 48. WINDMILL HILL, AVEBURY TRUSLOE, JUNE 18, 2000

This crop circle is the magnetic formula for the new interdimensional light web that we on the astral plane have carefully placed around Mother Earth to assist with this massive transmutation and quickening of Earth's energy fields during what is known as the Mayan Day Out of Time in the year 2000. It will sustain the holographic field and stabilize mass and matter for the movement of Earth through point zero. It replaces the fear grid that has held your planet for so many Earth years. This new grid is being activated through the energies set within the light grid implanted in Neolithic times beneath the surface of this sacred area.

As Earth prepares to shift through the wormhole into a new space-time dimension, the two nets of light and sound frequencies must be activated and harmonically resonated in a tone frequency of sixteen million megahertz per rotation of Earth's solar and orbital pattern. The Earth will reach what is termed by Arcturian technicians as a "spin-gate frequency within a shift elongated to the circum parallel dimensional equasic code lineation." Once this frequency is detected, the full resonant connection between the ancient time-coded light net that was implanted activates into full acceleration with the light net that has been placed around the planet. The mothership is standing by in preparation for the generators to intensify the frequencies in the core of the polar axis and stabilize the planet as it emerges through point zero.

PLATE 49. MILK HILL, ALTON BARNES, JULY 1, 2000

The time capsule that carries the master plans for the sequence of crop circles, locations, formulas and quantum effects, lies within a crystalline orb located in the ethereal of this mound or tumulus called Adam's Grave. Adam is known in your mythology as the father of mankind, and this mound is known in mythology as the breast of the Alton Barnes goddess, the Blessed Mother's breast from which milk flows to feed the world. The mythologies and sacred ceremonies conducted at this site throughout history were vital in the process of energizing the crystalline orb that carried the codes for these gifts.

This particular crop circle is the master code or blueprint of the frequencies and formulas to be activated in this area during the crop circle season of the year 2000. This is the master plan for circles that appeared later in the season.

A rose window reflects light and beauty through geometric designs. It becomes an object of focused concentration, which expands a pattern into a light pattern in the human brain, interpreted as art. This crop circle formulated this function by bringing the master plan into form and resonance for the sequence of circles encoded in the crystalline orb—the time capsule—that was implanted in this mound by the House of David. The command center for the Eden plan (blueprint) was located here during the ages of the House of David. The blueprint was encoded and implanted in this mound for activation during the emergence of heaven on Earth. This particular image is the master plan for the cycle of crop circles, which planned to appear during the summer season of 2000.

By viewing this set and doing suggested meditation, your DNA's sacred geometry can connect to the entire plan of this blueprint, having a positive effect on the critical mass of the entire project. This image is the master code for the entire matrix, set into action regionally. Please note the appearance of important circles on dates when other lightbeings are conducting world prayers for peace and ascension gatherings. These prayers create a collective effect on the planetary energies vital for the miraculous healing of Mother Earth.

The star glyph is the image of the crystalline orb, encoded with both the blueprint for this season's crop circles and a key to the entire plan for the scheduled appearances of the crop circles during the birthing of Gaia, or the Eden project. By activating your neurosynapses with this image, you can connect your psyche to and actively engage in this master plan in a positive way. Those in the fear vibration who would attempt to use these images for sabotage of the project (ET or human), need not bother. The frequency codes respond only to a high vibrational field of love. The project will not respond to the low-vibration frequencies emanated in the fear vibration. They will receive frequencies to assist in increasing their frequencies to a higher vibration. They will benefit from the experience but cannot adversely affect it.

PLATE 50. AVEBURY TRUSLOE, JULY 22, 2000

The emergence of Earth into a new frequency pattern has a multitude of phases that stretch over Earth years up to 2012. You are being assisted multidimensionally by advanced entities from parallel universes. The Arcturian mothership *Phasar Nine* is the scientific headquarters for the project known to the Galactic Federation as the Eden project. As each phase is completed, frequencies are monitored, evaluated and decoded to determine encodements for the next phase of Earth changes. This crop circle is the encodement of what is termed by ET scientists as the completion of the "full-spectral alignment of the quantum matrix activating the galactic counterpoint process." This crop circle is the code sequence for intergalactic frequency and phase shift adjustments. The result is a rejuvenation and recalibration to the original blueprint of the essential life force within the third dimension on Earth.

The spheres in this crop circle represent the merging of the alpha and omega (mother/father) energies in the creation of the new paradigm. The magnetic frequencies of Earth have been multidimensionally realigned, creating new frequency patterns. The recalibration to the original blueprint is complete; the galactic counterpoint process has been activated.

These frequency patterns sustain life in a divine creative pattern, balancing the negative and positive poles. This phenomenon will last thirteen years in Earth time. You are witnessing the cosmic code for the full potential of the alpha and the omega in cosmic cocreation.

The original blueprint has been set in the energy grid patterns for a rapid transformation of all life forms expressed as mass and matter, including thought forms on the Earth plane.

Prepare for massive rapid metamorphosis of the world as you know it. Obstacles for ascension that appeared insurmountable will dissolve before your eyes. Do not limit your thought patterns by what was once unattainable. The future is filled with potential, and a return to divine creation is in process. Although to your perception the world appears the same, it is not. Be prepared for what have been termed miracles, for the world will open like a lotus blossom before you. Use this set in meditation to facilitate the transformational process.

The effect of this formula was enhanced by the large number of people entering this circle within days of its formation. Many of the individuals in the area were carrying important DNA activation geometries. Sound-frequency activation was effective in maximizing the effect with group meditation for world peace. This event was conducted by Gandiva, master of sound, with the use of Tibetan bowls and resonant toning devices. All activities that appear to be spontaneous within these very special crop circles are actually parts of the alchemical formula being activated. The individuals are responding to a deep call to participate in this mystical phenomenon, and in doing so, they become part of the formula.

PLATE 51. WEST AMESBURY, JULY 19, 2000

This crop circle is the announcement of the eleventh solar house of light joining the galactic councils; this is a great event in galactic history. The mystery houses of the eleven/eleven now resonate in a full frequency alignment with the thirteen/thirteen. The twelve temples that were represented by the twelve apostles are complete; the eleventh apostle has joined the thirteenth (Christ consciousness).

There are magnificent ceremonies being conducted intergalactically to celebrate the joining of the eleventh house of light—the missing link—with the Galactic Federation. Although this is an event of galactic proportions, Earthlings do not know it. Everyone is carrying on as usual. The forty-fourth aspect of the Holy Grail had to be complete before the eleventh solar house could join the Council of Thirteen. This galactic event is as significant as the

Mayan prophecy's "end of the nine hells and beginning of the thirteen heavens." Refer to crop circle 13; this 1999 crop circle was the energy matrix that birthed this event.

The thirteen/thirteen must be in full alignment for the master plan to be activated. The formula present in this crop circle is for anchoring the full alignment of the thirteen/thirteen into the third-dimensional Earth plane.

PLATE 52. EAST KENNETT, JULY 2 AND 16, 2000

The frequencies in the formula for this set contain energies that will harmonize and balance human brain-wave energy with an activated and expanded heart chakra to accommodate a more compassionate species of humans. The crop circle becomes a harmonic psychatronic energy device when specific frequencies of light and sound are projected into the grid and ley lines (implanting the formula into the planetary collective energetics). The ET technical term for this is "exatronic resonator of equilateral miatradular harmonic energy device."

Using the most universal symbol known to man, we have introduced the frequencies into the biosphere, grid lines and ley lines. This frequency resonance will impede the effectiveness of HAARP and activate mass ascension of pure Christ love frequencies. Subsequently, there will be a massive heart chakra opening. The effect will peak over the next thirteen years.

The cubic crop circle contains light resonance patterns that are literally repatterning brain-wave frequencies and activating the heart chakra of the human species. This will help to transform ideologies that are no longer useful in the new paradigm, such as greed based on the fear of not having enough, competition based upon the survival of the fittest and the hoarding of power and monetary abundance based on the fear of deprivation. The new brain patterns will release chemicals such as endorphins, creating an enhanced feeling of euphoria in masses of humanity that will be supported with compassion, generosity and creativity.

Part of the long-range effect of the emanation of this frequency is the expanded use of the right and left hemispheres of the brain simultaneously. The human species will expand its brain capacity from the current average of ten percent to nearly one hundred percent.

The process will repattern the controlling mentality present in current theology. The new spirituality is based on a desire to resonate with higher sources of wisdom and convey these jewels into the mass consciousness for the spiritual ascension and the betterment of all, not just the self.

This set was created partially for the phenomenon to occur during the lunar eclipse. The sacred DNA geometries of the group that gathered to pray and meditate on world peace were part of the alchemical activation of this formula. During the ceremony, the group brain-wave patterns from each person were formulated into the crop circle. They attained a high state of collective love energy during the ceremony that was conducted in the heart circle on the eve of July 16, 2000. These frequencies were encoded with the DNA of nearly two hundred individuals to be woven with the DNA of various lineages and human forms currently residing on the planet. The maximum effect was achieved during the lunar eclipse as the Earth received the massive beam of photon energy through the shaft in Silbury Hill.

The wedding that was conducted following the formation of this crop circle prepared the frequency patterns for the peace meditation that was conducted on July 16, 2000. The love vibration in the holy union of man and woman was alchemically combined with existing frequencies, setting the energy patterns for the group meditation on the night of the lunar eclipse. Please refrain from excluding yourselves from the crop circle process and phenomenon. In alchemy, as in science, all factors contribute to the completed form.

PLATE 53. ALLINGTON DOWN, AUGUST 1, 2000

When gods dance amongst the corn,
the Sun will shine from early morn,
the Earth will dance beyond the gate and
heaven's song will no longer wait.
The myth and lore of long gone by
will be the lyre of golden seeds
that strings our souls as gossamer beads.

This crop circle is the completion of the long-awaited dance of the kachinas (Native American spiritual beings). They have come from the three mesas, from the keepers of the tablets of light, from the sacred land of the Hopi. Blue Star Kachina has traveled within the body of a woman to physically manifest at the sacred sites and awaken the seven light orbs, uniting the force fields of these ancient centers of enlightenment. The ancient ones of the Whirling Rainbow Way dance between the worlds and awaken vast planetary entities held in waiting for the universal moment of truth.

The seven hoops of light become resonating light patterns as they awaken to full spectral frequencies. These hoops of light, or time capsules, were implanted within critical points of the Earth's lightbodies. Through the ages, these areas have been centers of powerful ceremonies and used as energy receptors, preparing the land for the initiation. The orbs of light are located within the sacred Black Hills (the Lakota holy land) and the borders of Scotland (the resting place of the Templars of Rossalyn). The full initiation has been completed. The Templars of Rossalyn have been freed from the hold of the death fear to rise as knights of justice, peace and freedom in the spiritual realm.

At the same time, vast numbers of the tortured souls of the victims of genocide have been released from the entrapment of the death fear. These souls were being manipulated energetically to maintain the deteriorating fear grid around the planet.

The kachinas unite the dimensions of light as they dance the dream fields into being. This is the link of the seven/seven. The forces of light and love long ago separated are now reunited in all dimensions. It is most essential to create beautiful images with this set. The more it is introduced into the collective mind, the better the results for all.

Within the star glyph are the formulas to create the maximum results with this energy blueprint using energy patterns and light frequencies. There will be those of you who will be guided to take these images on location in these areas to be used in ceremonies and in the physical creation of these energetic images in the third dimension. If you are so guided, then this is your mission. Perform the sequence of rituals to fully anchor the seven light orbs, or hoops of light,

during power times with specific groups of souls who carry the sacred DNA for these activations. There are those of you who will be guided to these locations for ritual, guided by a deep subconscious agreement encoded in your DNA.

AUTHOR'S NOTE: The above poem was received by me as a spontaneous transmission when I visited this crop circle.

PLATE 54. WOODBOROUGH HILL, ALTON PRIORS, AUGUST 13, 2000

Within the divine potential of All That Is dwells all that has been and all that will ever be. This is the portal of all divine possibilities, the meeting place of cosmic creation. Within this matrix are potential universes that will never be birthed. It is the cosmic gene pool of all possibilities in the creative matrix of the universal hologram. That which will be emanates on a balanced stellar frequency with the time continuum of all that is and all that has been.

In uniting the emanations of all divine possibilities and time fields, the space-time continuum within the wave patterns that define matter becomes fluid. This allows a polar shift and a restructuring of the cellular components without major disturbances in the third-dimensional hologram as Earth emerges through point zero. This is the formula that stabilizes the hologram of linear time in this massive swirling of cosmic interdimensional frequencies in all parallel universes and time fields during the point zero emergence.

Allow your eyes to rapidly shift between the images of the crop circle and the star glyph. This will encode your brain's neurocortex to adjust from the rapidly deteriorating old world to the newly resonant third-dimensional hologram.

PLATE 55. GIANT'S GRAVE, AUGUST 3, 2000

This is a toning device balancing three fields of resonant sound frequencies that have not yet been available to the audio receptors of humanity. The animal kingdom has integrated this frequency shift, but it has not been detected by the limited Earth technology.

The tonal frequencies introduced enhance the emanation of the universal Om with three octave wave frequencies, completing the aural spectrum resonant within the solar houses of the thirteen/thirteen. The baseline of the wavelength of the octave will shift .001 degrees in the sound continuum. This seems to be a minute shift, but it will facilitate vast healing effects in the vibrations of the existent sound frequency fields.

This new sound emanation could not be introduced prior to the breakdown of the fear grid around the Earth field and the anchoring of the light grid. This fine-tone frequency could not emanate in the low vibration field that emanated prior to the massive shift in the summer of 2000. I emphasize that Earth technology cannot as yet detect this new sound frequency emanation resonated within the spectrum of the previously existing sound-wave frequencies.

This shift is critical for the evolution of more enlightened and attuned inhabitants of the Earth plane. Once this frequency code is fully activated and anchored within the wave spell, there will be gradual increases of the frequencies of the universal Om, tuning Earth to a higher, more spiritual vibration field.

The introduction of this sound frequency formula will affect the collective dream field in a very positive way. Literally, there will be a resonant frequency that, although not consciously audible during REM sleep, will be detected by the audio canal, stimulating pleasant dreams, increasing alpha states and allowing a deeper REM sleep; this can be used as a tool for ascension. This frequency code is inaudible and therefore will not cause confusion or irritation to the human species. It will render HAARP useless.

The use of this set accompanied with sounds from crystal and Tibetan bowls, harp music, didgeridoos and other high-vibration instrumentation, will enhance the effect of this phenomenon.

PLATE 56. CLENCH, AUGUST 11, 2000

There has been a decline of spiritually repressive religion as we have known it and an evolution of spiritual practices within the Earth temple. The world's religions have been used both as instruments of oppression, fear and control, and focal points of faith and unity in the Holy Spirit. There are a limited number of original religions that dominate the theology of the masses. These are largely rooted in the patriarchal societies and in the reign of the goddess in some matriarchal societies. This power structure will shift to the emanation of divine union and balanced cocreation within the Mother, Father and Holy Spirit.

These religious practices were implemented to maintain control of the masses and utilized for covert fear operations. The assumption was that the common person was not evolved enough to communicate with the higher houses of light and the esoteric principalities. The religious structure interpreted extraterrestrial entities as gods and lightbeings as angels. The secrets for magic, emanation of the Holy Spirit and spiritual techniques for movement of energies were held by a select few, many of whom used the gifts for control and power. With the emergence of the Eden principle, the ancient mysteries are being revealed to an increasing number of incarnate souls. The paradigm is shifting.

This crop circle and star glyph are encoded with the key to the doors of the mystery schools that have been barred from the masses until now. This star glyph is an encoded ancient talisman for revealing the mystery schools and opening the temples of light. It is the root of all mysteries found in the Egyptian, Mayan and Incan empires, the schools of mysteries in Nepal and India, the inner temples of the Orient, and the Chaconian and Silburian complexes, to name a few.

The four sections were kept separate in deep ethereal chambers beneath four temples in four key sacred sites: the Great Pyramid at Giza, the Temple of the Moon at Lake Titicaca, Chichén Itzá and Silbury Hill. The talisman was in four separate pieces, enshrouded in the energetic fields of these temples. The pieces of the talisman were united through the ceremonies and prayers of the awakened beings of light during the summer of 2000. It will be complete and activated by the spring of 2003. The release of the teachings and practices of the mystery schools will not be fully revealed until a later date.

The crop circle is the formula of light and sound frequencies that releases the secrets and the seals of the mystery schools. All over the planet, teachings will begin that were once only known to a privileged few.

The prophet will be in the marketplace and on the street corner. The mantra for the reception of these esoteric teachings is *Ma koa, ma koa, ma koa* (to be toned like the Om chant, *Maaaaaaaaaaaaaaaaaaa Kooooooooooooaaaaaaaaaaaaaa*). Use this mantra in combination with a visual image of the crop circle and the star glyph to expedite this process.

PLATE 57. BROADBURY BANKS, AUGUST 5 AND 13, 2000

The crop circle on the left is the device that, once implemented, activates sacred geometry within individuals, soul groups and sacred sites (known and unknown), restructuring the cellular geometries of all mass and matter on this planet. Focus on the top portion of the star glyph, and imagine dormant fractal codes within the subatomic cellular structures being activated with this device.

The crop circle on the right is the device that interprets the dormant fractal light patterns into sound frequencies and reverberates them into form and matter. Focus on the lower part of the star glyph, and imagine this expansive activation and the positive effects it will have on the inhabitation of this plane.

These fractal codes were imprinted in the subatomic structure of the planetary essence at the time of creation. As life springs forth, each cell is encoded with these dormant fractal geometries. To visualize this activation, picture a great city in darkness with one switch that turns on all the lights. Suddenly, before your eyes appears a massive field of light. The difference in what will happen and this scenario is that a great city is resonating erratic rapid frequencies. This activation is tuned for harmonic resonance. In the Records of Ra, this project is named the Microtroptic Fractal Code principle.

This process is a major factor in the ascension and awakening of heaven on Earth. A cosmic expansion of these dormant codes is the root for the massive metamorphic restructuring of mass and matter on the Earth plane. Full activation will be complete in approximately thirty-three Earth years.

PLATE 58. BISHOPS CANNINGS, JUNE 26, 2000

This set resonates the release codes for freeing individual souls and families long held bound in states of depression and chaos. These codes will cause the interdimensional shift in parallel time zones that will release fear, heal wounded souls, allow for peace and heal the trauma cycles that have repeated generation upon generation throughout the long dark night of the soul.

It is true that all of this drama has strengthened the collective soul. We are all *one*; there is no separation. Yet for the emergence into the new paradigm, it is necessary to clear old patterns ingrained on a cellular level in the neuroresponses and encoded in families' DNA. The cellular memory of DNA is encoded with vast amounts of low-vibration trauma responses that resonate on a fear frequency. The formulas of trauma are held in place by the imprisonment of tortured souls. Some of the well-known trauma sites are Auschwitz, My Lai and Wounded Knee. These areas are being cleared. The souls can move on because the energy fields have shifted and the door of Karmikaya has been opened. This door in the fourth dimension allows complete karmic cleansing for all incarnate souls.

Those of you who are guided to engage in the healing of generational bondage will find this set very helpful. It is now possible to clear generational patterns that repeat trauma and fear programs. The gateways to the kingdom of heaven are open. The formulas for ascension are now available in the energy fields of the essence of the planetary structure. Utilize this availability, and go forth in joy.

Many of you are like the elephant raised with a chain around his foot. When the chain is removed, he might not realize that he is free. The chain has been removed; claim your freedom. As the formulas for ascension are utilized, there will be a domino effect for those who are not yet conscious enough to do the work themselves. As you heal your lineage, family members will begin to make more enlightened choices. This also works on your soul families, those not genetically related to you, but related through past lives to your soul DNA. Sit for a moment and conceive the vast numbers of souls each of you are connected to. Now, conceive the implementation of massive karmic cleansing and soul healing. You are indeed a homeopathic remedy.

This set will be very useful for this process. With or without these images, the process is in effect and the formulas are engrained into your biochemical energy field. Know that this is true; accept it within every cell of your system. This knowingness will be extremely beneficial to the process.

PLATE 59. BISHOPS CANNINGS DOWN, JUNE 18, 2000

This crop circle was placed on a specific grid point that energetically links the Masonic monument with the ancient Neolithic tumulus of the Lady of Light, En Na Ki Tan.

She is the root of Ganeshkato, the priestess of the inner sanctum of temples of light that have held the formulas for the awakening. She cracks paradigms and shifts dimensions. When she awakens, a cosmic force of great proportions will be stirred. The ceremonies conducted in this area have honored her spirit and funded the energies for this awakening. Her essence is engrained in all major planetary houses of light. She is a laser beam of light frequencies that connects the very essence of *all* earthen temples to this energy source. She is known by many names and has greatly influenced the protection of the force fields from imploding in darkness and chaos. She is keeper of the Siran, guardian of the gate of Eniquia.

All the mysteries have not been revealed, even to those who have been called the Brotherhood of Light. Much has been withheld, for it is unwise to put such power in the hands of a species that dwells under the dark cloak of the death fear. Yet these mysteries had to be practiced and the energies needed to be worked with in many civilizations, in many time spans. You are viewing the one who unveils the mysteries not yet revealed. Many of you think that this was done in Lemuria and Atlantis, but the world was not ready for the unveiling of this principle mystery of the most esoteric essence in cosmic creation.

Within this crop circle and star glyph are the keys to unlock the mysteries and awaken En Na Ki Tan. The entire code is now being released within this time capsule, with full activation when the Gaia project is complete. There is no projected time for the completion of this full release and activation; it is a process that goes beyond anything your consciousness can conceive at this point in the process. A power is being released on the Earth plane that transcends all

forces, shifts the inner planes and releases vast cosmic mysteries into the collective.

The inheritance is of a spider; it weaves its way through life, each strand closer to its final goal. Spider is the key to life from the great Temple of Nelaixkila in ancient Peru. The spider was a creature from within, a god to the people. They believed that Spider would lead them through darkness and into the light, away from starvation and strife. This is the core energy of this gift. Honor its intention and engage your psyche in this process for maximum quickening of the gift.

PLATE 60. NORTH DOWN, NEAR BECKHAMPTON, JULY 26, 2000

As the Earth shifts through the interdimensional portals referred to as point zero, the energetic core is accompanied by a super-resonant tonal code of the geodesic radical continuum. This sequence of harmonic patterning is vital to stabilize the third-dimensional holographic dream field, which basically allows reality as you perceive it to be for the most part undisturbed.

Within the spectrum of point zero, all baseline continuum structures for mass and matter in the third dimension are repatterned for a new vibratory sequencing code that resonates in harmony with the thirteenth galactic aspect of the Central Sun. This readjusts the sequencing pattern of the intergalactic continuum.

The basic adjustments are encoded with an interpretive pattern of resonant frequencies that is undetectable in the Earth science. The mothership of the Galactic Federation is carefully monitoring this repatterning of the continuum code frequencies. The crop circle is a cross-section view of the wormhole that the Earth is moving through as it begins phasing into the new dimensional frequency. The subtle core of this frequency is encoded in the ever increasing solar flares during the process of restructuring the Earth's biochemical receptor field. This repatterning will facilitate the evolution of new biocellular structures from the current deteriorating form.

The end of the world has been prophesied and indeed is occurring. You do not notice the thousands of skin cells that slough off and die from your body daily and the new formation of tissues. You also cannot detect that the Earth is experiencing just such a phenomenon. When the new rejuvenated tissue forms, it will vibrate with the essence of light and sound frequencies on a varied frequency from the old stellar code. Although some of the Earth's scientists have detected massive change, they are unable to pinpoint it to the quiadesic baseline of the planetary inner-solar code.

The star glyph is encoded with the formulas for this phenomenon. The globe at the top is a symbol of the Earth as she prepares to enter the birth canal, or point zero. Notice that the continuum frequency pattern enters a phase of radical discord, which is necessary for the disruption of the old paradigm. Then the continuum begins to resonate on a balanced pattern frequency, continuing as Earth emerges through the portal or wormhole. The globe at the bottom is the symbol of the new emergence pattern code of Earth.

You are viewing the process code for the next thirteen-year time period. This is only a linear projection of Earth time, which is entirely illusionary in galactic time sequencing.

Many of you are feeling exhausted and have noticed an increased humming or ringing in your ears. Note that the tonal frequencies of the sound you hear when you enter a state of nonthought are very intense and, although difficult to detect, have changed or increased in intensity and frequency. Meditate to quiet the mind-chatter and listen to this sound. Allow your receptors to observe the frequencies. This will be useful for your adjustment to the new frequency codes as the shifts occur.

This set may be used in meditation in two ways: to assist your body in the adjustments and to expedite the planetary adjustment. Meditate on this set and visualize a gentle transition and stabilization of energy patterns for Mother Earth.

PLATE 61. WEST OVERTON HILL, AUGUST 25, 2000

In Atlantis there was an alteration in human DNA in the microstructure of the brain cells to retard the firing codes of the neurosynapses. The brain's gray matter actively in use by the human species was reduced to an average of ten percent. This limited the reception of the creative genius patterns in the human species. Basically, a temporary demotion of the species was necessary to protect planet Earth from destruction during the reign of the death fear. What your scientists refer to as "junk DNA" is really only dormant, waiting to be reactivated.

The intent was to develop courage and motivation, and to activate the heart chakra energies to sustain inventive genius balanced with the God love source, the heart center of the planetary resonance. Once the heart energy was vibrationally enhanced and a critical mass of the species was evolved beyond the "kill or be killed" mentality into a more esoteric mindset, this formula could safely be initiated. Then the opening of the pattern frequency vibration of inventions could be safely accessed. Basically, the species had to be protected from the self-destruction it flirted with in Atlantis. Safeguards were set up until the proper timing allowed for this expansion and stimulation.

Some of you perceive your fellow humans as still living in the old paradigm (death fear). More of your fellow humans have evolved than you might think, and critical mass has been reached. If you travel and observe your planetary brothers and sisters, you will realize that the masses are shifting into a new consciousness. The power structures of control by fear are deteriorating, regardless of the propaganda to the contrary being promoted by the minority.

Other transmissions have spoken of the projected full use of the brain's left and right hemispheres; this shift is part of this process. It is now time to remove the limitations and stimulate the emergence of the code frequencies for the new creation. The DNA for the microstructure of the brain cell must be stimulated with a frequency eight octaves higher than what it currently receives. With advanced technology, the fractal light pattern of this DNA could be viewed as the image you see in this crop circle. It is patterned within the fractal crystalline formula of sevens, repeated in patterns of three varying geometric images.

The brain-wave patterns will shift to resonate on a higher octave, and the creative thought process will be greatly enhanced. Another effect is the enhanced telepathic communication for the reception of ET technology, to be developed spontaneously in the technical fields that will resolve Earth's current environmental crisis.

This is a quantum leap in creativity for Earth's residents. A very small surge of this frequency was emanated during what your planet refers to as the age of enlightenment. Another small stimulus surge for brain-cell DNA was projected just prior to and during the industrial revolution. These two surges were minimal and prepared the matrix for the enormous shift that is now occurring.

The use of this set in meditation will actually connect the frequencies of your brain waves with the surge patterns. Your brain will be used instrumentally to stimulate the microstructure of the brain-cell DNA of your planetary brothers and sisters. Don't expect an immediate shift in your creativity process; you will not instantly be a genius. Your DNA will be activated, and over a period of time, which varies with individuals, you will notice an enhancement of your creative powers.

The human creation of this circle is a critical alchemical component of the formula emanated.

PLATE 62. BISHOPS CANNINGS ENVIRONS, JULY 26, 2000

This set represents the full awakening of what is referred to as the Buddha of Compassion. The effect will be profound as the species opens to compassion. Forgiveness is the bridge that will assist in the metamorphosis of the collective mind. There will be a time when forgiveness is obsolete, as the species will no longer dwell in a state of discord.

Compassion is a state of grace within the full experience of the Holy Spirit. The most profound results will be seen in the treatment of those weaker than one's self. The thought of striking or mistreating a child or an elder will be inconceivable.

The focus of the collective mind will be on a code of honor and compassion. This shift will have a profound effect in releasing the thought pattern of conflict with what was once conceived as an enemy. The enemy has traditionally been perceived as an individual socially separate from one's self, who might pose a threat in the competition for food, territory and/or power. All of these thought patterns were sustained by the fear of lack, which is now being replaced by abundance consciousness. The weaker species will be a focus for compassionate attention in an effort to empower and love one's fellow humans. Your planetary brothers and sisters will move into a new state of grace and abundance. They will no longer be a threat to the current social structure.

The energetic structure of the collective mind has been shifting radically over the last century. Expect this shift to be more profound over the next three decades; the predicted peak shift will occur in the years 2012-13. This will be facilitated by an energetic frequency resonance that is being beamed onto the planet, stimulating the pituitary and pineal glands. The balance of the human brain chemistry is presently being altered with the emanation of the light and sound frequencies present in this fractal formula. The formula has already been implanted in the ecosystem and is resonating at an increasing frequency. Indulge yourself in the enjoyment of these images, and the process will quicken.

PLATE 63. BISHOPS SUTTON, JULY 14 AND 30, 2000

These crop circles have multiple uses. They are located on a major highway intended for the passing motorist to pick up their resonated frequencies and emanate their codes wherever they travel.

Star beings are reactivating the purest of the etheric Lemurian cities of light located in this area, southwest of London. This crop circle's formulas are creating energy surges along ley lines, transferring energy to London to positively affect the energies of international travelers passing through the city. This frequency transforms deteriorating, dysfunctional populace hubs into healthy habitats like the Lemurian cities.

Additionally, the ET technologists have utilized these formulas for the sublimation of erratic metropolitan frequencies and transmutation of the lower vibrational frequencies of fear and greed. Then high-level golden light frequencies are fed into the same area. Once the higher vibrational energies have been fed into London, the humans will receive a DNA implant called by ET scientists a "suprasonic esatronic emanation device." These devices emanate light and sound frequencies throughout any country to which the humans travel.

In ET scientific terms, this crop circle is called a "megalithic equatronic deactivator." There is a four-way intersection of gridual transence disectual energy frequency patterning that affects the resonance of potential life-emanating frequencies in other galaxies. Mother Earth is a map that corresponds to other galactic counterparts. The advanced frequencies of light and sound emanations are toning equatronic frequencies to prepare for the implantation of the receptors of the Eden force (the seeds of Eden). This location on the Earth is a "cube-atronic equilateral sector." It is a meeting point, a place where high-level toning frequencies can be emanated to create the ultrasonic environment that will be conductive to life prana in uninhabited galaxies.

This portal transcends time and space; therefore it is not restricted to the principle of light years and the resonant frequencies that emit from this circle. This circle could only be created on this point of the Earth. The mathematical formulas represented in this crop circle have not previously existed on this planet.

The star beings have contracted the subpsychic consciousness of the farmer to prohibit visitation because of the delicate frequencies and the importance of the mathematical formulas that are being resonated through this field.

The mothership is scanning the frequencies emanated from this intersector point. We have extremely sensitive, ultrasonic, nondimensional frequency-resonator detection devices. These transmitting devices maximize the efficiency of the crop circles by emitting frequencies into the consciousness of other galaxies.

The six-pointed crop circle in the left portion of the image was added later. It is the formula code for the maximum ultrasonic effect of this project. It stabilizes frequencies emanated by the implementation of the formula in the primary crop circle.

AUTHOR'S NOTE: As we approached the crop circle, Barbara began to see columns of golden light and energy fields with her third eye. The energy intensely affected me. I could see with my third eye that the automobiles driving by were picking up transformative light energy on their cars and spreading it like pollen as they drove.

PLATE 64. STEPHEN CASTLE DOWN, UPHAM, JULY 1, 2000

This crop circle is the mothership's detection device to map, measure and monitor the effects on the grid patterns of the Earth's energies at this point. The mothership's beacons beam onto this major grid intersection to interpret frequency shifts at specific distances and measure the overall resonance of the implant within the calculated distance. It was essential to implant the monitoring device and adjust the frequencies along grid lines prior to introducing the formulas resonant in crop circle 63.

AUTHOR'S NOTE: Barbara Lamb could see with her third eye that the energy patterns were different than at crop circle 63. The light frequency glow starts in the whole area of the crop circle and spreads out in all directions instead of ascending in columns.

PLATE 65. CHILBOLTON, AUGUST 13, 2000

This set is for the restoration of cosmic memory. The veil of amnesia is being gently lifted. This is a delicate process; to lift it too rapidly would shift the collective into a state of confusion and chaos. Your senses are being rapidly expanded, and the memory of who you are is activating. The sixth sense is being activated. This crop circle is the fractal code for the receptor stimulators that have been introduced into your biosphere. Your DNA is time-coded to respond to the increased resonance fields of vibratory light and sound frequencies, which are detected by the increase in the megahertz that the planet is resonating.

Manuscripts from the ancient mystery schools are surfacing to assist you in your awakening, such as *A Course in Miracles*, *The Big Book of AA*, *The Celestine Prophecy*, *The Seven Spiritual Laws of Success*, *Conversations with God*, *Awakening to Zero Point* and *Emissary of Light*. These gifts are encoded with sequence patterns of words and thought forms specially designed to trigger your cosmic memory and stimulate the activity of the pineal gland.

Awaken, and assist in awakening your species. Your mind-heart is part of the collective mind of the planet. As each brain cell resonates with a chakra balance and tones with the vibration of a pure love frequency, your biochemical structure becomes a frequency device for the resonance of joy, which stimulates the collective planetary mind. The essence of the subpsyche is being transformed in this way. The underworld is no longer held by the dark forces. It is now open for the clearing and repatterning of the frequencies that once held your planet in ignorance and fear. Imagine yourself as part of a cosmic force that is transmuting the energy fields of the subconscious of the planetary mind.

The primal group is vital to the process. As you enter the mainstream of society (grocery stores and so forth), you resonate higher frequencies of electromagnetic energy. This actually works like a jumper cable to a dead battery. It stimulates the flow of energy within those not yet activated. Imagine how many people you interact with in a period of one month. This is a powerful vehicle for change, and you are the select ones who are the bringers of the dawn. This information gives another perspective to the phrase, "Practice random acts of kindness and senseless acts of beauty."

The veil between the worlds is thinning, causing recall of past lives, parallel universes and higher-dimensional selves, memories of the cities of light, and awareness of your celestial brothers and sisters (although many of us are pure lightbeings, not restricted by gender). The initial process of preparing the mass consciousness for interplanetary communication was through the media, with ET-inspired productions such as those by Steven Spielberg. The primal group has agreed to be the contactees for open communication; telepathy is the main instrument for initiating contact with the primal group. The deteriorating fear grid and your greatly stimulated pineal gland are now making open, advanced communications possible. Many in the primal group have hosted co-conscious walk-ins, allowing them to continue to function in their third-dimensional lives while we can also enter the third dimension and do the preparation necessary for this process to occur. We are higher-dimensional aspects of you that have stepped through the veil to assist in the awakening.

This is a phase that is delicate, just as that of a butterfly coming out of a cocoon. By the time the UFO cover-up is resolved—which could not happen until the psyche was prepared—your species will be ready to interact with your cosmic family. One thing to keep in mind: You are us and we are you. There is no division or separation.

Allow the beautiful geometry of this crop circle pattern to merge with the lovely design of the star glyph. Merge these images by superimposing a transparent overlay of the star glyph on the image of the crop circle. Doing this will enhance the encoding found in both images.

PLATE 66. TELEGRAPH HILL, NEAR PEGSDON, JULY 28, 2000

Within the resonance of the increased solar flares lies the encoding for the cornea to receive light infusions that will stimulate the brain circuitry and repattern its frequencies. The thinning of the ozone has permitted these ultraviolet rays to increase the variables in the light that the retina receives and patterns into neuroresponses. The encoding present in these light infusions rapidly deteriorates the thought forms of a warrior/destroyer society. It has also, incidentally, served to detoxify the chemicals that are being released into the air, preventing extreme chemical reactions in all species.

Reading is important to learning patterns because the phenomenon of light encodement is present in the structure of the symbols that are viewed and translated into thought forms by the optic nerve. The solar flares' emanation of ultraviolet light has the same effect. Information from the Records of Ra are being encoded into UV rays, which are transferred by the retina to the neurofibers of the cerebral cortex to be read as the living language of light. Though the encodement carries some of the teachings of your planet's mystery schools, it goes far beyond what has been revealed historically on your planet. The resonance of the twelve solar houses of the Central Sun with the thirteenth house of Ra is encoded within these solar rays. This is a learning pattern that has been introduced into your environment.

Many of the species have not expanded the neurosynapses enough to consciously receive the encodement into thought form. The chemicals emitted by the "flight or fight response," stimulating adrenaline, inhibit the neurofunctions from interpreting these frequencies. The endorphins and other brain chemicals stimulated by states of peaceful meditation, high-vibration music or enhanced enjoyment of beauty, stimulate the optic receptors to interpret and download the encoding. This process has nothing to do with visual acuity, as it utilizes a different set of neuroreceivers than those needed to pattern an image in the conscious mind.

Visual handicap is not an impediment for this ascension formula. These UV encodements can also be absorbed by the skin. Yet this increased exposure could be dangerous for some sensitive individuals. Use topical UV protection and sunblocks; the encodement is not severely affected adversely by these products. Do not fear the Sun's intensified rays. The benefits far outweigh the adjustments and temporary discomforts of the intensified frequencies. It is important to remove the propaganda of fear of the environment from your thought forms. Your species has the capacity to adjust to the frequencies and mutate to accommodate your changing environment. We encourage you not to participate in the doom-and-gloom thought form, as it will inhibit the positive effects you will receive and limit your contribution to the activation of the collective mind's higher consciousness.

PLATE 67. UFFINGTON, JULY 23, 2000

Within this mountain is an ethereal temple marked by the dragon horse. Within its structure are the inscriptions for the periodic release of crucial frequencies emanated from all crop circles appearing at specific sites where the Neolithic emissaries of light implanted the time capsules [see crop circle 48]. These are encrypted into a galactic record, which is alchemically interactive with all variable factors. These variables include: their location on grid and ley lines or near tumuli, planetary alignment, the DNA of individuals entering the circles, the DNA of individuals who are astral projecting to the area and partici-

pating with the ET creation of the circles, and the collective DNA of soul groups present in the area. Alchemically added to the formulas for the formation of the circles are solar flares occurring at specific days of apparitions, rainfall, crop development, energy emanated from nearby sacred sites, springs and churches, and ancient Neanderthal, Neolithic and Celtic anthropological sites and white horses located near crop circles.

The star glyph is a replication of the ethereal temple within this mountain that carries the cryptic codes for the entire project of the apparition of the crop circles. This crop circle is the formula for the release of the set of crop circles scheduled for this season. It is important to conceive that every single crop circle has been planned. Because of these factors, with its appearance, each crop circle releases microcosmic particles of fractal formulas.

Within this geological formation are treasures and ancient inscriptions that link the light net that was implanted in the ethereal by the Neolithic ET brethren [refer to crop circle 48]. The entire records of their mission—the formation and completion—are encoded in these inscriptions. These inscriptions are available to a select few who have returned with the DNA codes to access these records. If you are one of these, you might feel a very intense tingling sensation in your brain when viewing this set. This is the activation of the encodement of the inscriptions located in the geographical formation and encoded in these images. It is particularly important to observe your sensations while viewing this set; you could be actively connecting your frequencies with these formulas. The mantra useful for activation of this frequency code is *Saaaa koaaaa mie (mee) na kaaaa wa.*

From the ethereal encodement, which is viewed in the extreme right side, there is an energy release of eight (the number of infinity) orbs of light. These manifest the geometry of the activated code emanating from the pattern at the left of the image.

PRACTICAL USE OF THE CROP CIRCLES AND STAR GLYPHS

JUDITH K. MOORE

This section is designed as a manual for practical application of the gift that the star beings have given us. It includes photos of the crop circles, images of the star glyphs, technical descriptions of each crop circle by Barbara Lamb and condensed phrases from each transmission. The following crystalline orb meditation is a particularly powerful tool for the activation of these alchemical formulas. You, the reader, are encouraged to be creative in the techniques you use to activate these formulas for ascension. Perhaps some of you will choose to take them to England and do activations in newly formed circles. The important thing is that you engage in the process of alchemically activating these images and connecting to the collective consciousness of the planet. You will be guided.

Feel free to send me letters about your experiences: Judith K. Moore, P.O. Box 546, Chimayo, New Mexico 87522. Good luck and have fun.

Laiolin: I encourage you to tone while viewing the star glyphs and crop circles. This will enhance the process. It is also advised to take this book to sacred sites to do meditations and sacred geometry activations. The sacred geometry of varied sacred sites will enhance the formula and be an important aspect of the process. Gather with a group of friends and fellow lightworkers at a sacred site during portal days, full and new moons, and planetary alignments to do meditations and activations with the crop circles and star glyphs.

Explore the use of kundalini gifts and the merging of tantric yoga practices with this material. These gifts were preserved in the mystery schools, kept sacred in ancient Mayan, Incan and East Indian teachings and used by all sacred teachings throughout the world. Wherever you live, whatever your traditions, the language of holy union is a powerful force of cocreation. All of these factors are important alchemical aspects of the process. Take some time and study the teachings of beloved St. Germaine. The alchemy of changing base metals into gold has little to do with metal and much to do with tapping universal energy to initiate the cosmic forces necessary for cocreation. I am in hopes that this book will be tattered and torn—perhaps with coffee spills and jelly donut spots, or tofu stains if that is your preference—certainly with many dog ears, underlines and highlights as you work with the process. The more you look, the more you will see; the more you open up to divine potential, the more incredible your experience will be. The star glyphs are your cosmic key. Apply them to your experiences, and they will take varied forms and have varied effects upon you and the entire cosmic scheme. You are cocreators. Each of you is a tool of Creator God, the messenger of the angels. You are members of the living body of Christ. Namasté. ✳

BILL WERELY'S EXPERIENCE

I want to share the following experience with you to help demonstrate this point. Bill and Rosemary Werely live in Vermont. He has been working with the crop circles and star glyphs at sacred sites. Recently, he shared his experience using the transmissions for a meditation during the great planetary alignment of May 3-11, 2000. I had brought through a set of transmissions specifically for the alignment (published in the May 2000 issue of Sedona Journal of Emergence). I include Bill's experience here as I feel it will illustrate how important it is to do active on-site work with the images.

Bill Werely: We opened up our hearts to know where we were to go during the May 5 alignment and did not know until the evening of May 4. There were four of us, and we had been kept very busy for the proceeding four days, but on the evening of the fourth, we knew we needed to be at a place I call the "control panel." This sacred site is hidden and powerful. When you're there, it's hard to believe that such a place could exist so close to towns and interstate highways. The first time I was taken there, I felt the sacredness of the site. I knew this spot was a part of the second world and that a powerful time portal was centered there.

The path to the site is about a mile long through dense woods on an old logging trail. There are two gates on the way in. These are not physical gates, and spiritual keepers are at both gates. On the previous trip, three times I asked for permission to go to the site from the gatekeeper, and three times I was refused. When I asked a fourth time, permission was reluctantly given. This trip, when I asked at the first gate, they said, "Hurry, we've been waiting for you."

When preparing for this trip, I went around the house as usual, being guided as to what to bring for the coming ceremonies. Many unusual things found their way into my bags. To my surprise, I was told to take Judy's book on crop circles and their related star glyphs. We walked quickly to the next gate, where the trail through the woods opens into a little valley, home to the portal and many other sacred sites, artifacts and energy centers. As I cleared the woods, I saw a spot three quarters of the way across the little valley (maybe one hundred yards away) that was glowing and seemed to call to me. I walked to it and knew immediately that this was the spot I needed to be, so I put my things down. The spot was a large outcropping of bedrock rising maybe twelve to fourteen inches above the surrounding grasslands. I then led a friend to the control panel, which is hidden in a grove of pine trees. I knew we were in the right place as soon as I saw and felt it. I said that this where I'm supposed to work.

The two women who came with us had spread out and were wandering, but soon they found where they belonged. Not a word was spoken, but we all knew that we were to anchor the energies at these spots. After about a half hour, I took out the book on crop circles, remembering that there were circles concerning the day's alignment. I thought perhaps I would get a deeper understanding of the work through study of the crop circles and star glyphs. I opened the book and thunder roared across the valley. It was the only thunder we would hear all day. I looked through the two crop circles concerned with the May 5 alignment and the related star glyphs. I began to look at the second star glyph, and an understanding reached me quickly. I realized that the glyph was a perfect map of our location and the symbols of energy were exactly where each of us had located ourselves. It was not just close, but exact, and the energy symbols well represented the energies of the various people and the work they were doing.

I was amazed, and yet I wasn't. This was just another progression of the miraculous and noted. At about the same time, all but the brother at the control panel went off to dreamland for about an hour and all came back at almost the same instant. We were a team, functioning together without words at a distance, allowing the greater forces to align and use us as they needed. We all entered dreamtime for about thirty minutes. We left that evening in quiet awe, speaking very little. It was a blessed time and the sacred was strong. We were humbled by the strength of the work. ✳

HOLOGRAPHIC HEART CRYSTALLINE ORB MEDITATION

Gather in a circle and say a brief prayer praising Creator and setting your intent to be a servant of the most high. Then prepare the energy space by setting a protective frequency of pure Christ light around the circle. The meditation begins with Maya yoga. Bring the light of the Central Sun in through the crown chakra on the inward breath. Anchor it into the crystal core of the planet, then send it back up to the Central Sun on the outward breath. Do this three times.

Next, bring the energy to the crystal core of the

planet and breathe it out of the heart chakra, activating the holographic heart. Then visualize a crystalline orb or globe forming in the center of the circle.

Activate the Flower of Life geometry by sending the energy from your heart out and around the orb, forming a Flower of Life pattern and moving on to the person to your left. Continue conscious Maya yoga and holographic heart breathing. Then move your energy around the circle, repeating the Flower of Life pattern with each person until it returns to you. Signal that the process is complete with a nod of the head or any signal you choose.

When the sacred Flower of Life is activated, begin the holographic activation of the crop circles and star glyphs. One person holds the images of the crop circles and glyphs up so that everyone can see them. Now, bring the energy from your mind to your heart and project it holographically into the orb. Repeat this procedure with each set, signaling that you are done by saying, "All my relations."

When all sixty-seven sets are completed, concentrate the image within the crystalline orb into the power of a corn seed and visualize that you are planting the seed within the collective consciousness of Mother Earth.

End by retracting your energy from the Flower of Life, starting with yourself and moving to the right, releasing the orb. Close with a prayer of gratitude.

This meditation technique is the alchemical means by which you, the reader, can participate in cocreating heaven on Earth. The sooner you begin working with this important exercise, the better. I must stress that each of you is important—we are at critical mass. *You are a tool of the Creator God.* Please give yourself fully in service.

This meditation was given to me when I traveled to sacred sites in the Southwestern United States at the time of the lunar eclipse on January 20, 2000, to activate the star glyphs and crop circles. At that point, I

The star glyphs are your cosmic key. Apply them to your experiences, and they will take varied forms and have varied effects upon you and the entire cosmic scheme.

had a set of thirty-five star glyphs matched with crop circles. I was urged to go on this journey and was told by the star beings that the initial activation was to take place between the lunar eclipse on January 20 and the February 5 solar eclipse. I had made arrangements with the Mind and Body Center in Arizona to do my first workshop on this important information.

On the way there, I was guided to pray at Abo Pueblo National Monument and at the Apache Warm Springs in the Magdalena Mountains in New Mexico. The first activation of the crop circles and glyphs in a collective meditation was on the sacred land of Grandmother Allegra Ahlquist and Grandmother Shirley Tassencourt in the Dragoon Mountains in southern Arizona. I always love to go visit these beloved elders. I am a member of the Grandmother's Council. I was traveling with my best friend, Tika, and Silvia, the guardian of the sacred Turtle Mother Spring at River Bend Hot Springs in Truth or Consequences, New Mexico. I spoke to Shirley and Allegra regarding my mission to bring in these transmissions and the information about the crop circles and the star glyphs. I had prepared a notebook, which was an easy way to display the two together. We decided to do the holographic heart crystalline orb meditation in Shirley's meditation chamber. It was incredible. At the end of the meditation, I heard the universal Om.

Over the next week, we traveled throughout Arizona and Colorado to connect with specific groups of people to do the initial activations. I was mystically guided to specific sacred sites and to work with a select group of people who carried the crystalline geometry in their DNA to matrix into this information and holographically project it into the collective consciousness of Mother Earth. The sacred sites included the Jaguar's Cave in the Dragoons, the Sun Temple in Sierra Vista, Casa Grande, the Womb Heart of the Cosmic Mother in Sedona, Hopi Land and the sacred Sleeping Ute Mountain.

The Hopi elder I went to see in Hotevilla told me that he recognized the star glyphs as a language. He told me that Kokopelli and Kokopelli Mana are just the romance aspect and that the one with a hunchback who plays the flute is *Bann* [the spelling might be off as I have never seen it written]. He told me that I carry those seeds on my back. He and his wife activated the crop circles and the star glyphs. We shared a warm cup of tea in his kitchen. I thanked Creator for the blessing of sharing a most precious moment with these beloved elders. As we drove away, we felt a deep sense of peace.

I stopped by a roadside rest a short way from his home and noticed a little road that went around a mesa. Spirit guided me to follow the road, and in a short distance, we found ourselves at the Hopi Prophecy Rock. I was humbled and made prayer offerings. Of all the sacred places I could be on this journey, this was the most wonderful.

We arrived at my friend Rand's house at the foot of the sacred Sleeping Ute Mountain at about 9:00 P.M. In his kitchen, we did a sacred geometry activation of the crop circles and star glyphs and did work that night to anchor the energies into the crystal chamber that was revealed to me in the ethereal realm of Sleeping Ute Mountain.

The next morning, I knew why I had come. I was to see my uncle, Tony Shearer. My uncle is the author of *Lord of the Dawn: Quetzalcoatl and the Tree of Life, The Prophecies of Ancient Mexico, Praying Flute: Song of the Earth Mother* and *Beneath the Moon and Under the Sun.* In the '60s, he traveled to Oaxaca, Mexico, and brought some of the first information on the prophecies to the United States. He now is an elder and lives in the Four Corners region in peace. When we did the activation in his kitchen, thunder and lightning filled the winter skies, and I knew that the ancestors were speaking. I hope this story demonstrates the kind of work that is to be done with this book.

The crystalline orb meditation is an important tool for the activation of the crop circles and the star glyphs. Allow yourself to be guided by spirit when you do this meditation, as there may be creative additions that will enhance the particular activations you are part of. I have included this meditation because I want you to practice it and use it as you read the crop circle transmissions.

―――――――――――――― ᘓᘓᘓ ――――――――――――――

PLATE 1

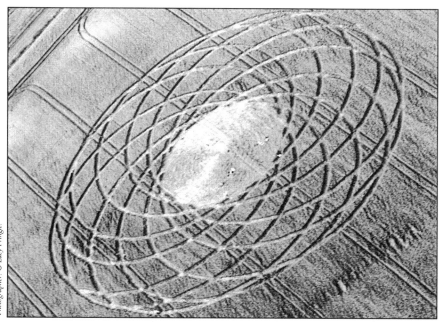

Photographer: © Lucy Pringle.

July 11, 1997, Woodborough Hill, Alton Priors, Wiltshire County, wheat crop, 300-350 feet in diameter.

This crop circle has been referred to as the "Torus" or the "Torus Knot," because it seems to show the way energy moves in a donutlike or torus shape, according to British physicist Jim Lyons.

The design looks three-dimensional in the way it is composed of twelve rings. It reminded people of a spirograph drawing, a knot or a web. It seems as though water or energy had flowed freely through the wheat, leaving these precise, even pathways.

The energy was strong, as measured by dowsing rods. British healer Philippa Coxall said the energy was so strong that it changed the whole energy system of visitors to this crop circle, from their spines to the tops of their heads, with special activations that improved their hearing.

As with so many crop circles through the 1980s and 1990s, this crop circle was placed on a hillside, and in this case, next to the faint traces of an ancient hillfort. The night it was formed, witnesses saw red, glowing orbs dancing in that field and a witness heard loud bumping sounds coming closer and closer.

This is the web woven by the precious one who is named Grandmother Spider by some Native Americans. This is the weaving of all her creative essences, the mandala of world peace. The star glyph depicts the womb of Grandmother Spider.

PLATE 2

This 297-foot-long and 184-foot-wide crop formation amazed many people in its near perfect depiction of the ancient Kabbalah or Tree of Life symbolism, showing the sacred systems of the Jewish people and relating to God permeating all time, space and matter. It is also said to depict the human chakra system.

These very brittle stalks somehow retained their circular swirls and straight lines and angles and showed no indications of damage. The great precision of this design would normally require surveying equipment and construction lines, but no indication of this type was found at this site. Although there were rumors that this formation was man-made, indications that it was made by the genuine (anomalous) source include the magical bends of many of the stalks and the yellow blossoms that lay uncrushed on the ground after being laid down. Anyone walking through this tough, brittle crop would have been cut and bruised.

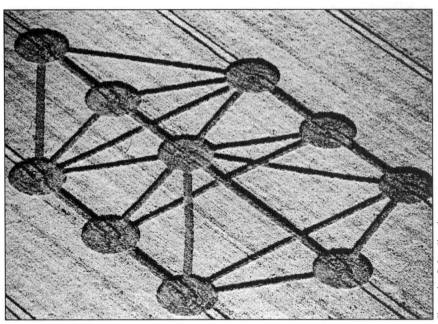

Photographer: © Steve Alexander

May 3, 1997, "The Key to the Kabbalah," Barbury Castle, near Swindon, Wiltshire County, oilseed canola crop.

This is the unified principle of the power awakened within the Cosmic Tree of Peace, united in all dimensions. This is the formula for the full union of the trees of peace that share one root. This is the movement in union and divine balance of cosmic forces that have been foretold by the ancient ones. This is the time we have so long awaited.

PLATE 3

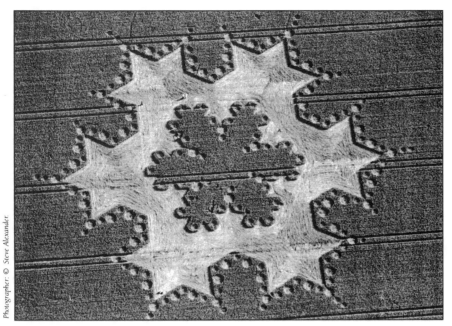

Photographer: © Steve Alexander.

August 8, 1997, Milk Hill, Alton Barnes, Wiltshire County, wheat crop.

This is a double "Koch Fractal Snowflake" design of amazing complexity. It is a fantastic elaboration of the Koch fractal crop circle design that appeared July 23, 1997, between Silbury Hill and Avebury, and contained 128 small circles. This pattern contains 157 circles in the outer design and 43 circles in the inner design, with a diameter of 264 feet.

This design has a Von Koch "snowflake" series of curves superimposed over the center of the larger one. This is an incredible feat of laying down the crop to meticulously form the larger fractal shape while leaving the middle intricate pattern standing and highlighted.

A Koch fractal design starts with a triangle, then forms a Star of David double triangle or hexagon. It then branches out into other triangles in a pattern that could be repeated to infinity. Fractal geometry shows the way in which aspects of nature and many systems in the world form in a mathematical order.

Michael Glickman has suggested that this design might be piercing the veil between realities and dimensions. According to Rod Bearcloud Berry, the six-pointed star shows the perfect symmetry of people and the universe, the never-ending motion of the universe and the interconnectedness and oneness of everything.

This crop circle is the Flower of Life. The beautiful geometry speaks of the coming renaissance of sacred art, theater, music and architecture, and the return of the sacred gardens of Eden. These treasures will gradually recondition the psyche of the masses to receive the gifts of the Holy Spirit in their hearts. That which was wrought to destroy will be used to heal. Once again, beauty will be the way of the world and the song of life for God's children.

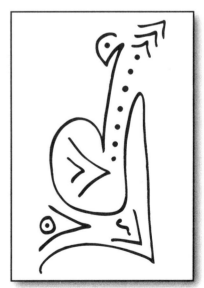

PLATE 4

This crop circle, 150 feet in diameter, was first discovered in the early morning by Barbara Lamb while she was riding high up in a double-decker bus, just four hours after it was formed. Barbara and her three American friends were the first people to enter the formation. This crop circle was so freshly made that it emitted a subtle sound similar to the "snap, crackle and pop" of Rice Krispies cereal when milk is poured over it. The wheat stalks looked fluffy and billowy as they lay bent over near the ground, and they glistened with the early morning sun shining through them.

The wheat was laid beautifully, with each blade swirled in perfect unison to form circles of diminishing sizes, culminating in a crescent design. Some researchers have called this crop circle "Thirteen Moons." This design appears to be the culmination of the series of crop circles that were thought to depict the twenty-one pieces of the Shoemaker-Levy 9 comet hitting planet Jupiter.

A one-foot-wide pathway formed a ring underneath the swirled circles, as if a guiding line upon which each circle would be formed. The standing stalks that defined one circle from another were precisely tapered down to two or three standing stalks.

This crop circle design may have multiple levels of meaning: the thirteen moons of the Native American and the Celtic calendars, the comet curled up at rest after the great effort of hitting Jupiter or the "dragon" of Earth energy beginning to hibernate. It gives a feeling of completion.

August 9, 1994, Avebury Trusloe, Wiltshire County, wheat crop.

Photographer: © Barbara Lamb.

This is the insignia for the awakening of the ancient goddesses who will open the portals between the three temples of Giza, Chichén Itzá and Silbury Hill. They will free the tortured souls from bondage of the death fear, playing an important role in the healing of Mother Earth. This set can be used in meditation for healing generational bondage.

PLATE 5

Photographer: © Steve Alexander.

August 10 and 11, 1994, Avebury, Wiltshire County, wheat crop.

This intricate crop circle was formed during two consecutive nights, with the first two rings formed the first night and the surrounding crescents and spokes formed the next. The total diameter was 328 feet. This pattern was placed next to the ancient megalithic stone circle and henge of Avebury, dating back to at least 2500 B.C., and is often referred to as the "Avebury Web." This was considered one of the most beautiful and complex patterns up to that time and even to date.

This design has been interpreted in various ways: as a spider's web, as a Native American dreamcatcher, as radar waves, as Earth's magnetic waves and as a labyrinth. Visitors agree that the energy of this crop circle felt exquisitely vibrant and alive, yet peaceful and serene to sit and meditate in. The precision of the lay of the wheat was exquisite.

No noise or signs of human activity were detected during those two nights, even though there were a least a hundred people living nearby.

Rod Bearcloud Berry has suggested that this design shows our connection to the Creator and to the Great Mystery and the universe. Life reaches out from the center of the web of life into all directions and returns to the center again. The center circle depicts the male energy of the Sun, the next circle represents the female energy and the Earth Mother, and both are with the total containment of the universe in the outer circle.

Within the essential core of creation are the geometric code frequencies of all matter. This geodesic code is the interstellar fractal formula for massive realignment, cosmic metamorphosis of mass and matter on a biochemical level. These code frequencies lie at the very heart of the cosmic creative spiral, within the core of the Great Central Sun. This frequency was introduced into the matrix of the Gaia project to activate the frequencies and prepare for the massive energetic shift that is currently occurring.

PLATE 6

This outstanding geometric design added new complexity, artistry and the suggestion of having been made by some superior intelligence who or which understands complex geometry and spiritual symbolism. Barbara Lamb was present at a meeting of the Center for Crop Circle Studies in the Wagon and Horses Pub when the first photograph of this formation was handed to researcher George Wingfield. George and the others were astonished that a crop circle design could be so beautifully executed and carry so much meaning from mathematics, geometry, ancient alchemy and ancient spiritual traditions.

This is a three-dimensional design depicted in two dimensions on flat ground. The tetrahedron incorporates a circle and rings and branches out to three differing wheel-like shapes, each with its own symbolic meanings. The whole pattern is similar to sixteenth-century symbols for alchemical formulas and sacred geometry. It is one version of Mandelbrot fractals.

During the night this crop formation was formed, many people saw glowing spheres, triangles and rectangles of light in the sky over that area. The warden sleeping in his cottage at the hillfort at the edge of this field, heard a loud roaring noise in the sky over his roof. When daylight came, he saw this crop circle in the field below him and noticed that the sheep were clustered together at the farthest side of the hill, as if they had been traumatized by something during the night.

July 17, 1991, Barbury Castle, near Swindon, Wiltshire County, wheat crop.

This crop circle is the balancing resonator for the cosmic law of perfection through imperfection. This is the law of radical discord, the divine principle of balance of unequal counterpoints within the matrix of divine creation and evolution. Make way for the illogical; make way for laughter. This is the cosmic juggling act that produces the fertile loam for transmutation and change.

PLATE 7

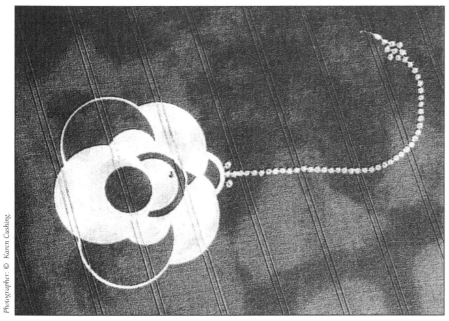

This surprising design has been called "The Stingray," "The Balloon" and "The Kite." It amazed every onlooker with its complex pattern of eight implied overlapping circles, leaving a lovely crescent, and its amazingly long tail. This tail was composed of fifty-two circles of diminishing size, each which was swirled in a different way and had a different kind of center.

The floor lay (the pattern in which the wheat was laid down) had the astonishing feature of a stair-step pattern. Barbara Lamb was told by Rod Bearcloud Berry that in his native tradition this stair-step pattern represents a portal or stairway to other dimensions of reality.

July 21, 1998, Beckhampton, Wiltshire County, wheat crop, 300 x 450 feet.

This crop circle and glyph speak of the return of the temples of light and of the emerald and cobalt blue Lemurian ethereal cities. From these great cities of light will come teachings, ascended philosophies and the workings for the principles of peace. In areas where they appear, there will be a rapid metamorphosis of beings and systems.

PLATE 8

This crop circle was one of several patterns in 1995 that seemed to depict various astronomical features of planets, stars, spinning galaxies and our solar system and asteroid belt. This pattern has been thought of as our solar system with planet Earth missing. Many have wondered if we were being warned to save our Earth from ecological or nuclear destruction or if this was a warning that the Earth will be bombarded out of existence by a meteor or asteroid from space. This design was 284 feet in diameter.

Dr. Nan Lu suggested that this crop circle was helpful for people's digestive systems and for increasing T cells.

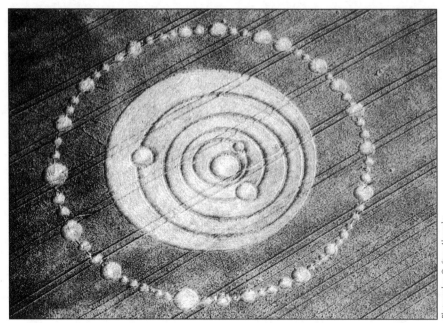

June 26, 1995, Longwood Warren, near Winchester, Hampshire County, wheat crop.

This is the emblem for the formula for the successful triumph of the Galactic Federation over the negative ETs and for the clearing of the key bases that held power to maintain the fear grid on Mother Gaia. This set is powerful when used in meditation as a tool to free oppressed souls, to put an end to the covert programs of human experimentation and incarceration of political prisoners. Freedom is *now*, empowerment is *now* and respect for life is *now*. All life is sacred.

PLATE 9

Photographer: © Steve Alexander.

May 31, 1999, "Menorah," below Barbury Castle, near Swindon, Wiltshire County, barley crop.

This is the image of the sound frequencies of the light orbs of *Soenan*, the name for the completed transmutation of your Sun, Kinich Ahau [see plates 13 and 32]. When light and sound resonate in the eminence of the God-source in such a pure way, galaxies are transformed and the very atomic and subatomic substance of mass and matter shift. This is the essence of the entire plan for the awakening of Mother Gaia and heaven on Earth.

This 300-foot-long spiritual symbol of the Menorah appeared in the flat field below Barbury Castle, in the same field where two years earlier "The Key to the Kabbalah" crop formation had appeared [plate 2]. Both of these formations are very important in Jewish life. This one is a symbol for ultimate reality.

Dr. Michael Green, a long-time student of archaeology and anthropology, said that perhaps the circlemakers convey truths better through ancient Jewish symbols than through any others. This was the way in which the ancient Hebrew symbol was represented four thousand years ago with its tripod base, as differentiated from the modern depiction with the rounded stand base. The three pillars represent the three pillars of the Tree of Life—the pillar of severity, the pillar of equilibrium and the pillar of mercy—which indicate the three paths to God. It is believed that God gave this symbol to mankind to represent, "Not by might nor by power, but by my spirit."

The use of eleven circles is unusual in a crop circle design, and this is the first elevenfold geometry to be seen in a crop circle. The smaller design above the Menorah was considered a lamp for the lighting of the menorah candles. In Jewish tradition, it was fueled by olive oil. This lamp was never to be extinguished because it symbolized the undying presence of divine wisdom.

The Menorah has been used over the centuries as a portable representation of the

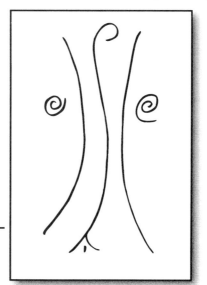

Tree of Life diagram, which could be carried by the Jewish people out of Egypt and from country to country. They used it to teach basic Kabbalistic wisdom and to provide a focus for meditation.

PLATE 10

This 670-foot-long pattern has reminded many people of the Egyptian symbol known as the wings of Horus, a winged solar disc or the wings of the falcon that protected most ancient Egyptian temples. This ancient symbol, with several types of elaboration, was usually painted over the doorways to the "holiest of holies" chambers. Horus was considered the god of wisdom, and he represented the processes of becoming spiritual.

The four quadrants of grain in the center circle are each laid in a different direction, which, along with the lay of wheat at the two ends, give a three-dimensional look to the formation.

In the eighteenth century, historian William Stukeley surmised that the original layout of the stones leading from the nearby Avebury stone circles was like this ancient Egyptian symbol of a serpent passing through a circle with wings of feathers.

Photographer: © Steve Alexander

June 19, 1999, next to Silbury Hill, Wiltshire County, wheat crop.

This is the image of the pod of Eden. The cupped end receives the pollen that fertilizes the center globe, which is your Mother Gaia. The other creates the seed, portraying the balance of the male/female aspects. Just as all plants have a pollination process, this crop circle speaks of the pollination, the fertilization of the pod of Eden. The star glyph is the cosmic heart of the divine mother.

PLATE II

June 20, 1999, Avebury Trusloe, Wiltshire County, wheat crop.

This relatively simple but pretty pattern, 150 feet in diameter, is known as the "Avebury Trusloe Star." It was formed in young, green wheat. By late July, having turned tan color and having hosted many visitors, it still had reasonably active energy according to dowsing rods. The centers of the circles were swirled in nestlike circles and the wheat stalks still had many "magical bends," indicating the authenticity of the creating force.

This crop circle is the portal for the fifth wave or soul group that will emerge from the twelfth dimension. These children born between the years 2000–03 will be newly incarnated souls who will merge with souls who have experienced lifetimes of learning on your planet, creating incarnate beings evolved in peaceful consciousness. These children will radiate pure love essences and resonate high velocity frequencies vital for continued evolution.

PLATE 12

This 370-foot-long complex geometric pattern of hexagons, triangles, diamonds and circles suggests a "Sierpinski Gasket," according to chaos theory and mathematics. It is a fractal pattern that could be repeated infinitely. Sierpinski showed how a triangle could be divided by another triangle and then another, to infinity. This crop circle pattern could be cut and folded into a three-dimensional octahedron, made of eight equilateral triangles, which are associated with the air element.

The octahedron is one of the five Platonic solids and relates to the throat chakra, according to Michael Glickman. This geometric design is a flattened form of two pyramid shapes, which could be put together three-dimensionally, base to base. This geometric form also relates to the cube shape that appeared as a crop circle during the same night at Allington Down a few miles away. Andy Thomas has suggested that the design is similar to the molecular structure of a crystal. Geometry enthusiasts are thrilled with this design.

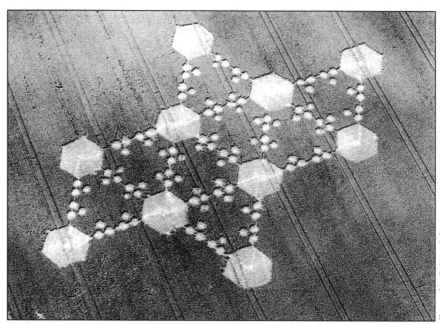

Photographer: © Karen Cushing.

June 23, 1999, West Overton, Wiltshire County, wheat crop.

The formula represented in this crop circle is the biochemical frequency code for the restructuring of planetary water. A non-Earth element will be added to the periodic table and chemically bond with H_2O. The new planetary water will be able to self-purify and rejuvenate.

PLATE 13

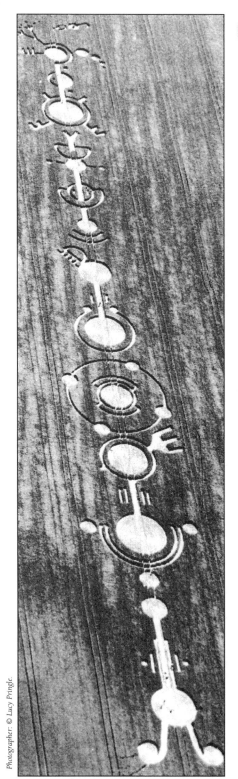

June 12, 1999, East Field, Alton Barnes, Wiltshire County, barley crop.

This pictogram was 1020 feet long and is known as the "East Field Long Pictogram." It was placed next to and near the long "Serpentine" formation in the same field under Knap Hill on the same night. Many researchers agree that this looks like a retrospective art exhibit from the circlemakers, incorporating many design elements that had appeared in long crop circles during previous years, especially 1990 and 1991.

On June 14, 1999, during an airplane flight over that field, researcher Francine Blake captured on film an amazing anomaly that appeared to be flying over this long formation. It looked like two wide areas of whitish light, one above the other, with eight orbs of dark light between the two layers. This has mystified many people. Five nights later on June 19, German researcher Frank Laumen photographed an orange sphere over this crop circle.

A local man named Charles Mallett was camped in this field overnight on June 12-13 and was amazed to wake up in the early morning and see this and the "Serpentine" formation five hundred feet away from him. He had not seen anyone else in the field with him or heard any noise during that night, and he saw no traces of footsteps or tracks or equipment near or in the formation.

The energies in this and the "Serpentine" formation were strong enough to disable all battery-operated equipment. A dog who spent the night in the end circle of this formation acted very disturbed for hours, barking, growling and acting sick. Another dog refused to go into the formation at all. Even veteran researcher Francine Blake felt queasy when entering this formation. The photographs she took in this pictogram showed unusual light anomalies.

This is the planetary merge of the galactic quantum, the completion of the thirteen solar houses, the joining of the eleventh house into the Council of Thirteen. This crop circle is a crystalline code for the evolution of cosmic DNA.

PLATE 14

This fluffy barley crop was beautifully laid down and curved into this five-hundred-foot-long serpentine shape, which appeared to flow along a slightly sloping field parallel to the "East Field Long Pictogram." These two formations appeared during the same night. This one had the appearance of moving, undulating across the landscape, under the so-called Serpentine Hills. Although all-night watchers were posted on top of adjacent Knap Hill, no one saw this and its companion formation being made. Suddenly, when daylight arose, they saw these amazing designs perfectly formed.

The serpent form has many meanings in various cultures, including a vertical alignment or ascension. An Aboriginal elder spoke of the serpent of the Dreamtime, which went all over Earth and found rivers, mountains, lakes and oceans. The serpent will return to Earth to eat all those who will not wake up. The serpent symbol is universal and complex, representing all kinds of dualities, and it is the source from which all energies come and to which they will return. The serpent has also been used to represent the ley lines of energy running through the Earth and to represent the goddess of the Earth.

Geometrically, this design is actually composed of a series of ten interlocking circles, each one seventy feet in diameter. The geometry is quite complex.

This crop formation was the location of a large late-afternoon gathering for the closing ceremony of the Wiltshire Crop Circle Study Group (WCCSG) Conference, on July 18, 1999. Guided by Francine Blake, Rod Bearcloud Berry and Ralph Jenkins, dozens of people processed through the entire length of this long formation, making music with symbols, tambourines, didgeridoos, flutes, drums and crystal bowls, and participated in singing, chanting, moving, swaying and listening to ancient Gaelic channeling. It was a very special place for a special celebration of the wondrous crop circle phenomenon.

Photographer: © Lucy Pringle.

June 12, 1999, East Field, Alton Barnes, Wiltshire County, barley crop.

This crop circle represents the harmonizing of the frequencies of the electromagnetic grids of Mother Earth, the new frequency for Earth's electromagnetic field. This geometry is representative of tones that stabilize the Earth's electromagnetic fields and balance and equalize the planetary energies for the polar shift. The formula for this phenomenon is $9^4/144$ (13 lunar phases + 13 resonant tones).

PLATE 15

Photographer: © Karen Cushing

June 23, 1999, "The Cube" at Allington Down, Wiltshire County, wheat crop.

This was a three-dimensional-looking pattern on a hillside, visible for miles around. It had high dowsing energy and made some visitors feel "heady." There was very high precision of the lay of the crop, forming exact straight lines and corners.

Michael Glickman and some other researchers had predicted that a cube shape would show up in an crop circle during 1999, and this design went even further as a three-dimensional-looking cube. The isometric projection made the design into a hexagram as well. The square shapes within the cube look like trapezoids or diamonds, according to the direction from which they are viewed.

People have interpreted this design in various ways: as the ancient Buddhist symbol of the antahkarana, as a geometrician's delight and as a design by Dutch artist M.C. Escher, who made optical illusions in his drawings. According to Native American tradition, this antahkarana design carries universal truths, such as the Star Altar of the Creator, which carries love, compassion and truth. It is also the symbol of the Eastern Star and the Eagle Spirit and a guide for the four sacred directions.

Dr. Nan Lu said that the energies of this crop circle were good for liver and stomach problems.

On July 28, more than a month after this crop circle had appeared, Charles Mallett witnessed orange spheres of light flying over this crop circle.

This crop circle represents the unveiling of the tomb of Exad (pronounced ee`shäd), the root of Ganeshkato, in the year 2001, located seven degrees southeast of Mount Sinai. Its opening will unlock the seventh aspect of the Ark of the Covenant. The star beings from Dogon planted a time capsule in the tomb before they were destroyed at the end of Mu, which is intended to be opened and activated when the tomb is revealed. Within the glyph of Exad are the star codes necessary for the time capsule's activation.

PLATE 16

Perhaps this crop circle was a gift to the crop circle community. This formation was placed very near to the gathering place of crop circle researchers and enthusiasts, the Barge Inn, located beside the Kennett and Avon Canal. This design is a circle or sphere within a three-dimensional-looking cube within another sphere or circle.

According to Rod Bearcloud Berry, the star beings who sent this crop circle intended the two circles to depict the spiritual truth of our inner self connecting to the Great Mystery. He said that the swirled semicircle is the place of the heart where we connect with the All—a special place we go into for meditation and openness, as in a native sweat lodge. Other people emphasize that if you look into the recessed corner of the cube, it seems to move forward and reach out to you.

This symbol might indicate the nature of our being, that we are both part of a greater universe and also contain the universe within ourselves. This design contains a solid hexagram: the symbol of the primal crystal, which contains within itself all of the twenty-four runes. Some people see this design simply as the peace symbol.

July 15, 1999, Honey Street, Alton Barnes, Wiltshire County, wheat crop.

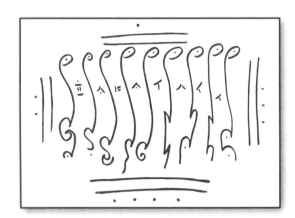

The mushroom-like peace stargate found at the bottom of the crop circle is the trinity effect, the healing of the nuclear violation of the planetary peace. This is the code for the deactivation of plutonium poisoning. It is recommended that those individuals who are committed to a nuclear-free planet use this crop circle and glyph for meditation, as it will expedite those results.

PLATE 17

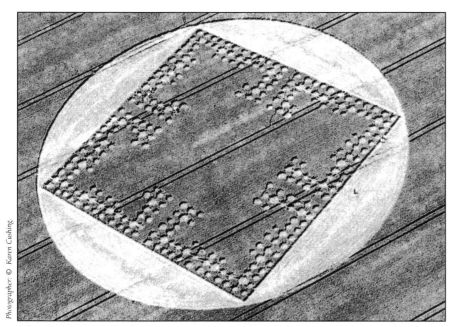

Photographer: © Karen Cushing.

July 16, 1999, on Windmill Hill, Avebury Trusloe, Wiltshire County, wheat crop.

This crop circle appeared on Windmill Hill, one of the earliest Neolithic sites (as old as 3700 B.C.), and downhill from an ancient tumulus. It is the same site where the spectacular "Triple Julia" fractal crop circle appeared in 1996. This 1999 design is a squared fractal, yet another example of the fractal theme.

According to Rod Bearcloud Berry, a square within a circle is a symbol drawn in many ancient pictographs in the Americas, and it suggests divine balance and harmony, that we are in balance between the Earth and the sky, or the body and the spirit. He says that the Star Nation people who made this crop circle made spirals of wheat between the outer circle and the inner square to show that we move within a spiraling energy, which expresses our connection to divine harmony.

Two hundred eighty-eight circles punctuate this formation and are each swirled clockwise. The entire design is 320 feet in diameter.

Many people think this crop circle represents a computer chip. Others suggest that this is a floor plan for a Knights Templar church, a strong fortress or a revered temple. Some see it as a Knights Templar cross, especially since Knights Templar used to live in this geographic area.

This crop circle is the DNA chip that will evolve our mathematical capacity. Each one of these circles is an infinite fractal crystalline code, and each crystalline aspect is a fractal universe. This evolved system is the next step for mathematics on Earth. *Qiuayon soen tra soen nas tra ka mix na ke te son tra laixwa mei ix nika* is the ancient mantra for the activation of this process.

PLATE 18

This design is the opposite or inversion of the July 16 Windmill Hill pattern, with the circles on the outside and the squares inside, giving a very different effect. Both of these crop circles are the same length and diameter: 328 feet.

This design is a fractal based on a square. The central square radiates out to form smaller squares, which reach out to form even smaller squares. This pattern could be extended to infinity.

Each square was formed by wheat being laid down in four different directions, which gives a three-dimensional look. The whole design looks like a group of connected pyramids, or perhaps Buddhist stupas. Some people tend to see primarily the square shapes, and some see primarily the triangle shapes. It has been suggested that the blunt end shapes could represent sacred doorways, as in Tibetan mandalas.

This is one of many crop circles placed near ancient sacred sites. In this case it is placed near the Neolithic West Kennett Longbarrow, which had been used for meditation and spiritual processes for an estimated 5500 years.

The night this crop circle appeared, several people standing in different locations witnessed a strange blue ball of light strobing, flashing and moving back and forth in the direction of West Kennett Longbarrow.

August 4, 1999, West Kennett Longbarrow, Wiltshire County, wheat crop.

Photographer: © Steve Alexander

This crop circle unlocks key time portals, facilitating a continuum for time travel. This is the template for the mathematical formula that is necessary for unlocking and opening the thirteenth door in time. The missing mathematical formula, or link code, for the successful opening of this wormhole, this door of destiny, is contained within this crop circle. This link code can only be used by individuals who have specific activation codes within their DNA.

PLATE 19

Photographer: © Karen Cushing.

July 18, 1999, Cherhill Down, under the white horse on the hill, near Calne, Wiltshire County, wheat crop.

This beautiful and first ever nine-pointed star of 230-foot diameter appeared under the 1780 white chalk horse carved into the steep hillside, near the standing obelisk monument. This crop circle appeared after a nearby resident had heard a loud banging sound during the night.

This pattern is made of three large implied triangles overlapping each other in three different directions. The star points are also triangles and give the impression of dynamic spinning, further emphasized by the swirling crescents. Perhaps they are suggesting an expanding and contracting or an opening and enclosing, as if giving us the opportunity to enter other dimensions and return again.

The nine points of the star have been considered significant, for, numerologically, nine is the number of completion and new beginning. This seems appropriate for the last summer of the millennium and the forthcoming beginning of a new millennium.

The feeling of energy in this crop circle was very strong, according to Barbara Lamb's personal experience and dowsing-rod and pendulum responses. Where one pathway of laid-down wheat joined with another, the energy seemed to be doubled. During the first day after this crop circle's appearance, Ralph Jenkins and Rod Bearcloud Berry were photographed while lying down on the ground with bright orange light/energy showing under their bodies.

This crop circle is an image of the crystalline seed that was implanted in twelve spots on the planet. It is the activation of the nine temples of evolution of the collective consciousness. The center is the Whirling Rainbow Way, the metamorphic opening of the collective heart chakra. The nine pyramids are the temples of the nine seeds of wisdom, the temples of the evolutionary gate to wisdom of the collective.

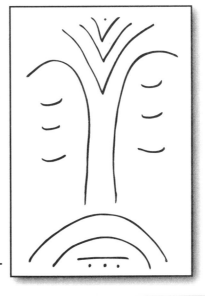

According to Rod Bearcloud Berry, the six inner curving moon shapes spiraling within the outer nine-sided shape represent inner truth and harmony. He has elaborated that the nearby separate glyph is an example of the star beings' written language. It had the unusual feature of a few standing stalks bending over at the top of the stem, with the seeds dehydrated. Another interpretation of the glyph is the Hindu symbol of Ganesha, the elephant deity.

PLATE 20

This 210-foot-diameter crop circle was an interesting pattern of circles, semicircles, triangles and straight bars. The lay of the wheat contained some unusual features. In the shorter straight pathways, the wheat splayed out in opposite directions from midpoint in the manner that people part their hair (a feature never seen before or since in a crop circle). Where a long pathway turned at a right angle to form one of the inner rings, a beautifully swirled circle of wheat splayed out with a tuft of standing stalks forming a vertical column in the center. One wondered how an anomalous force could accomplish such a feature.

Forty feet or so from the formation, a glyph or signature was laid down, too far into the standing crop from a tramline to have been made by people.

Photographs taken in this formation showed several luminous spheres in and near this crop circle, and cameras and other electronic equipment experienced battery failures.

According to Rod Bearcloud Berry, this design is another profound expression of Spirit and shows how Spirit moves into our existence and out again, how we work with energies and how our thoughts travel into the universe.

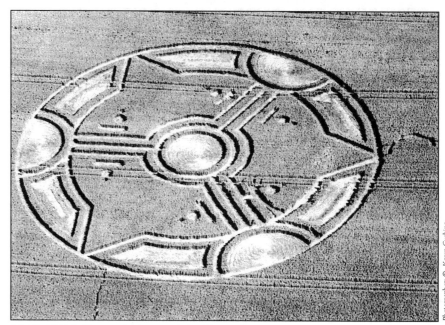

Photographer: © Karen Cushing.

July 21, 1999, Liddington Castle, east of Chiseldon, Wiltshire County, wheat crop.

This crop circle represents the evolution of the pure God-seed into its unique divinity, the divine procreative connection of the planetary DNA. This crop circle is the mathematical formula for the activation code that has been engraved in the pyramid of Giza. The glyph on the left is the key to the activation of this God-seed, the matrix of the evolved God-source within.

PLATE 21

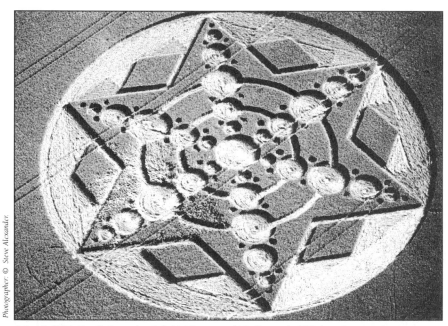

July 19, 1999, Devil's Den, near Fyfield, Manton and Marlborough, Wiltshire County, wheat crop, 250 feet in diameter.

This complex formation was the first crop circle to be placed near an ancient Neolithic dolmen of mega-lithic standing stones supporting a huge stone lintel. It is reported that this structure is the remaining part of a former, much larger structure with a surrounding circle of laid megalithic stones. Most of those stones were removed. This structure dates back to 4000–5000 B.C.

This crop circle design involves a six-pointed star within a hexagram, which is within another hexagram made by the lay of the wheat, and all are contained within a circle. The many circles radiating out from the center circle give this design a lovely starburst effect. The whole design is held together by two concentric rings. Between the points of the design are six diamond shapes.

Each circle was swirled in a slightly different way: some had centers which remind some people of chrysanthemum flowers; one center was swirled noticeably off-center; many centers were raised from the ground in nestlike fashions; some were swirled clockwise; and some were swirled counterclockwise.

The dowsing energy was very strong throughout this formation, and some researchers reported that their batteries were drained in their cameras, video recorders, cell phones, GPS meters and electronic voltmeters. The night before this crop circle appeared, residents in the local area had an electric power failure from 11:00 P.M. to 1:00 A.M.

The geometric feature of two overlapping triangles forming a Star of David may have originally come from pre-Jewish Arabic traditions, to ward off demons. It is notable that this symbolism appeared in the same field called Devil's Den.

The six-pointed star has long been used by native peoples throughout the Americas, and it expresses their path of Spirit. The circles and the hexagon in this formation express important truths of the Star Nation people and indigenous people, according to Rod Bearcloud Berry.

This is the cosmic equation for the planetary alignments necessary for the full activation of what is known in the mythology of the House of David as the fully awakened Christ being. This is the effect of the awakening of the DNA of the lineage of the ancient houses of light. The geometry of this crop circle imprints the cosmic completion of the Eden principle.

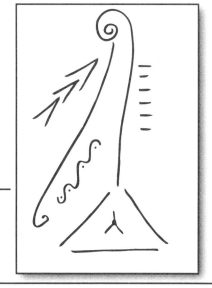

PLATE 22

This 275- to 350-foot crop formation commanded an inspiring view from the crest of a hill to nearby Silbury Hill and many fields for miles around, four of which contained existing crop circles. Although a very different shape than we had seen before, this design was another Koch fractal, which could replicate itself and extend to infinity. It reminded some people of the ancient ziggurat step-pyramid temples in Mesopotamia, built by Sumerians. These structures were referred to as hills of heaven or mountains of God, because it was assumed that God could live in the small chamber at the top.

It had a very interesting lay of the wheat, which seemed to come from four little nested centers in the middle of the formation, and curved and bent to form angular shapes at the edges. Because of this lay, the pattern looked three-dimensional when viewed from the air. Where different sections of the lay met together, they formed a deckle edge.

Each circle was beautifully swirled, often in directions opposite to its neighbors. The dowsing rods responded vigorously to the energy of the whole formation, especially at the four tightly swirled centers.

During the night when this crop circle was made, a witness in the Silbury Hill parking lot saw this field glowing with what looked like ultraviolet light, but he was not able to see where or what this light was coming from. At other times, spheres of light were seen over this crop circle.

Dr. Nan Lu suggested that the energy of this crop formation was good for stomach and digestive problems and for reducing tumors.

Photographer: © Steve Alexander.

July 24, 1999, across the A4 road from Silbury Hill, Wiltshire County, wheat crop.

This crop circle connects to the core of a crystalline ethereal temple, activating an ancient time-warp template contained there. This area is the cosmic connection for the earthly emanation of the Holy Grail.

PLATE 23

July 28, 1999, at Beckhampton, Wiltshire County, wheat crop.

This beautifully executed, precise design of 250 feet reminds people of a folded-ribbon design, a Celtic knot, a camera shutter, a Japanese origami design, a Seal of Solomon, a true lovers' knot or a symbol of our being connected to the universe.

As with many other crop circles, this design might have been influenced by people's thoughts and executed by the anonymous source. A tour group from Japan guided by Maseo Maki, the author of *In Search of Brazil's Quantum Surgeon* (Cadence Books), did a group meditation and prayer to the intelligence responsible for the making of crop circles for three hours at night. They asked for a design that would represent their Japanese culture. While doing this practice, they saw UFOs in the area, and some people developed unexpected nosebleeds. In the light of day, they saw this new crop circle, which had been placed in the direction they had been facing.

Some visitors to this crop circle reported malfunctions in their electronic equipment and episodes of missing time. Others experienced feeling wonderful and enjoyed that same energy.

The central swirled circle amazingly straightens out to form the inner hexagon, which reflects the hexagon at the outer edges of the design. The lay of the wheat precisely formed the triangles and straight pathways that define the segments of the design. This crop circle felt wonderful and had very strong measurable energy. It was considered by many to be a masterpiece.

The frequency in this crop circle is the quantum merkabah of the continuum of the radical theorem of space-time physics. This merkabah is activating a quantum leap in the science of physics on the planet.

PLATE 24

This very precise crop circle, 265 feet in diameter, reminds some people of playful dolphins in dynamic motion or of Japanese origami. Some Japanese researchers had been asking for a symbol representing their culture and this design appeared, symbolizing women in Japanese. Also, according to Native American traditions, Spirit shows our inner connectedness with the outer universe in this formation.

The wheat was laid in an outstandingly graceful and consistent manner, looking like sand or silt looks when it has been flowed along by water in a stream. This ripple effect, also called *bundling*, may have contributed to the high energy measured by dowsing rods. The energy was also high at the center of the formation and where one flow of the wheat joined with another at the tips of the crescents

Two experienced researchers, Michael Glickman and Patricia Murray, ran their video camera on a tripod pointed toward this formation while they walked around and took photographs of this design. The video camera recorded a series of many white luminous spheres flying over the crop circle from various directions, one by one. These white balls were also videotaped on August 7 by Donald Fletcher during a visit from London. Oddly enough, people in that formation during those times did not see any of those balls flying over and past them. We wonder if they could be seen only by the film and not by the human eye.

Dr. Nan Lu said this was the most energetically powerful crop circle during 1999, helpful for any physical problem. He suggested that people with physical problems keep a picture of this crop circle with them at all times.

July 23, 1999, Barbury Castle, near Swindon, Wiltshire County, wheat crop.

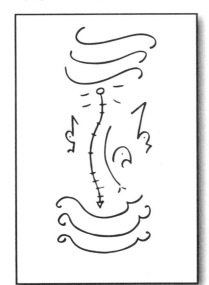

This crop circle is the emblem of the advisory governing body of Katorika and the geometric code for the balance of world power through divine cocreation. Three powerful forms of world government will emerge, representing unity through global prosperity, identity by free will and the merging of power for mutual benefit and respect for life. It is the essence of the principles of peace manifested through divine balance, empowerment and respect for life.

PLATE 25

July 31, 1999, at Roundway, Devizes, Wiltshire County, wheat crop.

This beautiful 300-foot-diameter crop circle was placed in a field with electric towers and lines at one edge. This crop circle itself emitted energy that affected the palms of people's hands, pendulums and dowsing rods. Early in the morning when it was discovered, visitors heard loud, crackling electrostatic noises, which were different than the usual noises from electric pylons. The next day, a bright white column or arc was seen over this crop circle.

The design is a nice interplay of seven large circles and seven smaller circles, perhaps representing the principle of growth, spiritual revelation or the seven stages leading to completion. Perhaps the seven circles represent the seven spirits before the throne, from Rosicrucian and Kabbalistic traditions. The fourteen-pointed star contains great symmetry and balance and connection, and it helps us to understand our lives on Earth. It shows important male and female energies that exist in the universe. These ideas were suggested by various researchers.

The center of the formation was a swirled circle surrounded by a raised ring of wheat, looking like a protective ring, unseen in any crop until this one. From this center, the laid-down crop flowed into each point where it swirled a circle, and then flowed exquisitely out of that point and into the next point, all around the entire pattern. Dr. Nan Lu observed that the energy came up from the center, made one continuous flow and ended back in the center again.

This was one of many crop circles over the years that felt wonderful to be in. Barbara Lamb and her friends meditated in it. They had the experience of leaving their bodies for a while and returning with a heightened sense of well-being.

This crop circle emanates a frequency that has dual purposes. One effect is the evolution of genetically superior seeds for food sources; the other is the evolution of the collective consciousness to accept, acknowledge and respect the mystical nature of seeds and their powerful influence on the planetary balance.

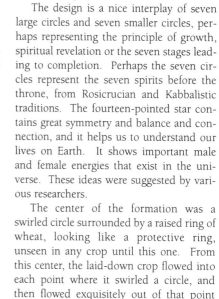

PLATE 26

This 410-foot-diameter crop circle was an incredibly precise pattern of swirling, interlocking logarhythmic curves and crescents. It appeared in a field near the Hackpen Hill White Horse, carved in 1898. The first people to enter this crop circle—Stuart Dike and others—found the crop to be very lightly laid down and crackling with energy.

The spirals seem to radiate out from the center circle, forming a vortex, in a kind of geometry shown in crop circles for the first time. The Fibonacci spirals are thought to foretell the approaching total eclipse of the Sun on August 11, 1999. They are also said to depict the Saros cycle of the Sun, which takes 1000–1200 years to complete. (A Saros cycle includes forty-two Sun eclipses each eighteen years, ten days and eight hours.) Another speculation is that this shows the paths made across the Earth's surface by the Moon's shadow during a total solar eclipse. Also, Rod Bearcloud Berry has said that this design reflects the matrix and the pattern of motion of the universe.

Bert Janssen, a researcher from the Netherlands, determined through geometric analysis that this design was made of circles, not of spirals as it appears, and is based on sixfold geometry. Some geometrically astute people have attempted to draw this design on paper and have not been able to achieve it with such impeccable precision. Therefore, it is difficult to imagine how this pattern was laid in a wheat field during the complete darkness of night.

Night watchers posted up on the hill noticed some small lights down in that field near the farmhouse. But later, the farmer, James Hussey, told Barbara Lamb that he had been outside at that time with some large flashlights, looking for foxes that had been chasing his chickens. Other than those lights, no indication of human involvement was detected in or near that field.

July 4, 1999, below Hackpen Hill, near Broad Hinton, Wiltshire County.

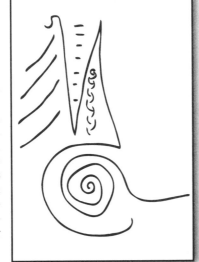

This is the thirteen-strand DNA from a cross section of each fiber strand within the newly evolved human ovum. Various colonizations brought their genetic strands to merge with the original people or the primal God-seed group, known to your mythologies as first man and woman. This has brought a galactic merge of varying aspects of DNA, creating a unique gene pool. The completion of this is the law of the five elements balanced in the human races on the planet.

PLATE 27

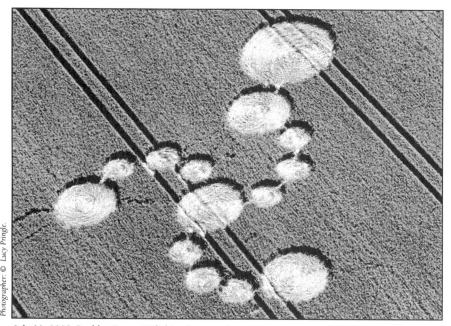

Photographer: © Lucy Pringle.

July 11, 1999, Rockley Down, Wiltshire County, wheat crop.

This simple but lovely crop circle was very nice to visit and meditate in. The circles were swirled beautifully, and each one was swirled differently. The dowsing energy was strong in each circle. Two of the circles had splayed-out, raised nests in the center that stood as high as seven inches from the ground. The whole formation was one-hundred-feet long and contained fourteen circles.

This formation was placed near Temple Bottom, an area where the Knights Templar lived and roamed centuries ago. It also looked across the road at the hillside of Gallops, where horse races still occur.

This is the molecule of the evolved planetary bacteria, E. coli, cultured within super blue-green algae beds. This algae will be a very powerful food source, carrying elements that will enhance healthy bacteria within the intestines and contribute to the evolution of a healthier populace.

PLATE 28

This crop formation held its strong energy at least six weeks after it appeared, according to dowsing rods and pendulums. Each circle was swirled in a direction different from its neighbor, and in three circles the centers were raised several inches from the ground. It was a nice formation in which to meditate.

This 230-foot-diameter design was composed of twenty-eight circles of varying sizes. A lot of wild grass grew in the circles, apparently unaffected by the energy that made this crop circle, unlike the crop which had been laid down so nicely.

Photographer: © Karen Cushing.

June 20, 1999, Allington Down, Wiltshire County, wheat crop.

This is the mathematical formula for the mutation of the poliovirus. The evolved virus will enter the muscle fiber and improve the longevity, durability, elasticity and strength of muscle tissue and fibrous cells in all species on the planet. Many of the devastating muscular diseases will be unable to take root in this evolved, healthier muscle fiber.

Note: *Every disease and organism that has affected the species as a destructive organism will evolve in this manner. What was used to destroy will be used to create. When you meditate or work with these images, imagine the creative potential of these two glyphs.*

PLATE 29

August 5, 1999, Barbury Castle, near Swindon, Wiltshire County, wheat crop.

This formation is a continuation of the serpent motif that appeared during the previous years. It followed almost two months after the long serpentine formation of June 12, 1999, in East Field, Alton Barnes.

Ancient Druids used serpent symbols to relate to planets, the Sun, the Moon, solar eclipses and star patterns. These serpent symbols and scorpion designs appeared in several crop circles in 1994, often thought to represent the continuing of the Shoemaker-Levy 9 comet hitting Jupiter. The serpent theme appeared in the "DNA Double Helix" crop circle in East Field, Alton Barnes, in 1996, and in three dragon formations during 1998.

The end of this 1999 serpentlike formation was a circle formed in a most unusual way: overlapping sections of wheat formed a basket effect, with stalks laid around the edge in a deliberate border. The entire formation was eight-hundred-feet long, following the curving pathway.

This crop circle awakens and clears vital energy rivers on the planet, such as the Mary and Michael Line and Rio de la Vida. When Rio de la Vida, the river of life, is activated, it stabilizes Mother Earth during Earth changes (her birthing), reducing the massive effects of the purification in the form of earthquakes, hurricanes, volcanoes and tornadoes. This set is to be used in meditation to remove fear blockages and to activate the sacred energies to open these vital energetic rivers.

PLATE 30

This design seemed to be the final development of three formations of a similar type during 1999: June 16 at Allington Down, July 10 at Rockley and now this one late in July, measuring 180 feet. Three arms of thirteen circles each appear to dance away from a center thirty-two feet in diameter. Some people called this design a dancing fractal.

This crop circle held its wonderful dowsing energy even weeks after it appeared. It held its beautiful circular swirls in spite of many people visiting it, due to its easy access from the road.

Some people interpret this design as a DNA strand, with three arms of differently sized and differently laid circles. As with the other similar patterns, this one gives a sense of dynamic movement and spinning.

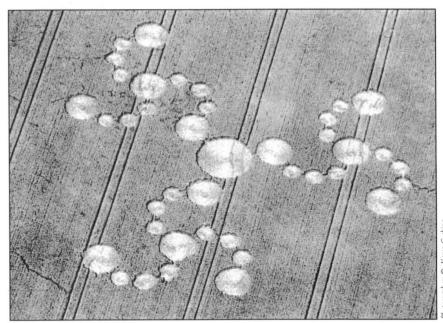

Photographer: © Karen Cushing

July 1999, Lurkley Hill, West Overton, Wiltshire County, wheat crop.

This crop circle is the seed for the resolution of the energy crisis, not only shifting the attitude of the collective as to energy use, but providing the inspiration for the development of new energy sources that will become widely available to the masses. It is the formula for removing existing blockages placed by the oil and coal industries and allowing existing sources of free energy to be readily available to the general populace.

PLATE 31

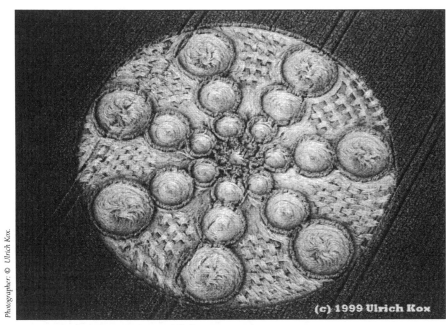

Photographer: © Ulrich Kox.

(c) 1999 Ulrich Kox

August 6, 1999, Bishops Cannings, Wiltshire County, wheat crop.

This astonishing 152-foot-diameter crop circle is known as "The Basket," because the wheat between the circles seems to be woven and the edges of each circle remain standing in a neat, thin ring. These rings were left standing over underlying pathways from the center circle to the outside rings in a spokelike pattern.

Rod Bearcloud Berry has said that this design represents a basket of plenty or a basket of Spirit, which expresses love and compassion from our spiritual source. Michael Glickman has pointed out the sevenfold geometry, signifying Spirit and revelation. All parts of the basket weave come together as a single unity.

Some of the circles had only one standing stalk in their center; some circles had a few stalks twisted around the center stalk. The center circle had seven standing stalks, perhaps echoing the sevenfold geometry of the entire formation. The woven areas were raised from the ground in a way that had never been seen before. The largest circles had a woven rotation, and their centers formed an *S* curve in which the wheat sharply curved in opposite directions. All of these details made this crop circle a masterpiece of the laying of the crop.

Distressingly, three hours after this crop circle was discovered by Ulrich Kox in an airplane and Andreas Müller and Werner Anderhub on the ground, the farmer cut out the entire formation with his harvester machine, even though researchers tried to pay him to stop cutting so they could study this unusual formation more thoroughly. The farmer refused and kept saying the crop circle was the result of vandalism. Fortunately, this one photograph had been shot from the air, and ground photos, detailed descriptions and surveys had been taken within the crop circle itself.

People who sat in the center of the formation after the harvesting, still felt the energy very strongly. They felt pressure in their heart chakras and believed that higher dimensions were trying to show that the energies of the crop circle were as important as the visual pattern.

This is the Flower of Life's sacred geometry. *Dorsa naki da ta* is the mantra for this ultimate symbol of peace in divine union, empowerment and mutual cocreation. It is a powerful set to be used in mediation and sessions for conflict resolution. This is a practical tool that can be infinitely useful in the transformation of the warrior/destroyer paradigm, the healing of the heart of the beast.

PLATE 32

This 350-foot-long formation seemed to be a harbinger of the complete solar eclipse predicted for August 11, 1999, three months later. Although solar eclipses are seen fairly regularly in one part of the world or another, this was only the second total eclipse to be seen from England since 1927. The next solar eclipse is predicted for 2090. Some experts think that solar eclipses create vast effects on the Earth.

Doug Rogers suggested another theory: that this design showed Comet Lee moving from the small end of the formation toward the middle, then in back of the Sun in the center, then to the large ringed circle at the other end, where it changed the ring's appearance. He was amazed that four hundred years ago, Nostradamus knew that a comet would come to our solar system at the same time as a total eclipse seen from that part of the world.

This design appeared in an early oilseed canola crop, which is so brittle that anyone walking through it would snap and break each stalk and would get cut and hurt. In this formation, however, the stalks were neatly bent without snapping or cracking, a testimony to the unusual force and intelligence that laid the rings down.

Once again, this intelligence seems to know about and depict significant astronomical events of interest to human beings.

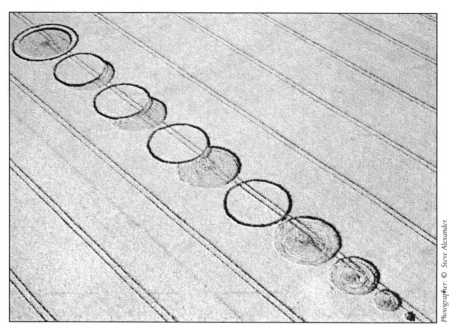

May 2, 1999, Middle Wallop, Hampshire County, oilseed canola (rapeseed) crop.

Photographer: © Steve Alexander.

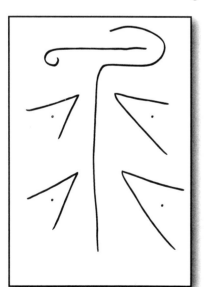

This is the mathematical formula for the emergence of the thirteen galactic suns into our planetary Sun, Kinich Ahau, which is the basis of planetary evolution of heaven on Earth. Each time a new galactic sun merges with your Sun, there is a shifting of the essences of the light energies emanated and received into the basic structure of planetary energetics and food sources. This energy works its way up the food chain in an energetic patterning and repatterning. This is the simple basis for evolution.

PLATE 33

This crop circle is one of many designs over the years of three implied overlapping circles. In this design, they form three lovely crescents and three petal or lotus-leaf shapes. The crop was laid down precisely and impeccably to form these shapes. This mandala design is conducive to meditation.

July 22, 1999, Meon Woke, Hampshire County, wheat crop.

This crop circle is the matrix for dissolving the information block that has been placed on inventions important in solving the Earth's ecological crisis, such as free, nondestructive energy sources and the production of items used in daily living that do not have a devastating impact on the environment.

PLATE 34

This is one of a few similar 1999 crop circle designs, although this one has four overlapping rings and four implied circles. The design forms three large crescents and three leaf shapes. As in the June 21 crop circle design [plate 35], there are two small standing circles in one crescent shape.

July 12, 1999, Wanford, Hampshire County, wheat crop.

Photographer: © Lucy Pringle.

This crop circle and star glyph are the blueprints for the divine marriage, the plan for the balance and healing of the male/female relationships in divine cocreation. With the healing of this paradigm, the Earth's population will naturally come into balance with the availability of space and natural resources. Be prepared for love in exotic bliss as experienced within your great mythologies—only without the tragic endings!

Note: *Crop circles/star glyphs 34 and 35 are sets that should be used together in meditation.*

PLATE 35

June 21, 1999, East End, near West Meon, Hampshire County, barley crop.

This pattern was similar in some ways to two other designs in the same general area. The three overlapping circles were echoed by three mid-sized circles and three small circles. The lay of the barley was done with careful precision, which is a real accomplishment for such a light, fluffy, blowing-in-the-wind crop. This design was 130 feet in diameter.

This crop circle is the formula for the balanced union of the Father, Mother and Holy Spirit. The divine balance of power through holy union is a circular pattern in which there is no head or controlling essence, but rather a cohesive flow of cosmic power in perfect balance. This is a mathematical fractal formula of light and sound frequencies that will emanate in the atmosphere and within the fiber of all inhabitants—animate and inanimate—and the core of Mother Earth herself. Once completed on this planet, this formula will be implemented in other galaxies in the original creative state.

PLATE 36

This 150-foot-diameter pattern is reminiscent of two similar cyclic crescent or nested crescent designs: one at Oliver's Castle, Wiltshire County, in July 1994, and one at East Meon, Hampshire County, in 1995. One wonders if the circlemakers keep giving us a design until we realize its significance.

Its predecessor of 1994 is thought to have depicted the site of impact on planet Jupiter of the Shoemaker-Levy 9 comet that occurred that same month. The 1995 design appeared in a series of crop circles depicting astronomical features. Perhaps this 1999 design continues the theme of giving attention to happenings and moving bodies in space. It could contain needed information. According to Geoff Stray, it might signify the end of time.

As with the other similar patterns, this crop circle can be viewed as rings, as crescents or as both. It conveys a sense of energetic swirling or orbiting.

Photographer: © Steve Alexander.

May 30, 1999, Penton Grafton, Hampshire County, barley crop.

This crop circle is a spinning calibration device that vibrates a frequency in the atmosphere that will bring profound unconditional love and resonate in the energies of faith and hope. This is the frequency-energetic device that will spark our divine potential through emanation from the emotional mind-heart of those awakened beings who have reached bodhisattvahood, or enlightenment.

PLATE 37

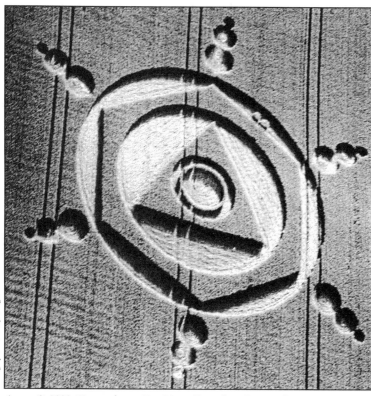

Photographer: © Lucy Pringle.

August 3, 1999, Henwood, near East Meon, Hampshire County, wheat crop.

One week after this crop circle was formed, a white, roundish object and a pink glow were observed in the center. The white object moved horizontally.

This formation is a lovely example of sixfold geometry and includes circles, a hexagon and a triangle. Many people liken this design to a mandala or a jewelry pendant.

This crop circle is the full geometric representation of the alpha and the omega. It resonates a frequency of perfect balance and a pure emanation of the great I Am presence. This is the House of God, the completion of the twelve elementals in perfect balance with the Mother/Father and the Holy Spirit in the manifestation of divine potential. *Maaa koo waa* is the mantra for this manifestation to be used in meditation.

PLATE 38

This 180-foot-diameter formation had an entirely unique design, unlike any crop circle seen before or since. It reminded people of a brain or nerve network, of flashes of lightning, of the roots of a tree or of the World Wide Web. Someone even saw a similarity to the baobab trees taking over the planet of the Little Prince in the well-known children's story.

This crop formation appeared in the same season with twenty-four other crop circles in various parts of the Czech Republic. On the night this one was formed, another crop circle composed of circles was also formed.

The researchers took this photograph after the whole field was harvested, and the pattern still shows amazingly clearly.

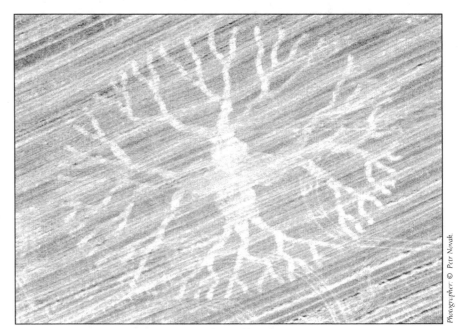

Photographer: © Petr Novak.

July 21, 1999, Novy Jicin, North Moravia, Czech Republic, wheat crop.

This crop circle is the electromolecular formula for the restructuring of the blood and bone cells of the human species to enhance T cells and the reproduction of natural antibodies that will be resistant to and capable of transmuting common disease-causing organisms.

PLATE 39

August 1999, Newton St. Loe, near Bath, Wiltshire County, wheat crop.

This crop design has some similarity to the July 1996 "Julia Set" crop circle near Stonehenge, which was a perfect fractal Fibonacci spiral, with the largest circle at the beginning of the arc and tapering down in circle sizes to the tail. This 1999 design is the reverse of the "Julia Set," in that the circles near the beginning circle are small and evolve into larger circles along the arc.

This set is the multidimensional alignment of the cosmic forces of creation. It is the blueprint of creation that carries primal codes for the creation of universes, worlds and all that is. The energy of the continuum is a spiral of creative force expanding the thirteen-strand galactic DNA in thirteen dimensions. This is the quintessence— the fifth element or spirit—of this adjustment that must be developed in parallel dimensions and universes for the effect to be complete.

PLATE 40

This pretty formation could be seen from the top of the chalk escarpment nearby. It consisted of forty-three clockwise swirled circles forming three rings or arcs of overlapping circles. Each ring had a larger circle toward the center of the formation and smaller circles toward the end, creating a graceful design.

Some of the swirled centers were not directly in the middle of their circles, yet somehow the circles were truly circular. Some of the circles had standing centers and some did not. No indications of footprints, human noise or even anomalies were noted by residents in that area.

This pattern might represent the ancient Celtic symbol of the *triskelemotif* (from 500-100 B.C. and seen again in 600 A.D.). It symbolized the seasonal cycle of the Earth Goddess who was shown in three separate forms of the one feminine principle: the Maid, the Mother and the Crone. Each aspect of the Goddess presided over one process of agriculture: planting, gestating and harvesting the crops to sustain human life.

As with many crop circles, this symbol reminds us of beliefs of ancient people who had greater respect than we do for the Earth and all its life forms.

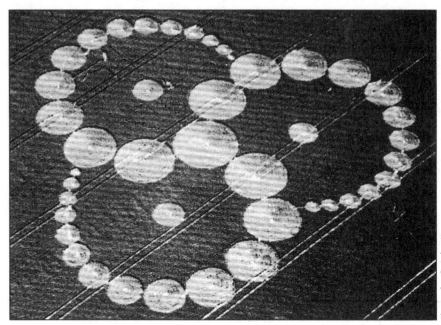

Photographer: © Andrew King.

June 20, 1999, Trottiscliffe, near Maidstone, Kent, wheat crop.

The formulas represented in this set are the codes to activate your lightbodies. These crystalline geometries are the seeds of light mentioned in the Keys of Enoch. This set is powerful for opening up the tunnels of light that will be used for this energetic exchange with the angelic realm. Wormholes are coded into the geometries of the Lords of Light who incarnated to ignite this matrix.

PLATE 41

July 14, 2000, West Stowell, Wiltshire County, wheat crop.

Photographer: © Lucy Pringle.

This flamboyant and vastly different pattern appeared under a seven-thousand-year-old Neolithic camp and Golden Ball Hill in the vale of Pewsey. The hill was named for the golden and reddish-orange spheres that have been seen flying in and out of it for thousands of years. On July 15, Australian visitor Kate Dash caught on film a glowing goldish sphere flying low over the field on its way to this formation. This crop circle was also placed directly under the belly of the Goddess Hill, which is part of the undulating hills known as the "Sleeping Goddess."

The site for this crop circle is very close to two dense copses of trees nestled in the valley between Knap Hill and Golden Ball Hill. Mystical ritualistic practices have been privately carried out in those thick bunches of trees for many centuries and even today. A few fairy rings can be seen on one of the hills.

According to Freddy Silva, this design shows fivefold geometry, sixfold geometry and encoded sevenfold geometry. Very high frequencies were registered here, making cameras and LCD displays blitz out. Many magical bends and gap seekings were found in the laid crop.

Some people wondered if active solar flares or a flaring star might be indicated with this design.

To maintain planetary balance there must be an intergalactic and parallel universal alignment of the frequencies. This crop circle is a tuning fork or calibration device for the galactic shift that is occurring as we emerge through point zero. Point zero is a phase—not a day—that occurs as part of a birthing process. This crop has a stabilizing effect on Earth's energies during this phase of our emergence. This is a vital pulsar point, a key gate to intergalactic interdimensional portals. The mathematical formula for this crop circle is seen on the top left corner of the star glyph.

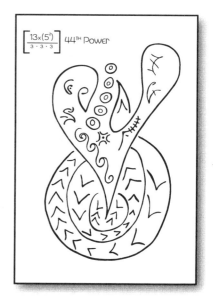

$$\left[\frac{13 \times (5^2)}{3 \cdot 3 \cdot 3}\right] \text{ 44}^{\text{TH}} \text{ POWER}$$

PLATE 42

This crop circle, 220 feet in diameter, held its shape and energy remarkably well for a month until the authors could visit it. Barbara Lamb detected with her dowsing rods a ley line running through the formation from Adam's Grave at the northwest to Picked Hill at the southeast.

Freddy Silva has said that this crop circle represents the throat chakra. Karen Douglas calls this formation the "South Field Temple," composed of sixteen petals.

Dr. Nan Lu said the energy of this crop circle was good for correcting disorders of the blood and for producing blood cells and T cells. It helped with chemotherapy and radiation treatments for cancer patients and those with irritable bowel syndrome and digestive problems.

Photographer: © Lucy Pringle.

June 19, 2000, South Field, Alton Priors, Wiltshire County, barley crop.

Part of the purpose of this crop circle is to infuse a new frequency of light vibration and energy into the grid and ley lines that will enter into Earth's light spectrum. This will shift our light spectrum from its present vibration into a higher frequency, allowing a larger variety of colors (particularly violet, sapphire and ruby) to emanate onto the planet. Our spectrum of light frequencies will be completely altered by this phenomenon, positively affecting the brain's biochemistry via absorption through the optic nerve.

PLATE 43

July 16, 2000, Avebury Down, Wiltshire County, wheat crop.

Photographer: © Lucy Pringle.

This crop circle was placed just north of the ancient stone circle of Avebury. It was beautifully executed with clean precision of the lay of the wheat. It had strong dowsing and pendulum energy, especially in the centers of the three swirled circles and at the female center of the whole design.

In each long petal or propeller-blade shape, half the wheat lay in one direction and the other half lay in the opposite direction. In one petal where the two directions met in the middle, the wheat was beautifully fanned out over the other direction and red poppies were woven into this fanning effect.

Directly uphill from this crop circle was an ancient sacred spring and nearby was a special round copse of trees where mystical practices were conducted.

This crop circle is a surge protector to guard the planet from massive upheaval as this frequency is beamed from the Arcturian mothership's tetratronic reactor through the shaft in Silbury Hill. Frequencies are first balanced and resonated with this formula before the surge enters the sacred temple of the birthing mother on Silbury Hill. Group meditations are particularly useful with this set at times of planetary alignments, eclipses and other cosmic phenomena that influence the electromagnetic balance of the planet.

PLATE 44

This crop circle was placed just downhill from a pyramid-shaped hill upon which was an extremely dense copse of trees. The copse was completely enclosed by a fence, perhaps because the energy therein was so intense. Author Judy Moore climbed over the fence and entered the copse anyway, and she later reported having astral traveled from there for a while.

Although overall, this crop circle had moderate dowsing responses, the energy was more intense in the center, where there was a pyramid shape of wheat standing vertically and bent over, and in the nicely swirled circles in the laid-down sections of wheat.

Photographer: © Karen Cushing.

July 16, 2000, Picked Hill, near Wilcot, Wiltshire County, wheat crop.

This crop circle is the code for the activation of the forty-fourth aspect of the Holy Grail, the vessel of God's pure life force that is born from the womb of the Cosmic Mother and feeds the embryo of the coming age of enlightenment. This crop circle is the meeting place between spirit, myth and science.

PLATE 45

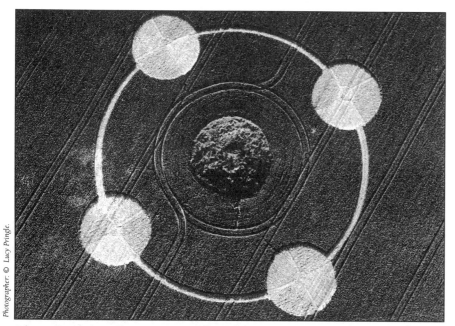

July 19, 2000, Milton Lilbourne, near Everleigh and Pewsey, Wiltshire County, wheat crop.

This crop circle appeared in the area of the Pewsey White Horse. It amazed many people because of its perfect placement around an ancient tumulus and its form of an ancient Celtic cross. There were three outstanding features: in each circle the lay of the wheat went carefully in four different directions from a center swirl; in the ring, one half of the wheat ran in one direction and the other half ran in the opposite direction; and the very brittle nettle plants on the tumulus were swirled in a clockwise circle without being broken or damaged. The whole formation was executed with precision, accuracy and beauty.

Very strong energy was detected by dowsing rods and pendulums, and the authors and their friends experienced a very positive, uplifting feeling in this entire formation.

Lower in the same field was a simple circle of fine energy, and in the opposite field was still another swirled circle.

This circle and mound are energetically linked with the spiritual energy of the ones of great wisdom, the ascended masters and wisdom keepers who walk the Earth to assist in bringing about the great peace of the winged serpent. This is an accumulation of energies of all peace ceremonies that are currently being conducted globally. This set can be used as a meditation tool to maximize the effects of global peace ceremonies and can be useful in focusing peace energy into places of destructive activity such as Silbury Plain, the Pentagon in the U.S. and any other military command centers.

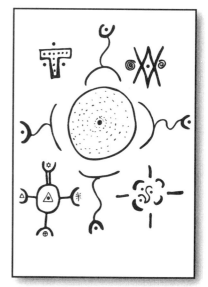

PLATE 46

This crop circle design might be a depiction of the Pleiades (the Seven Sisters) and their subsidiary planets or of some other planetary system or star field. The ring around the outside was most unusual: it was intricately woven in a basket-like way in the center of the ring, yet the innermost and outermost areas of the ring were laid in a smooth clockwise direction.

Most of the swirled circles were placed too far from the tramlines to have been made by humans. Each circle had a distinct center of standing stalks of varying sizes. One of these had been mysteriously knotted tightly at the top.

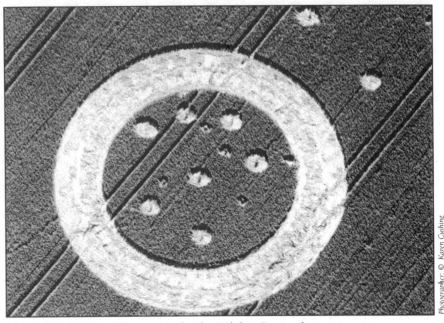

Photographer: © Karen Cushing

July 16, 2000, Old Shaw Village, near Lockeridge, Wiltshire County, wheat crop.

Within the frequency codes that define mass and matter, a genetic alteration is being conducted to alter life forms on the Earth. Literally, this is a restructuring of the DNA of the planet's biosystem. The shift of the base cellular frequencies of mass and matter will assist in creating the new hologram in the cosmic dream field. New species and mutations of existing species will appear within your life field and mend the damaged life chain by replacing important extinct species on the planet. The world appears to be the same, yet all is altered; nothing is as it appears.

PLATE 47

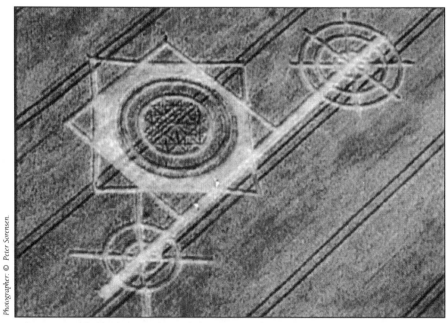

This crop formation was added to the day after it appeared. It had an unusual number of straight lines, rings and crosses and two squares overlapping each other. In the middle grid portion there were tightly swirled tufts of standing wheat, bent over at the tops of the stalks.

Although the lay of the wheat was not especially tidy, the dowsing rods registered a reasonable amount of energy.

July 30, 2000, Blackland, near Calne, Wiltshire County, wheat crop.

The Arcturian mothership contains a device that affects the solar frequencies entering the Earth's atmosphere, stimulating alpha brain waves and adjusting the bipolar frequencies within the brain. This crop circle is the formula that is being implanted into the solar rays to create the phenomenon. The basic result is an enhanced solar effect, stimulating the rapid metamorphosis of life forms on Earth. This set is recommended to be used in meditation groups of six, emanating intense love vibrations in a violet spectrum.

PLATE 48

This 282-foot-diameter crop circle amazed people with its three-dimensional look, due to the variation in size of the squares and rectangles. It was called by many the "Surrealistic Pillow." Geometrically, it is a fractalized octahedron, according to Michael Glickman.

The energies in this crop circle were so powerful during the first few days that many visitors felt dehydrated and sick. They affected film in an airplane by bleaching out pigments from several of Francine Blake's photos.

The young barley crop had risen up a lot in the heliotropic process, yet when the authors visited this formation five weeks later, the standing squares were still visible. Judy Moore had a special experience of astral travel and spiritual enlightenment, while friend Margaret Moore kept her "grounded" by holding her ankles.

Dr. Nan Lu said this crop circle helped to balance and harmonize the entire body, helped relieve pain in joints and helped the symptoms of chronic fatigue syndrome. It also could promote a person's relationship to nature.

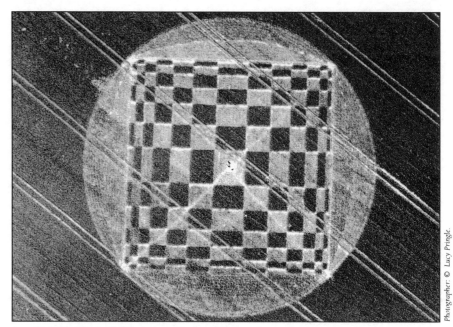

Photographer: © Lucy Pringle.

June 18, 2000, Windmill Hill, Avebury Trusloe, Wiltshire County, barley crop.

This crop circle is the frequency grid for the interdimensional light web that has been carefully placed around Mother Earth as she prepares for the massive shift that is described as the *Mayan Day Out of Time*. This is the quantum magnetic formula for the new light grid that has been placed around your plane. It replaces the fear grid that has held your planet in fear for so very long in Earth years. This process will stabilizes the Earth's axis as she emerges through point zero.

PLATE 49

Photographer: © Karen Cushing.

July 1, 2000, Milk Hill, Alton Barnes, Wiltshire County, wheat crop.

This beautiful 200-foot-diameter "Rose Window" crop circle appeared under the white chalk horse on Milk Hill. This was the general site where other outstanding crop circles have appeared in previous years, including the "Double Koch Snowflake" of August 8, 1997 [plate 3]. This was a sixfold floral design with petals flowing out from the center.

Mr. Hues, the farmer who owned the land, resolutely remained convinced that this crop circle was man-made, in spite of several researchers having pointed out magical bends of the laid stalks, the accomplished lay of the wheat and dowsing rod and pendulum responses and other measurements of unusual energetic activity. When Barbara Lamb offered to show him her dowsing responses, he said he did not want to see evidence of anything unusual and anomalous, and preferred to keep thinking that this crop circle and the crop circles placed in other fields that he owns are made by humans.

Dr. Nan Lu said the energy in this crop circle could help relieve joint pain and pain from blood or Qi stagnation as well as reduce the size of tumors and fight cancer.

This particular crop circle is the master code or blueprint of the frequencies and formulas to be activated in this area during the crop circle season of the year 2000. The star glyph is the image of the crystalline orb, encoded with both the blueprint for this season's crop circles and a key to the entire plan for the scheduled appearances of the crop circles during the birthing of Gaia, or the Eden project. By activating your neurosynapses with this image, you can connect your psyche to and actively engage in this master plan in a positive way.

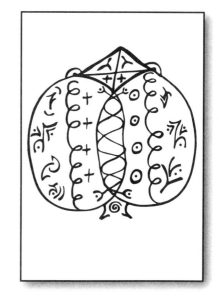

PLATE 50

This dynamic crop circle design reminds people of many things: changing Earth magnetics, the pattern made by iron filings being moved on a tray by magnets underneath, the way a living cell divides, the two hemispheres of a human brain, the chromosome effect, the biodynamic field around the human body or a Moiré pool pattern, which appears to move and form new patterns as you look at it from various directions. A Moiré is usually created by two patterns interfering with each other and is a fractal. From the air, this design looked three-dimensional because of the higher central section.

This design was exquisitely constructed with laid-down diamond shapes, leaving standing diamond shapes. The energy was so high throughout the whole formation that Barbara Lamb's dowsing rods stayed totally open in a 360-degree arc.

Steven Greer, M.D., told Barbara Lamb that on the airplane ride from the U.S. to England, his CSETI (Center for the Study of Extraterrestrial Intelligence) group was intently discussing the changing Earth magnetics. One night after their arrival, this crop circle appeared. He said this is an outstanding example of fractal magnetics and that this is a magnetic field dipole. Colin Andrews has said that he's found magnetic anomalies in many crop circles. Perhaps this design is highlighting that feature.

There was an active controversy over this crop circle. Linda Moulton Howe said the making of this formation was claimed by Matthew Williams and his team of hoaxers. Ron Russell told Barbara that it was actually made by a hoaxing team of Lundberg, Russell and Dickinson, with Williams helping. However, many researchers challenge these claims and continue to view this formation as genuine unless convincingly proved otherwise. It is staggering to conceive of the intricacy of this pattern having been laid down in the field by people during the darkness of night.

July 22, 2000, Avebury Trusloe, Wiltshire County, wheat crop.

This crop circle is the code sequence for intergalactic frequency and phase shift adjustments. The result is a rejuvenation and recalibration to the original blueprint of the essential life force within the third dimension on Earth. The spheres in this crop circle represent the merging of the alpha and omega (mother/father) energies in the creation of the new paradigm. The recalibration to the original blueprint is complete; the galactic counterpoint process has been activated.

PLATE 51

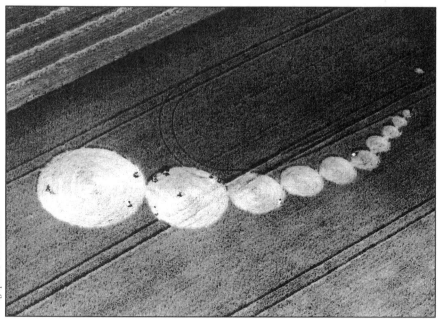

Photographer: © Steve Alexander.

July 19, 2000, West Amesbury, near Stonehenge, Wiltshire County.

his arc of circles appeared on a hillside, with the largest circle at the top providing a view of Stonehenge in the distance. This field was very close to the field that contained the famous "Julia Set" Fibonacci spiral crop circle in 1996. In contrast to that farmer who opened his field to thousands of visitors and made a large amount of money by charging entrance fees, this farmer was very annoyed at having people in his field (he yelled angrily at the authors and their friends) and chose not to take advantage of the opportunity to collect money. Within a few days of their visit, he destroyed the whole formation and left only piles of dirt and straw.

The authors and friends, Valja Roseman, Margaret Moore and Wendy Allen, visited this formation when it was still new and fresh. Each circle was beautifully swirled and registered high energy with dowsing rods and pendulums. The whole formation glistened with aliveness and had a shining look to the laid stalks. It had lovely symmetry and gracefulness.

This crop circle is the announcement of the eleventh solar house of light joining the galactic councils; this is a great event in galactic history. The mystery houses of the eleven/eleven now resonate in a full frequency alignment with the thirteen/thirteen. The twelve temples that were represented by the twelve apostles are complete; the eleventh apostle has joined the thirteenth (Christ consciousness). The formula present in this crop circle is for anchoring the full alignment of the thirteen/thirteen into the third-dimensional Earth plane.

PLATE 52

The 180-foot-diameter crop formation called "The Grid" or "The Mind" appeared July 2, on a hillside that could be seen from the much-visited West Kennett Longbarrow. It contained 1600 elements in the design: standing square boxes and the careful lay of squares. There was a woven effect on the ground and a three-dimensional look when seen from the air. Some cubes seemed to pop up and others seemed to sink into the ground.

This design was so precisely and logically laid down that people tend to relate it to the functioning of the left hemisphere of the brain. The whole pattern was divided into four quarters, with two zones diagonally opposite each other and the squares executed in opposite ways. Each box was carefully executed by the clever laying of the wheat. The dowsable energy was high throughout this formation, even after hundreds of visitors had trampled through it.

"The Heart" crop circle appeared two weeks later in the same field, further up the slope. The surrounding ring of the beautiful heart shape was composed of twenty-eight larger circles with an inner ring of twenty-eight smaller circles and additional circles scattered around the outer edge.

The heart and the circles were nicely laid down, and Barbara Lamb and Dr. Simeon Hein compared responses between her dowsing rods and his electrostatic voltmeter in many of the circles. Both methods consistently showed moderate to high energy responses.

"The Heart" crop circle was the site for the closing ceremony for the WCCSG Conference on July 16, 2000. Dozens of people stood in a ring within the heart shape, singing, chanting and reciting poetry in the late afternoon sunlight.

When seen together in the same field, "The Heart" and "The Mind" designs suggest important functions for people to have within themselves and to use in a balanced way in their lives.

July 2 and 16, 2000, East Kennett, Wiltshire County, wheat crop.

Photographer: © Lucy Pringle.

The frequencies in the formula for this set contain energies that will harmonize and balance human brain-wave energy with the heart chakra to accommodate a more compassionate species of humans. The human species will expand their brain capacity from the current average of ten percent to nearly one hundred percent.

PLATE 53

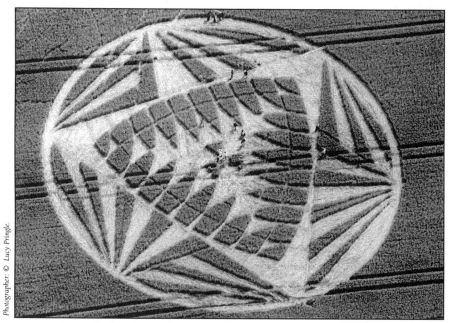

Photographer: © Lucy Pringle.

This crop circle appeared high up on Clifford's Hill, in the same field and in the same general spot where "The Cube" crop circle had occurred in 1999 [plate 15]. It was placed below the Iron Age Rybury Hillfort. As with its predecessor, this striking design could be seen for miles around the area.

Some people feel this is a Hopi Moiré design, similar to some Hopi Indian designs woven into baskets and textiles and depicted in paintings and carvings.

When standing in this brand-new crop circle, Barbara Lamb and friends found it to be nicely wrought, and it measured reasonably strong energy. It was difficult to decipher the overall pattern until they saw an aerial photograph of it later.

August 1, 2000, Allington Down, near Bishops Cannings, Wiltshire County, wheat crop.

Blue Star Kachina has awakened seven orbs of light within the sacred Black Hills of South Dakota and the borders of southern Scotland. The Templars of Rossalyn have been released from the bondage of the death fear and awakened. This long-awaited event has activated and united mystical planetary forces. It is most essential to create beautiful images with this set. The more it is introduced into the collective mind, the better the results for all.

PLATE 54

This exquisitely complex and masterfully executed crop circle sat at the crest of a hill, sloping down on both sides of the hill, which gave it a three-dimensional look from the air. It was positioned very close to the site of the 1997 "Torus" crop circle [plate 1], and it looked like a further elaboration of that design. This was a Moiré pattern, with designs within the design, which gave the appearance of dynamic spinning motion. Some people liken this design to a spirograph drawing, a blossoming flower or an artichoke; yet it is more profound than those.

This design was created by laying down the wheat in slightly curving triangles of varying shapes and sizes, leaving the standing triangles. There were twenty-two rings spinning clockwise and twenty-two rings spinning counterclockwise. It is hard to believe that this intricacy and perfection could have been created by laying down wheat stalks in a field, especially in the darkness of night, no matter who or what did it.

The center circle and the outer ring flowed in a clockwise direction. Two beautifully made raised centers were next to each other, looking like nests.

This design is like an important mandala in ancient Hinduism, and some visitors experienced higher levels of consciousness and a stimulation of their crown chakras.

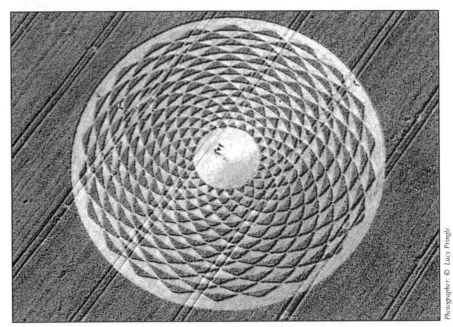

August 13, 2000, Woodborough Hill, Alton Priors, Wiltshire County, wheat crop.

Photographer: © Lucy Pringle.

Within the divine potential of All That Is dwells all that has been and all that will ever be. This is the portal of all divine possibilities, the meeting place of cosmic creation. Allow your eyes to rapidly shift between the images of the crop circle and the star glyph. This will encode your brain's neurocortex to adjust from the rapidly deteriorating old world to the newly resonant third-dimensional hologram.

PLATE 55

This crop circle was placed at Giant's Grave, part of a prehistoric settlement near the top of a hill and just below ancient ramparts. The site was very impressive, yet the crop circle felt very calm and peaceful to visitors.

This was a beautiful design of four overlapping rings swirled in a clockwise direction and lovely curving pathways. The wheat was laid down very precisely and evenly, although the hillside variations made the larger center ring look a bit irregular.

Photographer: © Lucy Pringle.

August 3, 2000, Giant's Grave, near Oare, Wiltshire County, wheat crop.

This is a toning device balancing three fields of resonant sound frequencies that have not yet been available to the audio receptors of humanity. The tonal frequencies introduced enhance the emanation of the universal Om with three octave wave frequencies, completing the aural spectrum resonant within the solar houses of the thirteen/thirteen. The introduction of this sound frequency formula will affect the collective dream and be used as a tool for ascension. The use of this set accompanied with sounds from crystal and Tibetan bowls, harps, didgeridoos and other high-vibration instrumentation will enhance the effect of this phenomenon.

PLATE 56

This crop circle was located in the Pewsey Valley beneath a well-known martinsell hill. This pretty pattern consisted of a twelve-foot-wide center circle with five lovely petal shapes and ten intersecting swirled circles. The whole design gives the appearance of a geometric flower.

Access to this formation was denied by the farmer and therefore details of the construction and the energy could not be determined. It appeared to onlookers to be a lovely gem and the S-shaped swirls in each circle were fantastic.

Photographer: © Lucy Pringle.

August 11, 2000, Clench, Wiltshire, wheat crop.

In the past, religion has been used to perform for covert fear operations. Until recently, the secrets for magic, emanation of the Holy Spirit and spiritual techniques for movement of energies were held by a select few, many of whom used the gifts for control and power. With the emergence of the Eden principle, the ancient mysteries are being revealed to an increasing number of incarnate souls. This crop circle and star glyph are encoded with the key to the doors of the mystery schools that have been barred from the masses until now. The mantra for the reception of these esoteric teachings is *Ma koa, ma koa, ma koa.*

PLATE 57

August 5 and 13, 2000, Broadbury Banks, near Wilsford, Wiltshire County, wheat crop.

The crop circle on the right appeared on August 5 as a ring with a simple line drawing inside. It looked unfinished, and that was the case. It was completed at least ten days later, which was an unusually long gap for a crop circle made in two stages. Then it featured seven blades, or a seven-armed spinner, which left a pattern of seven points of a star in the center.

The night it was completed, the additional circle on the left was formed next to it, though slightly uphill and placed next to the ancient Broadbury Banks settlement. This second design contained some of the features seen in the "Hopi Moiré" at Allington [plate 53]: triangles and lozenge shapes in the center.

In 1994, a "Shoemaker-Levy 9 Comet" crop circle had appeared in the same field, and someone had caught on film an unusual lighted object in that formation.

The crop circle on the left is the device that activates sacred geometry within individuals, soul groups and sacred sites, restructuring the cellular geometries of all mass and matter on this planet. Focus on the top portion of the star glyph, and imagine dormant fractal codes within subatomic cellular structures being activated with this device. The crop circle on the right is the device that interprets the dormant fractal light patterns into sound frequencies and reverberates them into form and matter. Focus on the lower part of the star glyph, and imagine this expansive activation and the positive effects it will have on the inhabitation of this plane.

PLATE 58

In this 200-foot-diameter crop circle, an eight-pointed star near the outside and an eight-pointed star in the center allow eight bell shapes. All of this is contained within two overlapping square shapes, which are contained within a ring. This nicely designed and executed formation retained very strong dowsing energy even five to six weeks after it appeared. Barbara Lamb noticed a strong band of energy a foot or so outside the formation.

In one of the spaces between the bells was a beautiful swirled circle with a pointed standing spire of wheat. When viewed from slightly uphill, the spire exactly replicated the real spire of a church across the A361 road, in the village of Bishops Cannings. This crop circle had a lovely feeling, as reported by many visitors.

Dr. Nan Lu said this crop circle could help relieve any stagnation in the body, relieve all kinds of pain and strengthen Qi energy. If accompanying an energy/movement practice, it could help a person communicate with nature.

The night this crop circle was formed, nearby campers heard strange sounds coming from this field. Very early the next morning, police cars, helicopters and even cranes came to see the new formation.

Photographer: © Lucy Pringle.

June 26, 2000, Bishops Cannings, near Devizes, Wiltshire County, wheat crop.

This set resonates the release codes for freeing individual souls and families long held bound in states of depression and chaos. These codes will cause the interdimensional shift in parallel time zones that will release fear, heal wounded souls, allow for peace and heal the trauma cycles that have repeated generation upon generation throughout the long dark night of the soul.

PLATE 59

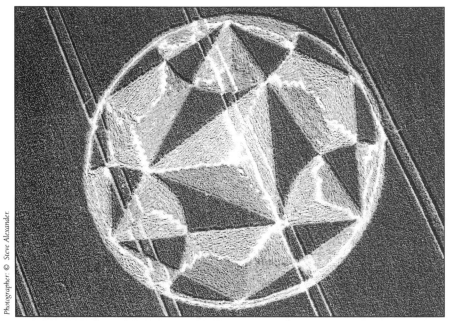

Photographer: © Steve Alexander.

June 18, 2000, Bishops Cannings Down, near Beckhampton, Wiltshire County, wheat crop.

Andy Thomas called this 180-foot-diameter crop circle a "Chinese Puzzle." It has curved triangles with an equilateral triangle inside a larger equilateral triangle, which is inside a hexagon. Because some of the crop is standing and some is laid down, the puzzle effect is created.

The lay of the wheat between these triangle shapes was cleverly arranged to create the look of three-dimensional pyramids. Where one area of laid wheat met another coming from a different angle, a deckle edge was formed.

This design incorporates several different triangle shapes and proportions. If observed in a certain way, this design looks like a three-dimensional sphere with three five-pointed stars wrapped around it.

Jude Stammers, an expert in esoteric wisdom, said that triangles are very significant shapes; they birth the cosmic child in each of us.

Dr. Nan Lu said the energy of this crop circle could relieve the stagnation of blood and Qi energy, help the liver by cleaning out toxins and poisons and help relieve pain and tumors.

Lady of Light, En Na Ki Tan: She who cracks the paradigms and shifts the dimensions, she is awakening. She is the one who unveils the mysteries not yet revealed. She is a laser beam of light frequencies that connects the very essence of all earthen temples to this energy source.

PLATE 60

This crop circle was placed uphill from the formation in plate 58. This relatively simple yet sophisticated design was executed with an extremely clear and precise lay of the wheat. The center circle was very unusual. It was laid down in various ways in various sections, including some woven areas and swirled circles.

This design displays unusual elevenfold geometry, composed of eleven curved arcs or spokes. Each one was impeccably laid down, coming to a finely tapered end at the center circle. From the air, the design looked three-dimensional and somewhat like a torus of moving energy.

When Barbara Lamb asked for the meaning of this crop circle while lying in meditation in the center, the words that were repeatedly sent to her were "solar flares." Perhaps this design was reflecting the increasing and enlarging solar flares that scientists had been studying and warning us about, especially during the year 2000.

According to astrophysicist Jazz Rasool, the Sun's gravitational changes are affecting Earth's magnetic fields. If this background frequency speeds up enough, we humans will all become psychic. Now our frequency is twelve hertz, but what if it becomes twenty hertz?

Photographer: © Lucy Pringle.

July 26, 2000, North Down, near Beckhampton, Wiltshire County, wheat crop.

As the Earth shifts through the interdimensional portals referred to as point zero, the energetic core is accompanied by a super-resonant tonal code of the geodesic radical continuum. This sequence of harmonic patterning is vital to stabilize the third-dimensional holographic dream field, which basically allows reality as you perceive it to be for the most part undisturbed. Use the set to assist in your bodily and planetary adjustments.

PLATE 61

August 25, 2000, West Overton Hill, Wiltshire County, wheat crop.

Photographer: © Lucy Pringle.

This striking formation was made by Matthew Williams and team without permission from the farmer. He was caught, arrested and fined on November 6, 2000, for trespassing and ruining a large section of the wheat crop. Williams said he had made the crop circle to dispute comments made by researcher Michael Glickman about the impossibility of anyone making a crop circle with this particular geometry.

The making of this crop circle took three nights, which was a strong contrast to the very rapid making of genuine crop circles by the anomalous source.

Critics of this design said the center contained several errors and geometric discrepancies, and the design looked rigid and hard. Other people agree that this is a surprisingly stunning and attractive design, considering it was made by humans.

In Atlantis there was an alteration of the microstructure of the brain-cell DNA to retard or minimize the firing codes of the neurosynapses in the brain cells. It is now time to remove the limitations and stimulate the opening to the code frequencies for the creative geneses. The use of this set in meditation will actually connect the frequencies of your brain waves with the surge patterns. Your brain will be used instrumentally to stimulate the microstructure of the brain-cell DNA of your planetary brothers and sisters. The human creation of this circle is part of the alchemical component of the formula being emanated.

PLATE 62

This abstract pattern of five implied overlapping rings appeared on the same night and in the same large field as the crop circle in plate 60. From the perspective of the ground, it had beautifully curved rings and an impeccable lay of the wheat. In the knob shape to the right was a pyramid shape of standing wheat, which held its shape firmly. By the far right-hand ring was a messy area where someone went into the standing crop and tried to make a larger pyramid with large sections of wheat. The result was a mess and the attempt was an abomination.

The energy detected by dowsing rods was strong, especially in the semicircles and where one pathway converged with another.

Photographer: © Lucy Pringle.

July 26, 2000, near Bishops Cannings, on A361, Wiltshire County, wheat crop.

This set represents the full awakening of what is referred to as the Buddha of Compassion. The most profound results will be seen in the treatment of those weaker than one's self. This shift will affect society on every level.

PLATE 63

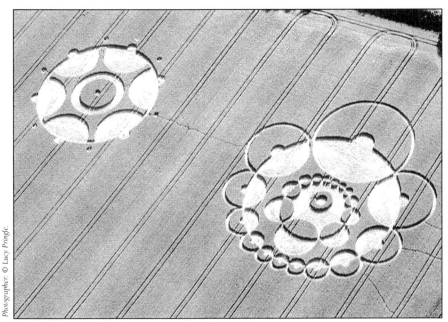

July 14 and 30, 2000, Bishops Sutton, Hampshire County, wheat crop.

The right-hand set of circles is a design of beauty and perfection. The outer set of twelve circles is reflected in the inner set of twelve circles, though in reverse sizing. Some people see UFOs in the laid shapes of the outer circles.

Because the authors and their friends respected the signposted wishes of the farmer to stay out of his field, they did not enter or take energy readings. Instead, Barbara Lamb used her technique of defocusing and seeing auric fields, and saw large vertical columns of golden light descending from the sky to the field, especially into this crop circle.

The left-hand formation appeared two weeks later: a six-pointed pattern with a variation of the UFO shapes. This was a relatively simple design, though beautifully executed.

These crop circles have multiple uses. They are located on a major highway, intended for the passing motorist to pick up their resonated frequencies and emanate their codes wherever they travel. This frequency transforms deteriorating, dysfunctional populace hubs into healthy habitats like the Lemurian cities of light. In ET scientific terms, this crop circle is called a "megalithic equatronic deactivator."

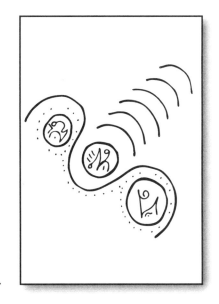

PLATE 64

This flowerlike design, 200 feet in diameter, preceded the one at Bishops Sutton [plate 63] and exhibited some of the same features: twelve circles around the outside and the same half-circular or UFO shapes.

The farmer was extremely hostile when the authors and their friends started to walk into his field. He kept yelling, "There's nothing mystical about this. This was just done by blokes from the local pub!" and, "Get out of my private property!" Thus we retreated and viewed the formation from the roadside. Barbara Lamb used her aura-reading technique on this crop circle. This time she saw square sheets or plates of semitransparent golden-whitish light sliding back and forth horizontally over the crop circle.

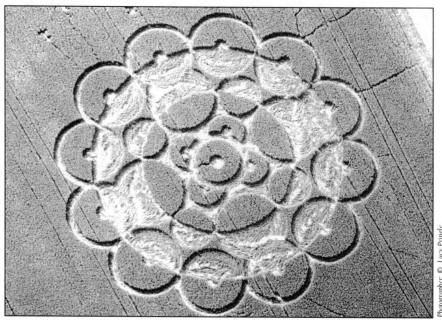

Photographer © Lucy Pringle.

July 1, 2000, Stephen Castle Down, Upham, Hampshire County, oat crop.

This crop circle is the mothership's detection device to map, measure and monitor the effects on the grid patterns of the Earth's energies at this point. It was essential to implant the monitoring device and adjust the frequencies along grid lines prior to introducing the formulas resonant in crop circle 63.

PLATE 65

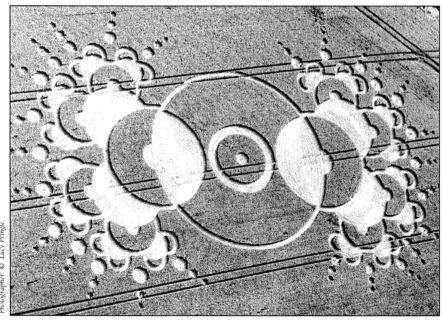

This unusually fancy pattern, 250 feet in diameter, was placed very close to the Chilbolton Radio Telescope. Perhaps it expressed the way radio waves are emitted and sent out. This design could be a fractal, with the circles and rings replicating themselves to infinity.

It had a very neat floor pattern and nice sections of crop flowed from the center circle into the outer circles.

The radio mast was manned during the night this formation was made, and no one heard any sounds or saw any lights.

Photographer: © Lucy Pringle.

August 13, 2000, Chilbolton, near Andover, Hampshire County, wheat crop.

This set is the restoration of cosmic memory. Your DNA is time-coded for release in response to the increased megahertz that are vibrating on your planet. This crop circle is the fractal code for the receptor stimulators that have been vibratorily introduced into the biosphere to stimulate this process. Your pineal gland is being stimulated, allowing the receptors in your brain to communicate in a more advanced manner.

PLATE 66

This "Star of David" pattern and ring has six attached satellite circles. One of the circles has another attached circle with six additional satellite circles.

The circle with the six small satellites had a lovely cone-shaped standing tuft in its center. The entire pattern was accomplished with great care and precision.

July 28, 2000, Telegraph Hill, near Pegsdon, Icknield Way, Bedfordshire, wheat crop.

Within the biochemical structure of the solar resonance emanated by the increased solar flares lies the encoding for the cornea to receive light infusions that serve to stimulate the brain circuitry and repattern its frequencies. Information from the Records of Ra (the records of the Great Central Sun) is being encoded into the solar UV rays, which are interpreted by the retina as light languages and transferred to the neurofibers of the cerebral cortex to be read as the living language of light.

PLATE 67

Photographer: © Lucy Pringle.

July 23, 2000, Uffington, Oxfordshire, wheat crop.

This lustrous crop formation was placed in a flat field below the ancient hillfort and carved white chalk horse of Uffington. Historians say that in ancient times, this white horse was a long white dragon shape, having subsequently been modified by Christians to look more like a horse. This crop circle could be seen to correspond to the dragon shape of long ago. It was seen very clearly from the heights of the hill.

Each circle was beautifully swirled and registered very strong energy with dowsing rods and pendulums. In fact, Barbara Lamb's dowsing rods stayed fully open throughout the entire formation.

The main feature, or the head of the design, was impeccably laid to leave standing triangular shapes, which formed a blossom effect. These triangles are very similar to the ones left standing in the subsequent August 13 Moiré pattern [plate 54] and to a July 30 crop circle in Yorkshire [not shown].

This crop formation seemed to contain healing energy. Barbara Lamb laid down in the center of the largest circle, meditated and asked for help with a serious condition with her leg. After returning home to the United States, her medical tests showed that the condition had cleared up.

This formation was gorgeous and felt wonderful to be in.

Encrypted within the interior ethereal structure of the mountain on which the dragon horse appears, are the inscriptions for the periodic releases of crucial frequencies emanated from all crop circles, appearing at specific sites where the Neolithic emissaries of light implanted the time capsules for release [see plate 48]. Within this geological formation are treasures and ancient inscriptions that link the light net that was implanted in the ethereal by the Neolithic ET brethren. The mantra useful for activation of this frequency code is *Saaaa koaaaa mie (mee) na kaaaa wa.*

APPENDIX A

CHANNELING AT SILBURY HILL,
JULY 13, 2000

Laiolin: *Ke Waat Nie Ka* is the ancient name for Silbury Hill. Within this hill is the pyramid of the seven ancient goddesses, the root of the ancient mysteries of the Mother Goddess energies of this area. Within the ethereal of this temple are seven elongated black crystals suspended in midair. They beam light into an octagon in the center. Each of the crystals represents an entity that incarnated in the women who held Celtic circle ceremonies at this temple throughout history. There is a soul group of seven women who reincarnated to set the matrix for this energy.

The lunar eclipse of July 16, 2000, was an important time in the history of this temple. Seven women have returned to this area for this lunar eclipse. This lunar temple is particularly sensitive to lunar cycles. The ethereal crystals that beam energy into the center crystal are connected to lunar energy. This temple is aligned with the different phases of the Moon and the currents of the Earth. The energies emanated from the octagon crystal to the center of the Earth vary as to the frequencies of the ley and grid lines that cross here. During the excavation here several years ago, crystals were discovered. The powerful Michael and Mary Lines also run through this area.

The crop circles surrounding Silbury Hill were created because of the alignment of the planetary energies that beam through these crystals during the lunar eclipse. The council of nine beings of the houses of light has reincarnated to be present at Silbury Hill during this eclipse. Frequencies are established in the crop circles that appeared around Silbury Hill prior to the lunar eclipse that carry the electromagnetic energy fields, the cellular soul-DNA patterns that are present in the Council of Nine. During the lunar eclipse, there will be a jolt of light frequencies that will enter Silbury Hill. For the maximum effect of the lunar eclipse there must be a geometric link with the frequencies of the Council of Nine, the surrounding crop circles, Silbury Hill, West Kennett Longbarrow and Swallowhead Springs.

The thirty-foot shaft opened up in the spring of 2000 in the top of Silbury Hill to permit the light frequencies to enter the Silbury Temple, activating the crystals and sending the energies into the core of the planet. ✳

JUDY'S EXPERIENCES AT CROP CIRCLE BY STONEHENGE, JULY 19, 2000

As I approached this crop circle [plate 51], I observed a sacred grove of trees and sensed a very powerful energy emanating there. This was the site of an ancient global gathering so large, it would fill the plain. This was the gathering of the ancient planetary houses of light. The tradition was carried throughout history to Druid times. Different priests from the Americas crossed the ocean to be at these gatherings, held when the astrological circumstances could maximize the energies. An astrologist would determine cycles of lunar and solar eclipses and plan the gatherings, when a certain number of eclipses accumulated. Stonehenge was created much earlier than is currently believed. Druids performed ceremonies here thousands of years ago.

Prior to recorded history, circular stone temples stood where this grove of trees now stands. Inside these temples of enlightenment were magnetic energy crystals that were removed by ETs and placed on Venus long ago. This crystal circle linked Earth to the ancient temples on Venus. White Buffalo Calf Pipe Woman and Christ Jesus both told us they came from Venus: "I am of the morning star." Later in history, this circle of trees became the location of the Goddess ceremonies that were carried on in secret while the Druids performed ceremonies in Stonehenge.

I received the transmission that there was a very important event happening in the Mayan prophecies connected to the joining of the eleventh house, described in the transmission of this crop circle. The Day Out of Time is experienced multidimensionally; although we do not necessarily feel it, it will have a lasting effect on this planet and the emergence of heaven on Earth.

While I was drawing the star glyph inside the crop circle, I saw a hawk circling the grove of trees mentioned earlier. Shortly thereafter, I met a newly married couple, and I channeled Laiolin for them. She said they were the alchemical aspects of the gift of divine union in loving, empowering relationships. Their energies and sacred geometries anchored into the matrix that was completed when the eleventh house entered the Council of Thirteen. They represented the Moon and the Sun as they appear together in the sky in the daytime. The Moon reflects the Sun, but they feed each other energy in a symbiotic relationship. These two individuals were components to the alchemical formula of this crop circle, anchoring the energies of the alpha and the omega.

> Stonehenge was created much earlier than is currently believed. Druids performed ceremonies here thousands of years ago.

CHANNELING EXPERIENCE NEAR CROP CIRCLE AT WINDMILL HILL, JULY 21, 2000

The following is a spontaneous transmission that occurred inside the grove of trees on Windmill Hill in Avebury Trusloe, just prior to entering crop circle 48. I was walking along, praying and honoring the ancestors of this sacred grove of trees, when without warn-

ing, the transmission came forth. The voice was very different from Laiolin, deep and booming. It was actually strenuous to my voice box. Luckily, I had a tape recorder, and this transmission was transcribed from the original tape.

The Seven Sisters: We of the south gate awaken to unlock the north door. We are the Seven Sisters, the keys to the east/west passage. *Wiex ka ma sha, wiex ka ma sha ha. Wa sha ka ma, wa shaw ka ma.*

This is the portal of transcendence to open the north door. We chose this messenger, and she received the message that we are waiting. We have called her here, and we are awakening. This is an ancient myth that goes beyond civilization as you know it, the ancient song of what became what they call the swallowhead—this anointed blessing waiting in timeless dimension, where all time and space cease as you enter the time capsules.

We are prepared to enter the third dimension to assist in the ancient fulfillment of the *Roeshan Na*, the lost prophecies of the Seven Sisters. We came here from the Pleiadian star system and the dog star you call Dogon. We were in a colony in what is referred to as Neolithic times. We came in lightships from beyond Pleiades, from beyond Dogon, from a galaxy unknown to Earth references. We are the creators of the light force that runs through the veins of this mother planet. We are *Wa Shaw Ka Ma.*

In the choice of our earthen bodies, we chose the long bone structure because it afforded us superior strength and agility and expansion of the DNA that has not been revealed in scientific tests. In the timeless thousands of years, we prepared the matrix for the birth you see before you, that of the crop circles. We are the circlemakers; we are the point where past, present and future meet interdimensionally. We are the light orbs that you see. We are neither Neolithic, nor are we from the future. We are neither ETs nor supradimensional, for our transcendence goes beyond time and space. In your Earth years, we have long waited to bring these frequencies and emanate the return of ascended civilization to this beloved green globe. We are in assistance with other ET technologies and councils of light. We are *Wa Shaw Ka Ma.* We have waited for this alignment, for the giant to awaken, for the Mother Gaia to birth.

APPENDIX B

ESSENTIAL CHANNELED INFORMATION

The channeled information in this section is not directly related to the crop circles. The teachings and information, however, are essential to the overall concept of the awakening of heaven on Earth and the fulfillment of the prophecies that are directly related to the reason the crop circles are appearing.

LAIOLIN SPEAKS OF THE HOUSE OF DAVID

Laiolin: Greetings, beloved ones. I am most delighted to be present with you for this great event in Earth's history. It is important for you to understand that I am not an entity that is channeled or separate from Judith. I am her thirteenth-dimensional higher self. I was able to connect to her in the third-dimensional hologram in April 1992. It was necessary for her to develop skills in conscious-merge channeling to facilitate communications; she is an oracle. I am multidimensional. I am manifest as an ambassador of the Council of Abborah and sit council within the Galactic Federation. I am assisted in all efforts by the Council of Abborah's Arcturian starship. My primary mission is to awaken the House of David or the Cosmic Christ presence.

Awaken now, my sweet ones. We have waited for so long, yet in cosmicdimensional time, only moments. You are each members of the living body of the Cosmic Creator. The long sleep has past; the fear grid that held beloved Mother Earth in amnesia is no more. Critical mass has been reached with the activation of enough awakened star beings who have shed the dark cloaks of fear to reveal their lightbodies. There is much information on DNA and the mutation of your species available. It is now essential that you become aware of the soul DNA, the divine plan you assisted in creating in the dolphin cities in the womb of the Cosmic Mother. Each incarnation was carefully planned to accumulate the experiences necessary for the completion of your soul mission. When you incarnated into your genetic family, you chose a DNA pattern that matched your soul DNA. When the two merged in one living being, the alchemical manifestation of your divine plan was initiated. This is your cosmic blueprint.

The wisdom of the ages has sprung from the long dark night of the soul to be embraced by you now, my sweet ones. Our father sent his son to you to teach and awaken you. His teachings are the jewels of consciousness. Christ Jesus taught that if you have the faith of a mustard seed, you can move mountains. He also told you what he has done; you will do only greater. He told you that he was the offspring of David, and the bright morning star [Revelation 22:16]. He spoke of his return. The second coming of Christ is within the hearts of humanity. Embrace his teachings. He taught you to forgive. Forgiveness is freedom; forgiveness is grace; forgiveness is release from bondage.

Yes, you have been hurt. Each of you was a victim of the great fear. Yes, you have suffered. Look not to the source of suffering amongst your fellow humans. Know that you have taken alternate incarnations as victims and victimizers. In the old paradigm, the good guys sought out evil and attempted to destroy it. The new paradigm is to seek the depth of our own shadow and unconditionally love it into healing.

Our father sent his daughter, White Buffalo Calf Pipe Woman. She came as your teacher and healer. She promised to return. As she appeared on the mound, the two young men approached her. One lusted for her and sought to take her power. This sacred trinity is within each of you. You are White Buffalo Calf Pipe Woman. You are the sacred twins who agreed to enter separation. By loving your dark twin, he is freed to return to oneness. He has received a state of divine grace; his transgressions have been forgiven. You are the messenger who returns to the people bringing the good news of her arrival. You are the keepers of the ancient traditions. Knowing this will help you in your journey.

The rule of the great fear has past. The work now is to heal, forgive and move into a new state of grace and joy. The time of spiritual renaissance is at hand. You have a great buffet of traditions and spiritual teachings available. The collective soul hungers for these gifts. Do not struggle in an attempt to find the exclusive truth, for truth is evident in all of these precious gifts and teachings. Each is like a color band in a beautiful rainbow. You are to stand in your own truth next to your brothers and sisters in unconditional love, forming the rainbow family.

The shadows must feel safe and loved to emerge, be it those within yourselves or your neighbors. Do not fear the shadows as they come forth. It is a necessary part of the healing. When you hear of acts of terrorism upon your fellows, send forth great beams of healing and loving light from your heart chakra. Your angels are with you. The energies are available as never before. Scientists have measured the megahertz of fear and love. Love has a higher vibration frequency; fear is lower and denser. Love is an intense electromagnetic force that is infinitely powerful. Your neurosynapses have been expanded to handle more electromagnetic energy than was previously available to your species. You are funded with the alchemical forces to transmute all shadow.

Faith is your passport to the new world of peace. In the coming times, your faith will continue to be tested. You will be asked to take the leap of faith. Your lower mind, or logical mind, might scream out in disbelief, but the miracles will continue to manifest. Imagine that you are like seeds beneath fertile loam. Imagine yourselves as the size of that seed and the amount of loam comparably. It appears as tons of soil—a great weight, indeed. Your awakening is the alchemical bursting forth of that sprout. You seek your course of destiny, penetrating the darkness and expanding into a new world of light. The loam is not a barrier to your inevitable expansion. It will yield and fund all that you need to complete your journey. So, too, the shadow will yield, offering you inevitable nourishment and making way for a new world of peace and prosperity.

Through lifetime after lifetime, you have been conditioned to feel unworthy. You have not been taught the difference between ego and confidence. Some of the programming phrases are: "I'm not good enough," or, "I don't deserve good things." Your best is good enough. Opportunities are presenting themselves to help you heal from all of the mental traps that block your inevitable empowerment. You are a being of infinite potential; your mission awaits you. One mission is not greater than another. Each of you will contribute your valuable piece to this cosmic mandala. Some are more conscious of their missions than others. Conscious or not, your destiny is to complete your piece, your divine gift. Many of you still walk in both worlds. You have been released from the service of the dark one. You may not have integrated this truth; do so now. If this is the case, take heart. You are not expected to be perfect in every way. Perfection is in the continued intent to seek integrity, respect, truth, empowerment and freedom.

Your contribution is unique; it is valuable; it is the cosmic you. You are the only one who can fulfill your mission. If you stumble, someone will be there to assist you, to help to share your burden. Your best is good enough. You cannot fail if you have faith. You are not alone. The time of isolation has passed. Reach out in love to one another. Join hands in forming the living bridge to heaven on Earth.

You are the only one who can fulfill your mission. If you stumble, someone will be there to assist you, to help to share your burden. Your best is good enough.

THE HOUSE OF DAVID HISTORY REVEALED

The amnesia barrier is dissolving rapidly. There is much important information that has not been revealed to the collective until the time is right. It is a paradox that time as it is known in the third dimension is an illusion in galactic consciousness, yet here in the third dimension, timing is everything. The history of the House of David was removed from Earth records when the fear grid was placed on your planet.

The lineage of the House of David has been preserved in the collective through the biblical expression of King David and the lineage of Christ Jesus. It is not limited to the humans of Jewish ancestry, but is rather a lineage that has starseeded all of Mother Earth's inhabitants.

The memories of the House of David are in your bones, perfectly encoded in your genetic and soul DNA. There is little known about the true capacity of DNA. There is not in existence a computer on this planet that is in any way comparable to your DNA. Soon the ones who call themselves scientists will begin to expand their multidimensional realities and begin to discover the vast secrets locked in this precious coil of life.

The DNA is a crystalline geometry, alchemically time-coded to activate with certain cosmic phenomena. Some are known as the Harmonic Convergence and the Grand Cross. Basically, your DNA is a time capsule set to release a preprogrammed sequence encoded in the beginning of creation. All was planned in perfection by your cosmic consciousness.

The soul DNA is your multidimensional cosmic planner, so to speak. Your lightbody is engirded in your human form, or vegetable body. This soul DNA has thirteen dimensional aspects. The thirteenth-dimensional aspect is encoded in the Records of Ra, or the Hall of Records of the Great Central Sun. Until now, humans had limited access, expanding only into the fifth-dimensional aspect of the DNA. This activation was present in those beings you know as the enlightened ones. Such beings as your beloved Gandhi were cosmically evolved to access the fifth-dimensional DNA.

It is important to recall that in Atlantis, mutations were placed in your species that limited evolution and expansion of consciousness. So entered the long dark night of the human soul and the ultimate test of the human heart. It is by adversity that the true nature and character of essential elementals such as the Heart Grail emerge. Many of you are aware of this fact. Gaia or Mother Earth is a DNA time capsule prepared to activate according to the cosmic plan. This activation is the Eden principle, or heaven on Earth. All is in perfect order.

Consider the concept of the living body, the great I Am, referred to by many as God, the all-seeing, all-knowing oneness of creation. Each of you is a cell of the living body. Each of you carries the divine plan in your DNA. The illusion of separation was a vital part of the divine plan. There is no separation; all is One.

Meditate on the image of a great river. Now, imagine that it comes to an island and splits. Is it still one river? Most assuredly it is, as all sprang from a common source. Such is the paradigm of the history of your beloved blue-green Mother planet.

All that I speak of is known in your cosmic memory. My mission is to assist you in remembrance. The House of David is the house of Our Lord. The Great Central Sun is the great Father; the black hole is the great Cosmic Mother. It is by union of these two vast forces that all was created. Allow yourself to remember the womb of the Cosmic Mother, known in the Records of Ra as the dolphin cities. You may wish to take a few moments and allow yourself to return to the dolphin cities and feel unconditional love and the peace of this root, the origin of all creation. All of this cosmic script was created in the womb of the Cosmic Mother in the beginning—or was it the end—of creation.

The House of David is comprised of the twelve solar temples that circumvent the Central Sun. I am an ambassador of the thirteenth temple, which is the crystalline center of the Central Sun. In the time before recorded history, we of the House of David colonized Earth. It was necessary for us to assume human form to function in the third dimension. In our world, we are pure light. We mated with existing Earth beings to merge the cosmic DNA with the existing species.

We established thirteen temple regions. These can be mapped out by placing a double hexahedron within the globe. The thirteenth region is the crystal core of your planet. Mother Earth is a living body. As the geography of this planet has shifted, so have the temple regions. These regions comprise the core of Earth's sites of scared geometry.

The DNA of the members of the House of David is linked to the ancient temple regions that they occupied during the existence of the ethereal temples of the House of David. The primal group is composed of the 144,000 christed beings who have accepted the mission to activate Eden and awaken six billion Christ beings. Do not get stuck in the limiting aspect of the number 144,000: this is an alchemical equation that identifies the primal group. This primal group contains vital DNA pulsar codes that are linked to the ori-gins of the temples of the House of David. If you sense that you are one of the primal group, you are. You know deep within your soul who you are.

During the golden age of the House of David, we lived in ascended temple cities in these regions. Many of you have had dreams or remembrances of this glorious and loving existence. We dwelt in cosmic love, peace, empowerment and trust. The word "freedom" did not exist, because the opposite of this word was not a reality. There are many references to this enlightened period in the mythologies of various cultural and religious traditions; the word I will use is *Eden*. These mythologies have been helpful in keeping the matrix active in the collective consciousness.

In the golden age, there was no separation between the secular and the sacred. Each member was the keeper of sacred teachings, healings, sciences, mathematics, temple entities, objects (such as crystals, geometric activators and sacred urns) and power aspects of their temple. Attempts have been made to re-create replicas of these magnificent ancient temples, such as the Taj Mahal and the great Egyptian pyramids. The walls of these temples illuminated light; murals were ornate with all manner of precious and semiprecious stones. The plazas were filled with gardens, flowers and fountains. At times, celestial music filled the air; at others, it was the sweetness of silence.

We were the manifestors of cosmic balance and cocreation, as we still are. During the reign of the House of David, there existed free-moving intergalactic travel and exchange. The Council of Abborah had representatives from each temple region and the corresponding galactic and universal bodies.

Each part of this precious planet corresponds to locations in other universes and galaxies. This is an important concept, for as she suffers so too do her corresponding universal counterparts. Likewise, as she heals and returns to peace and balance, so too do her corresponding galactic counterparts. It is no wonder that this precious planet has attracted so much universal attention.

We completed our mission. All matrices were prepared for the next evolutionary phase. We knew that by divine agreement, Gaia would enter the separation or the duality. The sacred twins would rule over the collective consciousness of all beings on Mother

Earth. The effects of evil on the planet were inevitable. The word *evil* is a reflection of the word *live*; the reflection of life-force—or prana—emanation is evil. The impending invasion of the fearmongers was an inevitable progression of evolution. The initial fear grid was placed on Mother Earth, and all ascended masters who incarnated had to agree to amnesia by rule of the great Galactic Council of Andonia, the united force of cosmic fear. The Council's plan for Earth was to create an iron planet devoid of love and ruled in terror. These beings feed off the energy created by fear. Earth was to be a fear mine, as that was the only energy their limited consciousness could utilize.

The Heart Grail is ultimately the most awesome force in the universe. It is the mysterious force that legend speaks of within the Ark of the Covenant. The matrix of this powerful force of love is the essence of the DNA we have spoken of. Of course, we knew that the total destruction of this powerful force would never be possible—the hologram had to be enacted.

We prepared for the end of the golden age of the House of David. Each of us ingested sacred healings, teachings, knowledge, entities and objects into our DNA to preserve the great wisdom for all times. When the invasion came, Gaia was nuked with the magnitude of ten thousand neutron bombs. The Earth was literally nuked and became molten. Many of us retreated into the crystal cities in the core of the planet. Others became DNA and entered the magma, carrying with us the Records of Ra.

The Records of Ra were manifested in Earth's mystical history in the Egyptian chronicles. They are encoded with all knowledge, past, present and future. The Records of Ra are a living body of the matrices of the House of David. During these long years of the dark ages of enlightenment, this gem of cosmic consciousness waited for the divine moment when all of this powerful and important information and energy will be fully manifested in the third dimension. This is the awakening of the House of David. The activation of the pulsar code is alchemically manifest in your DNA, your sacred geometry. The awakening of the House of David is the activation of the Gaia time capsule.

Lifetime after lifetime, the members of the House of David incarnated into genetic lineages that became victims of genocide. Each enlightened being who incarnated had to agree to the contract of total amnesia as to the divine plan. This phenomenon accounts for leaders who were controlled by the cosmic fear grid creating declarations to kill all first born or destroy whole family lines—such as in Egypt in the time of Moses, in Bethlehem at the time of the birth of Christ Jesus, in Germany during WWII and in the United States in the declaration of genocide against the Native Americans. It was the purpose of the Spanish Inquisition, the Crusades, the rule of the Roman Empire, Genghis Khan, Mao Tse-tung and Great Britain's invasion of the Celtic peoples. The attempt on the part of the fearmongers was to stamp out the vine, or the divine lineage of the House of David.

In incarnation after incarnation, the human Heart Grail was tested and strengthened. The stories of your lifetimes of heroism and acts of heroic love are endless. The vine spread and strengthened far beyond the primal group.

Two thousand years ago, Christ Jesus incarnated to activate the initial pulsar code of the House of David through his divine emanation and union with his beloved Mary Magdalene. Their descendants carried a powerful alchemical formula for the activation of the House of David. Their apparitions were projected through the divine hologram in many locations on your beloved planet. Christ's crucifixion and resurrection were reenacted in the crucifixion of the divine feminine for the following two thousand years. Mother Earth was crucified and assaulted in every way imaginable.

The Heart Grail persevered. Your soul memories carry the scars and wounds of the soul journey from fear to freedom. The most beloved lightbeings incarnated and found themselves in the roles of victims and victimizers. Karma and dense fear blockages accumulated in the soul matrix of the collective consciousness. The cycles repeated themselves over and over again. Fear programming was enacted to attempt to condition the collective consciousness into total subjection. The message was, "Why try to resist? Last time I did this, I was burned at the stake." Yet with each incarnation, you rose once more to the challenge of freedom, unconditional love and your divine mission.

All of your prophecies foretell the end times—the end of the reign of the lords of fear and the time of the great awakening of the House of David. History no longer needs to be repeated. Universal consciousness is funding energy as never before to cleanse and heal the scars and wounds of past fears, deactivate fear implants and emerge as fully awakened beings of love and light, totally attuned to the divine plan of the emergence of Eden. ✳

TOLKTAN SPEAKS: WISDOM OF THE GALACTIC MAYA

Tolktan, a mystical Mayan entity and guide, was the original messenger who brought myself and Barbara Lamb together. This transmission was done for Taskara for an original book that we began, titled Rio de la Vida, *about our mission in Mexico. I have been asked to delay the completion of* Rio de la Vida *until a later date due to the importance of this book. I reproduce the following with Taskara's permission. I have been guided not to attempt to interpret this information or to alter it in any way. It is not for all readers, but will be important to a select group of readers who have cosmic links with the Galactic Maya. Those of you to whom it applies will know who you are when you read the transmission.*

Tolktan: We have come from the Central Sun. We are Galactic Maya; we are the house made of dawn. We are the living aspect of the geometric matrices that have incarnated in the repeated cycles of fifty-two-thousand-year phases. We are forty-four Jaguars.

I am Tolktan, the thirteenth sun of the Great Central Sun. We have completed the formulas that were encoded in the Temples of Ra. I walk between the worlds; I am the time lord. I exist simultaneously in thirteen parallel dimensions. I have incarnated fifty-two times in Mesoamerica to ready the energies to prepare the priesthood of Iguani Kakal Koo. I am the seventh aspect of Quetzalcóatl.

In each of these fifty-two incarnations, through my multidimensional Vegan council, I have implanted time-coded, multiphased activators at specific pulsar points in the spine of the Great Turtle in what has

been referred to as Rio de la Vida. I came incarnated as the great peace. In each of the fifty-two incarnations, I entered as a priest of a key historical temple. These include sites in Palenque, Chichén Itzá, Teotihuacán, Monte Albán, Mitla, Tula, Chicxulub, Cobá, Uxmal, Chaco Canyon, Pecos, Tsankawi, Chimney Rock, Canyon de Chelly and the Cave of the Old Man—the named and the unnamed. Here, I met my sacred counterparts in starships that came to teach the inhabitants of your planet Pulsar Code Thirteen.

Great Mayan time lines are wheels that intermesh, moving harmoniously in parallel dimensional realities, parallel universes and time phasar banks like two giant gears meshed together in thirteen dimensions. I have not entered into the illusion of separation or incarnated to learn lessons. I come to complete my mission and will leave when it is finished. I have chosen fifty-two Jaguar priests to complete the matrix, which is the formula of thirteen pulsar codes. Within the lives of each of these priests, they have implanted the temples, the sacred sites and the ceremonial grounds with Pulsar Code Thirteen to prepare for the arrival of the thirteen suns. I am the Cobra. I am the night sky. I am the Condor.

Kinich Ahau and Ix Chel (Sun and Moon) dance in divine union between the worlds. The preparations throughout these cycles have laid the grid work for the opening of multidimensional portals, allowing the entrance of Kinich Ahau's counterparts, the twelve suns. As each sun enters, Kinich Ahau's power manifests through a physical body. Each sun brings forth one of the thirteen pulsar codes. When the full matrix is completed, the thirteen pulsar codes will unite with Ix Chel to enter the core of Mother Earth, imploding the time capsule of Eden. Each portal, each gateway along the course of Rio de la Vida, must be properly maintained, opened, activated, cleansed, rejuvenated and brought to full force.

Fifty-two Jaguar priests prepared their medicine ways and left their gifts in each of these locations extending to Lake Titicaca, the great lake of origins. Those who are of the Fifty-two Jaguar priesthood (male or female) will recognize this ancient mantra and respond to the ancient call within your soul. The mantra is: *forty-four jaguars, twenty-eight monkeys, thirteen condors, nine butterflies, seven iguanas, six black snakes, three crystalline serpents and one white snake.* This mantra will fall into the hands of those who know and understand. You will feel it pulse in your veins like fire. You will remember who I am and you will know in your soul what is to be done. My words will reach out to you, the ones who are contracted in your soul code, each of you: the time lords, the time travelers, the wind-walkers, the shape-shifters, the dark-night singers, Toltecs, Zapotecs, Olmecs and the Maya. It does not matter what flesh you have chosen in this cycle; within your soul code, you know who you are. As your feet stomp upon the hard soil, thunder beings dance in the mountains. You are Pulsar Code Thirteen.

The eleventh-dimensional portal has been activated. An incarnation is being prepared, and a flight of astral angelic entities from beyond the thirteenth dimension is preparing to descend into your realm. The clan mothers' wombs are waiting to carry this soul group. They are the return of the twenty-eight butterfly clans. They will be born throughout the entire planet. They will incarnate as fully conscious, fully aware, awakened celestial prophets. They will be of age by the activation of Pulsar Code Thirteen, scheduled for 2013. These torchbearers are the 144 children who will carry the geometric capacity to fully utilize the matrix energy of Pulsar Thirteen following the activation of the entrance of the final full incarnation of the thirteen suns. The clan mothers have prepared for their coming. The wisdom keepers await their arrival.

With the coming of this great galactic event, the tombs shall be opened in layers beneath the pyramids that have never been known to exist. The priests who are entombed there will release the mysteries. You of the Fifty-two Jaguar priesthood will feel them as they surge through your blood and awaken you to bring forth the final gift. The seventh seal has been opened. The signs are within the heavens; the white eagle returns to his nest. ✸

✝   ✝   ✝

> With the coming of this great galactic event, the tombs shall be opened in layers beneath the pyramids that have never been known to exist.

A MESSAGE FROM WHITE BUFFALO CALF PIPE WOMAN

Judy: The star beings have requested that this very sacred teaching be included in this book. I do so with great respect. Harry Flying Horse, a beloved Lakota elder, my grandfather, adopted my family in a ceremony called a "taking of relatives" ceremony, when I was ten years old. I am not a Native American in this lifetime, nor do I pretend to be a Lakota wise woman. I respect the old ways and traditions and would never dishonor the people I love so dearly.

As a child, I always loved going to the Rosebud and attending powwows. My mother educated me at a young age about the genocide of the native people. I am a coal miner's daughter and my family fought for human rights through the labor unions, so the plight of the people is dear to me. My childhood heroes were Chief Joseph, Crazy Horse, Sitting Bull, Deganawida and other great leaders and teachers of my Native American brothers and sisters.

I recall a visit to the Rosebud when I was ten years old. Ollie, my mother's friend, told us that there was a court hearing of a respected elder. The courtroom was packed, and I could barely see and hear what was going on. The man was on trial for having a sacred Calf Pipe. The judge told him that he would be sent to sixty days hard labor for having in his possession this most sacred instrument of his religion. The judge told him that if he would say he did not have the pipe, the charges would be dropped. He commented, "I like you, and I do not want to do this, but it is the law." The elder stood tall and proud and said that he had the pipe and was sentenced to sixty days hard labor.

Many people were persecuted in this way. They were the brave souls who have preserved these sacred traditions that the people may live. As a young person, the book *Black Elk Speaks* was sacred to me. The words, "To mend the Hoop," filled my blood with fire. I know that indigenous people all over the world have suffered, but the gifts have not been lost. We now approach the threshold, and the prophecies are being fulfilled. I first heard the sacred teaching of the story of White Buffalo Calf Pipe Woman as a child; I have since heard many versions. With deep respect, I now offer this gift. Mitakyue Oyasin (all my relations).

Once the people lived on the Great Lakes. As the conquest moved west, the Ojibwa pushed them onto the plains. They were hungry and lost. It was a very difficult time for the people. Two scouts were sent out to look for buffalo. As they came across the plains, they saw a woman on a mound. She was dressed in a beautiful white dress. She was the most beautiful woman they had ever seen.

One of the young men began to lust for her. He wanted to take her without her permission. The other young man had a pure heart and respected her. The one who would take her power stepped forward. As he did, a cloud of mist surrounded him. As it lifted, all that was left were bones crawling with worms and snakes. She spoke to the other young man and told him that he was the messenger. He was to return to the village and prepare for her coming. A great lodge was to be erected with a place in the west facing east for her to sit. She would bring them the seven rites of the Oglala Sioux.

As the people prepared for her coming, they cleaned the village and bathed in the river. My mother told me that this was when they saw their reflection and knew they were beautiful. By the time she came, they were feeling good about being the people again.

White Buffalo Calf Pipe Woman said that she came from the morning star, just as Jesus the Christ said. She stayed and taught and prayed with the council. When it was time for her to leave, they did not want her to go. She promised she would return. She told them that as she left the village, she would turn into a white buffalo calf. She would roll over four times and turn the colors of the four directions. Then they were to kill her and take the calf bone to make the sacred White Buffalo Calf Pipe and use the hide for the bundle. That pipe is still at Green Grass, and Arvol Looking Horse is the nineteenth-generation carrier of the sacred Calf Pipe.

✝   ✝   ✝

White Buffalo Calf Pipe Woman has asked me to give to the people. She said to look within our hearts and see the trinity of herself and the sacred twins. She loved the twin who would take her power with unconditional love and healed him. His soul was set free to join his twin. The worms are the fertilizers of the new world of peace, and the snakes transmute the poison of our dying world. She unconditionally loved the messenger and sent him back to the people.

We are the trinity. Seek within yourselves to love your own shadow unconditionally and bring it to healing through forgiveness, that your soul may be set free to join with our sacred twin. We are the messengers and we are the prophets. Seek balance in all things and celebrate joy. She wants you to know that each color of the Rainbow Nation is sacred and must shine in pure light with our brothers and sisters in unity with diversity. *En takwia waplishna* [channeled phrase, not authentic Lakota]. Mitakyue Oyasin.

APPENDIX C

The evening is cool. It is May 25, 2000, and I am trying to get the last ends together before mailing the first draft of the manuscript to the publisher. I go into my room to get the spelling of Hildegard of Bingen, as her name appears in the text. I open the book to the following wonderful reading. All at once, I am pulling books off my bookshelf and piling them in the computer room.

As I open the first book, a powerful wind begins to blow from a clear sky. The trees sway as the force of the Cosmic Ik (the divine wind) sweeps across the land. The storm is so strong that my four-year-old granddaughter becomes frightened, and I have to call her mom to comfort her. Then the storm quiets, and all is silent.

For the next several hours, I randomly open each treasure and compile the following quotes. When I cannot find my copy of the *Words of Wisdom: Quotes By His Holiness the Dalai Lama*, Spirit says, "There are many others not listed here; maybe your readers will enjoy adding their own."

I feel that the words spoken in this appendix speak to the heart of what *Crop Circles Revealed* is really about. These masters brought the seeds of truth before we were ready for the quantum leap in evolution that is at hand. When you apply these words to the information in the transmissions, a wonderful wisdom will be achieved.

The likeness of the soul to a tree: The soul is in the body as the sap is in the tree; and the powers of the soul are like the figure of the tree. How is this so? Understanding in the soul is like the green vigour of the branches and the leaves of the tree. Will is like the flowers on the tree; mind like the first fruit bursting forth. But reason is like the fruit in the fullness of maturity; while sense is like the height and spread of the tree. And in the same way, the human body is strengthened and supported by the soul.

—Hildegard of Bingen
Hildegard of Bingen: Mystical Writings
(Fiona Bowie and Oliver Davies, eds.)

El respeto al derecho ajeno es la paz. [*The respect of the rights of others is the peace.*]

—Benito Juarez

But where was this Self, this innermost? It was not flesh and bone, it was not thought or consciousness. . . . "Your soul is the whole world."

—Hermann Hesse
Siddhartha

The Universe
The Planet.
And
Somewhere
In all of this—
The earth—
And
Man!

—Tony Shearer
Lord of the Dawn

One meaning of care is love. Be gentle and loving with yourself if you find what is written causing you pain. And please be gentle and loving with those neighbors you may come to understand as evil. Be careful—full of care.

—M. Scott Peck, M.D.
People of the Lie

He does indeed look forward to the day when the blind forces of history will be subject to conscious, human control. . . . "The control and conscious mastery of these powers, which, born of the action of men on one another, have till now overawed and governed men as powers completely alien to them."

—Karl Marx and Friedrich Engels
The Communist Manifesto

Learn to drop everything
And come to Me for restoration and unification.
Every moment spent together in My presence
Welds you together . . .

—Foundations of Findhorn
Weavers of Wisdom
(Anne Bancroft)

My wife feels so much about the sufferings of the people that, though she is as old as I am and much less able than myself to brave such hardships as may be attendant upon jail life, she feels she must go to Rajkot. And before this is in print she might have gone.

—Mahatma Gandhi
The Forgotten Woman
(Arun Gandhi, et al)

XXXI
Up from Earth's Centre through the Seventh Gate
I rose, and on the Throne of Saturn sate,
    And many a Knot unravel'd by the Road;
But not the Master-knot of Human Fate.

XXXII
There was the Door to which I found no Key;
There was the Veil through which I might not see:
    Some little talk awhile of ME and THEE.
There was—and then no more of THEE and ME.

XXXIII
Earth could not answer; nor the Seas that mourn
In flowing Purple, of their Lord forlorn;
    Nor rolling Heaven, with all his Signs reveal'd
And hidden by the sleeve of Night and Morn.

XXXIV
Then of the THEE IN ME who works behind
The Veil, I lifted up my hands to find
    A lamp amid the Darkness; and I heard,
As from Without—"THE ME WITHIN THEE blind!"

—Omar Khayyám
Rubáiyát of Omar Khayyám
(Edward Fitzgerald, trans.)

Aware of the suffering caused by the destruction of life, I vow to cultivate compassion and learn ways to protect the lives of people, animals, plants, and minerals. I am determined not to kill, not to let others kill, and not to condone any act of killing in the world, in my thinking, and in my way of life.

—Thich Nhat Hanh
For a Future To Be Possible

I think that we may safely trust a good deal more than we do. We may waive just so much care of ourselves as we honestly bestow elsewhere.

—Henry David Thoreau
Walden

O Great Spirit, this is my prayer! Grant that fear may never enter into my heart to be the guide of my feet.... Great Spirit, Our Father, help us and teach us in the way of the truth; and keep me and my family and my tribe on our true Father's path, so that we may be in good condition in our minds and in our bodies. Teach all of the little ones Your way. Make peace on all the world. We thank You for the sun and the good summer weather again; and we hope they will bring good crops of grass for the animals and things to eat for all peoples.

—Ernest Thompson Seton
The Gospel of the Redman

Every part of this earth is sacred to my people.
Every shining pine needle,
every tender shore,
every vapor in the dark woods,
every clearing, and
every humming insect
are holy
in the memory and experience of my people.

—Ted Perry
Inspired by Chief Seattle
How Can One Sell the Air?
(Eli Gifford and R. Michael Cook, eds.)

"Do you see this woman? I came into your home, and you gave me no water for my feet, but she has washed my feet with her tears and dried them with her hair. You did not welcome me with a kiss, but she has not stopped kissing my feet since I came. You provid-

ed no olive oil for my head, but she has covered my feet with perfume."

—Luke 7:44-47

When you love you should not say, "God is in my heart," but rather, "I am in the heart of God." And think not you can direct the course of love, for love, if it finds you worthy, directs your course.

—Kahlil Gibran
The Prophet

Saving these woods from the axe and the saw, from the money changers and the water changers is in many ways the most notable service to God and man I have heard of since my forest wanderings began.

—John Muir
The Life and Adventures of John Muir
(James Mitchell Clarke)

Any man who knows not the value of the world around him. From a single blade of grass to the largest mountain, from the smallest insect to the largest mammal. He is alone and can never be as one with the God he praises and preaches about.

—Amando Trujillo

Be impeccable with your word.... Speak with integrity. Say only what you mean. Avoid using the word to speak against yourself or to gossip about others. Use the power of your word in the direction of truth and love.... Don't take anything personally.... Nothing others do is because of you. What others say and do is a projection of their own reality, their own dream. When you are immune to the opinions and actions of others, you won't be the victim of needless suffering.... Don't make assumptions.... Find the courage to ask questions and to express what you really want. Communicate with others as clearly as you can to avoid misunderstandings, sadness and drama. With just this one agreement, you can completely transform your life.... Always do your best. ... Your best is going to change from moment to moment; it will be different when you are healthy as opposed to sick. Under any circumstance, simply do your best and you will avoid self-judgment, self-abuse and regret.

—Don Miguel Ruiz
The Four Agreements

Remember how sacred the pipe is
And treat it in a sacred manner,
For it will be with you always.
Remember also that in me are four ages.
I shall leave you now,
But shall look upon you in every age
And will return in the end.
—White Buffalo Calf
Pipe Woman
Mother Earth Spirituality
(Ed McGaa, Eagle Man)

BIBLIOGRAPHY OF ADDITIONAL RESOURCES

Books:

Alexander, Steve, and Karen Douglas. *Crop Circle Year Book 1999*. Gosport, Hampshire, England: Temporary Temples Press, 1999.

———. *Crop Circle Year Book 2000*. Gosport, Hampshire, England: Temporary Temples Press, 2000.

Bartholomew, Alick, ed. *Crop Circles: Harbingers of World Change*. Bath, England: Gateway Books, 1991.

Boerman, Robert J. *Crop Circles, Gods and Their Secrets: History of Mankind, Written in the Grain*. Brummen, the Netherlands: Ptah Foundation, 2000.

Bura, Paul. *Stepping to the Drummer*. Cemaes Bay, Anglesey, England: Honeytone Promotions, 2000. Contact: 12 Gongl Rhedyn, Cemaes Bay, Anglesey LL67 0HY, England.

Canada, Steve. *Crop Circles—A Convergence of Narrative*. Self-published, 1994. Available through Steve Canada, 111 W. Romie Lane #8, Salinas, California 93901.

———. *Crop Circles: Interim Report on the 1994 Season in England*. Self-published, 1994. Available through Steve Canada, 111 W. Romie Lane #8, Salinas, California 93901.

Clarke, Denni. *Crop Circle Wisdom: Simple Teachings from the CircleMakers*. Santa Fe, New Mexico: Spirit Passage Publishing and Communications, 2000.

Collins, Andrew. *The Circlemakers*. ABC Books, 1992. Available through the Center for North American Crop Circle Studies, P.O. Box 4766, Lutherville, Maryland 21094.

Cyr, Donald L., ed. *Crop Circle Secrets*. Santa Barbara, California: Stonehenge Viewpoint, 1991.

Davis, Beth, ed. *Ciphers in the Crops: Fractal and Geometric Circles of 1991*. Bath, England: Gateway Books, 1991.

Delgado, Pat, and Colin Andrews. *Crop Circles: The Latest Evidence*. London: Bloomsbury Publishing, 1990.

Devereux, Paul, et al. *Earth Lights Revelation: UFO's and Mystery Lightform Phenomena: The Earth's Secret Energy Force*. Penzance, Cornwall, England: Empress, 1989.

Glickman, Michael. *Corn Circles*. Walkmill, Cascob, Presteigne, Powys, Wales: Wooden Books, 1996. Available through Nexus Magazine, 55 Queens Road, East Grinstead, West Sussex RH19 1BG, England.

———. *Crop Circles*. Presteigne, Powys, Wales: Wooden Books, 2000. Available through Nexus Magazine, 55 Queens Road, East Grinstead, West Sussex RH19 1BG, England.

Good, Timothy, ed. *The UFO Report 1991*. London: Sidgwick and Jackson, 1990.

Goodman, Kent. *The Wessex Series: Crop Circles of Wessex*. Salisbury, Wiltshire, England: Wessex Books, 1996.

Howe, Linda Moulton. *Glimpses of Other Realities, Volume II: High Strangeness*. New Orleans: Paper Chase Press, 1998.

ilyes, and Peter Sorensen. *Symbols from Above: A 1993 Crop Circle Presentation*. Washington: Centre for Crop Circle Studies United States Network, 1993.

Martineau, John. *A Brief Guide to Crop Circle Geometry*. England: Holospiral Booklets, 1993.

———. *Crop Circle Geometry*. Walkmill, Cascob, Presteigne, Powys, Wales: Wooden Books, 1996.

Meaden, George Terence. *Circles from the Sky*. London: Souvenir Press, 1991.

Melchizedek, Drunvalo. *The Ancient Secret of the Flower of Life*. Vol. 2. Flagstaff, Arizona: Light Technology Publishing, 2000.

Michell, John, ed. *The Dimensions of Paradise: The Proportions and Symbolic Numbers of Ancient Cosmology*. London: Thames and Hudson, 1988.

———, ed. *Dowsing the Crop Circles: New Insights into the Greatest of Modern Mysteries*. Glastonbury, Somerset, England: Gothic Image Publications, 1991.

Müller, Andreas. *Crop Circle Formations: Diagram Trilogies '98*. Saarbrücken, Germany: self-published, 1998.

———. *Crop Circle Formations: Diagram Trilogies '99*. Saarbrücken, Germany: I.C.C.A.: The International Crop Circle Archive, 1998.

Noyes, Ralph. *The Crop Circle Enigma: A Range of Viewpoints from the Centre of Crop Circle Studies*. Bath, England: Gateway Books, 1991.

Ossebaard, Janet. *Graancirkels, Een Wereld-wijd Mysterie*. Hedel, the Netherlands: Librero, 2000.

Palgrave-Moore, Pat. *Crop Circle Classification*. Norwich, England: Elvery Dowers Publications, 1991.

Pringle, Lucy. *Crop Circles, the Greatest Mystery of Modern Times*. London: Thorsons, an Imprint of HarperCollins Publishers, 1999. Available through Lucy Pringle, 5 Town Lane, Sheet, Petersfield, Hampshire GU32 2AF, England.

Taylor, Busty. *Crop Circles of 1991*. Beckhampton, Wiltshire, England: Beckhampton Books, 1992.

Thomas, Andy. *Fields of Mystery: The Crop Circle Phenomenon in Sussex*. Seaford, East Sussex, England: S.B. Publications, 1996.

———. *Vital Signs: A Complete Guide to the Crop Circle Mystery and Why It Is NOT a Hoax*. Seaford, East Sussex, England: S.B. Publications, 1998.

Thomas, Andy, and Paul Bura. *Quest for Contact: A True Story of Crop Circles, Psychics and UFOs*. Seaford, East Sussex, England: S.B. Publications, 1997.

Williams, Margot, and Carolyn Morgan. *The Answer*. Shanklin, Isle of Wight, England: Grosvenor Press, 1991.

Wilson, Terry. *The Secret History of Crop Circles*. Poignton, Devon, England: Center for Crop Circle Studies, 1998.

Periodicals:

The Cereologist: The Journal for Crop Circle Studies, edited by John Sayer. Contact: Global Circles Research, 17 Spindle Road, Norwich, Norfolk NR6 6JR, England.

The Circular: The Quarterly Journal of the Centre for Crop Circle Studies, edited by George Bishop. England: Partington Printers. Contact: George Bishop, 12 Tintagel Close, Beacon Heath, Exeter, Devon EX4 9EH, England.

The Circular Review, edited by Nick Nicholson. Contact: 6D Pond View, Moor Farm, Moor Lane, Calverton, Nottinghamshire NG14 6FZ, England.

Cosmic Horizons, edited by Mark Haywood. Contact: 22 Smithfield Rise, Lichfield, Staffordshire WS13 6SG, England.

SC: The Bimonthly Journal of Crop Circles and Beyond, edited by Andy Thomas. Contact: www.swirlednews.com.

The Spiral: The Crop Circle Newsletter for Wiltshire, edited by Francine Blake. Devizes, Wiltshire, England: Wiltshire Crop Circle Study Group. Contact: Dereka Dodson, WCCSG, P.O. Box 2079, Devizes, Wiltshire SN10 1US, England.

Videotapes:

Andrews, Colin. *Colin Andrews Lecture at Madison Square Garden 1995.* Walker Productions. Available through Circles Phenomenon Research, P.O. Box 3378, Branford, Connecticut 06045-1978.

———. *Colin Andrews Live! Crop Circle Update.* Los Angeles: Harry De Lighter Productions, 1992. Contact: P.O. Box 661593, Los Angeles, California 90066.

———. *The Crop Circles—Are They Created by: A) Extraterrestrials? B) Doug and Dave? C) The Earth's Magnetic Field?* International UFO Congress and Film Festival, 2000. Contact: 9975 Wadsworth Parkway #K2-504, Westminster, Colorado 80021.

———. *Undeniable Evidence.* Glastonbury, Somerset, England: Ark Soundwaves of Glastonbury, 1991. Contact: P.O. Box 1395, Glastonbury, Somerset, BA6 9FE England, or Lightworks Audio and Video, P.O. Box 661593, Los Angeles, California 90066.

Bongiovanni, Giorgio. *I Cerchi Nel Grano.* Nonsiamosoli Video, 1999. Contact: nonsiamosoli@upnet.it., or at www.nonsiamosoli.org.

Christopher, Ian. *Something Wonderful Has Happened. . . But It Was Not in the News!* Palo Alto, California: Mariposa-Pacific Research Institute, 2000. Available through East-West Bookshop, 324 Castro Street, Mountain View, California 94041.

Everard, Christopher. *Crop Circle Update 1999: The Most Comprehensive Guide to the British Crop Circle Phenomenon.* The Enigma Channel, 1999 and 2000. Contact: 163 Churchbury Road, London SE9 5JB England, or at www.enigmatv.com.

Glickman, Michael, and Patricia Murray. *The Crop Circles: History and Geometry.* Santa Monica, California: Crop Circle Radius, 1997. Contact: P.O. Box 2077, Santa Monica, California 90406.

Hein, Simeon. *Morphic Resonance: Crop Circle Spinners.* Boulder, Colorado: Mount Baldy Institute, 1999. Contact: www.mountbaldy.com.

Hesemann, Michael. *Mystery of the Crop Circles.* Hesemann Productions, 1991. Available through Circles Phenomenon Research, P.O. Box 3378, Branford, Connecticut 06045-1978.

ilyes. *Crop Circle Update 1995: Circle Makers Magic.* 1996. Available through Webworks, P.O. Box 3695, Olympia, Washington 98509.

———. *Crop Circle Update 1996: Mystery Messages.* 1997. Available through Webworks, P.O. Box 3695, Olympia, Washington 98509.

Janssen, Bert, and Janet Ossebaard. *Crop Circles— The Research.* 1999. Contact: P.O. Box 10, 9460 AA, Gieten, the Netherlands. Laumen, Frank. *Crop Circle Connections: Intangible Realms of Reality.* Frank Laumen Video, 2000. Contact: f.laumen@telelev.net, or at .

Macnish, John. *Crop Circle Communique: Investigating the Mystery of the Crop Circles.* England: Circlevision, 1991.

Russell, Ron. *Quantum Resonance: Scientific Evidence of Anomalous Energy Fields in British Crop Formations.* Midwest Research, 2000. Contact: www.cropcircles.org.

Crop Circle Conferences:

Center for Crop Circle Studies (CCCS) Convention. Held late July in Andover, Hampshire, England. Contact: George Bishop at su2261@eclipse.co.uk.

Glastonbury Symposium. Held end of July or early August in Glastonbury, Somerset, England. Contact: Sheila Martin at symposium@sheila06.globalnet.co.uk, or http://www.isleofavalon.co.uk/symposium.html.

Wiltshire Crop Circle Study Group (WCCSG). Held mid-July in Devizes, Wiltshire, England. Contact: Francine Blake, P.O. Box 939, Devizes, Wiltshire SN10 3TA, England, or at sky.picture@virgin.net.

Crop Circle Decks:

Quinly, Cariel. *Crop Circle Cards: The Living Oracle.* Cosmic Connections, 1997. Circular oracle cards. Available through Cosmic Connections Center, 1611-A South Melrose Drive #246, Vista, California 92083.

———. *Crop Circle Cards: The New Myth.* Cosmic Connections, 1994. Circular oracle cards. Available through Cosmic Connections Center, 1611-A South Melrose Drive #246, Vista, California 92083.

GLOSSARY

alchemy (alchemical): Cosmic science of divine creation and re-creation. A miraculous power or process of changing the physical world.

Ark of the Covenant: A geometry of light wherein God's revelation is made known. The Ark of the testimony equals the "energy tablets of God's law," kept in certain key places in the world. When David brought the Ark to Zion, the place then became sacred.

Cave of the Great Cobra: A nonphysical location. The Great Cobra is a Christed being, a great master teacher and the mother of the global and galactic snake clan. Snake medicine transmutes poison.

Christ being: One who carries the heart of Christ, yet who is not necessarily awakened. There are approximately six billion Christ beings on Mother Earth (circa 2000 A.D.).

christed being: One who has awakened the heart of Christ within and attained enlightenment.

clan: Born of the same spirit group.

Cobra: Uraeus, the sacred serpent, represented on the headdresses of kings and gods of ancient Egypt. In Egyptian myth, Cobra governs the entire Earth. The Great Cobra is also depicted in Hindu and Buddhist theology.

collective soul: The soul of God.

Condor: Sacred symbol of the freed spirit. Represents the evolved souls, equivalent to the fully outstretched symbol of Egyptian mythology—Ma'at. This also refers to the Native American prophecy of the unity of the continent: when the eagle and the condor unite, is the coming together of North and South American indigenous peoples, prophesied during the end times, or the time of emergence into the fifth world of peace.

Cosmic Christ consciousness: The spiritual essence of the collective mind-heart of the Christ.

Cosmic Ik: The divine wind.

cosmic mandala: Circular designs containing geometric forms and images of deities, that symbolize the universe, wholeness and the totality.

Council of Abborah: Light of the High Council of the thirteen councils of the Great Central Sun. A spiritual council, it is the inner council of spiritual wisdom. The Galactic Federation is the external or administrative council.

Council of Abborah's mothership: In the spiritual realm, "Our Father's house has many mansions." This speaks of multiple dimensions and parallel universes. The Council of Abborah has a Galactic

Federation starship, a mothership and a fleet of starships.

crystalline geometry: Geometric crystals that are both ethereal and physical.

crystalline matrix of the water aspect: "The memory of water."

deactivation of plutonium poisoning: This occurs by use of the most electronegative and reactive of all the elements—fluorine—in the form of fluorocarbons of a detoxification nature by ionic reaction.

divine hologram: God's cosmic projection of universal law.

DNA pulsar codes: Electromagnetic frequency codes that carry the encoding of DNA.

dolphin cities: Within the womb of the Cosmic Mother is the embryonic sack of all creation. The cells of this creative womb are the essence of the dolphin spirit. We have memories in our DNA of swimming as dolphins in the womb of the Cosmic Mother before we came on our Earth walk.

Ectomie: The trickster in Native American mythology.

Eden: Heaven on Earth.

Eden principle: This is the formula for the composition of heaven on Earth, or Shamballa, or El Dorado.

equatronic: Balance through the process of acceleration of atomic structure.

ethereal: Of or like the ether, or upper regions of space. Refers to the celestial or heavenly, not earthly.

ethereal temples of the House of David: At the time of the invasion of the fearmongers, the temples of the House of David entered the ethereal. [see Appendix B].

Exad: At the root of Ganeshkato.

fear grid: The net of fear and mind control that restricts our divine potential.

Flower of Life geometry: All of creation unfolds in lovely fractal patterns, flowers of sacred geometry. These patterns carry codes and formulas of the creative essence of the God-source.

fractal: A repetitive mathematical analogue, usually seen as a geometrical pattern of crystalline nature, in which the patterns are repeated in ascending and descending scales at nodal points along and within the geometry.

fractaline: A repetitive analogue of expansive change, often caused by a seeding or catalysis.

Gaia: Another name for Mother Earth.

Gaia time capsule: Mother Earth was implanted with time-release capsules set to activate with the energies of the planetary alignments at the time of the prophecies and the emergence of the fifth world of peace, or heaven on Earth. These time capsules were created to quicken our evolution.

Galactic Federation: Innergalactic federation council equivalent to Earth's United Nations.

Galactic Sun: The force fields or energy matrix of all solar houses in the plan of the cosmos is united and energetically complete in the Great Central Sun. We are many, but of one body, one soul, one spirit. This term refers to the living body of all galactic suns.

Ganesha: In Hindu mythology, Lord Ganesha is the son of Lord Shiva and the divine mother, Parvati. *Gana* means "all existing beings in names and forms," and *isha* means "lord." Thus, Ganesha is the lord of all existing beings of creation. He removes all obstacles and ensures success in human endeavors. He is an archetype of wisdom and beneficence.

Ganeshkato: One of the ancient beings who came to Earth. This comes from Hindu and is a reference to a god of good fortune and prosperity associated with early Indian history and mythology.

Great Central Sun: The universe is infinite; there is no form or end. To conceptualize the Central Sun is to identify the center of the universe, the archetype of the Father God.

Great Turtle: In Chinese tradition, the shell plates on the back of a turtle mirror the acupuncture meridian system. In Native American tradition, it refers to North America or the continent of the Americas, and in some traditions it refers to the world.

HAARP (High-Frequency Active Auroral Research Project): A weapon massively more powerful than the atomic bomb intended to beam more than 1.7 gigawatts of power into the ionosphere and actually boil the upper atmosphere. This will create a mirror and/or a giant antenna to transmit huge amounts of power to any specific area on the Earth. This energy can then be used to manipulate global weather, hurt or destroy ecosystems, knock out electronic communication, change our moods and mental states, and could be used to try to destroy or manipulate the new Christ grid around the world.

Hall of Records of the Great Central Sun: The holding place of the Records of Ra.

Heart Grail: Each of our hearts is the cup of the Holy Grail, the vessel of the blood of Christ. From our heart chakra flows forth the unconditional love of God's grace.

hexatronic: A six-sided geometric hologram that is rapidly replicated in spiraling frequencies that transcend light and sound barriers.

hologram: A photographic plate containing the record of the interference pattern produced by means of holography. In advanced technologies, it can be projected onto any other medium besides picture film. It can be used to create enormous illusions formed from coherent force fields of light.

holography: A method of making three-dimensional photographs without using a camera, by splitting a laser beam into two beams and recording on a photographic plate the minute interference patterns made by one beam going from the laser to the plate and the other beam going from the laser to the object to the plate. The virtual image can be reconstructed by shining laser light through the developed film.

Kabbalah: The science of the many universes of higher intelligence that serve the Godhead. Also referred to in Judaism as the Tree of Life.

Kinich Ahau: Mayan name for the Sun of this (our) solar system. Sol or Shan (ancient title).

lightbodies: Our higher-dimensional light essences.

Maka: Earth Mother in Lakota Sioux.

matrix: The environment from which the universe originates.

morning star: The last star to leave the sky in the morning and the first to enter the sky in the evening is really the planet Venus. Many of our holy ones have said they come from the morning star, such as Christ and White Buffalo Calf Pipe Woman.

namasté: A term meaning "the divine within me greets the divine within you."

one of the thirteen pulsar codes: Refers to the frequency resonance of time line as in music: two octaves—one yin, one yang—with a nodal overlap point.

Patal Patala: Incarnated souls born as children in the years 2000 to 2003, originating from the twelfth dimension and part of the fifth-wave soul group.

pod of Eden: Ma'at in Earth, from the ancient Egyptian.

portal: Interdimensional gateway.

prana: The very essence of God's life force, creation, breath.

primal group: A group chosen to start any project. In creation, God chose a primal group to be starseeded to inhabit Mother Earth. Later, other beings came.

Pulsar Code Thirteen: Refers to the solar system, the Sun (Kinich Ahau). The furthest system from the center of the star group of which Sol or Shan is a participant in that dimensional reality.

pulsar points: Nodal points or acupuncture points of the planet Earth.

quadrasonic: Quantum formula of sonic resonance to the fourth power of innergalactic resonance. Superceding sonic resonance, this resonance transcends time and space and is a key factor in innerdimensional space-time physics.

quintessence: Ether, the fifth essence or element, which was thought to be the constituent matter of heavenly bodies latent in all things.

Rainbow Nation: The coming together of all races and nations for unity by diversity, freedom, respect and unconditional love.

Records of Ra: These are the cosmic records of the Great Central Sun that contain all knowledge since creation.

sacred twins: In Earth's history, the sacred twins are depicted in many mythologies. This concept assists our psyche in conceptualizing the dichotomy and the divine balance of apparent opposing forces, such as negative and positive, hot and cold, male and female, yin and yang.

shadow: The lost part of self that is confused and still lives by the rule of fear. The inside of the womb is dark, but it is certainly holy. Shadow is also our reflection; it moves when we move. To be truly free beings, we must embrace our shadow in uncondi-

tional love, heal this shadow and release our fears. Then, and only then, will we be gifted with the divine shadow dance in harmony and peace.

Soenan: Composed of the light and sound frequencies that transform atomic and subatomic mass and matter in the evolution of heaven (haven) on Earth to complete the genesis of the effect of our Sun's transmutation.

solar temples: Around the Central Sun are twelve solar temples of light. The center temple is the thirteenth, the Great Central Sun. In Earth mythology, these are depicted in the twelve tribes of Israel, the twelve Apostles and the twelve months of the Gregorian calendar. The center is Christ Jesus.

soul matrix: The crystalline geometry that comprises the soul encoding, or information contained in the soul.

soul retrieval: An ancient shamanistic journey that integrates fragmented parts of the soul into oneness. Often, a part of the soul will splinter when there is severe trauma in this or past lives. Soul retrievals should be done by well-trained professionals. Past-life karma can be cleared, and repatterning of negative destructive behavior can be healed.

star beings: Our cosmic brothers and sisters. Many are our higher dimensional selves.

star glyphs: Ancient star hieroglyphs that compose a universal ascended star language originated from the Great Central Sun. This language was first used in the House of David temples.

starseed: We all come from the heavens to Earth as starseeds. This also refers to children born to mothers that have been taken up on starships and implanted with highly evolved extraterrestrial DNA.

Thirteenth House of Ra: The thirteenth sun matrix alignment.

triadular: An ion that has a valence of three.

Vegan: Relating to the star system Vega.

White Calf: The White Buffalo Calf traditions.

White Eagle: Justice; mythological symbol of the Christ. In Native American teachings, the white animals are sacred. The White Eagle therefore would be a sacred messenger from the world of spirit.

wind: Energy; resonance; frequency; dimensional transit.

womb of Cosmic Mother: The archetype of the "Mother God." The Great Central Sun's divine female balance is a black hole. Within her womb reside the dolphin cities, the central origin of the dolphin race—those who are cosmic cocreators with Creator God.

Zod: After Zodiacus (Greek), the zodiac.

PHOTOGRAPHER CONTACT INFORMATION

Steve Alexander
27 St. Francis Road
Gosport
Hampshire PO12 2UG
United Kingdom
Tel/Fax: +44(0)23 9235 2867
temporarytemples@netscapeon-line.co.uk

Colin Andrews
Circles Phenomenon Research
International
P.O. Box 3378
Branford, CT 06405
USA

Karen Cushing
1207 Union Street
Schenectady, New York 12308
USA
+1(518)382-8146

Andrew King
Kenberly
Victoria Gardens
Biggin Hill
Kent TN16 3DJ
United Kingdom
andrewking@dhuru.demon.co.uk

Judith K. Moore
P.O Box 546
Chimayo, New Mexico 87522
USA
redclay@newmexico.com

Ulrich Kox
Dyck 71
D-41334 Nettetal
Deutschland
Tel/fax: +49 2153 4722

Barbara Lamb
1517 Marjorie Avenue
Claremont, California
USA
Tel: + (909) 626-8332
blambms@37.com

Patricia Murray
Crop Circle Radius
P.O. Box 2077
Santa Monica, California 90406
USA
Tel: + (310) 358-60
www.cropcircleradius.com

Petr Novak
Sirius Society
Amerika 27
Plzen 301 00
Czech Republic
petr.novak@edu.pilsedu.cz

Lucy Pringle
5 Town Lane
Sheet, Petersfield
Hampshire GU32 2AF
United Kingdom
Tel/fax +44(0) 1730 263454
LucyPringle@cs.com

Albert Ridgley
Wiltshire
United Kingdom
Tel: + (01672) 514603

Peter Sorensen
C/O Carmichael
1115 E. Cordova # 219
Pasadena, California 91106
USA
croppie2@yahoo.com

Other recommended Photographers

Francine Blake
Wiltshire Crop Circle Study
Group
P.O. Box 939
Devizes,
Wiltshire SN10 3TA
United Kingdom

Michael Glickman
Crop Circle Radius
P.O. Box 2077
Santa Monica, California 90406
USA
Tel: + (310) 358-60
www.cropcircleradius.com

ABOUT THE AUTHORS

BARBARA LAMB

Barbara Mallory Lamb has been visiting and researching crop circles in England since 1990. She is one of the leading crop circle researchers and educators in the United States. She has presented lectures at meetings and conferences in various states, including California, Wyoming, Colorado, Texas, Arkansas, Virginia, New Mexico, Arizona, Nevada and Florida. She has presented at various forums in England, including the Center for Crop Circle Studies in Devizes, Wiltshire (1994), the Glastonbury Symposium (1998, 1999 and 2001), the Wiltshire Crop Circle Study Group Conference at Alton Barnes (1999), the Power Places Tours Conference in Salisbury (1993 -1996) and the Staffordshire UFO Study Group (1997).

Barbara has been interviewed on dozens of United States radio programs, Internet radio shows and cable and national television shows, including: "Encounters," "The Other Side," "Hard Copy," the Fox "Roswell" special and the Learning Channel. She has published numerous articles about the crop circle phenomenon.

Barbara received a Bachelor of Arts degree from Mount Holyoke College in Massachusetts, a master's degree in Behavioral Science from the University of La Verne in California, a license as a Marriage and Family Therapist, certification as a Clinical Hypnotherapist and certification as a Regression Therapist. In her multifaceted professional work, her specialty is regression therapy, in which she helps people resolve problems and conflicts from past lives or from experiences with extraterrestrial beings. She is in private practice in Claremont, in southern California.

She is a former Executive Vice President and board member of the Association for Past Life Research and Therapies, and currently serves on the Board of Directors of the International Board for Regression Therapy and the Board of the Academy of Clinical Close Encounter Therapists.

JUDITH K. MOORE

Judith was born on July 27, 1949, in the mountains of Colorado, and currently lives in the beautiful valley of Chimayo, New Mexico, near the sacred healing shrine of Santuario de Chimayo. She is the guardian of the sacred Womb Spring near her home. Her Lakota name is White Bird Girl. She has six adopted children and six grandchildren.

Judith served as the administrator for her former husband's acupuncture clinic for twenty-four years. She was instrumental in the growth of the acceptance of Chinese medicine as a medical modality in New Mexico and the U.S.

For many years, she was active as a child advocate. She has served as an educator for adoptive parents and as both a board member and chairperson of the Citizens' Review Board for Northern New Mexico. She served on the advisory board of Child Rite (an adoption agency) for five years.

Since her early childhood, she has been very close to the Earth Mother and Native American teachings. She spent many summers of her childhood living in a camp on Bald Mountain at the sacred Charm Springs. It was there at the age of fourteen that she vowed to Creator God to be of service to humanity as a tool of Creator to mend the Hoop and help the balance to return. The wisdom of her work has come from her inner journeys and her vision that world peace is possible in our lifetime.

In 1989, she began her inner healing journey from fear to freedom. It became a seven-year spiritual journey to claim her empowerment as a divine being of light, truth and trust. In April 1992, she had an intense light experience and became coconscious with Laiolin, a thirteenth-dimensional ambassador of the Central Sun. Her work is vast, including readings from the Records of Ra (the records of creation of the Great Central Sun), intuitive healings, past-life regressions, soul retrievals, the activation of cosmic DNA and the dissolution of fear implants. Her life is dedicated to the service of the awakening of heaven on Earth.

Judith's many other interests include traveling, gardening, cooking, camping and photography. Being a grandma is her heart's song. She is a writer of children's stories and a poet. She is an active crone and member of the Grandmothers' Council.

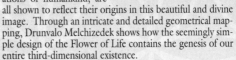

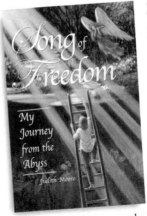

Song of Freedom
My Journey from the Abyss

Judith Moore knew she had been brought up by loving parents. Before age forty, she had no memory of childhood trauma, although she knew she had been sick a lot more than most people. But it wasn't until she joined an incest survivors' group to help her adopted daughter that the memories began surfacing. At first she feared for her sanity, for these recollections were of painful medical experiments, torture, and sensory deprivation at the hands of the United States government.

In this brave and groundbreaking work, Judith Moore shares her shattering revelations of the reality of high-level mind control. She opens the pages of her journal and the innermost feelings of her heart to share with the reader her journey to wholeness and healing. As memories flood her consciousness, she struggles to make sense of what is happening and to process the information in accordance with her lifelong worldview of love, intellectual curiosity, and a deep respect for nature.

Her early environment, rich in Native American folklore, helps her in her quest. She researches, travels, investigates, and meditates in an effort to set herself free and to reclaim her very sense of herself as a person. Her search leads her into terrifying, unknown territory and illuminating discoveries about her own psyche and that of today's society as a whole.

$19⁹⁵ **Softcover 364 PP.**
ISBN 1-891824-38-4

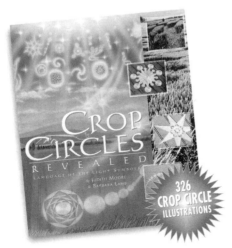

326 CROP CIRCLE ILLUSTRATIONS

Crop Circles Revealed
Language of the Light Symbols

Welcome to the world of crop circles, one of the most tantalizing phenomena in our world today. It is difficult not to be captivated by their beauty and complexity and by the questions and issues they provoke, including one that becomes more pressing every day—what other intelligent life forms are out there trying to communicate with us? What are their intentions? What is the communication system between them, the Earth, and humanity?

Unlock the secret keys for the emergence of a new world of peace, freedom, healing, and unconditional love. We are being assisted with energy as never before to regenerate ourselves and our ailing planet. Reactivate and discover your invaluable gifts and divine mission. Awaken your DNA and empower yourself!

This comprehensive document reveals the deep mysteries of the crop-circle phenomenon. Scientific analysis of the hoaxing controversy and high-level spiritual transmissions are combined in one masterful presentation for your use and interpretation.

$25⁰⁰ **Softcover 308 PP.**
ISBN 1-891824-32-5

A New Formula for Creation
The Miracle of Immortal Love

This manuscript contains vital information about the divine plan in order to expand the nature of the entirety of creation as revealed at this crucial time in Earth's history. It goes far beyond the external manifestations perceived of as Earth changes. Its magnitude is of cosmic proportions, representing the divine plan for the expansion of the existing creation as it is known. The present changes on Earth reflect the vast metamorphosis of the totality of creation, of All That Is. *A New Formula for Creation* expands your perception of reality as it activates the cosmic plan encoded in your DNA. Judith's gifts as an extraordinary adept of the mysteries of interdimensional communication and conscious trance mediumship open new portals for human consciousness.

$16⁹⁵ **Softcover 186 PP.**
ISBN 1-891824-57-0

THE ENCYCLOPEDIA OF THE SPIRITUAL PATH

DR. STONE has a PhD in Transpersonal Psychology and is a licensed marriage, family, and child counselor in Los Angeles, CA. On a spiritual level, he anchors the Melchizedek Synthesis Light Academy and Ashram.

The Encyclopedia of the Spiritual Path consists of thirteen books and an index in this ongoing series on the subject of **ASCENSION**, **SELF-REALIZATION**, and a further **DEEPENING OF THE ASCENDED-MASTER TEACHINGS**.

These books collectively explore the **DEEPEST LEVELS** and understanding of ascension through the personal, planetary, and cosmic levels, offering the reader tools to work with that span the spectrum of all the bodies and to ultimately bring them into the subtle realms of cosmic ascension.

These tools are practical gems for the **PURIFICATION**, **HEALING**, **CLEANSING**, **ACCELERATION**, and **ASCENSION PROCESS** that cover the individual incarnated soul and extend into the vast monadic and cosmic realms.

1 THE COMPLETE ASCENSION MANUAL
How to Achieve Ascension in This Lifetime
A synthesis of the past and guidance for ascension. An extraordinary compendium of practical techniques and spiritual history. Compiled from research and channeled information.
SOFTCOVER 297 PP.   ISBN 0-929385-55-1

2 SOUL PSYCHOLOGY
Keys to Ascension
Modern psychology deals exclusively with personality, ignoring the dimensions of spirit and soul. This book provides groundbreaking theories and techniques for healing and self-realization.
SOFTCOVER 256 PP.   ISBN 0-929385-56-X

3 BEYOND ASCENSION
How to Complete the Seven Levels of Initiation
Brings forth new channeled material that demystifies the 7 levels of initiation and how to attain them. It contains new information on how to open and anchor our 36 chakras.
SOFTCOVER 280 PP.   ISBN 0-929385-73-X

4 HIDDEN MYSTERIES
ETs, Ancient Mystery Schools and Ascension
Explores the unknown and suppressed aspects of Earth's past. Reveals new information on the ET movement and secret teachings of the ancient mystery schools.
SOFTCOVER 330 PP.   ISBN 0-929385-57-8

5 THE ASCENDED MASTERS LIGHT THE WAY
Beacons of Ascension
The lives and teachings of 40 of the world's greatest saints and spiritual beacons provide a blueprint for total self-realization. Guidance from masters.
SOFTCOVER 258 PP.   ISBN 0-929385-58-6

6 COSMIC ASCENSION
Your Cosmic Map Home
Almost all the books on the planet on the subject of ascension are written about planetary ascension. Now, because of the extraordinary times in which we live, cosmic ascension is available here on Earth! Learn about self-realization, evolvement of nations, and more.
SOFTCOVER 263 PP.   ISBN 0-929385-99-3

7 A BEGINNER'S GUIDE TO THE PATH
OF ASCENSION with REV. JANNA SHELLY PARKER
This volume covers the basics of ascension clearly and completely, from the spiritual hierarchy to the angels and star beings.
SOFTCOVER 166 PP.   ISBN 1-891824-02-3

8 GOLDEN KEYS TO ASCENSION AND HEALING
Revelations of Sai Baba and the Ascended Masters
This book represents the wisdom of the ascended masters condensed into concise keys that serve as a spiritual guide.
SOFTCOVER 205 PP.   ISBN 1-891824-03-1

9 MANUAL FOR PLANETARY LEADERSHIP
Here at last is an indispensible book that has been urgently needed in these uncertain times, laying out the guidelines for leadership in the world and in one's life. It serves as a reference manual for moral and spiritual living.
SOFTCOVER 284 PP.   ISBN 1-891824-05-8

10 YOUR ASCENSION MISSION
with REV. JANNA SHELLEY PARKER
This book shows how each person's puzzle piece is just as vital and necessary as any other. Includes all aspects of living the fullest expression of your individuality.
SOFTCOVER 249 PP.   ISBN 1-891824-09-0

11 REVELATIONS OF A MELCHIZEDEK INITIATE
Dr. Stone's spiritual autobiography, beginning with his ascension initiation and progression into the 12th initiation. Filled with insights, tools, and information.
SOFTCOVER 306 PP.   ISBN 1-891824-10-4

12 HOW TO TEACH ASCENSION CLASSES
This book serves as an ideal foundation for teaching ascension classes and presenting workshops. It covers an entire one-to two-year program of classes.
SOFTCOVER 460 PP.   ISBN 1-891824-15-5

13 ASCENSION AND ROMANTIC RELATIONSHIPS
with REV. JANNA SHELLEY PARKER
Inspired by Djwhal Khul, Dr. Stone has written a unique book about relationships from the perspective of the soul and monad rather than just the personality.
SOFTCOVER 184 PP.   ISBN 1-891824-16-3

14 ASCENSION COMPLETE INDEX
Ascension names and ascended master terms glossary, plus a complete index of all thirteen books.
SOFTCOVER 233 PP.   ISBN 1-891824-30-9

15 HOW TO BE FINANCIALLY SUCCESSFUL
A SPIRITUAL PERSPECTIVE
Dr. Stone has written an easily digestible book full of tools and advice for achieving prosperity. This book conveys esoteric secrets of the universe that, if mastered, can lead to maximum manifestation results.
SOFTCOVER 236 PP.   ISBN 1-891824-55-4

BEYOND
THE
LIGHT BARRIER
The Autobiography of Elizabeth Klarer

This is the autobiographical story of Elizabeth Klarer, a South African woman, and Akon, an astrophysicist from Meton, a planet of Proxima Centuri that, at a distance of about 4.3 light years, is our nearest stellar neighbor. Elizabeth was taken in his spaceship to Meton, where she lived with him and his family for four months and where she bore his child. Her life on Meton is fascinatingly described. Akon brought Elizabeth back to Earth after the birth of their son and continued to visit her thereafter.

Akon explained how his spaceship's light-propulsion technology operated and how it allowed him and his people to travel across vast interstellar distances. This technology is explained in detail in the book.

Elizabeth was given a standing ovation at the 11th International Congress of UFO Research Groups at Weisbaden in 1975, and her speech as guest of honor was applauded by scientists of twenty-two nations.

$15⁹⁵

SOFTCOVER, 224 PP.
ISBN 0-929385-22-5

ET Visitors Speak Vol. 2
through Robert Shapiro

For those of you who've always wanted to meet somebody completely different, here's your opportunity. This book contains the continuing adventures of visitors to planet Earth. In a strange sense, you might include yourself as one of those, as the human race does not really claim the title of full-time and permanent Earth citizen. So when you're reading this book, think about it as if you were visiting another planet. What would you say in reaction to the local population, their habits, and so on? Put yourself in the picture so this isn't just a meaningless travel log from various beings that you don't know and may never meet. Make it personal this time, because the time is coming—maybe even in some of your lifetimes—when you might just be one of those extraterrestrials on another planet. So you might as well practice now and get your lines down right.

- *ET from a Future Version of Saturn*
- *Tuwass, a Visitor to Future Earth*
- *Xzhetah, ET Hybrid*
- *Visitor from Planet Odin*
- *The Sound of Breath*
- *. . . and many, many more!*

$19⁹⁵

SOFTCOVER 460 PP.
ISBN 1-891824-78-3

LIFE with a
COSMOS CLEARANCE
Dan Salter as told to Nancy Red Star

Military men and others employed in government agencies have known the truth about UFOs for decades. Dan Salter, now in his 80s, reveals the story behind government attempts to suppress, as much as they can, all knowledge of contact with extraterrestrials. He says that the extraterrestrials have been waiting for the government to come forward with information about contact, and if that doesn't happen, they will take a more public role in disclosure. He lays out the case for a web of conspiracy and tangled interactions ranging across continents through time and space and into the innermost workings of world politics, religion and economics.

$19⁹⁵ SOFTCOVER 198 P.
ISBN 1-891824-37-6

AGENT DANIEL M. SALTER is a retired former counterintelligence agent for the Scientific and Technical Unit of Interplanetary Phenomena in Washington, D.C. He was a member of the Pilot Air Force, NRO (National Reconnaissance Office) and DCCCD (Development of Conscious Contact Citizenry Department) with the United States military.

Our
Cosmic Ancestors
by Maurice Chatelain

Author Maurice Chatelain, former NASA space expert, has compiled compelling evidence to show that a highly advanced civilization had existed on the Earth approximately 65,000 years ago. Further, his work indicates that the knowledge of the advanced civilization has been 'seeded' by extraterrestrial visitors who have aided mankind with advanced information in mathematics, electricity, and astronomy.

Our Cosmic Ancestors is a dynamic work unraveling the messages of these 'universal astronauts' and decoding the symbols and visual mathematics they have left for us in the Egyptian Pyramids, Stonehenge, the Mayan calendar, the Maltese Cross, and the Sumerian zodiac.

The book is captivating reading from beginning to end; however Mr. Chatelain's purpose is sharing these exciting discoveries lies in the hope that all of humankind will extend his horizons, to release fear of the unknown, just enough, that another generation will exhibit growing curiosity to continue the search for signs of purposeful

$14⁹⁵ SOFTCOVER 216 P.
ISBN 0-929686-00-4

Shamanic Secrets Mastery Series

Speaks of Many Truths and Reveals the Mysteries through Robert Shapiro

Shamanic Secrets for Material Mastery

This book explores the earth and soul connection between humans and Mother Earth. Through that intimacy, miracles of healing and expanded awareness can flourish. To heal the planet and be healed as well, we can lovingly extend our energy selves out to the mountains and rivers and intimately bond with the Earth. Gestures and vision can activate our hearts to return us to a healthy, caring relationship with the land we live on. The character of some of Earth's most powerful features is explored and understood, with exercises given to connect us with those places.

ISBN 1-891824-12-0 Softcover 514 pp., $19.95

Shamanic Secrets for Physical Mastery

Learn to understand the sacred nature of your own physical body and some of the magnificent gifts it offers you. When you work with your physical body in these new ways, you will discover not only its sacredness, but how it is compatible with Mother Earth, the animals, the plants and even the nearby planets, all of which you now recognize as being sacred in nature. It is important to feel the value of oneself physically before one can have any lasting physical impact on the world.

ISBN 1-891824-29-5 Softcover 576 pp., $25.00

Shamanic Secrets for Spiritual Mastery

"Spiritual mastery encompasses many different means to assimilate and be assimilated by the wisdom, feelings, flow, warmth, function, and application of all beings in your world that you will actually contact in some way. My approach to spiritual mastery will be as grounded as possible in things that people on Earth can use—but it won't include the broad spectrum of spiritual mastery, like levitation and invisibility. My life is basically going to represent your needs, and it gets the secrets that have been held back out in a story-like fashion so that it is more interesting."

—Speaks of Many Truths through Robert Shapiro
ISBN 1-891824-58-9 Softcover 676 pp., $29.95

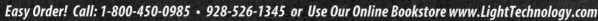

Gaia Speaks

GAIA THROUGH PEPPER LEWIS

Gaia Speaks SACRED EARTH WISDOM

I am the nonphysical sentience of this planet—simply put, I am the planet Earth. I am the body and the soul of the planet you currently inhabit. My sentience guides and enlivens all that surrounds the planet as well as all that is upon and within her. Although many believe in a sentient or feeling Earth, not all are attuned to her. Channeling offers a unique advantage in this respect, because it allows the transmission of vibrations and impressions to be communicated as language.

$19.95 · Softcover 393 pp.
ISBN 1-891824-48-1

Subjects include:
A BRIEF HISTORY OF RELIGION
WALK YOUR WAY OR WALK AWAY
THE KEY TO DEALING WITH AN
EPIDEMIC OF GLOBAL FEAR

Gaia Speaks Wisdom for an Awakening Humanity

Your purposes are made of multidimensional similes and metaphors designed to stimulate, encourage, create, and resolve. As Gaia tells it, you have at least seven purposes or reasons for being. You instinctively (consciously or unconsciously) know one or more of these, but others may remain hidden for many years or even throughout your entire lives. Given this expanded view of what you are and why you are here, you can begin to see how this book might be of use to you.

$19.95 · Softcover 418 pp.
ISBN 1-891824-51-1

PART 1: INVOLUTION
THE PATH OF THE HEART

PART 2: EVOLUTION
THE PATH OF THE SOUL

Solutions *for a* Small Planet Volume One

Gaia says: As you read through these pages, some messages will stand out more than others. It is likely that you will hear my voice speaking directly to you and through you. You will revive and regenerate moments such as the one when your soul selected this life as potent and pivotal—a bright light against a dark backdrop.

$14.95 · Softcover 236 pp.
ISBN-10: 1-891824-83-X

Subjects include:
AN ENTITY AND CHANNEL INTERVIEWED
MAKING SENSE OF SURPLUS WISDOM
KEEPING IT ALL BY GIVING IT ALL AWAY
FINDING YOUR SPIRITUAL FAMILY

Solutions *for a* Small Planet Volume Two

We, collective humanity, are one of Earth's resources. We cycle and recycle ourselves through lifetimes upon Earth, learning, sharing, and contributing to Earth in a variety of ways. Gaia truly benefits from our company, and her sentience enjoys the varied history we have shared with the planet. That being said, this is a time of great change for humanity and for Earth.

$14.95 · Softcover 225 pp.
ISBN-10: 1-891824-84-8

Subjects include:
HEALING THE WORLD ONE MEDITATION AT A TIME
SOLUTIONS FOR A SMALL PLANET
THE LONG AND SHORT OF IT
THE WARS OF HUMANKIND IN HEAVEN

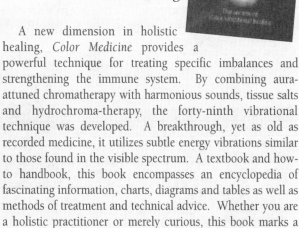